D0350194

15.00

Wagner Nights

CALIFORNIA STUDIES IN 19TH-CENTURY MUSIC
Joseph Kerman, General Editor

BY THE SAME AUTHOR

Conversations with Arrau

Understanding Toscanini

The Ivory Trade: Piano Competitions and the Business of Music

Wagner Nights

AN AMERICAN HISTORY

JOSEPH HOROWITZ

UNIVERSITY OF CALIFORNIA PRESS

BERKELEY   LOS ANGELES   LONDON

The letters of M. Carey Thomas are quoted
by permission of the Bryn Mawr College Archives.

University of California Press
Berkeley and Los Angeles, California
University of California Press, Ltd.
London, England
© 1994 by
The Regents of the University of California

Library of Congress Cataloging-in-Publication Data

Horowitz, Joseph, 1948–
    Wagner nights : an American history / Joseph Horowitz.
        p.   cm. — (California studies in 19th century music ; 9)
    Includes bibliographical references and index.
    ISBN 0–520–08394–6
    1. Wagner, Richard, 1813–1883—Appreciation—United States.
2. Music—United States—19th century—History and criticism.
3. Music and society.   I. Title.   II. Series.
ML410.W13H7   1994
782.1'092—dc20   93-42410
                                                            CIP
                                                            MN

Printed in the United States of America
9   8   7   6   5   4   3   2   1

The paper used in this publication meets the minimum
requirements of American National Standard for Information
Sciences—Permanence of Paper for Printed Library
Materials, ANSI Z39.48–1984.

For Stephanie

This our nineteenth century is commonly
esteemed a prosaic, a material, an unimaginative age.
Compared with foregoing periods, it is called blind to beauty
and careless of ideals. Its amusements are frivolous or sordid,
and what mental activity it spares from the making of money
it devotes to science and not to art. These strictures . . . have
certainly much truth to back them. But leaving out of sight
many minor facts which tell in the contrary direction, there
is one great opposing fact of such importance that by itself
alone it calls for at least a partial reversal of the verdict we
pass upon ourselves as children of a nonartistic time.
This fact is the place that music—most unpractical,
most unprosaic, most ideal of the arts—has held
in nineteenth-century life.

—Mariana Van Rensselaer,
Harper's, March 1883

Anton Seidl, 1895.

CONTENTS

ILLUSTRATIONS

frontis. Anton Seidl (New York Philharmonic)

(*following p. 124*)

1. Carl Bergmann (New York Philharmonic)
2. Theodore Thomas (New York Philharmonic)
3. Leopold Damrosch (New York Philharmonic)
4. Walter Damrosch (New York Philharmonic)
5. Anton Seidl (Music Division, The New York Public Library for the Performing Arts, Astor, Lenox and Tilden Foundations)
6. Anton Seidl (New York Philharmonic)
7. Anton Seidl (New York Philharmonic)
8. The Metropolitan Opera House (Music Division, The New York Public Library for the Performing Arts, Astor, Lenox and Tilden Foundations)
9. Henry Krehbiel (Music Division, The New York Public Library for the Performing Arts, Astor, Lenox and Tilden Foundations)
10. The Brighton Beach program cover for 1889 (The Brooklyn Historical Society)
11. A letter from Anton Seidl to Laura Langford (The Brooklyn Historical Society)
12. Brighton Beach (The Brooklyn Historical Society)
13. Anton Seidl's funeral (Music Division, The New York Public Library for the Performing Arts, Astor, Lenox and Tilden Foundations)
14. Albert Niemann as Tannhäuser (Music Division, The New York Public Library for the Performing Arts, Astor, Lenox, and Tilden Foundations)

ACKNOWLEDGMENTS

This book germinated in the fall of 1990, when I was a Visiting Professor at the Institute for Studies in American Music at Brooklyn College—which means I am one of multitudes of scholars in music indebted to Wiley Hitchcock for guidance and support.

As in the past, the New York Public Library, still a great institution, anchored my research. I am especially grateful to the splendid staff of the Music Research Division of the Performing Arts Library at Lincoln Center.

The Seidl Society archive, at the Brooklyn Historical Society, proved an astounding find. I may have been the first person in a century to disturb the precious letters, clippings, and programs contained therein. Clara Lamers, of the Historical Society's library, was always attentive to my needs. So were John Pennino and Robert Tuggle of the Metropolitan Opera Archives, and Barbara Haws of the New York Philharmonic Archives. The clippings, letters, and scores of the Anton Seidl archive at Columbia University's Butler Library added detail and depth to the materials at my disposal.

Of my friends and colleagues who read *Wagner Nights* in manuscript, Robert Bailey was remarkably thorough. Others who offered valuable feedback included David Hamilton, Helen Horowitz, Joseph Kerman, David Large, Vera Lawrence, Lawrence Levine, Carol Oja, Burton Peretti, David Schiff, Ruth Solie, and Jeffrey Swann. I'm sure I'm leaving other names out; my apologies.

I relied on Tom Bender and Kathleen Hulser for advice about American history, and on Mike Beckerman and Robert Winter for advice on Dvořák in America. My agent, Elizabeth Kaplan, always manages to be patient with me. Doris Kretschmer and Erika Büky of the University of California Press also proved adept at catering to authorial anxieties; they could not have been more cooperative.

My parents have long tolerated my solitary habits and moods. A greater burden of understanding fell on my wife and son, from whom *Wagner Nights* took away time and attention. Thank you, Agnes and Bernie.

A note on opera titles: I have opted for those most familiar in the United States, whether in English, German, French, or Italian. I say *The Flying Dutchman*, not *Der fliegende Holländer*, and *Die Meistersinger*, not *The Mastersingers*.

INTRODUCTION

WAGNERISM AND AMERICA

Wagner is a bewilderingly protean figure. Is there another artist who wears so many faces? Who embodies such a self-contradictory diversity of programs and problems? Wagner encapsulates the Romantic decades he inhabits; he also resonates mightily with aspects of decades to come. At any moment, his fate in performance reveals something about an era, a people, a time and place.

We connote this multifariousness of cause and effect by the term "Wagnerism"—or *wagnérisme*, or *Wagnerismus*. It was not a unified campaign, but a heuristic ideology, a means and a mirror. Aesthetically, it was both progressive and reactionary. Politically, it was of the left and of the right. Philosophically, it was utopian and parochial. Wagner himself was all of these. He wrote prolifically on music, politics, and philosophy. His essays "Art and Revolution" (1849), "The Artwork of the Future" (1849), and "Opera and Drama" (1851) made him famous even before his "Music of the Future"* became widely known.

If Wagnerism had a core, it was a core of disillusionment with the status quo, with the industrial revolution and its legacy of science, technology, and allegedly sterile rationality. Romain Rolland spoke for the Wagnerite legions when he wrote: "Cramped by the artificiality of a town, far from action, or nature, or any strong or real life, we expanded under the influence of this noble music—music which flowed from a heart filled with understanding of the world and the breath of nature. In *Die Meistersinger*, in *Tristan*, and in *Siegfried*, we went to find the joy, the love, and the vigor that we so lacked."[1]

---

*Wagner neither coined nor cared for the term "Music of the Future" (*Zukunftsmusik*). By the late nineteenth century, however, this phrase was commonly used to refer to his music, and also to that of Liszt and other "progressive" composers—and I have so used it as well.

Wagnerism as a necessary crusade—a cultural movement, empowered, in Rolland's words, "to see and judge the whole world in the light of Bayreuth"—peaked in the late nineteenth century and ended by World War I. It had its own periodicals, its own poetics, its own riots. Its practitioners included George Bernard Shaw in England, Karl Huysmans in France, Friedrich Nietzsche in Germany, Gabriele D'Annunzio in Italy, Alexandr Blok in Russia. If Wagnerism in the United States produced no advocates of comparable world importance, it was nothing if not urgent and enveloping. The cult of Wagner dominated America's musical high culture, and helped shape its intellectual life, throughout the closing decades of the century. It powerfully infiltrated the women's movement—most American Wagnerites were female—and amassed a vast and impressive literature of books, pamphlets, and articles. The bouts of high passion and intense cogitation it inspired testified to the impact of performers of genius, gathered about the conductor Anton Seidl. He inculcated the Wagner canon in New York and Brooklyn, Boston and Cincinnati, Dayton and Peoria. "The remembrance of his work will never be wiped out among us," wrote the critic August Spanuth. "While the name of Wagner lives the name of Anton Seidl will live," wrote the soprano Lillian Nordica. Brooklyn was expected to erect a statue in his memory.[2]

But Seidl and the cult of Wagner were soon forgotten. A leading historian of American music once described the period in question as "characterized by the cult of the fashionable, the worship of the conventional, the emulation of the elegant, the cultivation of the trite and artificial, the indulgence of sentimentality, and the predominance of superficiality." Another prominent commentator has written: "After the Civil War, the greatest single controlling influence in American intellectual life came to be that exerted by a powerful small group, the big-business class. . . . The 'almighty dollar' became the standard of value, infecting the country with contempt for things of the spirit." More recently, the program booklet for the New York Philharmonic, which Seidl led to dizzy heights of achievement and acclaim, has reported that prior to the arrival of Gustav Mahler in 1909, sixty-seven years of concerts had "not produced a high standard of music-making." According to James Levine, the current artistic director of the Metropolitan Opera, where Seidl and Wagner once presided in glory, it was Arturo Toscanini who in 1908 brought to the Met "a whole new standard of performance."[3]

Why have America's Wagnerian decades been forgotten? Partly because Seidl left neither important compositions, like Mahler, nor recordings, like Toscanini. More fundamentally: the twentieth century, modernism, and the Great War against Germany wrought a sea change within a generation. The resulting future is with us still. It is the aim of this book to recapture the unremembered past.

A further, prosaic explanation of our forgetfulness is that American Wagnerism has barely been studied. Joseph Mussulman devotes a chapter to it in *Music in the Cultured Generation* (1971). The compendium *Wagnerism in European Culture and Politics* (1984) includes a single contribution, by Anne Dzamba Sessa, on "British and American Wagnerites." There is Harold Briggs's 1989 dissertation, *Richard Wagner and American Music-Literary Activity from 1850 to 1920*. And that is all. No European Wagner movement has been comparably neglected. We too readily accept the frequent European verdict that America was and remains a frontier outpost, a cultural backwater. What is more, the Gilded Age—the period beginning with the Civil War and ending at the turn of the century—suffers from a bad reputation that maligns its high culture. One prominent recent study of "Culture and Society in the Gilded Age," Alan Trachtenberg's *The Incorporation of America* (1982), typically omits all mention of Seidl—or Leopold Damrosch, or Theodore Thomas, or other leading culture-bearers, all inspirational and effective, considered in the pages to come. Only with Lawrence Levine's *Highbrow/Lowbrow: The Emergence of Cultural Hierarchy in America* (1988) have our historians begun to appreciate what kind of music American orchestras and opera companies were making before 1900.

Present-day scholars and intellectuals tend to ignore Seidl, Damrosch, and Thomas because they ignore classical music—and for this I cannot really blame them. In the United States one hundred years ago, however, classical music was as vital and contemporary as today's music business is insular and anachronistic. One hundred years ago, general intellectual discourse routinely focused on the purposes of opera, on the merits of Italian versus German singers, on the Music of the Future, on whether Americans were "musical." Many writers proclaimed music the highest, most ineffable of the arts. One cannot fully fathom the life of the mind in Gilded Age America without knowing something about America's remarkable musical institutions and the social and aesthetic purposes they served.

It follows that music critics, one hundred years ago, were influential, not marginal, purveyors of taste and opinion. In fact, I doubt if any European city ever hosted a more distinguished group of music journalists than the one headed by Henry Krehbiel, James Gibbons Huneker, and William J. Henderson, the outstanding New York critics of the Wagnerite era. Krehbiel, their acknowledged "dean," is a daunting figure, caustic and pontifical, and of vast and varied learning. Beside him, Huneker—a virtuoso stylist, a harbinger of modernism, an authority on literature and painting—is (like the virtuoso Virgil Thomson of a later period) cavalier; and Henderson, a pleasanter arbiter, is less thorough. As Krehbiel is the central chronicler of America's Wagner cult—and as he deserves more posthumous attention than he has received—he requires an introduction in this Introduction.

He was born in Ann Arbor in 1854, to German-born parents. He spoke English and German with equal fluency (and later acquired a reading knowledge of French, Italian, Russian, and Latin). He studied law in Cincinnati, but wound up a reporter and critic for the *Cincinnati Gazette*. An insatiable autodidact in the American manner, he was self-taught in music, and he taught himself well. He was music critic for the *New York Tribune* from 1880 until his death in 1923. During this period, he was also well known as a lecturer and program annotator. He completed the first English-language edition of Thayer's *Life of Beethoven*—the monumental task of his last years—and wrote a dozen books, including an influential study of African American folksong, a popular music-appreciation text, primers for famous operas and piano works, a scholarly examination of the Wagner operas, and a two-volume history of opera in New York not superseded by later writers. He also translated operas from French and German, composed exercises for the violin, and edited collections of songs and arias.

Though Krehbiel's taste was increasingly conservative, his conservatism is shrewd, never thoughtless. Assessing new works by Puccini and Richard Strauss, he is always cogent; assessing singers and instrumentalists new to New York, he seems clairvoyant; his verdicts hold. So do those of his friend Henderson—of the *New York Times*, later of the *New York Sun*—with whom he nearly always agreed. Krehbiel's other friends included Seidl and his leading soprano, Lilli Lehmann, who later remarked: "A whole chapter would not be too much to devote to American criticism in recognition of all that it has done for German opera and German artists in an unselfish and unprejudiced way. . . . The critics were incessantly interested in conferences, which impressed many, even us artists, in the preparatory work necessary to quicken the understanding of Wagner's text and music. In this they succeeded brilliantly."[4] Krehbiel disliked Mahler but got along well with Dvořák. These personal relationships had significant consequences. No subsequent New York critic played so influential a role within the city's community of artists— and no subsequent critic so deserved such a role.

Two obstacles impede proper appreciation of Krehbiel—and hence of American Wagnerism—today. The first is the density and circumlocution of his prose. The second is his insistence on the moral function of art, which prejudiced him against modernism. Like Henderson, unlike Huneker, Krehbiel is ever of his time. He exemplifies the reigning "genteel tradition." I here invoke a term coined by George Santayana in 1911[5] (and still applied today) to describe— and deride—the intellectual world of turn-of-the-century America. It stigmatizes the high-cultural life of the Gilded Age as a feeble footnote to the exploits of Morgan, Carnegie, and the Vanderbilts, "grandmotherly in that sedate, spectacled wonder with which it gazed at this terrible world and said how beautiful and how interesting it all was."[6] Santayana's disdain was buttressed by an infamous 1886 credo—that America's writers should "concern themselves with the more smiling aspects of life, which are the more American"—that its author, William Dean Howells, himself effectively disavowed. The ostensible voice of gentility is sweetly deluded, pretentiously noble, prudish and pure. It pretends not to notice the flophouse and the slum. It serenades an audience of housewives, ministers, and professors. It embalms a world of feeling and experience to which Isolde's death-orgasm, Sieglinde's incest, and Alberich's brutal factory were—or should have been—anathema.

Santayana accused genteel custodians of culture, philosophically inclined toward a sanguine idealism, of denying the realities they aspired to mold and elevate. And the Gilded Age was, truly, a time of harsh and intractable contradictions: between capital and labor, progress and economic depression. Its symbols included the railroads and the trusts—and the immigrant ghetto, a cesspool of crime and disease. Haymarket, Homestead, and Pullman were merely the most famous of its violent workers' protests. The city epitomized American affluence and poverty, hope and despair. "It is a beautiful island, long, narrow, magnificently populated, and with such a wealth of life and interest as no island in the whole world before has ever possessed," wrote Theodore Dreiser of Manhattan. "The sad part of it is, however, that the island and its beauty are, to a certain extent, a snare. Its seeming loveliness, which promises so much to the innocent eye, is not always easy of realization." According to Jacob Riis, three-quarters of Manhattan's population of more than a million lived in thirty-seven thousand tenements, "hot beds of the epidemics that carry death of rich and poor alike; the nurseries of pauperism and crime that fill our jails and police courts; that throw off a scum of forty thousand human wrecks to island asylums and workhouses year by year."[7]

Women of the middle and upper classes experienced a crisis of confinement and disutility. Restrictions on travel (no solo journeys), on attire (layers of restrictive undergarments), on self-expression (no discussion of sexual needs) contributed to an epidemic of "neurasthenia"—by which term doctors diagnosed nervous prostration and other symptoms of irrelevance. Meanwhile, evolutionary science turned the universe into mechanistic atoms, mere chemical and biological matter. This information was esoteric, but its impact was not: traditional sources of identity were confounded, traditional orthodoxies of faith abandoned. What Henry Adams termed the "disappearance of religion" was a common experience. Adams also wrote of himself: "Of all studies, the one he would rather have avoided was that of his own mind. He knew no tragedy so heartrending as introspection. . . . Ever since 1870 friends by the score had fallen victim to it." To Howells in 1890, the human personality seemed an onion which was "nothing but hulls, that you keep peeling off, one after another, till you think you have got down to the heart at last, and then you have got down to nothing."[8]

The city's new cultural landmarks—museums, libraries, opera houses, orchestras—were equally symptoms of the age. To caustic commentators of a subsequent era, they seemed monuments to evasion and complacency, or a ploy to mesmerize and subdue the masses. And yet, sympathetically observed, the genteel intellectuals, and their monuments and institutions, are not so smug and complacent. From our vantage point in the late twentieth century, writers like Krehbiel—in the *Atlantic*, the *Century*, and *Harper's*, in the better newspapers—addressed an enviably large and literate public. Their purposes were not hermetic. Public discussion of the arts, of politics, of religion and philosophy—including such issues as the extermination of the Indian, the oppression of women, and the vices of capitalism—was vigorous and eloquent. America's rifts and tensions were not blandly transcended. Free thinkers, free lovers, spiritualists of every stripe preached psychic and physical health. Socialism was rampant. So, by the 1890s, was cocaine: doctors prescribed it, cigarettes and medicines incorporated it.

The closing decades of the century were a particular time of ferment. John Higham, in a landmark 1970 essay, summarized the "Reorientation of American Culture in the 1890s" in terms of a "hunger to break out," to shatter "the gathering restrictions of a highly industrialized society."[9] One signature phenomenon of the new quest for spontaneity was the New Woman, who rode a bicycle, played tennis, and even smoked cigarettes; who pursued new personal roles and a gamut of social causes. More recently, Jackson Lears, in his influential *No Place of Grace* (1981), documents a craving for "intense experience" beginning around 1880. Santayana notwithstanding, the United States did experience a fin de siècle.

All this forms the context for America's Wagner cult. Wagner offered an avenue of intense spiritual experience, a surrogate for religion or cocaine, a song of redemption to set beside Emerson and Whitman. It was both intellectually and emotionally vitalizing. It spoke to America's women. At the same time, the Americanization of Wagner was a quintessential genteel enterprise. Traditional culture-bearers such as Krehbiel crafted a meliorist Wagner who practiced uplift and was never—as in France, England, or Russia—decadent, modernist, or politically risqué. Wagnerism in the United States was distinctively humanist, an antidote to materialism, scientism, and urban anomie.

This book, then, has a multiple thesis. It documents a Wagner movement more conservative and parochial than the Wagner movements of Europe. It documents a genteel tradition, absorbing Wagnerism, more formidable and resilient than conventional wisdom allows. And it documents a more hidden, more disruptive Wagnerian strain that activated emerging New Women. Wagnerism elaborates in surprising ways the Gilded Age portraits of Higham, Lears, and other cultural historians. It reveals both suspected American limitations and unsuspected American strengths.

A first history of American Wagnerism, *Wagner Nights* makes no attempt to be comprehensive. I focus on the period 1880 to 1900, the apex of the Wagner cult, and on New York, its capital. One inevitable result is a book-within-a-book about the United States career of Anton Seidl, which begins in 1885 and ends in 1898, and which until now has been neglected even by students of music in America. My narrative is flanked, fore and aft, by more cursory consideration of the 1860s and 1870s, and of the period between 1900 and World War I.

Following a Prelude, set in 1898, the book proceeds chronologically. Of Wagner's "First Missionaries" (Chapter 2), the most important is Carl Bergmann. The "Master Builder" (Chapter 3) is Theodore Thomas, who succeeded Bergmann as conductor of the New York Philharmonic and later became the first conductor of the Chicago Orchestra. Leopold Damrosch, who "Germanized" the Metropolitan Opera (Chapter 4), is a third New World Wagner missionary preceding Seidl, or "The Coming of the Disciple" (Chapter 5). Tracking Seidl in New York, I consider the reception and interpretation of *Tristan und Isolde* (Chapter 6), *Der Ring des Nibelungen* (Chapter 8), and *Parsifal* (Chapter 10). Displaced at the Met, Seidl went into "Partial Eclipse" (Chapter 9) and wound up conducting the New York Philharmonic. Another previously undocumented episode in his Wagner crusade unfolded in Brooklyn, where the women of the Seidl Society presented Wagner concerts at the Academy of Music—and also at Coney Island, where Seidl conducted in the summer, and where "Wagner Nights" (Chapter 11) filled the three-thousand-seat Brighton Beach musical pavilion. "Protofeminism" (Chapter 12) is my central attempt to fathom the relationship between Wagnerism and the New Woman. "*Parsifal* Revisited" (Chapter 14) observes Wagnerism in an adulterated late phase. "Enter Modernism" (Chapter 15) takes stock of the Wagner cult at its point of demise in comparison to the Wagner cults of Europe; this is the closest I come to summarizing my findings. "Secularization" (Chapter 16) briefly surveys the post–World War I decades, and discovers only Wagner, not Wagnerism. I close not with a conclusion but with a reconsideration of the Gilded Age, raising topics for further inquiry. An Appendix summarizes the Wagner operas and lists important first performances.

Some readers will doubtless want to skip over more purely musical matters in favor of investigating the Seidlites or, in the Postlude, issues of anti-Semitism and (following Lawrence Levine) sacralization. Others will want to skip everything extramusical, and read only about the Wagner stars Lilli Lehmann and Albert Niemann (in Chapter 5), or about Seidl as a Wagner interpreter (in Chapter 7). This is precisely the schism I try to counteract. Read the whole book.

As in my previous studies of America's borrowed musical high culture—in *Understanding Toscanini* and *The Ivory Trade*—I draw inspiration from de Tocqueville: "It is therefore not true to assert that men living in democratic times are naturally indifferent to science, literature, and the arts; only it must be acknowledged that they cultivate them after their own fashion and bring to the task their own peculiar qualifications and deficiencies."[10]

PRELUDE

A Gilded Age Funeral

By 11 A.M. a crowd had begun to assemble at 30 East 62nd Street. Many of the mourners were fulsomely upholstered ladies of social standing—whose grief, however, was not merely formal. Others, black in top hats and tailcoats, were men who conversed in German. The day was overcast and drizzly.

At 12:30 the doors of the three-story brownstone were opened. The crowd, now two hundred strong clogging sidewalk and street, stirred to attention. The coffin appeared, strewn with violets and white lilies, borne on the shoulders of recognizable persons of distinction. These included Richard Watson Gilder, the editor of the magazine the *Century,* and the reform leader Carl Schurz; the German American banker James Speyer and the physician William H. Draper; the music critics Henry T. Finck, Henry Krehbiel, and Albert Steinberg; the composers Edward MacDowell and Xavier Scharwenka; the pianist Rafael Joseffy; the violinist Eugene Ysaÿe. They maneuvered down the steps and set the casket in the horse-drawn hearse. A large escort formed. The solemn carriages proceeded east for a block, then turned south abreast Central Park.

The view down Fifth Avenue was imposing. Here were the city's newest and most fashionable residences, palatial edifices whose ponderous mass and encrusted Gothic and Renaissance, French and Italian facades proclaimed acquired taste and gargantuan ambition, financial nerve and cultural instability. The four-year-old Metropolitan Club, on the left, was a marble palazzo. Across the street to the south and fronting the Plaza at 59th Street were the Savoy and New Netherlands Hotels, of which the latter, six years old, was the "tallest hotel in the world." South of the Plaza the cortege passed Vanderbilt Row, whose four family mansions mingled a stately opulence with gaudy turrets-and-flags splendor. St. Patrick's Cathedral, conspicuous for its pair of towering, tapered spires, was one of a series of new Fifth Avenue churches.

By the time the hearse reached the Moorish towers and Saracenic arches of the two-thousand-seat Temple Emanu-El, its route was crowded by an assortment of onlookers, curious and devout. By the time it reached the Croton Reservoir, whose forty-four-foot "Egyptian" granite walls stretched from 42nd Street to 40th, the route was mobbed. A hundred-piece band—a German musical army, volunteers from the Musical Union under the direction of Victor Herbert and Nahan Franco—had assembled at the 40th Street corner. The dark euphony of its massed winds and muffled drums, in the Funeral March from Beethoven's Op. 26 Piano Sonata, doubled the dismal weather.

The band, the horse-drawn hearse, the pallbearers and bereaved friends headed west, flanked by throngs of spectators, the men hatless in the rain. Their destination, straddling Broadway between 39th and 40th streets, was the Metropolitan Opera House, a scene of chaos. The vestibule had been clogged since eleven. Several women had fainted in the crush. One hundred fifty patrolmen had arrived to restore a degree of order, inside and out, before the house was opened a few minutes past midday, with six policemen stationed at every door. For fully ten minutes, the inrushing women formed a surging, smothering human mass. Many who lacked tickets gained entrance by clasping hands with ticketholders. Within fifteen minutes, every downstairs seat was occupied, with women outnumbering men twenty to one. The crowd poured upstairs. Standees were packed five and six rows deep. In box 40, where she had been accustomed to listening with her husband when he was not conducting, the widow—barely composed, a large, handsome woman with gentle eyes—sat beside her physician and a few close friends. The house contained about four thousand people. Its normal capacity was thirty-three hundred. Some fifteen thousand had applied for tickets.

The cortege arrived at the 40th Street entrance at 1:15. The pall-bearers removed the bier and conveyed it into the awesome horse-shoe auditorium, whose Family Circle, five stories aloft, inclined beyond the back wall toward some remote Valhalla. Upon the casket's appearance, the audience, overflowing two tiers of boxes and three balconies, arose with a sudden loud rustle of furniture and clothes. All heads were bowed. The procession moved down the left aisle. The band of honor, now onstage, played a dirge.

From the railing to the stage, the pit had been floored over, car-peted, and encircled with black cloth. Masses of harmonized flowers blanketed both this platform and the stage. Jean and Edouard de Reszke had contributed a wreath of four thousand violets. Nellie Melba had sent another nearly two feet in diameter. A rose wreath from Lillian Nordica quoted Isolde: "Gebrochen der Blick! Still das Herz! Nicht eines Atems flücht'ges Wehn! Muss sie nun jammernd vor dir stehn."* A music stand in white roses and violets, near the head of the coffin, bore an open score on which appeared portraits of Richard Wagner and the departed, with the inscription "Vereint auf Ewig."†

The casket was placed on a black flowered catafalque several feet high; draped in an American flag, it marked the conductor's place. The stage, lit by candles in great candelabra, was set as the cathedral from Gounod's *Faust*. There sat mourners and friends, a male cho-rus, the German band, and the New York Philharmonic Orchestra. This was the memorial service for Anton Seidl, dead three days before, March 28, 1898, at the age of forty-seven.

The first of two orchestral selections, led by the Philharmonic's concertmaster, Richard Arnold, was the *Adagio lamentoso* from Tchaikovsky's Sixth Symphony.

Carl Schurz, the designated eulogist, could not bring himself to speak. His place, on the stage of the Metropolitan Opera House, was taken by Henry Krehbiel. The other speaker was a Unitarian minis-ter, the Reverend Merle St. Croix Wright. Though Seidl had been a

---

*"His eyes dimmed! His heart still! Not the fleeting stir of breath! Must she now stand before you, mourning?"

†"Forever united."

Roman Catholic, his insistence on cremation and the absence of final rites dictated that no priest could preside.

From the sad, candle-lit stage, the Reverend Wright hurled his speech into the auditorium.

> Today we honor a man who first honored himself, who honored us, honored our city and our country by making America a worthy member of the great international musical family. He, as director of the opera, had the courage to give music a new birth, and he may justly be called the premier of the music of America. . . . He was a foreigner, but of that class of foreigners who make a country native to our souls—a citizen of this country preferring America and by America preferred. He was a leader perpetual in the everlasting war against evil, selfishness, and lust, his only thought to uplift and ennoble men.

Krehbiel now arose to read a dispatch from Colonel Robert G. Ingersoll, famous for his oratory and his atheism, and a devoted friend of the deceased:

> In the noon and zenith of his career, in the flush and glory of success, Anton Seidl, the greatest orchestral leader of all time, the perfect interpreter of Wagner, of all his subtlety and sympathy, his heroism and grandeur, his intensity and limitless passion, his wondrous harmonies that tell of all there is in life, and touch the longings and the hopes of every heart, has passed from the shores of sound to the realm of silence, borne by the mysterious and resistless tide that ever ebbs but never flows. . . .
>
> We will mourn for him, we will honor him, not in words, but in the language that he used. Anton Seidl is dead. Play the great funeral march. Envelop him in music. Let its wailing waves cover him. Let its wild and mournful winds sigh and moan above him. Give his face to its kisses and its tears. Play the great funeral march, music as profound as death. That will express our sorrow—that will voice our love, our hope, and that will tell of the life, the triumph, the genius, the death of Anton Seidl.

The musicians, led by Henry Schmitt, now began again. The soft timpani taps, the tense, tragic murmur of the low strings seamlessly joined the mortuary ambience—then convulsively transformed it. Upon the pounding, shuddering tread of Siegfried's dirge were superimposed heroic memories of the departed: his legendary strength, his naive ardor, the heedless energy of his doomed exploits. In another time, in another place, this thundering meta-imagery would have seemed a preposterous memorial tribute. On this occasion, the imagery seemed right. Temperamentally, Anton Seidl had been no Siegfried. But he had been Siegfried's—and Wagner's—instrument. And this labor had been heroic. At the Metropolitan, he would lead Wagner three and four times a week. At Coney Island, in the summers, he would conduct two concerts a day, seven days a week, giving the overtures to *The Flying Dutchman*, *Tannhäuser*, and *Die Meistersinger*, the *Tristan* Prelude, love music, and *Liebestod*, and dozens of excerpts from *The Ring of the Nibelung*. His first American concert audiences were sometimes pathetically small. He never enjoyed the services of a permanent orchestra. He kept his own counsel, and did not tire. When he arrived in the United States, only *Lohengrin*, of the Wagner operas, was a repertory staple. When he died, a dozen years later, the Wagner canon was a holy and a necessary cause. Hearing Siegfried's Funeral Music, four thousand mourners, eyes riveted on the raised, flowered coffin, heard all of this. A mere handful had ever met Anton Seidl. They experienced his loss as an American calamity.[1]

For nearly a week, every metropolitan daily chronicled Anton Seidl's final hours, the evolving funeral plans, the memorial services and statements, the cremation. Critics reviewed his achievements in Europe and America, and pondered the consequences of his departure. Henry Finck of the *New York Post*, a Wagnerite prone to blatant and reckless enthusiasms, at one point called Seidl's American career "the most important 12 years in the history of music in America."[2] Other assessments, if more restrained, were no less worshipful. Considering that many Americans had heard Hans Richter and

Hermann Levi abroad, considering that Arthur Nikisch, of the Berlin Philharmonic, was familiar in Boston and New York, there was nothing parochial about this posthumous veneration. Rather, what distinguished the New World perspective was an intense gratitude. Americans grieved for Seidl as a great conductor, but also as a friend.

Of the memorial essayists, none was more eloquent than James Gibbons Huneker, who was neither sentimental nor a Wagnerite. Seidl's passing revealed in Huneker an uncharacteristic humility, an unsuspected susceptibility to reverence.

> Without any apparent volition on his part he made one feel that he was a distinguished man—a man among men.
>
> His funeral was more impressive than any music drama ever seen or heard at Bayreuth. The Metropolitan Opera House was for the moment transformed into a huge mortuary chamber. It was extremely picturesque, yet sincerely solemn. The trappings of woe were not exhibited for their mere bravery. A genuine grief absorbed every person in the building, and when Henry Edward Krehbiel read Robert G. Ingersoll's dispatch the quaver in his voice, a thousand times more significant than the rhetorical phrases he uttered, set many sobbing. . . . It was overwhelmingly touching. . . .
>
> Alas! that Anton Seidl is dead.[3]

The most affecting tribute from Seidl's colleagues was signed by the American soprano Lillian Nordica (née Norton), whose Isolde and Brünnhilde Seidl had coached:

> In sustaining his ideals by untiring effort there never seemed with Mr. Seidl any thought that he was doing more than the humblest would have done to secure a proper standard of performance. His sincerity, like his enthusiasm, was infectious; if the one aroused those engaged to more vital interest the other helped make that interest of the enduring kind. When a man of such high purpose comes into the world he impresses an influence extending so far beyond his time that it is not given to us to estimate it.[4]

Seidl's passing left a vacuum. At the Metropolitan, he had presided over the German repertoire. In the concert hall, he had led the bulk of New York's symphonic programs. Brooklyn's *Daily Eagle* worried: "His death leaves New York in the almost anomalous position of being without an available music director—a humiliating circumstance when the size and wealth and cultivation are considered. . . . The place of Mr. Seidl will not be readily occupied again."[5]

A mere generation after Seidl's death, only old-timers could recall when Brooklyn's Seidl Society spoke of fostering a regular summer Wagner festival, an "American Bayreuth." The *Musical Courier* remembered, as a curiosity, a time when Wagner was "in fashion," when a conductor named Seidl magnetized "an immense audience of music lovers [from] all over the country who flocked to New York," when "middle-aged women in their enthusiasm stood up in the chairs and screamed their delight . . . for what seemed hours."[6]

The Wagner cult had expired. America itself had changed.

1

The Ascendancy

During the last week of January 1880, Richard Wagner was in a terrible mood. The weather was rainy and cold—the most severe Neapolitan winter in memory. His physician had declared him fit; he declared his repugnance for all medicines. His Bayreuth Festival had buried him in debt—even King Ludwig seemed unwilling to help. All of Germany was misruled, mismanaged. He read to Cosima an account of Goethe's death. "So beautiful!" he exclaimed. "What was wrong was the time, his country. Thus does a great and noble man die." He pondered Wahnfried, the Festspielhaus—his life's work, all in vain. "Were I to point out what, beyond the general sufferings of existence, is particularly painful, it would be the necessity of keeping some sort of contact with the world. Oh, for Tribschen! Oh, for the children's childhood days, for the days of complete withdrawal! Then came fame, then the children grew up, while we two were armed for only one thing—the tranquility of love and creative work." One morning, before breakfast, he went to the piano and played the Pilgrims' Chorus from *Tannhäuser*. Cosima thanked him in tears. He remarked: "Yes, people ought to respect me for having expressed the spirit of Christianity in this—and, what is more, freed of all sectarianism." He complained of social isolation: "Nobody belongs to us. And yet we have behaved reasonably enough." Over dinner at Prince Ouroussof's, he startled the company by observing that he had no idea why Russia had not granted him a pension. One morning he awoke to ask Cosima the name of the last conqueror of Asia, about whom Corneille had written a play. She could not remember.

"Bajazet." "What brought that to mind?" "Because at the moment I am so interested in nomadic peoples." His thoughts harped on emigration.[1]

Cosima kept anxious watch. Richard was fatigued, Richard was depressed, Richard slept poorly, Richard had no appetite. He suffered from fits of shivering, from erysipelas, from rheumatic catarrh. He came down with a skin rash, then an eye infection. On February 1, she confided to her diary: "It is years since I have seen him as he was yesterday. Today the eye inflammation is worse, and it is tormenting him." She also reported: "He wants to move to America (Minnesota) . . . he can no longer tolerate the situation here in Germany. . . . Again and again he keeps coming back to America, says it is the only place on the whole map which he can gaze upon with any pleasure. 'What the Greeks were among the peoples of this earth, this continent is among its countries.'"[2]

In the days that followed, Wagner announced that he intended to collect the heads of German professors. This would prove that there were no true Germans among them, the heroic tribes having perished through migration. In conversation about the Paris Commune, he conceded that it included men of integrity but derided its pipe dream that the power of property could be destroyed. He denounced Italian opera for its monotony and poverty of invention. Driving through Naples, he declared it "the only big city for me!"; encountering congestion and long delays, he grew testy. The open air made his skin turn red. His eyes were badly strained. He dreamt that Cosima was against him. He thought of his money-raising schemes and felt trapped: "Escape from these 15-mark contributions!" He asked to have a map of North America. "Yes, they will outstrip us. We are a sinking crew."[3]

Wagner's thoughts turned to the family dentist, Dr. Newell Jenkins. Dr. Jenkins was a wise and widely traveled man. With Wagner, he was accustomed to taking long walks and conversing on all subjects except music—which, to Wagner's relief, did not fall within the wide orbit of his enthusiasms. Dr. Jenkins was amazed by Wagner's intellectual powers. He was impressed by his "red-blooded" republicanism and his intense curiosity about all things American. He had once offered to help Wagner undertake a concert tour of America. It was to this American friend, residing in Dresden, that Wagner now wrote from Naples on February 8. "I feel as though my patience will soon run out with regard to my hopes for Germany and her future," he began, "and that I may have cause to regret not having transplanted the seed of my artistic ideas to a fertile and more helpful soil in years long past. It is not impossible that I may yet decide to emigrate to America."[4]

The plan, Wagner explained, was to take along his entire family plus his latest artistic offspring: the festival play *Parsifal.* An American Wagner association would be formed and would place one million dollars at his disposal. Half this sum would be used to settle the Wagners "in some climatically beneficial state of the Union." The other half would be deposited "in a state bank as a capital investment at 5 percent." The association would also raise funds for an annual Wagner festival. Replacing Bayreuth, it would mount model performances of the Wagner canon, beginning with the premiere of *Parsifal.* In return, America "would secure my services for all time. . . . Whatever I do in the future, whether as performance manager or as a creative artist, would belong to the American nation, free of charge." The letter concluded: "Would you be good enough to think this over a little, and if it seems to you a good idea, let me know your views."

For two decades Wagner had cast evasive glances toward the New World. The almighty dollar had already enticed the likes of Jenny Lind and Henriette Sontag, Anton Rubinstein and Hans von Bülow. Soon, it would seduce Tchaikovsky, Busoni, and Mahler. And America was virgin. It had no Napoleons or Bismarcks, no princes or kings, no creditors or cultural bureaucrats.

At first, Wagner's transatlantic gaze was inquisitive yet wary. In 1849, banned from Germany for his role in the recent Dresden uprising, he wrote from exile in Zurich: "America for me now and always can be of only financial interest: but if circumstances here at home remain such that I finally run out of air to breathe, I might finally cast an eye in the direction of America, but only to become a craftsman there—albeit with a baton in my hand—which would at least ensure me a better income there than it would here." Taking stock of his political views some three years later, he found only "the bloodiest hatred for our entire civilization." "That I ever set store by the workers as workers is something I must now atone for grievously: with the noises they make these workers are the wretchedest slaves, whom anyone can control nowadays if he promises them plenty of 'work.' A slave mentality has taken root in everything with us. . . . I am now thinking a good deal of America! Not because I might find what I am looking for there, but because the ground there is easier to plant. . . . I am planning to make a start soon on my great Nibelung trilogy. But I shall *perform* it only on the banks of the Mississippi."[5]

By January 1854, Wagner was aware that Boston's Germania Musical Society had given its first all-Wagner concert the month before. "They urge me to come over and inform me that the interest in my works is growing," he wrote Liszt, "and that I could make a great deal of money with concert performances." But America still seemed inimical—"as impossible as it is ludicrous"—to his artistic needs. In 1855, he was offered a six-month American tour as a conductor. "Ten years ago I might have considered such an undertaking," he now wrote Liszt, "but it would be callous for me to make such detours for a living, especially now, when I am fit for one pursuit only, to devote myself to my very own affair, my [*Ring of the Nibelung*]."

By the end of 1858, still in Switzerland, he had finished *Das Rheingold* and *Die Walküre* of the Nibelung tetralogy and was working on *Tristan und Isolde*. He still had no regular income. A Frankfurt concert agent conveyed an invitation from New York. Wagner dithered: he felt "somewhat indifferent" to the fate of his operas in America; conducting there would be lucrative yet "somewhat uncongenial." By March 1859, however, he had decided to spend five months in New York: "I am gradually taking a more serious view of the matter, and have submitted my conditions," he reported to Karl Kindworth, whom he proposed as second conductor. But these conditions were rejected. "Quite honestly, I do not think much of your American ideas," counseled Liszt.[6]

In 1873, Chicago invited Wagner to help superintend the production of his operas; Wagner declined because he doubted Chicago could supply the right audience. In 1874, Wagner asked Dexter Smith, editor of New York's *Staats-Zeitung*, to establish an American Wagner festival to help support Bayreuth. In 1876, he composed a march on commission from Philadelphia's Centennial Exposition. The accumulated debts of the Bayreuth Festival, begun that summer with the first *Ring*, forced abandonment of a planned 1877 festival in favor of a London concert tour—whose profits, however, were meager. With his health declining—"I am dragging myself from place to place with my entire nervous system in a state of seemingly irrevocable collapse"—Wagner now adopted a revised view of the United States: less an expedient source of capital, more a potential homeland. The German response to his goals and needs had been insufficient. No groundswell had acclaimed the new spirit of the *Ring*; instead, Wagner's essential audience, as Nietzsche was to stress, was a privileged elite. Responding to an 1877 offer from the American impresario Bernard Ullman, Wagner threatened to liquidate his Bayreuth assets and "set sail across the ocean with my entire family, and never again return to Germany." King Ludwig, who in 1864 had rescued Wagner from exile and begun subsidizing his affairs, responded: "I implore you, by the love and friendship which has united us all these years, to abandon this *dreadful* plan. All Germans would be indelibly stained, were they to allow the departure of their greatest man. . . . Your roses will not grow on America's sterile soil, where selfishness, lovelessness, and Mammon hold sway."[7]

Though Ludwig guaranteed Bayreuth's survival, Wagner's bitterness was deeply implanted—and so were notions of a new home in a New World. His 1880 letter to Dr. Jenkins propelled these notions to their maximum potential bounty: a million-dollar stipend, an American Bayreuth. En route to Constantinople, Jenkins stopped in Naples with the intention of gently exposing this fantasy, yet found Wagner and Cosima so deluded about America that his arguments had no force. That summer, he wrote to John Sullivan Dwight, confidentially conveying an English translation of Wagner's letter and begging Dwight's advice. Dwight replied that Wagner's American plan, excited reports of which were already widely circulating, had affected "almost every one who has read it, even those inclined to Wagnerism, as an extraordinary and almost insane proposal."[8]

By the fall, Wagner, while still envisioning a North American tour, was reassuring Ludwig that only Bayreuth's stage could be consecrated for *Parsifal*. It was duly performed there on July 26, 1882. Wagner died in Venice—not Minnesota—seven months later.

And yet the conjunction of Wagner and America was less farfetched a century ago than one would imagine.

We have grown accustomed—too accustomed—to stigmatizing the cultural life of the Gilded Age as timid and "genteel." In music, however, the genteel tradition eventually produced critics of outstanding power and discernment, of whom I have already mentioned Henry Krehbiel and William J. Henderson. Their common precursor, less remarkable in all respects save influence, was the same John Sullivan Dwight to whom Dr. Newell Jenkins appealed for help in counseling his friend Richard Wagner. A onetime Unitarian minister, subsequently a member of the utopian Brook Farm community, Dwight for three decades edited *Dwight's Journal of Music*, until its termination in 1881 the leading American periodical of its kind. Ralph Waldo Emerson, to whose transcendentalists Dwight once belonged and who pronounced "culture" the "word of ambition at the present day," was one inspiration for Dwight's crusade against decadence and materialism. Another was Matthew Arnold, who urged men "to try and know the best that is known and thought in the world"—and so set standards and uplift taste. Culture and morality, to thinkers of Dwight's persuasion, were intimately bound. "Moral" meant orderly, temperate, decent. Truth was *intellectualized* beauty. The best music connected to the life of the mind—not vulgar programmatic content. Emotion was suspect.[9]

Wagner's music was known to be blatantly programmatic, blatantly emotional. Its wandering melodies and opulent instrumentation sounded sensuous. Its harmonic and structural convolutions defeated symmetry and logic. His librettos added further grounds for objection. Though a Wagnerite, John G. Hassard of the *New York Tribune* presented a body of outraged opinion when he deplored the *Ring*'s "gross divinities" and "incestuous heroes."[10] Finally, Wagner himself was irascible, egotistic, rebellious. He had joined the Dresden rebels. He had cuckolded his friend Hans von Bülow— whose first wife, Cosima, became Wagner's second. In an age when music was disparaged as ladies' stuff, when breeding, religiosity, and *manliness* were trumpeted virtues of the genteel Mendelssohn, Wagner's nervous, hyperbolic style, his relatively short stature, his addiction to silks and perfumes and ribbons were all likely symptoms of a proscribed effeminacy.

A genteel tradition shackled by conventional expectations was no figment of George Santayana's imagination. But especially by 1880, when Wagner set his sights on Minnesota, it was not nearly as shackled as the stereotype suggests. In fact, discourse on the arts, if conservatively biased, was informed and nuanced. As early as the 1850s, Dwight plentifully supplied his readers with discussions of Wagner's life and theories and with translated extracts from Wagner's writings, as well as with reviews of Wagner's music. Positive opinion was not excluded. Negative opinion was neither casual nor arbitrary. One 1858 critique, for instance, does not quarrel in principle with Wagner's signature tunes, but finds their deployment in *Lohengrin* "exceedingly clumsy." The same review plausibly maintains that, of *Lohengrin*'s three long acts, the third is musically the most successful, containing "much that is beautiful."[11] Dwight himself first reacted to Wagner with a combination of shock, confusion, and admiration. Over time, however, his tentative judgments hardened into opposition to Wagnerian "formlessness" and iconoclasm.

A twenty-eight-page article in the April 1873 *North American Review* by John Knowles Paine, himself a leading (and by no means negligible) composer of genteel inclination, condemns Wagner as a godless rebel—but the arguments are meticulous. In addition to reviewing the events of Wagner's life, Paine scrutinizes three texts— "Art and Revolution," "The Artwork of the Future," and "Opera and Drama"—that had contributed, as he remarks, to "a greater commotion in the musical world than even [that caused by] his music, except perhaps the very recent operas. . . . Year by year the war of opinion has grown more fierce and general, and finally has divided the musical world into two hostile camps." Wagner, who "took an active part" in the revolutionary movements of 1848–49, was "a violent radical in politics." Concomitantly, "The modest aim of Wagner's writings is a complete revolution in art, society, politics, and religion." In contrast to Beethoven, whose compositions are pervaded by "deep religious feeling and moral tone," Wagner was a declared enemy of Christianity. His essays were "a strange mixture of truth and error, in which the error predominates." His "total and irreverent denial of the inestimable good which Christianity has done and will continue to do" linked him with "other violent agitators and enthusiasts . . . who seem out of joint with the world."

In a more analytical mode, Paine debunks Wagner by subjecting overheated Wagnerian rhetoric to cold logic, buttressed with citations from August Ambros, Otto Jahn, Adolph Marx, and Friedrich Schlegel. Addressing the *Gesamtkunstwerk*—Wagner's union of the arts—Paine majestically observes: "There is in truth nothing eminently new or original in the idea. Music, poetry, and dance have from time immemorial appeared conjointly in the drama, in one form or another, accompanied to some extent by the other fine arts." He proceeds to argue at length that "every fine art is complete in itself." Paine next contests Wagner's attempt to "wed poetry and music in perfectly equality," observing that

> the movement of the feelings, through the agency of music, is far more expanded in duration than the motive supplied by the words. A dramatic text cannot content itself with a repetition of the same thought, but must proceed from one thought to another, in order to sustain the progress of the action. Now if the music follows the poem strictly, syllable after syllable, word after word, without the privilege of dwelling here and there upon the sense of a passage, it cannot fulfill its highest object, which is to express the emotional principle to the utmost.

Paine equally takes issue with Wagnerian "infinite melody" and leitmotifs, and with the notion that only myth can be the source of "ideal drama." He acknowledges the present popularity, in Germany and the Netherlands, of "Wagner's most *musical* operas," *The Flying Dutchman, Tannhäuser, Lohengrin,* and *Die Meistersinger.* He notes that *Tristan und Isolde,* "from which airs and concerted melodies were banished, has not survived its production at Munich in 1865." In sum, Wagner is a clear and present danger, "a man of wonderful energy and talent [and] at the same time one whose head and heart are not entirely right. . . . As art-loving Americans let us hope that it will be the mission of our own country to rejuvenate the life of music; may it be vouchsafed to her to lift the veil that now shrouds the future of this beautiful art!"

If Dwight's criticism was never this sustained, his stiffening resistance to the "Music of the Future" had by 1880 grown greatly embattled;[12] he died an anachronism in 1893. By then, Wagner's ascendancy was unstoppable, his appeal irresistible. And yet Wagner did not shatter the genteel code. To a remarkable degree, its latter-day adherents reconstrued Wagner as one of their own.

One inevitable topic of the raging Wagner debate was Wagner the man. Was he immoral, licentious, unbridled? In 1869, *Dwight's Journal* called Wagner's essay "Judaism in Music" "ignoble" and "small-minded."[13] Paine, as we have just seen, branded Wagner a violent revolutionary. More perfect Wagnerites were more forgiving.

Even Dwight admired Wagner's heroic self-reliance, and his practicality as a man of the theater. A more emphatic Wagner advocate, influential on both sides of the Atlantic, was the German-born scholar Francis Hueffer, who moved to London in 1869. Writing in the *Century* in November 1874, Hueffer declared Wagner's reputation—notwithstanding the "ill-disguised hostility" of certain writers—already "established beyond dispute." Wagner, Hueffer stressed, "is not negative only"; he was less a rebel than a progressive reformer, embodying "character"—a genteel codeword for moral rectitude—as well as genius. "He has overthrown much, but his reconstructions are vaster and more harmonious than the old fabric." Had Wagner been born to a higher station, he might have made a "great statesman." Rather, copying a quintessential New World scenario, his life was struggle, his success hard-earned. Beethoven was "the load-star [*sic*] of our master's early aspirations." His political activism was an outgrowth of early discouragements, of a "morbid despondency, in which change at any price seemed a relief. In this mood, and more from a sense of antagonism to things existing than from any distinct political persuasion," Wagner took on active part in the revolutionary risings of 1848 and 1849. Anyway, that revolt was no nihilistic deviation, but a "dream of liberty."

Hueffer at times seems disingenuous. His synopsis of *Tristan und Isolde*, for instance, is confined to act 1, avoiding the carnal second act and the suicidal eroticism of act 3. The disturbing fatality of the love potion is cleverly soft-pedaled: it is a "symbol of irresistible love, which to speak with the Psalmist, is 'strong as death' and knows no fetter." The whole of *Tristan*, moreover, closely follows a respectable medieval source: Gottfried von Strassburg's "immortal epic."

The same year he wrote for the *Century*, Hueffer in London published a book-length study, *Richard Wagner and the Music of the Future*. No American Wagnerite had yet undertaken such a thorough and sanitizing portrait. But the portrait was congealing. In February 1874 William Foster Apthorp surveyed Wagner's writing for the *Atlantic* and inferred heroic self-control: "Even under his most turgid bombast, amid his most sensuous metaphors, we can always trace a fixed principle resolutely worked out, without wavering or hesitation." For other American observers, the "invincible perseverance" and "unquenchable enthusiasm" Apthorp admired in Wagner's essays were seen applied in more worldly ways. Few Americans had ever met Wagner. They had incompletely sampled his music. But his vigorous financial overtures and his building and subscription schemes were well-known. Josiah Gilbert Holland, writing in 1876 of Bayreuth's drive-to-fruition, perceived entrepreneurial prowess: "The power that rules the world is the power of ideas. Any man with genius enough to conceive a vital and germinal idea, and vitality enough to push it, is a master, sure of his triumph. He has that within him which gives a crowning significance to his life. To possess a great idea is to have a mission. It is to know what to do. It is to have a path and a goal."[14]

If such praise of Wagner the statesmanlike visionary, disciplined thinker, and inspirational businessman distorted the truth, other components of the Wagner agenda completely supported Gilded Age mores. Wagner made Art a religion. Here he insisted on pure acts and principles. He denounced Italian and French opera as meretricious, artificial, opportunistic, unholy. High-minded aesthetes of the Gilded Age felt the same way. Donizetti's "hurdy-gurdy tunes" and the opulent spectacles of Meyerbeer offended them. Krehbiel, who revered Mozart, found the libretto to *The Magic Flute* frivolous. Music "should be more of a brave inspiration than an indolent luxury," wrote Samuel Osgood in *Harper's.* "The modern opera is morally and intellectually a monstrosity, and Wagner . . . is probably right in his onslaught upon it, and in his plea for wedding the divine art of song to good sense and manhood, instead of leaving it to the foolish doggerel of the pattern librettos and the harlotry and ruffianism of the pattern heroes and heroines."[15]

Finally, the core affinity between Wagner and America was that Wagner was, if not exactly a moralist, a Victorian meliorist. Like the genteel critics of industrial capitalism, he inveighed against decadent aristocrats, greedy materialists, and depraved utilitarians. He preached uplift: new social vision, new spiritual awareness. Like America's Spencerians and Darwinians, whose agendas he otherwise contradicted, he believed in evolutionary progress, organic betterment. Like Ralph Waldo Emerson and John Sullivan Dwight, he perceived himself as a cultural missionary embattled by philistines and businessmen. This is why, compared to subsequent generations of American Wagnerites, Americans of the Gilded Age were predisposed to listen to what Wagner was saying; even before they knew him as a musician, they took him seriously as a thinker.

In fact, what Wagner wrote was at first far better known than what he composed—and nowhere more so than in the United States.

Partly, this imbalance resulted from the many practical problems afflicting Wagner production in the composer's lifetime. The vocal and orchestral assignments were, more than controversial, almost incomprehensibly long and difficult—which is why Wagner jealously discouraged unauthorized and incompletely prepared stagings. A second factor was Wagner's own production schedule. Following his relatively swift early output—*Rienzi* was finished in 1840, *The Flying Dutchman* in 1841, *Tannhäuser* in 1845, *Lohengrin* in 1848—he stopped composing for more than five years. This was a period of personal and artistic stock-taking. It was also the period during which, as a necessary by-product, he wrote much of his best-known and most influential prose. Of his remaining stage works—his mature operas, a radical departure even from his own past practice—*Tristan* was finished only in 1859, *Die Meistersinger* in 1867, the *Ring* (*Das Rheingold, Die Walküre, Siegfried, Götterdämmerung*) in 1874, *Parsifal* in 1882.

As of 1880, when Wagner considered emigrating to Minnesota, only *The Flying Dutchman*, *Tannhäuser*, *Lohengrin*, and *Die Walküre* had been mounted in the United States. But Wagner's writings were already widely read in intellectual circles. Dwight first published Wagner in translation in 1853. In 1871, the *Gesammelte Schriften und Dichtungen* began appearing. Four years later, Edward L. Burlingame published a dozen translated essays from the collected works as *Art, Life and Theories of Richard Wagner*. Of special interest, four years after that, was "The Work and Mission of My Life"—Wagner's only address to American readers, a two-part, thirty-seven-page article in the *North American Review*.*[16] This proved an autobiographical primer cunningly interlaced with a manifesto whose inevitable thesis was Wagner's special relationship to the New World.

Wagner's writings, so potent in his lifetime, are too readily dismissed today. Their faults are obvious: prolixity and circumlocution, egocentricity and inflamed personal bias. But only an equally biased reader could deny the intellectual energy animating Wagner's world of ideas. And the ideas themselves, if not always original, are deployed with a marvelous resourcefulness—in relation to one

---

* It is generally assumed that Wagner's essay was overseen, if not actually written, by his disciple Hans von Wolzogen.

another, to the times, and (always the ultimate purpose) to the author's urgent rationalization of the historic and personal necessities governing his life in art. Wagner the essayist is an indispensable mentor to conductors and singing actors, an inspirational analyst of late Beethoven, a shrewd critic of contemporary opera. If his 1879 essay for the *North American Review* is a relatively undistinguished effort, it remains deeply informative. For reasons both psychological and material, Wagner had to convince Americans, and himself, that they needed and deserved one another. His appeal to Americans illuminates his inherent appeal to America.

Naturally, the essay bristles with disdain for an ungrateful and unsupportive Germany. A "great German revival" seemed heralded by individual artistic geniuses: Goethe, Schiller, Mozart, Beethoven. But "they found no great public, no nation, to which they could speak in their own language." Rather, German princes and aristocrats were reactionary blockheads, insensitive to the timeliness of a national art based in the theater as a public agency of social reform. And there was an influential foreign element—a race of "go-betweens," of "mediators and negotiators" (that is, Jews): Meyerbeer's historical operas, a "mishmash of styles and methods," and Mendelssohn's shallow concert works, all elegance and delicacy, completed the estrangement of Germans from their own truest cultural expression. Repelled, Wagner removed himself to Paris, whose decadent cultural life he found even more alienating. In Dresden (where he was Kapellmeister, and where *Rienzi*, *The Flying Dutchman*, and *Tannhäuser* were first performed), he felt "utterly alone," a victim of a petty and conservative school of criticism that prevented the public "from exercising anything like a spontaneous, independent judgment." Increasingly scornful of the political status quo (his acquaintances included Mikhail Bakunin), he took up with the Dresden revolutionaries of 1849—and wound up in exile. He now composed the *Ring*, *Tristan*, and *Die Meistersinger*. In Bavaria King Ludwig undertook to elevate aesthetic culture. Great plans were laid for Munich. A malicious opposition emerged. In 1876, five years after German unification, a permanent Wagner theater was founded in the Upper Franconian town of Bayreuth, "far from all the tumult of the world"; "it would have been amply worthy of the support of our young Imperial Government. . . . But the powers that rule in Germany, neglectful as ever of the interest of true art, saw in my efforts now, as they had always seen before, nothing but the expression of the most extreme personal ambition. . . . Never has such a work been carried out amid great difficulties and anxieties, or amid more petty hindrances, than beset this 'ideal theatre' at Baireuth."

This is where America came in. The German spirit had deserted Germany—yet persevered. In accordance with a "law of history," the strongest Teutonic races had been the very ones which had broken away from their own soil, implanting Germanic civilization in England, France, Normandy, Lombardy, and Andalusia. And now a true Germanic race, in immigration, was "working out the future of America." True, the United States had "no history behind it" with which to buttress a life of culture. "Yet in spite of this . . . the New World always awakened hope in me, as hope is always aroused when one looks at anything really strong. . . . The German mind can there develop in activity and freedom, unoppressed by the wretched burdens left upon it by its melancholy history!" Wagner concludes:

> *German music* already unites the nations of the world—even to those beyond the sea—by an ideal bond. Our great masters . . . have made it certain that this alone can ever be the true, natural, living world-language. . . . Let us see to it that the original, pure, vigorous style of this great German music—and of that visible form, the universal drama, in which its spirit is best revealed—shall be preserved to it; so that the influence of the German mind, upon a world which will always need that influence, shall not be perverted and false and therefore worthless, but true, noble, and vigorous, and therefore in the highest degree salutary, beneficent, and broadening in its effect.
>
> Such is the wish and hope of the German artist who has here sought to give, to such sympathetic readers as he may find beyond the sea, the story of his ideal and the story of his life; and who now bids them farewell, in the hope that they and he may some time meet again, as earnest co-workers in the domain of ideal, spiritual progress.

The skein of ideas and arguments is characteristic. Wagner is a nationalist and yet an internationalist. He celebrates German unification, yet dismisses Germany as an impostor nation. He hates all princes, especially if German, but loves Ludwig. He resents political authority—*Kunst* alone defines a nation's identity—yet reviles the state's failure to subsidize its artists. He dislikes the French and the Jews (and also all Christians) but trusts the people. He disdains all that is worldly and material but obsesses over money, which he pursues both knowingly and naively.

What is finally remarkable about this thicket of inconsistencies is that Wagner is always, after his fashion, sincere, not merely cynical. All his pronouncements, however fleeting, are passionately felt, buttressed by intense experience. Cunning and deluded, pragmatic and idealistic, he seethes and shakes with the talents and energies of a dozen normal men. Every reading, every interpretation untangles him a different way. In America, as in Germany, his ideological applications would prove as potent and contradictory as the man himself.

2

The First Missionaries

agner's paean to the Germanization of American culture was both misguided and informed. German music would never "unite the nations of the world." But in the United States, circa 1880, many agreed that the only universal music was German. And, to a remarkable degree, America remained a musical colony of Germany until World War I—which suggests both a predisposition to Wagner and the absence of a strong native heritage to stand in the way.

Louis Moreau Gottschalk, America's first important pianist, and something of a Germanophobe, remarked in 1862 while in St. Louis: "I was introduced to an old German musician with uncombed hair, bushy beard, in constitution like a bear, in disposition the amenity of a boar at bay to a pack of hounds. I know this type; it is found everywhere." A year later Gottschalk summarized: "All the musicians in the United States are German."[1]

German and Austrian immigrants already numbered 200,000 at the time of the American Revolution. Their influx crested in the 1850s and 1880s. For immigration generally, the decade of the 1850s was a watershed: the foreign-born population grew by 84 percent, the German-born population by 118 percent. In Cincinnati, 30 percent of the inhabitants spoke German. In New York's Kleindeutschland—with Vienna and Berlin, one of three capitals of the German-speaking world—more than 100,000 German speakers were also German-born—about 15 percent of the total population. As of 1890, German-born New Yorkers were the city's largest foreign-born contingent, outnumbering the Irish 211,000 to 190,000; according to the country-of-birth-of-mother criterion used by the Census Bureau, *27 percent* of New York's 1,515,301 inhabitants were "Germans." According to Baedecker's 1893 guide, if the children of foreign-born parents were excluded, "probably not more than one-fourth or one-fifth of the inhabitants [of New York City could] be described as native Americans."* New York was a "foreign" city whose immigrant intellectuals discussed Schopenhauer and Dostoyevsky and spouted Proudhon and Marx.[2]

Compared to the English, the Germans of late-nineteenth-century America were gregarious. They were also clannish. They did not readily assimilate. Discrimination made German workers seek German neighborhoods and employers. Such wealthy German Americans as William Steinway, whose Steinway pianos already enjoyed a formidable international reputation, were equally intent on maintaining a *Deutschtum*. Germans established their own churches, their own newspapers, their own schools and libraries. In such cities as Chicago, Cincinnati, Milwaukee, New York, Philadelphia, and St. Paul, the German theater achieved professional status. But it was music that indelibly stamped German American culture. The arriving Prussians and Franconians, Saxons and Bavarians swarmed with singers and instrumentalists. They sang and played in their parlors, in beer gardens, in smoky theaters and makeshift concert halls. No German institution was more characteristic than the singing society, which, as New York's *Staats-Zeitung* once summarized, united "the worker, the businessman and the politician [and erased] the social distinctions which divide the German element."[3] Philadelphia acquired a *Gesangverein* in 1835, Baltimore one in 1836. New York's elite Liederkranz began in 1847; its members would include Schurz and Steinway. Cincinnati had its Liedertafel, Charleston its Teutonenbund. The *Gesangvereine* held balls, picnics, carnivals, and poetry readings. They spawned Cecilia clubs, Schubert societies, and Beethoven *Vereine*. German music festivals dotted the map as far afield as Galveston and San Antonio. Germans also held annual singing competitions, or *Sängerfeste*.

---

*These population figures for "New York" precede the annexation of the Bronx, Queens, Brooklyn, and Staten Island in 1898.

Competitors from rival cities would often travel great distances. The programs ranged from folksongs and *Heimatlieder* to overtures and excerpts from operas and oratorios.[4]

Germans claimed to have cured the United States of the English condition of being a *Land ohne Musik*. Americans less resented than welcomed this cure. To aesthetes and intellectuals of the Gilded Age, Germany was a nation of clean streets and prompt trains, of science and medicine, philosophy and jurisprudence. To legions of culture lovers, it was the nation of Beethoven. No less than the Germans', their rites were devotional. The Germans loved to preach; Dwight and his brethren loved to worship. In the New World, German literature and theater were necessarily admired from afar. German music, transcending language, was assimilated with amazing thoroughness and speed. Wrote George William Curtis in *Harper's*: "Some future poet will say that of all of the good fairies who came to the birth of the free nation, none was more generous than Teutonia, who brought the refining, elevating, humanizing gift of music."[5]

An early German beachhead was the New York Philharmonic, founded in 1842—the same year as Vienna's Philharmonic, and forty years before Berlin's. The orchestra's prime movers were German-born or trained. Four out of ten players—and by 1855, seven out of ten, and by 1892, more than nine out of ten—were of German extraction. As of 1875, German music comprised 80 percent of the repertoire. The orchestra's prospectus intoned: "The chief object will be, to elevate the Art, improve musical taste, and gratify those already acquainted with classic musical compositions, by performing the Great Symphonies and Overtures of Beethoven, Mozart, Haydn, Spohr, Mendelssohn, and other great Masters, with a strength and precision hitherto unknown in this country."[6]

Embodying democratic ideals its immigrant members associated with their new homeland, the orchestra was a self-governing musicians' cooperative. Initially, its audience consisted exclusively of subscribers, their families, and a limited number of their friends. By the second season William B. Astor and other social scions, less alienated than seduced by the Philharmonic's foreign pedigree, began signing on. In 1851, nonsubscribers—described in the by-laws as "strangers"—were declared admissible. In 1852, Theodore Eisfeld, born in Wolfenbüttel, became the first conductor to lead an entire season.

This record of growth and social penetration is in one respect misleading. Throughout the nineteenth century, the Philharmonic was a part-time orchestra. For decades, its seasons consisted of no more than half a dozen concerts, plus public rehearsals. And yet the German beachhead expanded even while the Philharmonic did not.

It should not be imagined that the new orchestra occupied a vacuum. As early as 1840, musical performances could be heard in New York practically every day of the year.[7] In season (September to May), concerts were given two to four times a week. Operatic fare ranged from Beethoven and Bellini to burlesques, ballad operas, and musical comedies. The majority of these offerings, even the operas, blended into a panoply of recreation and entertainment; a distinct highbrow stratum had yet to form. Ballyhoo was a New World specialty. Imported singers and instrumentalists courted the American dollar—and were themselves flamboyantly courted, feted, and showcased. P. T. Barnum presented Jenny Lind as a virtual angel descended from heaven; her stage-managed New York welcome included a torchlight parade with two hundred musicians and twenty brigades of firemen. A second singing sensation, Henriette Sontag, innocently ignited a riot when her "public serenade" degenerated into public combat between parading musicians and a screaming mob unwilling to relinquish space under Sontag's balcony.

Lind and Sontag—and also Ole Bull, who could bow all four violin strings at once, Leopold de Meyer, known as the "Lion Pianist," and Henri Herz, whose recitals were illuminated by a thousand candles—represented a species of popular spectacle whose antitheses were the devotional concerts of chamber, choral, and symphonic music launched by the arriving Germans. As they grew in numbers, the Germans grew in influence. Meanwhile, American audiences were becoming both more sophisticated and more snobbish. In 1864—around the time he remarked that all musicians in the United States were German—Gottschalk also had occasion to observe: "I am daily astonished at the rapidity with which the taste for music is developed and is developing in the United States. At the time of my first return from Europe . . . grand movements, tours de force, and noise had alone the privilege in piano music. . . . I was the *first* American pianist, not by my artistic worth, but in chronological order. . . . Now piano concerts are chronic. . . . From whatever cause the American taste is becoming purer, and with that remarkable rapidity we cite through our whole progress." Other observers were equally impressed; audiences who once craved virtuosic stunts and "Yankee Doodle" variations had begun to clamor for masterworks and great composers.[8]

One crucial factor was the conductor Carl Bergmann, who first led the New York Philharmonic in 1858. Bergmann was the Philharmonic's most potent artistic personality for more than three decades. He also happened to be America's first potent advocate of the music of Richard Wagner.

The conducting activities of Carl Bergmann and Theodore Thomas intertwined, and so have their reputations. Thomas, fourteen years Bergmann's junior, frequently played the violin under Bergmann's baton. Bergmann was initially the cellist in the historic chamber-music concerts of Thomas and the pianist William Mason. It was Thomas who brought the work Bergmann had helped begin to a plateau of high fruition. And the best-known account of Bergmann's own achievement is Thomas's own, in his autobiography. It is not flattering:

> Bergmann was a talented musician and a fair 'cello player. . . . He lacked most of the qualities of a first-rank conductor, but he had one great redeeming quality for those days which soon brought him into prominence. He possessed an artistic nature, and was in sympathy with the so-called "Zukunft Musik" ["Music of the Future"]. He lacked the force, however, to make an impression, and had no standard. He derived his principal inspiration from our chamber music practice. His readings of Beethoven's works showed clearly that he had no tradition, and that it was not based on study. I remember

well one morning, after we had been playing the Schumann string quartets for the first time, his saying to me: "You have lifted the veil from our eyes to-day." It was after this that he brought out hitherto unknown orchestral works by Schumann.

And, Thomas adds, Bergmann never practiced.[9]

Thomas himself was phenomenally industrious. He could also be jealous and cruel. His assessment of Bergmann may be accurate, but it is ungenerous. Reviews and descriptions of Bergmann's concerts leave no doubt that he did possess "the force to make an impression." He may have been lazy, erratic, and insufficiently schooled. But he was anything but innocuous. Mason judged him "an excellent, though not a great, conductor."[10]

The story of Bergmann's American career begins with the Germania Musical Society of Berlin. This was an orchestra of twenty-five young Germans who came together in 1848 with the conviction that democracy was "the most complete principle of human society" and with the motto "One for all, and all for one." The private orchestras they had manned, and the nobility that owned and enjoyed them, were jeopardized by political turmoil. The Germanians' constitution stipulated self-government, "equal rights, equal duties, equal rewards." Naturally, they resolved to set sail for America.

In England, where they stopped first, they proved their mettle. They were urged to stay in London, but were set on reaching the New World. In New York, they established new standards. They toured extensively. When in 1850 their conductor, Carl Lenschow, chose to remain in Baltimore to head the *Gesangverein*, Carl Bergmann, then a cellist with the orchestra, took his place. Fleeing Europe following his involvement in the uprisings of 1848–49, he had emigrated to New York in 1849 at the age of twenty-eight. Under Bergmann, the Germania Society acquired a more dynamic approach to interpretation, as well as a braver repertoire. Bergmann championed Wagner and Liszt. He also programmed quantities of Beethoven and Mendelssohn. Eventually, the Germanians gave over nine hundred concerts in the United States.[11]

It was with the Germania orchestra that Bergmann led the first known American Wagner performance—of the *Tannhäuser* "Finale," in Boston on November 27, 1852. In October and November of the following year, Bergmann and the Germanians, in Boston again, gave first American performances of the overtures to *Tannhäuser* and *Rienzi*. And it was in Boston, on December 3, 1853, that Bergmann led America's first "Wagner Night"—of which Wagner himself, as we have seen, was apprised. The program included the overtures to *Rienzi* and *Tannhäuser*, plus excerpts from *Tannhäuser* and *Lohengrin*. *Dwight's Journal* had heralded the event by publishing, in five installments beginning November 19, Dwight's English translation of Liszt's enthusiastic *Tannhäuser* analysis. Of the concert itself, Dwight reported that the program was not "judicious," much of the music proving "fatiguing and monotonous." The *Rienzi* Overture was criticized for the "noisy commonplaces" of its second half. The *Tannhäuser* Overture, already "wonderfully popular" and performed with "the utmost spiritual delicacy and precision," was judged "strikingly imaginative and beautiful." The *Lohengrin* excerpts were praised for their "unique and spiritual beauty." On another occasion, Dwight wrote of the Germanians: "Music is religion to these men." He called their success "a moral triumph."[12]

When the Germania Musical Society disbanded in 1854, Bergmann settled in New York. There he scored the pivotal success of his career on April 21, 1855. Theodore Eisfeld had fallen ill, and Bergmann was enlisted to replace him for a Philharmonic concert at Niblo's Garden. His rendition of the *Tannhäuser* Overture took musical New York by storm. In his autobiography, Thomas recalled: "It sounded little as we know it to-day, but it shook up the dry bones and made the dust fly, anyway!" At the time, the *New York Musical Review* reported: "It was one of the best symphonic performances we have ever had in New York." The Philharmonic's directors responded by engaging Bergmann to lead all the orchestra's concerts in 1855–56, commencing a twenty-year relationship.[13]

But Bergmann's most remarkable 1856 concerts were eleven undertaken with his own, smaller orchestra, of which Thomas was concertmaster. Played to packed houses, the series exuded an unquenchable eagerness to sample the newest, most important music. The programs were not only fresh, but—for their time— notably concentrated. Theodore Hagen, who excitedly praised

Bergmann's work in the *New York Musical Review*, represented one body of progressive opinion when, after the first concert, he unfavorably compared the "thin" and "simple" discourse of Mozart's *Jupiter* Symphony to the romantic drama of Beethoven's *Egmont* Overture. Other Beethoven pieces on Bergmann's series were the Second and Eighth Symphonies, and the *Coriolan* and Third *Leonore* Overture. The Mendelssohn selections included the Violin Concerto (with Thomas as soloist), the A minor Symphony (not yet called the *Scottish*), the *Rondo brillant*, and the *Fingal's Cave* and *Athalie* Overtures. Schubert's big C major Symphony was given, as were, for the first time in the United States, Schumann's *Manfred* Overture, Fourth Symphony, and Op. 52 Overture, Scherzo, and Finale. Of Berlioz there were American premieres of the *Waverly* and *Roman Carnival* Overtures. The audience's passionate applause secured repeat performances of the *Roman Carnival* and Schumann Fourth. But it was Wagner that Bergmann could not program often enough. The "Grand March" from *Tannhäuser*—presumably, the Entrance of the Guests—was encored and twice reprogrammed. So was the Bridal Procession from *Lohengrin*.[14]

Three years later, on April 4, 1859,* Bergmann conducted the whole of *Tannhäuser*—the first American staging of a Wagner opera. The hall, on the Bowery, was New York's German-language Stadttheater, which held twenty-five hundred people and whose fare ranged from Goethe and Schiller to popular melodramas and farces. Visitors from other neighborhoods found it a dirty place where vendors strolled the aisles hawking beer. But contemporary sources describe the *Tannhäuser* premiere as a creditable performance. The chorus, drawn from New York's *Gesangvereine* (of which the Arion was since 1854 led by Bergmann), was strong and well prepared; the orchestra was nearly as good; the solo singers were not. The listeners were mostly, but by no means exclusively, German. W. J. Henderson and other after-the-fact chroniclers were in error in reporting that only the German press paid attention. The *New York Evening Post*, for instance, ran a review including this informed analysis of a work

---

*Some references (e.g., *The Dictionary of American Biography*) incorrectly give the date as August 27, 1859.

that "has excited the most exaggerated criticism, both laudatory and condemnatory":

> The general idea . . . is the struggle between the pleasure of senses and the conviction of duty. It is but a romanticized epitome of the similar trials in every day real life. And as to the music—that wonderful "Music of the Future" about which there is so much talk!—most people seem to think that is nothing but a mass of incoherent orchestration and chaotic vocalization, utterly destitute of sustained melody. But this is not the case with "Tannhäuser," which contains some truly beautiful melodic inspirations. The great feature of the work lies, however, in the orchestration, in which the composer seems to have almost exhausted the powers of the orchestra. . . . There is one noble march, with a chorus of finely-marked melody. . . . The choral strains of the pilgrims are noble and majestic. . . . But to all these beauties are contrasted dismal wastes of dreary recitative. For the solo singers there are no decided melodies, if we except one baritone and one soprano song; and the declamatory style requires the closest attention to the words to be appreciated. The concerted pieces are also sometimes spun out, as if the composer were trying after effects he could not produce—as though he formed an ideal he could not realize. The magnificent tenor scene in the last act is one of the finest specimens of declamatory music ever written; yet its great length, and the utter absence of anything approaching melody, makes it, with all its power, rather tedious.

Another non-German report of America's first *Tannhäuser* was that of the highbrow diarist George Templeton Strong. Though antipathetic to opera generally, he found the work "decidedly impressive," with an "unusually good" plot and libretto. "Dramatically considered, it's the best opera I know; the only one, rather, that's not beneath contempt." He already liked and knew the overture; elsewhere, he found a "lack of fluent melody," and "gold instrumental effects" that were "original rather than beautiful." He also recorded: "A great crowd, Teutonic and generally frowzy. . . . Lager beer and cakes handed round between acts. Audience grimly attentive to the music, which is grim likewise. . . . Performance was not to be found fault with, though the principal 'artistes' would have been sniffed at by the Academy of Music habitues. Orchestra unimpeachable. Chorus the best I ever heard in opera. Mise en scene most careful and elaborate. It was a very satisfactory evening and did Deutschland credit."[15] *Tannhäuser* was given four times* and withdrawn. Not until 1877 would it acquire a more luxurious venue and a more affluent, more "refined" constituency.†

With his Arion Society, Bergmann performed Wagner's cantata *Das Liebesmahl der Apostel*. With the Philharmonic, he led a recitative and chorus from *Rienzi* (1859), the *Lohengrin* Prelude (1859 and 1864), the *Rienzi* Overture (1861), and *The Flying Dutchman* Overture (1863), all the time alternating on the podium with Theodore Eisfeld. Upon Eisfeld's retirement in 1865, Bergmann became the sole conductor. In addition to repeating the Wagner excerpts in which he had previously led the Philharmonic, he now programmed the Prelude to *Tristan und Isolde* (1866 and 1875), the *Faust* Overture (1866), the Prelude to *Die Meistersinger* (1871), and choral excerpts from *Lohengrin* (1869) and *Die Meistersinger* (1870). By 1873, however, his laziness and lager consumption were topics of loud complaint. His mood dipped, his health decayed, his drinking increased. Only the orchestra's affection for him prolonged his tenure. On March 17, 1876, he could not rehearse. His resignation was requested six days later. Then his wife died. According to the *New York Tribune's* obituary of August 14, 1876: "From that time he rapidly declined in health and spirits, living a solitary and retired life, and shunning the company of his former associates. About a week ago he was obliged to seek refuge at the German Hospital, where he died on Thursday night at 11 o'clock." The funeral, at the Aschenbrödel Hall, was a German affair. *Dwight's* reported:

> The services were entirely musical; no minister was present and no burial service was read. As the coffin was borne from the house the members of the Arion Society entoned Bergmann's favorite song, the "Pilgrim's Chorus" from Wagner's *Tannhäuser*, accompanied by

* Not six, as is sometimes reported.

† Nothing is more suggestive of the popular aroma of America's first *Tannhäuser* than the performance, four months later, of a *Tannhäuser* burlesque at the same theater. (See George Odell, *Annals of the New York Stage* [New York, 1937], vol. 7.)

a band from the Aschenbrödel Society. . . . Through some misunderstanding, the news of his death did not reach many of his musical associates, who would otherwise have attended the funeral, and therefore the number present was comparatively small.

Three months later, a memorial concert was given at Steinway Hall. R. Ogden Doremus, formerly president of the New York Philharmonic and a partner in the city's social and intellectual leadership, eulogized:

> His gifts included the "Sacred Fire"; and the genius to communicate the inspiration to all under his control, that auditors may thrill with the electric rendering. A conductor . . . labors in vain if he lacks this magnetic influence. . . . There must emanate from [him] a mysterious power . . . similar to that possessed by a great military chieftain as he triumphantly leads his army to victory. The city mourns the loss of a great teacher.[16]

Frédéric Ritter, in his 1883 history *Music in America*, remembered Carl Bergmann as, "at the height of his American career, the most respected and admired musical leader in America." But Bergmann's name faded fast. Only twenty-two years later, W. J. Henderson felt called upon to remind American readers "Who Discovered Wagner."

BERGMANN THE PIONEER WAGNERIAN

To him is due all credit for the introduction of the works of both Wagner and Liszt to America. . . . There is a story of a music-lover who went to Bergmann and complained of his continual performances of Wagner.

"Mr. Bergmann," said this visitor, "the people do not like Wagner."

"Oh, they don't like Wagner?" responded Bergmann. "Then they must hear him till they do!"

Henderson summarized that "one thing is beyond denial. The records show that the first to fight for a recognition of Wagner in America was that doughty champion of his ideas, Carl Bergmann. He drove the plow into the earth and sowed the first seed in soil that proved remarkably fertile. Others brought to a high state of cultivation the field which he opened."[17]

America's promise, Wagner had written in 1879, was that of a country with "no history behind it"—of a culture unburdened by accumulated taste and tradition. Wagner's own reception in the New World shows that this was thinking both wishful and true. It bears stressing that Bergmann and the Germanians fled Germany at the same moment that Wagner did, and for much the same reason. The democratic ideals of the New York Philharmonic, seven years earlier, likewise repudiated Old World ways.

Again and again, American audiences of the Gilded Age proved adventurous. Touring the United States, the Germania orchestra initially failed to thrive. One reason became apparent in Baltimore, whose German population insisted on more "serious" programming. The orchestra now played Beethoven, Mendelssohn, Weber, and Liszt—and began to prosper.* Describing his chamber music concerts of the 1850s, Theodore Thomas explained the conservative taste of two colleagues by noting that "they were still somewhat under the influence of their European training. But Bergmann and I had had no training."[18]

Bergmann's 1853 Boston performance of excerpts from *Lohengrin* came just three years after Liszt had given the premiere in Weimar. His 1866 performance of the *Tristan* Prelude, with the Philharmonic, followed by exactly nine months the *Tristan* premiere in Munich.† Thomas had already conducted the same work with his

---

*In stylish New Orleans, the Belgian violin virtuoso Henri Vieuxtemps offered programs of operatic fantasies, "Yankee Doodle" variations, and the like on tour in 1844—and found himself importuned to play Haydn, Mozart, Beethoven, and Hummel. (See John H. Baron, "Vieuxtemps [and Ole Bull] in New Orleans," *American Music*, Summer 1990.)

†Although Bülow first led the prelude in concert in 1859.

orchestra a month before. The *New York Musical Review* proudly observed: "The attention of every body was roused to the highest pitch by the prospect of listening to the celebrated introduction to 'Tristan and Isolde,' the latest production of the much abused Richard Wagner, and a work of art which according to the German journals has given much more offense than pleasure. . . . There are not more than two or three cities in Europe where this piece has as yet been performed."[19]

It would be false to claim that Americans spared Wagner the vituperation that made the European press, in Hans von Bülow's opinion, his "bitterest enemy." Ritter, for example, complains of "the insane vigor and illogical reasoning" of Wagner's American enemies, and continues: "People who had never heard a note of Wagner's music, had never witnessed the performance of a Wagner music-drama, had never taken the trouble—provided they had the necessary practical knowledge to do so—to study the score of any of Wagner's published works, were loud in their denunciations." William Henry Fry was one prominent composer and critic who, in the 1850s and 1860s, found Wagner unmelodious and arid. Richard Grant White, an influential and versatile essayist, rejected the Wagnerian *Gesamtkunstwerk*. A writer for Cincinnati's *Commercial Advertiser*, in one 1868 diatribe, likened the *Rienzi* Overture to "a brigade of bedlamites in a rolling mill with a nail factory attachment." And there was always Dwight. Yet it is no coincidence that, during the 1880s, the fervently Wagnerian *Musical Courier*, edited by Marc Blumenberg and Otto Floersheim, supplanted *Dwight's Journal* as the leading national digest of musical reportage and opinion. By the 1890s, Wagner's genius had become an American article of faith. It was, moreover, as faithfully asserted that America had welcomed Wagner earlier and better than any foreign land. Had Wagner emigrated to the United States in 1880, it was said, he would have been more enthusiastically greeted than anywhere in Europe. Gustav Kobbé, recalling the 1855 American invitation Wagner spurned, put it this way:

[The offer] was one of the most remarkable facts in the history of Wagnerism. It was in line with Wagner's contention that recognition of his music was retarded by those whose understanding was obscured by the knowledge of the conventional in music. A New York audience, unfettered by musical traditions, hears one of his overtures, and the effect produced by it is such that shortly afterward he received a handsome offer to come over here. Considering the comparative musical culture of Europe and America, it can truly be said that Wagner's genius was recognized here far earlier in his career than it was abroad.

American audiences, Josiah Gilbert Holland summarized in the *Century*, "had less to unlearn than those who knew more."[20]

By the time Bergmann died, Theodore Thomas had eclipsed him as an influential proponent of the Music of the Future. Thomas's Wagner advocacy would peak after 1880. Meanwhile, other advocates helped sustain Wagner's lively and controversial presence in American musical affairs.

The leading Wagner conductor to visit the United States in these years was Hans von Bülow, who had led the premieres of *Tristan* and *Die Meistersinger*. Bülow did no conducting on his American tour of 1875–76; he did, however, play Liszt's piano transcriptions of the Pilgrim's Chorus from *Tannhäuser* and the Spinning Chorus from *The Flying Dutchman*. Though a scathing observer of human affairs, Bülow praised American audiences for their "spirit of reverence," for being "quick to perceive" and "desirous to be taught."*[21]

Theodore Eisfeld, who first led the New York Philharmonic in 1849, and who shared the Philharmonic podium with Bergmann from 1854 to 1865, was a less magnetic performer than Bergmann—Thomas called him a "time-beater" who "would make corrections in the harmonies of master-works he did not understand"—yet ventured readily onto new terrain. With the Philharmonic, Eisfeld led

---

*The most extravagant of all keyboard transcriptions of Wagner was surely Louis Moreau Gottschalk's version of the *Tannhäuser* Pilgrims' Chorus for up to sixteen pianos.

the *Faust* Overture (1857, 1860, 1863), the *Tannhäuser* Overture (1858, 1861, 1863), Elisabeth's Prayer (1860), and the *Rienzi* Overture (1863).[22]

In the 1870s, America's most notable conductor of staged performances of Wagner was Adolf Neuendorff. Born in Hamburg in 1843, he arrived in New York in 1854, and served as concertmaster and then chorus master at the same Stadttheater where Bergmann had led *Tannhäuser* in 1859. When a new Stadttheater was opened on the Bowery in 1864, Neuendorff became its opera director. In this capacity, he led *Tannhäuser* in 1870 and then, on April 3, 1871, the American premiere of *Lohengrin*. In 1876, Neuendorff went to Bayreuth for the first *Ring*, about which he wrote in New York's *Staats-Zeitung*. The following year, he presided over a Wagner festival at New York's most respectable venue for opera prior to the building of the Metropolitan Opera in 1883: the forty-six-hundred-seat Academy of Music at 14th Street and Irving Place. Here, he led multiple performances of *Tannhäuser*, *Lohengrin*, and *The Flying Dutchman* (its first German-language performance in the United States, the premiere, in Italian, having been given on November 8, 1876, at Philadelphia's Academy of Music). The festival's pièce de résistance was America's first *Die Walküre*, on April 2 and 3. Neuendorff again presented *Die Walküre* at a Wagner festival in Boston the same month. On March 5, 1878, at the Academy of Music, he conducted the first American *Rienzi*. He led the New York Philharmonic in 1878–79; the repertoire included Wotan's Farewell. He resettled in Boston, then returned to New York as music director of Temple Emanu-El and also, in 1886, conducted for the Met.

According to Ritter, in *Music in America*, America's first *Lohengrin* was "very creditable. . . . There were life, enthusiasm, an agreeable freshness, and commendable effort on the part of the performers." The chorus was good. The orchestra, "though rather small, was of excellent quality, and played with vim." The flavor of the occasion is also conveyed in an account in the *Century*. The Stadttheater is a dusty place with "dingy benches." Neuendorff is glimpsed in rehearsal: "By dint of much shouting and many gestures, [he] kept his orchestra up to the work, and drilled the singers in their parts, and, as the morning wore away, evolved order and harmony out of a chaos of discordant sounds." At the performance, the theater is

> crowded with hot, talkative, eager Germans, and nearly all the notable musicians of the city—except the Italians, who will not hear German music if they can help it.
>
> At a quarter past eight the lights were turned up, motherly dames put their half-sucked oranges away, a glow of pleasure suffused the faces of the shining, red-handed damsels, and a great crowd of men, smelling of tobacco, came in from the lobby. Then there climbed quickly into the conductor's chair the slim and restless young Neuendorff, who, before he was fairly in his place, gave an impetuous jerk of his head, rapped on the desk, threw his arms right and left over the orchestra, and so set the performance at once a-going.

As for the work itself:

> This splendid drama [is] interwoven with the most poetical and delicious of [Wagner's] music, and embroidered with the most brilliant and fanciful orchestration.
>
> It is the fashion to say that the obstinate prophet of the new musical revelation has no perception of beauty, and there are cultivated people who make believe they do not like even such musical splendors as the overture to "Tannhäuser." But they must be dull and perverse spirits who cannot feel in this exquisite romance of the Holy Grail the true flavor of poetry, the rare gifts of a great intellect and fine sensibilities. The delicious verses in which Tennyson tells of the famous quest by Sir Percivale and his companions, are not so nearly perfect in their way as the closing scene of this opera, when the Knight . . . repeats the legend of the Blessed Cup, and declares his name and rank. With mingled awe, and rapture, and sadness, he begins the mysterious narration in a low voice, half monologue, half song. The wonderful orchestral accompaniment grows more and more eloquent; the declamation becomes impassioned. . . .
>
> We do not envy the man who can hear and see this closing scene unmoved.

> And what shall we say of American enthusiasm for art, and enter-
> prise in its cultivation, when a work like this has had to wait twenty
> years to be heard at all on this side of the Atlantic, and at last is only
> heard in the Bowery?

And yet neither London nor Paris had yet heard *Lohengrin*.[23]

Henry Krehbiel, in *Chapters of Opera*, recalls Neuendorff as "a man of indefatigable energy and enterprise." But Neuendorff the conductor was not admired, nor were the stagings over which he presided. His 1877 *Tannhäuser* offered the Venusberg scene with no corps de ballet. Of his 1877 *Die Walküre*, Krehbiel writes: "Memories of that production were painful when they were not amusing"; Gustav Kobbé refuses even to consider it a "real performance."[24] At the same time, Neuendorff's *Die Walküre* offered Americans their first opportunity to experience something like mature Wagnerian music drama. Neuendorff was a provincial but indispensable contributor to the Wagner cause. Like Bergmann before him, he helped navigate out of German American byways and toward the fashionable cultural mainstream.

A landmark event, in this progression from dingy benches to cushioned seats, was the first American *Lohengrin* to be given in Italian—about which the redoubtable W. J. Henderson wrote in 1905: "The opera has never had a greater cast." The Lohengrin for the first performance, on March 23, 1874, was Italo Campanini, who had sung the role in Italy as early as 1871, and who would later open the Metropolitan Opera as Faust. Christine Nilsson, a famous Marguerite, was Elsa. Annie Louise Cary—who that day became the first American woman to sing a Wagner role in the United States— and Giuseppe Del Puente were Ortrud and Telramund. Emanuele Muzio conducted. The impresario was the formidable Maurice Strakosch, whose sister-in-law and sometime client was Adelina Patti and whose stellar company—the other singers included Victor Maurel, Victor Capoul, and Romano Nannetti—was hailed by the *Century* as "the most thoroughly well-organized troupe yet heard in America." With *Aida*, *Lohengrin* was the triumphant novelty of Strakosch's season at the New York Academy of Music. When he took it to Boston a year later with a somewhat different cast, the

Atlantic called it "the first instance of a dramatic work of Wagner's being presented to our . . . public in anything approaching the spirit the composer and poet intended." Of the orchestra, the writer noted: "The exceptionally full score was absolutely filled. The three flutes, three bassoons, English-horn, and bass-clarinet were all palpably there. . . . We have never heard an opera orchestra play so well in Boston." Two areas of complaint were the chorus (of "distracted and distracting cacophonists") and the Italianate singing and acting. Even so, the polish of Strakosch's *Lohengrin* was new.[25]

Another Wagner production marking the exodus from the German ghetto was America's first English-language *Flying Dutchman*, given at New York's Academy of Music on January 26, 1877. The company was headed by the important American soprano Clara Louise Kellogg, whose Senta was warmly acclaimed. In her memoirs, Kellogg recalls that the work was prepared without "any traditions [or] impressions to help us." Not even at the Stadttheater could anyone be found who had heard it given abroad.

> One thing I had particular difficulty in learning how to handle [was] Wagner's trick of long pauses. There is a passage almost immediately after the spinning song . . . during which Senta stands at the door and thinks about the Flying Dutchman, preceding his appearance. Then he comes, and they stand still and look at each other while a spell grows between them. . . . The music, so far as Siegfried Behrens, my [music] director at the time, and I could see, had no meaning whatever. It was just a long, intermittent mumble, continuing for eighteen bars with one slight interruption of thirds. I had not yet been entirely converted to innovations such as this and did not fully appreciate the value of so extreme a pause. I knew, of course, that repose added dignity; but this seemed too much. . . .
>
> Finally Behrens looked up Wagner's own brochure on the subject of his operas and came to me, still doubtful, but somewhat reassured.
>
> "Wagner says," he explained, "not to be disturbed by long intervals. If both singers could stand absolutely still, this pause would hold the public double the length of time."
>
> We tried to stand "absolutely still." It was an exceedingly difficult thing to do. . . . "I have *got* to hold it! I have *got* to hold it!" I

kept saying to myself, tightening every muscle as if I were actually pulling on a wire stretched between myself and the audience. I almost auto-hypnotised myself; which probably helped me to understand the Norwegian girl's own condition of auto-hypnotism! An inspiration led me to grasp the back of an old Dutch chair on the stage. That chair helped me greatly, and, as affairs turned out, I held the audience quite as firmly as I held the chair!

Afterwards I learned the wonderful telling-power of these "waits" and the great dignity that they lend to a scene. There is no hurry in Wagner.[26]

Everything about Wagner—the acting style, the declamation, the orchestration, the dramatic density—seemed new, yet was rapidly assimilated. German Americans assimilated Wagner first. America's Italians acquired a taste for *Lohengrin*. At the Academy of Music, those native-born Americans who ostentatiously patronized opera spurned opera in English as unpedigreed; that Kellogg successfully undertook Wagner in English suggests a further, fledgling Wagner constituency.

Kellogg and Strakosch, Carl Bergmann and Adolf Neuendorff, all contributed to the Wagner juggernaut. But its eventual engine was Theodore Thomas. More than any other individual, he powered Wagner toward the bastions of genteel culture. In a brief decade or two, Bergmann's Stadttheater and Neuendorff's Wagner festival would seem quaint antecedents. The new Wagner precincts would be Carnegie Hall and the Metropolitan Opera—and also Chicago's Orchestra Hall, which Thomas would help to build. No less than the Wagner cult he absorbed and advanced, Thomas was born a German but grew up an American.

3

The Master Builder

The travels—and travails—of Theodore Thomas comprise one of the great and characteristic personal sagas of American history.[1] He was born in Esens, Germany, in 1835. Ten years later, he came to New York with his parents. By 1849, he was touring the South by himself as "Master T. T.," the prodigy violinist; he acted as his own manager, publicist, and ticket taker. As a teenager, he played in New York's orchestras, including the Philharmonic. At the age of twenty, he was named first violinist of the new "Mason and Bergmann" chamber music concerts, which two seasons later became the "Mason and Thomas" concerts. He first led an orchestra of his own in 1862. Beginning in 1864, Theodore Thomas's concerts were a regular—often nightly—feature of New York's concert life. As a point of pride, Thomas insisted that his musicians were the best to be found. Busy though it was, his orchestra could not offer them steady employment unless it traveled—and so it did. Thomas's core itinerary of twenty-eight cities in twelve states became known as the Thomas Highway. Thomas byways included communities where railroad stations and churches were the only places to perform. A tireless organizer, Thomas was equally a thorough musician. Discriminating visitors were amazed by the discipline and dedication of his players. Anton Rubinstein toured with Thomas in 1872–73 and declared: "When he accompanies me with his orchestra, it is as though he could divine my thoughts, and then as though his orchestra could divine his. . . . I know of but one orchestra that can compare with that of Theodore Thomas, and that is the orchestra of the national conservatory of Paris."[2] Thomas's tours implanted the specifically American ideal of the "symphony orchestra," in contrast to the pit orchestras of Europe. He preached: "A symphony orchestra shows the culture of a community, not opera." America believed him.

As a personality, Thomas was a timely combination of traits German and American. He was religiously devoted to German masters and masterworks. He called his concerts "sermons in tones" and repudiated popular music as a sensual indulgence having "more or less the devil in it." He was stern, autocratic; William Mason called him "born to command." His integrity was truculent. The soprano Lilli Lehmann, who reported of Thomas's orchestras that she had never before encountered such unified bowings, smooth blends, and perfect intonation, summarized that he was "a man, take him all in all, to whom I would like to erect a monument, for he was a sound kernel in a rough shell, and music, that is his ideal art, was as exalted to him as mine is to me."[3]

Thomas's melioristic fervor endeared him to John Sullivan Dwight and other dour moralists of genteel persuasion. His appeal to others less genteel depended on his "masculinity," counteracting Gilded Age stereotypes of effete high culture. The embodiment of Teddy Roosevelt's "strenuous life," he was known to harden his body with icy baths and gymnastics every morning. According to the critic Richard Aldrich, "he could take up almost any of his subordinates and lay him upon the table without apparent effort."[4] A cultural frontiersman, he relished the taming and tilling of a musical wilderness. On his earliest tours as a teenaged prodigy, he traveled on horseback and packed a pistol. No less than the pioneer type celebrated by Frederick Jackson Turner in his influential "frontier thesis" of 1893, he was sturdy, pragmatic, dominating. Self-educated, self-reliant, he was a self-made man in the American mold.

Finally, in an era of regnant commerce and industry, of scientific management and "time-study" efficiency, Thomas was a forceful and self-possessed administrator. According to his friend, the critic George Upton, he was "not given to the emotional or sentimental," and "disapproved of the eccentricities of dress and manner affected by some musicians." In the opinion of Chicago's *Evening Post*, he looked "more like a substantial banker than one of the four most renowned conductors in the world." The same article continued with these remarkable observations:

> The high condition of discipline of [his orchestra] is the result not only of Thomas' organizing faculty, but of his own strict subordination of the artistic element in his temperament to the practical. . . . [When he conducts,] you will find it difficult to detect the least outward symptom of an inward change even in the most sharply contrasted music. . . . The composition, the orchestra, the performance are merely so many incidents of the day's experiences. He lays down the baton as calmly as he takes it up, acknowledges applause with the imperturbability of a [Nellie] Melba and goes on his way serene and passionless, wondering, doubtless, how long it will be before the public he is educating even against its whim—like a pedagogue his refractory pupils—will get within gunshot of his own ideals of a community musically cultured.

And Thomas exuded a competitiveness as fierce as any oil baron's. His enemies called him brutal.[5]

Van Wyck Brooks, in a famous 1915 formulation, remarked that only the American mind fused "saintliness" and "shrewdness" so that each became "the sanction of the other."[6] *Kultur*-bearer, frontiersman, captain of musical industry, Theodore Thomas was the Gilded Age personified.

Thomas's eventual goal was to canonize the German masters and transcend the rabble. His 1882 "Philharmonic Creed" stressed the promulgation of "only standard works, both of the new and old masters," and rejected "experimenting with the musical sensation of the hour." Earlier, however, his missionary agenda had been less conservative.

For years, the Thomas orchestra visited backwater locales to tutor the unlearned. Thomas seduced converts with overtures and dances before subjecting them to symphonies one movement at a time. Even in New York, his outdoor concerts tolerated such "little extravagances" as piccolo players in the trees (for the *Linnet* Polka) and a tuba in the shrubbery (for the *Carnival of Venice*). Performing Schumann's *Träumerei* (a transcription for violins, violas, and cellos), he diminished the dynamic so the tune grew fainter until the players were moving their bows without touching the strings. According to one 1877 account: "Of a sudden [the listeners] awoke to the fact that Mr. Thomas had laid down his baton and there was no sound. For the last minute there had been none. . . . So strong was the spell, these thralls had believed they still heard that marvelous elfin melody. A strange gasping noise arose as two thousand people suddenly recovered their breath and consciousness, and then looked at one another to see if all this were real."[7]

Such musical epiphanies complemented the traveling lecturers of the Lyceum movement and the band concerts of Patrick Gilmore and other ambitious leaders whose programs included operatic snatches. (Gilmore frequently led excerpts from *Tannhäuser*, *Lohengrin*, and *Rienzi*.) Thomas's repertoire tenaciously aspired to elevate taste. Of such composers of the "modern school" as Wagner, Liszt, and Berlioz, Thomas said in 1865: "[They] represent the growth and effort of our own times, and are eclectically interesting for that reason. Their intrinsic merits, also, give them the right to be heard." The "two pillars" of his programs were Beethoven and Wagner. As he explained late in life:

> In earlier years [my concerts] always included a Beethoven number; first, because Beethoven is the nearest to us in spirit; second, because he expresses more than any other composer; and third, because he has reached the highest pinnacle in instrumental music. . . . His place was always in the first part of the programme.
>
> I have always believed in climaxes, also in giving people the most recent musical productions, and Wagner is the composer who satisfies both these essentials. Like Beethoven, he also answers a double purpose. He represents the modern spirit, and his effective scoring makes the desired climax. Wagner excites his hearers, especially the younger generation, and interests the less musical. . . .

The effect of these composers on the public was plainly apparent. So I placed them where they belonged, and then filled out the rest of the programme so as to keep within a certain limit of time, have each piece prepare for the one to follow, observe a steady crescendo, never allow an anticlimax, and "keep a trump" for the last.[8]

Thomas's debut program as a symphonic conductor, on May 13, 1862, included the American premiere of *The Flying Dutchman* Overture. The *New York World* commented: "Most of the audience expected dreary wastes of dissonant harmony and were agreeably surprised to find not merely defined ideas but actual bits of melody." But the *New York Daily Tribune* found the overture "ingeniously destitute of melody. Ghastly rumpus was its main feature." When on February 10, 1866, Thomas gave the first American performance of the *Tristan* Prelude—a performance I have already mentioned in comparing first performances in the United States and Europe—the *Times* found it "absolutely without significance and unintelligible." The *New York Musical Review* countered: "It is the longest musical breath ever taken. The virtuosity with which it is accomplished is really astounding."[9] Seven months later, on October 20, Thomas led the American premiere of the *Meistersinger* Overture.

Thomas's eight summer seasons at New York's Central Park Garden, comprising 1,127 concerts beginning in 1868, were a landmark effort. The venue, just south of Frederick Law Olmsted's new Central Park, was an impressive auditorium, with tables as well as boxes, adjoining a large dining room and garden space. The Thomas orchestra performed nightly. Beer and refreshments were served; the air was perfumed both with flowers and tobacco. At first, the programs stressed light music. Within a few seasons, full symphonies and concertos were performed as a matter of course. Of Beethoven, Thomas gave all nine symphonies except for the choral finale of the Ninth, plus several concertos. He performed Schubert's last two symphonies, symphonies and concertos by Mendelssohn, both Brahms serenades (the First Symphony was not finished until 1876), and the Schumann symphonies, all four of which he gave repeatedly.

Ezra Schabas, in his biography of the conductor, remarks: "Thanks to these concerts, New York became the English-speaking capital (if not *the* capital) of the symphonic world. August Manns in London and Jules-Etienne Pasdeloup in Paris led their orchestras in many concerts, but neither group had the finish of Thomas's ensemble. The famed Leipzig Gewandhaus Orchestra, conducted by Carl Reinecke, did not give anywhere near as many concerts year-round."[10]

The first "Wagner night" at Central Park Garden took place September 19, 1871. The first all-Wagner program, on September 17, 1872, featured the American premiere of the Ride of the Valkyries. The public responded by leaping onto chairs and shouting. The same night, at a post-concert banquet, Thomas announced he was founding a New York Wagner *Verein* to help raise funds for the first *Ring* at Bayreuth.

During these years, as well, Thomas gave first American performances of the linked Prelude and *Verklärung* (later dubbed the *Liebestod*) from *Tristan* (December 6, 1871) and of Wotan's Farewell (January 8, 1875). In an 1873 essay, he credited Wagner's growing popularity to "the persistence of one man"—meaning himself—"to whom the introduction of Wagner is mainly due in this country."[11] According to one well-worn anecdote: when told that people complained they did not like Wagner, Thomas pounded the table and said he would program Wagner until they did. As we have seen, the same story was told of Carl Bergmann.

Thomas never met Wagner. During the summer of 1867, he tried unsuccessfully to see him while in Europe, where he never conducted. In 1871, he asked Wagner for permission to program excerpts from the uncompleted *Ring*; Wagner turned him down. Wagner knew Thomas by reputation. He was also familiar with American copyright laws, which failed to protect foreign composers. In 1873, Thomas's Wagner *Verein* donated $10,000 to Bayreuth; three years later, in 1876, it sent some members of Thomas's orchestra there for the first *Ring*.[12] This was also the year of America's Centennial Exposition in Philadelphia—which became the occasion, finally, for substantive communication between the composer and his American champion.

The exposition was an event of grand proportion and expenditure. Hard times notwithstanding, the federal government contributed almost $11.5 million—one percent of the annual budget. Some one hundred seventy buildings were erected on four hundred fifty acres. Fifty countries participated. Eight million Americans—out of a total population of forty-six million—are believed to have attended. Thomas was named director of music. He proposed that two works be commissioned from American composers: a hymn by John Knowles Paine to verses by John Greenleaf Whittier, and a cantata by Dudley Buck with words by Sidney Lanier. And he suggested, as a third commission, a new work by Richard Wagner—a ceremonial march in the style of the festive processionals of *Tannhäuser* and *Die Meistersinger*.

The Women's Centennial Executive Committee, whose responsibilities included music, approved Thomas's plan. Thomas himself wrote to Wagner about it. The response was encouraging. The ensuing negotiations—over money, over performance and publication prerogatives—grew suspicious and confused. For Thomas, what began as a privilege became a frustrating and disillusioning obligation—not least when the *Centennial March* arrived in April 1876 and proved instantly forgettable. This did not dissuade J. R. H. Hassard of the *New York Tribune* from observing:

> The MS., consisting of 33 large and closely written pages, was all in the composer's own hand. A more beautiful musical autograph is rarely seen. Every note is as clear and elegant and symmetrical as print. The characters are fine but distinct and regular, and the expression marks are made with extreme care. The mere manual labor of transcribing such a score must have filled seven or eight long days of steady application.
>
> . . . The effects [of the march] are produced by the interweaving of subjects, rather than by the individual character of the subjects themselves. Judged from this point of view, the work is a master-piece.[13]

The premiere took place on the morning of May 10, a hot and humid day, as part of the opening ceremonies. A stage had been constructed along the front of the Main Building. The Thomas orchestra was expanded to one hundred fifty players; a chorus of one thousand also took part. President Grant, members of Congress, and justices of the Supreme Court were present. Imperturbable in his morning suit and silk top hat, Thomas led eight national airs followed by the new march. Most in the crowd, which stretched half a mile down the fairgrounds, could not hear. Hassard called the *Centennial March* "rich and elaborate." The *Herald* thought it "noble" and "grand." The *New York Times* more accurately reported: "It is altogether devoid of the pomp and circumstance which should characterize an achievement of this sort, and all its beauties as a specimen of orchestral writing do not make amends for the lack of thought which has made recourse to scholastic treatment of a single theme necessary throughout." Wagner himself is reported to have said of the *Centennial March* that its best feature was its five-thousand-dollar price tag—an exorbitant sum, even had the music been better.*[14]

In this context of gratitude and exploitation, praise and rebuke—of New World deference and assertion, naiveté and sophistication—the President's speech proved apt. He said:

> One hundred years ago our country was new and but partially settled. Our necessities compelled us to chiefly expend our means and time in felling forests, subduing prairies, building dwellings, factories, ships, docks, warehouses, roads, canals, machinery, etc. . . .

*Wagner also said of the *Centennial March*: "Unless the subject absorbs me completely, I cannot produce twenty bars worth listening to"—an excuse that deserves to be taken seriously. Wagner was dependent upon dramatic ideas—on characters and situations—for musical inspiration. The idea of the United States evoked little for him. According to Anton Seidl, he even obtained a collection of American tunes, but to no avail. Seidl also reported that the march incorporates allusions to the Revolutionary War and to patriotic Philadelphia socialites strewing palm branches before General Washington. (See Henry Finck, *Wagner and His Work* [New York, 1893; rpt. 1968], vol. 1, p. 508; Finck, *Anton Seidl: A Memorial by His Friends* [New York, 1899; rpt. 1903], p. 9.)

Burdened by these great primal works of necessity which could not be delayed, we have yet done what this exhibition will show in the direction of rivaling older and more advanced nations in medicine and theology; in science, literature and the fine arts, while proud of what we have done, we regret that we have not done more.[15]

The exposition celebrated a progressive civilization of factories and machines. Amid the looms, lathes, presses, and pumps of Machinery Hall, the Remington Arms Company displayed its new "typewriter," Thomas Edison his "multiplex" telegraph, Alexander Graham Bell his telephone. The majestic Corliss Double Walking-Beam Steam Engine, thirty feet high, powered the entire ensemble. "It is still in these things of iron and steel that the national genius most freely speaks by," wrote William Dean Howells. He found the Corliss engine a thing of "vast and almost silent grandeur," of "unerring intelligence."[16] But the endeavors of the women's committee petered out. The fairgoers preferred machinery to music. Reduced to paying his musicians out of his own pocket, Thomas was left twenty thousand dollars in debt. The sheriff seized his baton, his inkstand, and his library, including Wagner's march, to be sold at auction—where a Thomas loyalist bought everything for fourteen hundred dollars and returned it free of charge.

Of Thomas's wounds, the most painful may have been his disappointment in Wagner, with whom he never again corresponded. To culture-bearers of genteel precept, a great artist exuded "character." Great books, great paintings, great symphonies were infused with moral content. Wagner, unlike Beethoven, was no moral hero. And yet Thomas continued to perform him. With his own orchestra, he gave the first American performance of the *Siegfried Idyll* in 1878. As conductor of the New York Philharmonic from 1877 to 1891, he played Wagner, often with vocal soloists, thirty-four times on seventy-four programs. By April 24, 1880, he had given virtually all of act 3 of *Götterdämmerung*. Of *Das Rheingold*, he offered all of scene 1, Loge's scene 2 narrative, and the close of scene 4. Of *Die Walküre*, he gave the Ride and Wotan's Farewell, of *Siegfried*, the forging songs. He led the Philharmonic in the Prelude to *Parsifal* on November 11, 1882—less than four months after the first *Parsifal* at Bayreuth.[17]

Apart from the Philharmonic concerts, Thomas during these years presided over gargantuan Wagner festivals in New York and other cities. These events belonged as much to America's established choral tradition as to its Wagner cult. One element common to both was the German American *Singverein*. Thomas's activities in Cincinnati, where he led the May Festival, were an early focus of his choral work. In 1882, he presided over a New York festival, at the Seventh Regiment Armory Drill Hall, whose three thousand singers came from as far away as Worcester, Reading, and Baltimore, and whose players, from as far away as Chicago and Cincinnati, totaled one hundred violins, thirty-six violas, thirty-six cellos, and forty double basses, plus complementary winds and percussion. Of the vocal soloists, the most heralded was Wagner's Bayreuth Brünnhilde, Amalie Materna, who upon arriving was serenaded below her hotel room by a military band before being escorted downstairs by Thomas to meet the musicians. According to Thomas himself, the festival's huge orchestra so successfully negotiated Mozart's *Jupiter* Symphony "as to perfectly reproduce the relative proportions, the coloring, the exact sentiment of a symphony written for thirty or forty instruments. . . . The orchestral tone [had] a purity and sonority that is only obtained by immense musical forces." But the festival's high point, in Thomas's opinion, was Materna's rendering of the immolation scene from *Götterdämmerung*, which "created the greatest excitement I have ever witnessed, and made many converts to the Wagner music dramas." George W. Curtis, in *Harper's*, called the 1882 festival an occasion of "legitimate grandeur . . . the high-water mark in the musical annals of the country."[18]

Two years later, Thomas mounted a Wagner festival and took it on tour. The first stop was Boston, where he gave six concerts in four days. In addition to a gargantuan orchestra and chorus, he engaged three principal singers from the Bayreuth *Parsifal* a year before: Materna (who sang Isolde, Brünnhilde, and Kundry), Hermann Winkelmann (Tannhäuser, Siegfried, Walther, Tristan, Parsifal), and Emil Scaria (Wotan, Sachs, Pogner, Gurnemanz). Audiences of up to eight thousand were offered lengthy program notes, libretto translations, and a Wagner handbook prepared by Henry T. Finck. Other cities on the tour, whose programs were predominantly, but not exclusively, Wagnerian, were Baltimore, Chicago, Montreal, New York, Philadelphia, Portland (Maine), Richmond, and Washington.

The Thomas festivals and similar events capitalized on the popular appeal of the choral movement, with its middle-class base. They encouraged local participation and forestalled the cleavage between audience and performer, "amateur" and "professional." And yet performances of *Messiah* and *Israel in Egypt*, the Ninth Symphony and *Missa solemnis* bred an elitist sophistication that was bound to rebel against "bigger is better" in favor of more modest forces and more proper halls. Reviewing the 1884 Cincinnati May Festival, Henry Krehbiel wrote: "[Cincinnati's] motive has always been something higher than the sensationalism which is the too frequent product of the tendency to combination which now pervades almost all social, commercial, artistic and political activities." Following Thomas's Wagner festival in Chicago two months later, the *News* cautioned: "A musical festival is not a circus," and the *Saturday Evening Herald* wrote: "Monster affairs are of [no] benefit to the cause of musical culture."[19]

Thomas, too, was tiring of such exertions. The populist phase of his career—his "missionary" work—was abating in stages. Previously, he had never taken much interest in conducting opera. Now, his espousal of Wagner, and the public's response, changed his mind. It was rumored that the new Metropolitan Opera would stage Wagner's operas. Thomas hoped his Wagner festivals would validate his candidacy to conduct them. In his memoirs, he mentions an offer to conduct an American Wagner company including Materna, Winkelmann, and Scaria:

> At first I refused, as the promoters of the project wished to put it into effect immediately. After consultation, however, they agreed to my conditions, and I consented. These conditions were that the plan should not be carried out until 1885–86, and that I should spend the intermediate year in Europe, studying and familiarizing myself with the German opera, and especially with the Wagner music-dramas as given in Germany. The three singers also agreed to this arrangement, and Winkelmann and Scaria kept faith with us in the matter. Materna did not. She accepted an engagement with the

Metropolitan Opera Company, which was formed the next season, and our enterprise, consequently, was abandoned.[20]

In fact, Thomas never conducted at the Met. But he did become a prominent operatic conductor—an enterprise both short-lived and significant.

In 1833 Philip Hone, an important New York City diarist (and one-time mayor), reported the opening of a new house for Italian opera: "The performance occupied four hours—much too long, according to my notion, to listen to a language which one does not understand. . . . Will this splendid and refined amusement be supported in New York? I am doubtful." That Italian opera was supported was partly due to the presence of many Italians, partly to the presence of people who preferred opera in "a language which one does not understand." Hone understood: "The real charm of the opera is this—it is an exclusive and extravagant recreation, and, above all, it is the fashion."[21]

Opera in English, however, had a strong start. English ballad opera, a species of topical spoken drama with interpolated songs, was already performed in America in the eighteenth century. Before the Civil War, English versions of Mozart, Bellini, Donizetti, Rossini, and Verdi were popular. The Pyne and Harrison English Opera Company, one of many, toured from New York to Cincinnati and Chicago, from Boston to Mobile and New Orleans, performing five hundred times between 1854 and 1856. Though German opera in German was a later development, *Die Zauberflöte, Fidelio, Der Freischütz,* and *Oberon* had all been mounted in English by 1840. Meanwhile, English-language grand operas were written by a series of Americans, beginning in 1845 with William Henry Fry. According to one tally, there were nearly sixty English opera troupes in the United States between 1847 and 1860.[22]

As of 1900, however, English-language opera had alienated afflu-ent snobs—not to mention Germans and Italians—who preferred foreign languages. And yet far-sighted observers were still hoping that opera in English would thrive in the United States. For one thing, dozens of Americans had become important opera singers. For another, opera in the vernacular was a normal occurrence in countries like Germany (where *Faust* was given in German), Italy (where *Lohengrin* was given in Italian), and France (where *Rigoletto* was given in French). It was Henry Krehbiel's sensible conviction that only once Americans accepted opera in English would they adequately embrace opera as a fine theatrical art. At the same time, important operas would finally be composed by Americans. The fashionables who craved prima donnas, who came late and left early, would once and for all be displaced. Krehbiel did not wholeheartedly espouse opera in translation; hearing Wagner in English, he missed "some of the bone and sinew of the drama."* And yet he maintained that, on balance, opera in America would remain "experimental" until "the vernacular becomes the language of the performances and native talent provides both works and interpreters. The day is still far distant, but it will come."[23]

One formidable attempt to hasten its coming occurred in 1885 with the founding of the American Opera Company. This was the brainchild of Mrs. Jeannette Thurber, who the same year founded the National Conservatory of Music with similar goals in mind. She aspired to cut the cultural umbilical cord to Europe: to cultivate American-born, American-trained composers, conductors, singers, and instrumentalists. Her touring American Opera would perform only in English, and at reasonable prices. It would mainly rely on American singers. It would downplay vocal glamour and stress ensemble, production values, and a fine ballet and chorus. For an orchestra, she procured the best: Theodore Thomas's. And Theodore Thomas, whose 1884 Wagner tour she had helped support, would be her conductor.

The enterprise was nothing if not ambitious, and so were its claims. According to the prospectus, Thurber had assembled "the

---

*Wagner himself endorsed Wagner in English. (See, e.g., Stewart Spencer and Barry Millington, eds. and trans., *Selected Letters of Richard Wagner* [New York, 1987], p. 807.) So did Anton Seidl.

largest regularly trained chorus ever employed in grand opera in America," "the largest ballet corps ever presented in grand opera in America," "four thousand new and correct costumes for which no expense has been spared in fabric or manufacture," "armor, properties, and paraphernalia" made "from models designed by the best authorities," and scenery "painted by the most eminent scenic artists in America."[24] Equally ambitious was Thomas's decision to open the first season, on January 4, 1886, with the American premiere of Hermann Goetz's *Taming of the Shrew*. The remainder of the repertoire, mounted first in New York and then on tour, included two Wagner works Thomas favored: *The Flying Dutchman*, given eighteen times, and fifteen performances of a sumptuous *Lohengrin*, with three hundred costumes.

On balance, the season was an artistic success. In particular, the company's assault on what its literature termed "the pernicious star system" was timely and complete. Gilded Age intellectuals believed, with Krehbiel, in both German opera and opera in English— that the first would prove conducive to the second; that Italian opera, whose expensive singers sapped financial resource and artistic nerve, would give way to an integrated musical-dramatic whole. A columnist for the *Century* wrote approvingly of the American Opera Company in May 1886: "Close knitting together of all the parts . . . was the clear note of the representations. . . . [Thomas] plays operas as he would a symphony." Curtis wrote in *Harper's* the same month: "The opera that began with Malibran, and which has charmed generations, ended, and the German and American opera, vigorous and triumphant, sits supreme."[25]

In Boston, where intellectual bias against the star system was especially thorough, Mrs. Thurber's company especially triumphed. Of the two Wagner productions, *Lohengrin* "was performed as never before in Boston." All the artists "entered thoroughly into the spirit of the work." The chorus was fresh-voiced and well drilled, as well as "handsomely and picturesquely dressed and disposed in judicious masses and cleverly scattered groups." One feature "without precedent at a performance of 'Lohengrin' in our local experience" was "the close and sympathetic interest manifested by the audience . . . due to the fact that the listeners understood what was sung." The crowning contribution came from Thomas's "unrivalled" orchestra, compared to which "the great Bayreuth festival orchestra can show immense perfection of drill, but not such uniformly fine executive material." "We have never heard the orchestral score of 'Lohengrin' played as magnificently as on this occasion. . . . There was scarcely a flaw in the instrumental work from beginning to end."

As for *The Flying Dutchman* in Boston, "a more generally satisfactory performance of the opera cannot now be recalled." "The music is familiar from oft-repeated presentations on the concert platform, and the opera itself has been frequently given on the operatic stage in German, English, and Italian versions. Previous presentations in this country have not, however, created any great amount of enthusiasm for the opera, but the wholly admirable manner in which it was presented last night ought to go far to commend it very strongly to the music-loving public." "It goes without saying that the orchestral score was given with . . . perfection and brilliancy." "The scenes painted by Garpard Maeder afford a setting of rare picturesque beauty, and the application of the latest improvements and mechanical devices for stage effects give some of the most novel and striking reproductions of nature's phenomena. In the storm scene the lightning was almost terrifying in its realism." "The closing scene, with the wreck of the vessel and the apotheosis of the lovers, was managed with remarkable skill." In sum: "Never before has grand opera been presented in this city in so complete a manner as by this troupe. We have usually had a few good singers, a poor chorus of ancient singers, a meagre orchestra of musicians who had but little enthusiasm for their work, and a poverty of scenic illustration that was often laughable. None of these faults could be laid at the door of the American Company."[26]

But as the cumbersome Spring tour proceeded, with three hundred members in tow, much went wrong. Lavish expenditures were unrealistically combined with low prices. Contractual disputes sapped morale. Audiences in some cities insisted on the missing vocal stars, or lacked sophistication to understand the aims being pursued. As the "National Opera Company"—a ploy to hide assets from its creditors—the troupe struggled through a second season, whose even more ambitious, even less realistic route reached the

West Coast. By mid-1887 the National Opera was penniless, and its members, Thomas included, were suing for their wages.

To Krehbiel, who sympathized with its aims, the American Opera Company was boastful and naive. To the affluent who, notwithstanding an initial enthusiasm, failed to back or patronize it, the American Opera was irresponsible as business and insufficiently exotic as art. Thomas himself was left embittered by the episode; in his memoirs he complained of "peculiarities of management which neither art nor business could long endure. . . . Toward the close it was either a disgrace or a calamity to everyone connected with it." But Thomas himself was not blameless. Though he aspired to conduct opera as an extension of his Wagner advocacy, he retained a moralistic antipathy to the stage. His orchestra was frequently criticized for dominating the singers, whom he straightjacketed and bullied. His credo remained: "A symphony orchestra shows the culture of a community, not opera."[27]

Though opera in English did not end with the American Opera Company, the great American opera was never written. America continued to produce important opera singers—and yet singers whose inexperience singing in their own language shortchanged their potential as singing actors. For audiences and artists alike, opera as theater remained primarily an Old World preoccupation. The outcome for Wagner in America was not crucial so long as German-speakers abounded. After World War I—after Wagner's American heyday—the audience for Wagner would inevitably embrace "the pernicious star system." Flagstad would become the new Patti.

Thomas was tired. He craved, once and for all, a permanent, full-time orchestra such as Henry Higginson's Boston Symphony—an orchestra New York, with its part-time Philharmonic, had never offered him. The offer came in 1891, from Chicago. Thomas accepted. New York bade him farewell at a testimonial banquet at Delmonico's Restaurant on April 22. George William Curtis rose to propose the health of a public benefactor—an artist whose devotion to a beautiful, refining, and ennobling art has greatly distinguished his name and given great distinction to the city in which he lives— the health of the central figure of the musical life of New York for a generation, and your hearts go before my tongue in saluting Theodore Thomas. . . .

It is because of the dignity of his career, its absolute fidelity to a high ideal, its total freedom from charlatanry of every kind that his service to this city has been so signal a public benefit and that his departure is a public misfortune.[28]

Four months later, Thomas led the last in a series of farewell concerts at Madison Square Garden. It ended with the *Tannhäuser* Overture. Two months after that, on October 17, he led the first concert of his new Chicago Orchestra, later the Chicago Symphony. The program began with Wagner's *Faust* Overture.

In fourteen Chicago seasons, 164 of the 274 subscription programs Thomas led included works by Wagner. Yet the Thomas-Wagner equation faded. Thomas found that popular enthusiasm for Wagner had accustomed people "to strong doses of excitement, and contrast, and everything without these tonic properties was regarded with indifference. Indeed, the announcement of a symphony was enough to keep many persons from going to a concert." And Thomas's own taste was changing. As the Wagner wave foamed and crested, he increasingly stood apart in more settled waters. He had never been the type of Wagnerite who—like Theodore Hagen of New York's *Musical Review* in the 1850s, or Henry Finck of the *New York Evening Post* after 1881—used Wagner as a club to bludgeon Mozart and other early masters. "The strongest Wagnerites are unmusical people," he declared in 1887. "They dwell upon what they call his dramatic power and leave out the musical part." "I have neither sympathy not patience with those so-called 'musicians' whose education begins and ends with Wagner," he fulminated five years later. In 1904, months before his death, he set down his final thoughts on music and performance. Of Berlioz's program music he now wrote: "He . . . tried to replace soul by adopting a text which should interest the listener and to cover up the lack of musical expression with material effects . . . his works were interesting for a time." Of Wagner he said: "The necessity for calling attention to his works no longer exists, nor does he suffer from being neglected, and besides, much of his music is not suitable or legitimate for concert purposes." Thomas continued:

> Wagner . . . expanded everything, but . . . without soul. . . . He made a great impression on the world by his combination of intellect and passion, or sensuousness. He touched greatness in "Siegfried's Death March," but even in this chiefly by his intellect. Wagner did not care for humanity, but in his later life he became sentimental, as is shown in his "Parsifal"—though the Flower Maiden scene shows that he remained sensuous to the last.

In the same essay, Thomas turned his back on the "monster American halls and theaters" in which he once mounted his festivals. He espoused "purity of style" and predicted a time "in which the various periods will be adequately represented, in halls of different sizes, and with orchestras selected for the purpose."[29]

In certain respects, this conservative drift was timely. The beer-and-tobacco audiences of Bergmann's first *Tannhäuser*, the polkas, waltzes, and arboreal flutists of Thomas's Central Park Garden concerts, were already relics from another era. As never before, great music was an occasion for secular religious rites. As never before, its repertoire showcased Beethoven and other dead masters. Thomas complained of having prostituted his art and talents. He was losing his onetime faith "that the people would enjoy and support the best in art when continually set before them in a clear and intelligent manner." As Thomas's wife, Rose Fay, later remarked: "A little experience taught him that neither children nor what are called 'wage-workers' were sufficiently advanced intellectually to be able to appreciate the class of music which was his specialty. . . . He longed to play to an audience which could understand his best, without any more preparatory effort. . . . Missionary work did not appeal to him as it had in former years." Thomas himself said of his Chicago Orchestra: "One does not buy a Krupp cannon to shoot sparrows."[30]

He had never seemed so little the frontiersman, so much the "substantial banker" the *Chicago Evening Post* perceived. In Chicago, a city of rude and astonishing growth, his backers bore names like Field, McCormick, Armour, Otis, Sprague, Swift, and Pullman. Their wealth ensured his orchestra's prized permanence.

If Thomas had grown disillusioned with the broad public he once courted, and with the Wagner with whom he once corresponded, a third disappointment exacerbated these two. In New York, he had been displaced by another conductor, a Wagner specialist. This was the bitter reality underlying Thomas's explanation, in his memoirs, for the disbanding of his orchestra in 1888: the musicians "thought that New York would not allow our organization to be abandoned after so many years of service, but would raise an endowment fund and make it a permanent institution. New York, however, was now absorbed in its new operatic venture, and did nothing at all." Six pages later, he adds: "New York had now gone backwards, and the musical standard of the East was set by the Boston Orchestra."[31]

Anton Seidl was the man who led New York "backwards." He exemplified those "so-called musicians" whose musical education "began and ended with Wagner." Not only was Wagner's music his bible; so were Wagner's views on conducting, espousing a newly subjective approach to interpretation, a new flexibility of pulse, an expanded range of tempo and dynamics. Thomas's conducting was not of this type; in this regard, his growing conservatism was not timely but old-fashioned. His problems as an operatic conductor, the resistance he encountered from such singers as Materna, his failure to establish a personal rapport with Wagner, exposed a rigidity increasingly at odds with the contemporary moment.

He was no mere Kapellmeister. His dignity, diligence, conviction, personal authority, and natural musical ability made him a figure of world stature. In the Music of the Future, he was not merely polished but majestic. The pianist Emil Sauer, a pupil of Liszt's, tellingly described him as a "full-blooded musician of the Hans Richter type" who (like Richter) offered "convincing proof that shades of expression and tonal effects may be produced without hysterics, contortions, and such foolery." But as the century drew toward a close—as Wagner and Schoenberg explored the limits of tonality, and Debussy began his quest for a trance-state of iridescent, self-sufficient sound; as writers like Proust and Joyce, Ibsen and Strindberg were discovered and championed in America by James Gibbons Huneker—Thomas's vaunted self-control came to seem not ennobling (a favorite Gilded Age adjective) but retarding. Wagner was orgasmic, Dionysian. Thomas, who once said of *Tristan*, "I do not believe this music will ever be popular," spurned the "sensuous." He recommended his Chicago concerts for "rest and relaxation," an antidote to "nervous strain."[32]

He died, in 1905, an institution—telephone operators told callers "Theodore Thomas is dead" before inquiring "Number, please"— but also an anachronism. The *New York Times*'s obituary called him an ideal exemplar of "the older generation of music lovers," versus "the 'modern' conductor that has evolved from Wagner's influence." Six years later, the *Musical Courier* declared him "a human metronome, a drill master who never yielded for a moment to a flexible or emotional indiscretion, as he would have called it."[33]

Thinking even of the painters Albert Pinkham Ryder and Thomas Eakins, who transcended brown sobrieties, Lewis Mumford wrote of the "Brown Decades," 1865 to 1895: "The prevailing palette . . . ran most easily through the gamut from yellow brown to dark sienna. In the best work of the period these somber autumnal colours took on a new loveliness: a warm russet brown." If the Brown Decades "began with the mourning note of Lincoln's funeral," they ended, "like a sun thrusting through the clouds, in the golden portal of Louis Sullivan's Transportation Building at the Chicago World's Fair in 1893."[34] With his prudish dignity and stolid flair, Theodore Thomas validated Wagner for the Gilded Age. More than introducing Wagner's music, he made it respectable. He turned it brown, even russet brown. For Wagner in America, the golden portal—the thrusting sunlight of Brünnhilde's Awakening—awaited a different Siegfried.

4

Germanized Opera

Opera in nineteenth-century America was many things.
A box at the opera, quipped Henry James, was "the only
approach to the implication of the tiara known in American
law," the "great vessel of social salvation." Opera was also a cheap
and popular entertainment, merging with ballad opera, musical comedy, and farce. It is said to have helped solidify New York's patriciate
by 1850. The same year, Jenny Lind's American debut tour, master-
minded by Phineas T. Barnum, enthralled audiences at New York's
Castle Garden, at the White House, and in a Wisconsin pork
butcher's shed. Opera was elevated; it appealed to progressive taste.
"Everybody goes, and nob and snob, Fifth Avenue and Chatham
Street, sit side by side on the hard benches," grumbled George
Templeton Strong in 1851. Opera was elegant: its rituals included
promenading one's diamonds and interpolating delicious Italianisms
in suave conversation. Opera was sinful: Boston banned *Rigoletto*,
Brooklyn outlawed *Traviata*. Opera was exotic: its incomprehensible
French, German, or Italian conferred the sort of snob appeal Mark
Twain claimed he observed in an Italian hotel register bearing such
signatures as "John P. Whitcomb, Etats Unis" and "Wm. L. Ains-
worth, travailleur." Less socially ambitious theatergoers preferred
English-language adaptations of *La cenerentola* and *The Marriage of
Figaro* that cheerfully altered the originals, adding or subtracting
arias, even characters.[1]

Operatic culture was vigorous and diverse. On February 24, 1847,
Walt Whitman informed readers of his *Brooklyn Daily Eagle* column
of their opportunities to enjoy operas "neatly got up on a small

scale" at the Olympic Theater (tonight, *Fra Diavolo*); to attend Italian opera (tonight, *Lucrezia Borgia*) on Chambers Street; to sample the troupe from Havana giving opera twice a week at the Park Theater. New Orleans, home of the nation's first permanent opera company, offered fourteen performances of nine different operas during one April week in 1836. Theodore Thomas was not the only observer to remark:

> The beginning of the fifties brought over to this country not only instrumentalists, but the most brilliant, finished, and mature vocalists of the world, such as Jenny Lind and Sontag, besides a large number of eminent Italian singers, among them Mario, Grisi, Bosio, Alboni, and others. I doubt if there were ever brought together in any part of the world a larger number of talented vocalists than were gathered in New York between 1850 and the early sixties.[2]

The first New York venue to centralize all this activity was the Academy of Music on 14th Street. Opened in 1854, burnt down and rebuilt in 1866, it was the city's leading opera house for nearly three decades. Among its resident impresarios was Maurice Strakosch. As we have seen, his 1874 *Lohengrin*, with Campanini and Nilsson—and also Clara Louise Kellogg's English-language *Flying Dutchman* of 1877, Adolf Neuendorff's Wagner festival of 1877, and the first American *Rienzi* in 1878, all at the Academy—boosted German opera from the Bowery and lower Broadway. In 1878, the Academy finally acquired an impresario with staying power: James Henry Mapleson, whose artistic stable included Campanini, Adelina Patti, and Francesco Tamagno, and who toured as far west as Chicago, Cincinnati, and St. Louis. "Colonel" Mapleson was a colorful figure. Krehbiel called his attempt to stage a "spontaneous" torchlight serenade for Patti as "the most painful affair that I have ever witnessed." Huneker testified that Mapleson conducted business—frequently, the business of deferred fees—by "smearing his singers" with "the unguent of fat praise." When flattery failed, so, sometimes, did the Colonel's pocketbook.[3]

The principal problem with opera at the Academy, however, had nothing to do with Mapleson: there were only eighteen boxes—far too few to satisfy the demand for ostentation. "The world of fashion was still content to reassemble every winter in the shabby red and gold boxes of the sociable old Academy," Edith Wharton later remarked. "Conservatives cherished it for . . . keeping out the 'new people.'"[4] And so the "new people" built an opera house of their own. The 3,615-seat Metropolitan Opera House, between 39th and 40th streets, Broadway and Seventh Avenue, was a clumsy building with a shallow stage, minimal stage machinery, and flawed sight lines and acoustics. But its five-tiered horseshoe auditorium was breathtakingly vast—104 feet long from the proscenium to the back of the center box. And there were 122 boxes.* The owners of the new theater—the stockholders, who were also boxholders—would not themselves produce opera. Rather, they would lease the premises to impresarios, whose activities they would monitor. The first of these, for the 1883–84 season, was Henry E. Abbey, a theatrical producer contracted for "first class opera" in Italian.

Abbey ordered lavish sets and costumes and lavish casts. The opening night featured *Faust* with Nilsson (for whom Abbey had outbid Mapleson at two thousand dollars per performance), Campanini, and Franco Novara—all of whom, according to Krehbiel, "had been heard in the opera many times when their powers were greater." But never before had the Jewel Song been rewarded with a sash of hammered gold bay leaves and berries, with medallions in the form of Tragedy and Comedy as clasps, handed to Nilsson during her ovation. The Met's second night was a triumph for twenty-five-year-old Marcella Sembrich as Lucia. The remainder of the repertoire included a single Wagner work—*Lohengrin*, of course. Like everything else, it was heard in Italian, with Nilsson and Campanini. Krehbiel reported: "The opera attracted the most numerous and brilliant audience since the opening night, and remained one of the most pronounced successes of the season."[5]

---

*After the fire of 1892, there were seventy-four boxes plus an "omnibus box" of four rows, two sections.

But the total financial picture was bleak. One reason was that Abbey had overpriced the house. In so "foreign" a city, some potential operagoers were Italian and German immigrants who could not afford Abbey's three-dollar balcony seats, or the two-dollar seats in the front half of the Himalayan Family Circle.

Abbey apparently offered to undertake a second season. Instead, the board chose a less opulent, more practical strategy: a season of opera in German. Whereas for Italian opera luminaries like Nilsson and Sembrich were both necessary and expensive, in German opera a skilled ensemble mattered. What is more, the best singers were already employed year-round by the court operas of their homeland, from which they could be borrowed for reasonable sums; any two would cost less than Nilsson alone.[6] To capitalize on the clamor for Wagner, the house was scaled down from Abbey's initial $6 top to $3 for the 562 downstairs "parquet" seats; the 1,700 balcony and family circle seats cost from $1.50 to 50 cents.

Never had German opera experienced so mighty or fortuitous an American boon. Faced with the possibility, under Abbey, of an additional assessment of at least three thousand dollars per box, the Metropolitan Opera, the nation's largest, became a German house. For seven seasons, not a note would be warbled in Italian or French. If the financial dividends would please the boxholders, the artistic consequences would startle and perplex them. And yet New York— and not only its swarming Germans—was ready.

Passing over Theodore Thomas, the Metropolitan entrusted its 1884–85 season to Leopold Damrosch, whose candidacy was influentially supported by his friend James Roosevelt, president of the Met board of directors. Damrosch had conceived a plausible German opera plan. For French and Italian operas (sung in German), he could use Abbey's sets and costumes. For the *Ring* operas, he would copy Bayreuth's sets and costumes. His salary would be ten thousand dollars. The boxholders would pick up the deficits, if any.

Damrosch was fifty-two years old. Unlike Thomas (but rather like Gustav Mahler, who would arrive at the Met in 1907), he was a small, high-strung man of Jewish extraction, and deeply cultivated. His rabbinical beard emphasized his expressive Semitic features. At his parents' insistence, he had started out as a doctor. He switched to music by 1857—the year he became concertmaster of Liszt's court orchestra at Weimar. This exposure to Wagner's great friend and apostle was doubtless inspirational. From 1858 to 1871 Damrosch conducted in Breslau. He came to New York in 1871 to lead the Arion Chorus once conducted by Carl Bergmann. He formed his own Oratorio Society two years later. In 1876 he went to Bayreuth to attend the *Ring*. The same year, he succeeded Bergmann as conductor of the New York Philharmonic, where his repertoire included the entire first act of *Die Walküre* and excerpts from act 3 of *Götterdämmerung*, and also first American performances of Saint-Saëns's G minor Piano Concerto, Goldmark's *Rustic Wedding* Symphony, and a formidable helping from Berlioz's *The Trojans*. Such brave programing was one reason attendance plummeted. Replaced at the Philharmonic by Thomas, Damrosch formed his own orchestra, named the New York Symphony in 1878. In 1880, with this orchestra, he gave the first American performances of *Siegfried* act 3. In 1881, he expanded his singers and players to an army of 1,450 and booked the new Seventh Regiment Armory. Here, during a five-day festival anticipating Thomas's even more grandiose Armory doings a year later, he directed *Messiah*, Beethoven's Ninth, Rubinstein's oratorio *Tower of Babel*, and the American premiere of the Berlioz Requiem.

According to a well-known anecdote, Thomas once told Damrosch: "Whoever crosses my path, I crush." But Damrosch was as clever a mouse as Thomas was an arrogant lion. In one skirmish, in 1877, Damrosch had copyists work day and night to prepare parts for Brahms's First Symphony; he beat Thomas to the American premiere by six days. Beginning in 1882, Damrosch began to tour his orchestra to Midwestern cities Thomas considered his own. As a conductor, he was less polished, more excitable than his poised rival. His beat lost precision in moments of high feeling. Rehearsing the

St. Matthew Passion, he was reduced to tears. Frédéric Ritter remembered Damrosch as "a gifted, thorough musician" and "a broad-minded, educated man." Damrosch's devotion to the Music of the Future fired his plan for the Metropolitan. But he had remarkably little experience conducting opera.[7]

The company Damrosch now assembled eschewed glamour; only Materna's was a famous name. The season of twenty-one weeks (November 17 to April 18, including visits to Chicago, Cincinnati, and Boston) surveyed fourteen operas by Auber, Beethoven, Boïeldieu, Gluck, Halévy, Meyerbeer, Mozart, Rossini, Verdi, Wagner, and Weber—a misleading list, given that forty-four of the 101 performances were of *Tannhäuser*, *Lohengrin*, and *Die Walküre*.[8]

The novelty of it all bears stressing. New York knew Wagner, but nothing like these months of staged performances by a stable Wagner troupe. Never before had Americans so experienced opera as theater. For New York intellectuals, Wagner infused the dramatic ideals of a Goethe or Shakespeare, counteracting divas whose excessive fees, according to Curtis, revealed "the nature of Italian opera as a fabulous luxury."[9] On the same stage where Christine Nilsson had been rewarded with real jewels during the ovation for her Jewel Song, jewels and jewel songs, arias and ovations were banished by Wagner rites.

The revolutionary emphasis on dramatic integrity was taken for granted not only by Damrosch, but by his singers. The second night of the season, Marianne Brandt, a Bayreuth Kundry, was Beethoven's Leonore. Krehbiel later wrote: "On its musical side her performance was thrillingly effective, but on its histrionic it rose to grandeur. Every word of her few speeches, every note of her songs, every look of her eyes and expression of her face was an exposition of that world of tenderness which filled the heart of Leonore. . . . There was nothing of the petty theatrical in Fräulein Brandt." Nine days later, signaling the new esprit de corps, Brandt took the tiny role of Hedwige in *William Tell*. Materna's first appearance, on January 5, was as Elisabeth in *Tannhäuser*, a work still little-known in New York, except for its overture and choruses. Notwithstanding her many appearances with Thomas, this was her American stage debut. She performed, one reviewer marveled, "like a play-actress." Every word told. The opera itself, while well known to many, seemed renewed.[10]

But the season's centerpiece and triumph was *Die Walküre*, previously seen only in Adolf Neuendorff's lamentable stagings at the Academy. Damrosch rehearsed it for months. The company was consumed by the example of Bayreuth. Beginning with the first performance, on January 30, *Die Walküre* was given five times in eight days. The work itself was as great a novelty as any performance could be: no arias, no chorus, no ballet, no pauses for applause. Wagner had fashioned a mythological music drama for forces that must have seemed equally mythic: an orchestra of one hundred, including four trumpets, eight horns (four doubling on Wagner tubas), five trombones, and tuba; singers with the power and stamina to surmount the torrents of sound thus produced.

Anchoring Damrosch's cast was Materna's Brünnhilde—a role she had learned from Wagner himself. Wagner insisted on singers who could act. Though the poses he prescribed may today seem histrionic, he outlawed stereotypical stage deportment. As Brünnhilde, Materna at the Met seemed to contemporary observers the embodiment of art concealing art. Both the impetuous abandon of the role, and its underside of daughterly tenderness, absorbed her fully. The rest of the cast included Anton Schott's Siegmund, Auguste Seidl-Kraus's Sieglinde, and Josef Staudigl's Wotan. Brandt both sang Fricka and joined the Valkyrie choir as Gerhilde. Damrosch's orchestra was called "a constant wonder," the best ever heard from a New York pit. The stage director, also imported from Germany, was the experienced Wilhelm Hock. He marginally departed from the Bayreuth model, replacing Hunding's door with romantic draperies and costuming the Valkyries more colorfully. His magic fire was admired, as was the cloudswept mountain duel closing act 2. Unlike Wagner, who used painted projections, he did not attempt the Valkyries' ride.

Not the least remarkable aspect of the Met's first German season was its audience. True, some of the boxholders, as Krehbiel put it, "hankered for the fleshpots of Egypt"—their bursts of conversation provoked hisses from the devout. And yet the devotional mode prevailed. *Die Walküre*, in particular, was accorded an "almost painful attention." Though the performances ran for more than four hours, and "nervous exhaustion" caused fatigue during acts 2 and 3, no one left early. Damrosch's liberal cuts were not deplored by Krehbiel and other purists. Rather, the true believers sought true audiences, whose concentration inspired the performers.[11]

The logic of the Damrosch scheme relied not only on reduced expenditure, but belief in Wagner and the hunger for Wagner. The season's attendance justified this faith. For *Die Walküre*, the company's most popular, most lucrative offering, speculators bought the good seats and resold them for nearly twice what their messenger boys had paid. What is more, the huge houses, according to impressions in the press, were not always predominantly German. Even boxholders were caught up in the excitement. Audiences for *Lohengrin*, *Tannhäuser*, and *Die Walküre* were described as "brilliant." In January 1885, Damrosch signed a contract for a second German season. Meanwhile, at the Academy, Mapleson's Wagnerless operation—"Wagner spells ruin," the colonel had mispredicted—was failing.

The deep meanings of these developments were plumbed by the Wagnerites. The new order stemmed not from Bellini, Donizetti, and Rossini, but from Gluck, Mozart, Beethoven, and Weber. Fashion no longer called the tune but cheerfully obeyed or impotently groused. Italian opera "had received its quietus"—a Krehbiel proclamation that, however parochial, proved remarkably valid for the moment.[12]

And this despite the sudden death of Leopold Damrosch on February 15, 1885. He had expired of pneumonia at the age of fifty-two. Until he fell ill on February 10, he had conducted every performance of the opera season: fifty-two assignments in twelve weeks. Nor had he relinquished his Oratorio Society or New York Symphony. His funeral took place at the Metropolitan, which was draped in black inside and out. Henry Ward Beecher delivered a eulogy. Wilhelm Hock rendered the final farewell, in German, to the casket. A performance of Siegfried's Funeral Music, still barely ten years old, followed.

It fell to Leopold's twenty-three-year-old son, Walter, to finish the season. While his poise was admired, and while his podium career would span six decades, Walter Damrosch was never a major conductor, and his rise was rapidly squelched. Another unsuccessful candidate to run the company was the tenor Anton Schott, whose reorganization plan included Wagner in English with German singers "quick to learn your language." Instead—again bypassing Theodore Thomas, conspicuous for his absence at Leopold's funeral—the Metropolitan sent Walter to Europe to find a suitable replacement for his father. Forty-one years later Henry Finck would savagely quip that Walter's contract for Anton Seidl, delivered upon his return, constituted the "supreme achievement" of his life in music. Edmund Stanton, whom the directors had named manager, also took part in negotiating contracts for Seidl, for a new chorus, and for such important singers as Lilli Lehmann and Emil Fischer.[13]

By his own frequent testimony, Seidl was decisively shaped by the six years he lived with the Wagner family in Bayreuth. "My mode of thought, the manner in which I . . . conceived anything, the vigor with which I . . . attempted everything, all had their origin in that gracious and blessed house," he told Krehbiel in 1887.[14]

Born in Budapest on May 7, 1850, he studied piano and composition at the Leipzig Conservatory, then the hub of German musical life. He followed the conductor and Wagner protégé Hans Richter to Pest. With Richter, he attended the laying of the cornerstone of the Bayreuth Festspielhaus in 1872. The stone was lowered with a casket containing a telegram from the King of Bavaria. Wagner struck three blows with a hammer and turned away, teary-eyed and pale. Later in the day, Friedrich Nietzsche observed him "turning inward on himself a look which it is beyond the power of words to describe. . . . We know that in moments of supreme danger or at decisive turning-points in their lives men see their whole life's experience concentrated into one swift inner vision, and have an intensified perception of all that is recent and all that is most remote." A concert that afternoon featured the "Wach' auf" chorus from *Die Meistersinger* and Beethoven's Ninth under Wagner's baton.

Seidl was overwhelmed. He resolved, as he related to Krehbiel, "at any cost to get near to Wagner."[15]

Fortuitously, Wagner needed an assistant. Richter recommended Seidl. Wagner became Seidl's second father. A slender, smooth-faced twenty-two-year-old Parsifal, Seidl was Wagner's amanuensis, his companion at the piano, at mealtimes, on walks. Every night at seven, he joined the family for music, conversation, and readings of essays and literature. These evenings left "the most vivid recollections of my life. In one of them it was often possible for me to learn more than all the conservatories or great musicians could offer. To hear the master . . . talk about Bach, Beethoven, Mozart, Weber, Marschner, Spontini, or Auber and Rossini, explain their music, occasionally illustrating what he said at the pianoforte or by singing . . . was so instructive and so amazing to me that I saw everything in a strange, magical sort of light."

On one such evening, shortly after Seidl's arrival on September 28, 1872, Wagner "entered the room, bowed with mock solemnity and modesty to the company and begged their kind indulgence and mild judgment on [a] new work. Then with a comically serious face he seated himself at the piano and the reading began. . . . I [then] enjoyed the first privilege vouchsafed to mortal man to hear the mighty, cataclysmic sounds of the funeral music and the broad, world-redeeming harmonies of Brünnhilde's last address in the 'Götterdämmerung.'"[16]

Cosima Wagner's diary eavesdrops on the growing intimacy of master and disciple. "R. goes through Mozart's symphonies with Herr Seidl; Mozart was a great chromaticist, R. says, but rarely gave expression to his nature; R. indignant that Seidl does not know the subject thoroughly." R. goes through *Tannhäuser* act 1 with Herr Seidl, and discusses shortening the first scene; Cosima demurs. R. plays Mozart's G minor Symphony with Herr Seidl—a four-hand performance provoked by dismissive comments about the work; of the first and second movement themes R. indignantly exclaims: "They should be set in diamonds!" Again at the keyboard, they play through great chunks of *Parsifal*, which R. is now composing, with one or both singing Gurnemanz, Parsifal, Amfortas. These sessions—"splendid, blessed hours such as no public performance could ever provide," according to Cosima—are dubbed by Wagner his "studies with Seidl." On February 23, 1878, the duettists play through the *Siegfried Idyll*; R. laughs that what distinguishes him from other composers is that he cannot compose without inspiration, whereas they can: a great advantage. A month later, he chides Herr Seidl about the correct tempos for Beethoven's *Pastoral* Symphony ("What on earth do they learn in Leipzig?"). The topic of his April 1 disquisition is Spontini, whose *Olympie* Overture Seidl does not know. April 15, Seidl plays whist with Wagner, Cosima, and Liszt; R. "does the teaching." By May 21, 1878, Herr Seidl has become "friend Seidl." A day later, R. is wheeled about the Wahnfried grounds in a new carriage; the "horses" include Seidl and the children. May 29, the after-dinner reading, attended by Seidl, is from *Macbeth*; as always, R. takes all the parts. June 6, Cosima and R. serenade friend Seidl at his window with the ditty "Harlequin, thou must perish!" By June 8, the day of a country outing, friend Seidl is "uncle" to the children. July 11, accompanying Ferdinand Jäger in the forging song from *Siegfried*, friend Seidl is chided for getting the tempos wrong.[17]

Initially, Seidl was one of Wagner's copyists. He also helped Wagner with his correspondence. With Wagner's encouragement, he took up conducting a local amateur orchestra, whose performances—including one of Wagner's *Das Liebesmahl der Apostel*—Wagner attended. On Christmas 1874, Wagner inscribed a score of *Das Rheingold* with the punning verses:

Auf der Welt ist alles eitel:
Wer kein Maass hat, trinkt sein Seidl.
Anton nur ist's ganz gelungen:
Von der Sohle bis zum Scheitel,
Hat er sich hineingesungen
In den Ring des Nibelungen.*[18]

---

* Translated by Henry Finck: "In this world all things are idle, / Hast no mug? [In German, *Seidl*] / Then take your Seidl. / Anton only has succeeded: / From the head down to his lung / He alone himself has sung / Into the Ring of the Nibelung."

When Wagner went to Berlin to conduct two concerts, Seidl went as his assistant. Franz Fridberg of the *Berliner Tageblatt* later reported of "Wagner's right hand":

> He was, in fact, the real conductor of our rehearsals. It was impossible to conceive all that this young man from Budapest heard and knew by heart. Before Wagner himself had noted errors in his own music, Seidl could be seen flying over chairs and desks to correct the blunder. The Master viewed the actions of his young famulus with paternal love, and repeatedly I heard him murmur, "Ho, he! What would I do without my Seidl?" If Seidl disappeared for a moment, and things began to go a bit at sixes and sevens, Wagner would look about anxiously and cry, "Help, Seidl!" and Seidl would come with flying leaps to set things to rights.[19]

During the long preparations for the first *Ring*, Seidl coached some of the principal singers as well as the male chorus for *Götterdämmerung* act 2. He was responsible for implementing many details of the staging, and operated the "swimming machine" carrying Lilli Lehmann, as Woglinde. Richter conducted; Seidl was his de facto understudy, of whom Wagner later wrote in a testimonial letter: "He has proved himself eminently capable at the rehearsals as well as at the performances, so that in case of necessity I should have considered it possible at any moment to put the directorship entirely in his hands, all the more because his leadership of orchestral concerts during several years has conclusively proven his qualifications as an energetic and careful conductor."[20]

Seidl subsequently scouted Wagner productions in Munich and Leipzig, conveying detailed reports to the anxious composer. Attending rehearsals for the first Leipzig performances of *Das Rheingold* and *Die Walküre* in April 1878, he zealously hounded the company's manager, Angelo Neumann; only Richter's counsel quieted his mistrust. When Neumann proceeded to prepare *Siegfried* and *Götterdämmerung*, Wagner prevailed upon him to employ Seidl to help ready them, arguing: "Believe me when I tell you that no one (be he ever so gifted and painstaking) who has not learned all these things thoroughly *here under me* in Bayreuth can carry out my plans with absolute fidelity. The news I get from Munich of the last performance of *Siegfried* (and coming from such a source [i.e., Seidl] I am forced to believe it) makes me very anxious as to this production." Neumann later wrote: "At the very first rehearsal Seidl proved his extraordinary talents . . . , and any one with artistic sympathies could understand his wild desire to be allowed to conduct the works he felt himself so fully master of. He pleaded with Wagner to insist upon it I should give him the baton for the *Ring*." Wagner, in turn, pleaded with Neumann: "None of the other conductors has such a clear understanding of my tempi, and the harmony between the music and the action. I have coached Seidel [*sic*] personally, and he will conduct your Nibelungen as no other can. If my word for this is not sufficient, then I shall *never* express my opinion to you again!" He expressed his opinion again three months later, following the announcement of the departure for Hamburg of Neumann's conductor, Josef Sucher: "My every wish would be gratified if you would consent (in pursuance of your course of striving for perfection) to appoint to your vacant position of conductor this young musician, in whom I have more confidence than in any other."[21]

In January 1879 it was arranged: at the age of twenty-eight, Seidl became chief conductor of Neumann's Leipzig Opera. The collaboration was propitious; a former singer, Neumann was himself a devoted and visionary Wagnerite. In the summer of 1881, Seidl and Neumann introduced the *Ring* to Berlin with four complete cycles. Attending rehearsals against Neumann's wishes, Wagner himself underwent cycles of depression and elation, fitness and illness, excitement and fatigue. According to Cosima, he greeted Seidl "as a pearl" but complained about the singing and acting; Materna, whose Brünnhilde gesticulated too much, was twice reduced to tears. The following January, Leipzig presented its first *Tristan und Isolde*, about which Wagner wrote to Neumann: "You are aware that I had made up my mind to allow this problematic work to be given . . . only under my personal supervision: now it has succeeded without me— and that astonishes me! Well, good luck! I certainly discover in Seidl hidden faculties which only require a fostering warmth to surprise even me."[22] Seidl was reportedly Wagner's choice to conduct the first *Parsifal* that July in Bayreuth; but an agreement with King Ludwig reserved the work for his gifted Munich Kapellmeister, Hermann Levi.

Beginning in September 1882, Neumann took a touring Wagner company, under Seidl, through Holland, Belgium, Switzerland, Germany, Austria, Hungary, Italy, and England. Its 135 stage performances and 58 concerts both introduced the *Ring* and insured its best possible reception. The ensemble included such artists as Materna, Brandt, Auguste Kraus, Albert Niemann, and Schott—all of whom would appear at the Metropolitan Opera by 1886. The orchestra gradually mastered the difficult scores. Neumann's Brussels *Ring*, in early 1883, was attended by Lalo, Massenet, and the leading French critics. As would later occur in Italy, encores—as of Mime's "Sorglose Schmiede," in *Das Rheingold*—were demanded and given. Then on the morning of February 14, having arrived in Aix-la-Chapelle (today's Aachen) with his technical staff and chorus, Neumann was informed of Wagner's death in Venice the day before. Seidl honored his commitment to give *Das Rheingold* that evening. "Tears were streaming from his eyes during the performance," according to a member of the company. Following the Entrance of the Gods, the audience stood for the Funeral Music from *Götterdämmerung*. Paul Geissler, Neumann's assistant conductor, completed the Aix *Ring* while Seidl and Neumann joined the mourners who received Wagner's body at the Bayreuth train station. An observer reported that Seidl "could not conceal his grief as did the older people who endeavored to console him."[23] When Neumann's Wagner tour reached Venice two months later, Seidl's orchestra, deployed in Venetian gondolas of state, played Siegfried's Funeral Music before the Palazzo Vendramin, where Wagner had died. The company's singers occupied six smaller boats.

Later that year, Neumann and Seidl moved from Leipzig to the Bremen Opera. The following February, Seidl married the soprano Auguste Kraus. In an 1899 memoir, she described her husband-to-be and his courtship:

At Amsterdam I was to sing the part of Eva in the [*Meistersinger*] quintet for the first time in the concert hall. . . . I told the conductor, "kindly excuse me if I make any blunders, for I found it absolutely impossible to get the music." Then you should have heard him telling me before the whole orchestra, "That is no excuse; when it is a question of the *Meistersinger* you ought to have gone from one music store to another until you found it." I retorted, somewhat sharply, that it was not my duty to go hunting scores. . . . He answered, sarcastically, "Of course, a spoiled Viennese princess like you doesn't need to do such a thing." I was furious. . . . My dear Tony acknowledged to me later on that he had been angry only because he knew well that I was perfectly familiar with the quintet, and that once for all he had wished to drive such whims out of my head—"Prima Donna whims" he called them. . . .

According to Mrs. Seidl's account of the Wagner troupe, Seidl was prone to oversleep and arrive late at the train station. He was forgetful and would lose canes, hats, overshoes, and umbrellas. He remained "modest and retiring" even in Italy, where he was lionized like no other member of the company. In Bologna, he appeared at her door, "visibly embarrassed, with a beautiful bouquet which he had gathered for me with his own hands. He asked me if I would consent to become his partner in life and share with him pleasure and sorrow. I do not know myself how love for him crept into my heart without my being aware of it, but I felt it was a love such as we experience but once in a lifetime." The Seidls were married in Frankfurt, where Auguste was singing. Seidl "had not the remotest idea" how to procure a wedding bouquet, but managed. The couple proceeded to Bremen, to find their apartment filled with flowers. The orchestra serenaded them that night. The chorus turned up the following morning.

In later years, Seidl would tell friends and reporters that Wagner himself had urged him to settle in the United States. According to Mrs. Seidl's memoirs, her husband "dreamed so often about America that an irresistible power drew him towards that country, and he felt convinced that he would find there a fine opening for his work." When Leopold Damrosch offered her a contract to appear at the Met in 1884, she agreed only so that she could appraise her husband's possibilities in the New World. Then Damrosch died, and Seidl was engaged. According to Mrs. Seidl: "The moment he saw the [New York] harbor he was delighted; the elevated railroad he found imposing; even the large telegraph poles seemed to him beautiful. We were still in the carriage when he exclaimed: 'This is magnificent! I feel that I shall get along well here.'"[24]

5

The Coming of the Disciple

The implausible speed and magnitude of Seidl's American impact become plausible in relation to what had gone before. America was avidly acquainted with Wagner, but mainly as a concert composer. He was esteemed as a musical dramatist, but most often encountered via orchestral extracts. The flourishing operatic culture was predominantly Italian. Prior to its surprise 1884 incursion at the Metropolitan, German opera remained a sporadic or provincial presence.

The leading Wagner conductors were Theodore Thomas and Leopold Damrosch. Thomas mistrusted the theater. He mistrusted singers. Damrosch's allegiance to the Music of the Future was more consuming. He attended the 1876 Bayreuth *Ring*. Eight years later, he eagerly descended from the concert platform to the opera pit. He rehearsed his first *Die Walküre*, a labor of love, for months.

Seidl, at thirty-five, was already a seasoned opera conductor. Unlike Thomas or Damrosch, he was also a superb pianist, accustomed to coaching Wagner's own singers. He had helped prepare the Bayreuth *Ring* Damrosch attended. He had led *Die Walküre* and the other *Ring* operas dozens of times.

Much as fledgling painters visit museums to copy masterpieces of art, fledgling conductors and composers benefit from copying the orchestral scores of a master musician. The activity of inking every string figuration, every clarinet note, every accent and crescendo is a learning experience more painstaking and permanent than any acquired by the scanning ear or eye. Seidl had spent years copying full scores and parts for Wagner, sewing every strand of the complex sonic tapestry. At the keyboard, he had played and sung at Wagner's side, absorbing a second imprint, in performance, of the music he had written out.

"He gave us a new Wagner—the real Wagner," wrote James Gibbons Huneker. "We all thought we knew [*Lohengrin*] perfectly well," testified the critic Albert Steinberg, "and yet . . . many of us were greatly puzzled. Not alone were the climaxes built up in a strange manner, the melos brought out in a more plastic fashion, and a hundred lovely poetic details supplied that were formerly missing, but the opera . . . sounded differently."[1] This encomium—the familiar made new—is so abused today that only with difficulty can we recapture its meaning. When we think "*Lohengrin*," we refer to conventions of interpretation culled from myriad broadcasts, recordings, and live performances—to a binding mainstream experience of the work. In 1885, when Seidl first led *Lohengrin* at the Met, those in the audience who had heard it most likely had only heard one or two others conduct it. And those conductors would themselves have seldom encountered *Lohengrin* as listeners. In 1885, different *Lohengrin* readings *were* likely to sound completely different.

And Seidl was different—not a nervous musician, like Damrosch, or stoically placid, like Thomas. He was poised and mysterious, undemonstrative and impassioned. With his remote manner, Gothic features, and flowing hair, he was priestly, mysterious, charismatic. He was rumored to be an atheist, and Liszt's illegitimate son. Huneker wrote: "His eyes alone were eloquent when his other features were sphinx-like—brown, almost black; . . . they riveted his men with a glance of steel."[2]

"Magnetic" and "electric" are two adjectives that recur in reviews of Seidl at the Met. Three other general attributes of his conducting bear stressing. First, he was a man of the theater. He knew all the vocal parts and all the words. He maintained eye contact with the singers. He worried over every detail of the staging. He harmonized voice and orchestra. Lilli Lehmann considered him "a leader of singers, who felt and breathed with them." According to Edouard and Jean de Reszke, he possessed an instinct which is indeed rare among orchestral conductors of the modern school; he understood singing, seemed to know by intuition exactly what the singer would do in every case and always helped him to do it well. But he did not accomplish this by following the singer slavishly. There are many conductors who can follow a singer in a ritardando such as singers love to make at the close of a musical phrase, but there are few who know exactly how to catch up the rhythm again and restore the equilibrium, as Seidl did, without apparently affecting the shape of the musical period in the least.[3]

A second predominant attribute of Seidl's conducting—and a necessary condition for the first—was fluidity. He did not beat a steady pulse. "Herr Seidl not only attends to every mark of shading and expression with a watchful eye," wrote Henry Finck, "but he indulges in various minute modifications of tempo, which are indicated by the emotional character of the music; and this is what gives so much life and meaning to his 'reading' of a score." To which Boston's William Foster Apthorp added, after a performance of *Tristan und Isolde*:

> the orchestral performance, taken by itself, was a marvel of beauty; such delicacy of shading is exceedingly rare. It was not merely that succession of crass contrasts between fortissimo and pianissimo which sometimes parades under the name of "shading," but a hardly interrupted series of the more subtle and delicate nuances in dynamics and tempo. It reminded one of what [Wilhelm] Gericke once said of Wagner's conducting *Lohengrin* in Vienna: "The most striking thing about it was the surpassing delicacy of all the effects; modification of force and tempo were almost incessant, but were for the most part modifications by a hair's breadth only."[4]

Thirdly, Seidl was a master of climax, a calibrator of harmonic and structural stress who preferred paragraphs to other conductors' words and sentences. According to the *Musical Courier*:

> No conductor that we have ever heard could build up such massive climaxes, such overpowering, such thrilling altitudes of tone. His breadth . . . was no less wonderful. With him there was the abiding

sense of foundational security; his accelerandos were never feverish, a calm logic prevailed from the first bar to the last, yet he was a master of the whirlwind and rode it with a repose that was almost appalling.

Krehbiel confirmed:

> He attained his climaxes, in which the piling of Pelion on Ossa by other men was exceeded, by the most patient and reposeful accumulation of material, its proper adjustment, and its firm maintenance . . . when once it had been gained. The more furious the tempest of passion which he worked up, the more firmly did he hold the forces in rein until the moment arrived when they were to be loosed, so that all should be swept away in the *mêlée*. None of his *confrères* of Bayreuthean antecedents can work so directly, so elementally, upon an audience as did he.[5]

The sum total was a new type of conductor of whom Seidl was America's first important exemplar (the second being Arthur Nikisch, who arrived in Boston in 1889). The progenitor of the new type was Richard Wagner. In his essay "On Conducting" (1869), Wagner dismissed both the self-effacing time-beaters of his day and the elegant Mendelssohn. In his brisk, polished Beethoven performances, with the Leipzig Gewandhaus Orchestra, Mendelssohn mistook his own discreet aesthetic for "Beethovenian classicism." The new podium type Wagner prophesied embodied Lisztian license and charisma. With improvisatory abandon, he would seize extremes of tempo and dynamics. For Wagner, the "pure Allegro" cannot be too fast; and the "pure Adagio" cannot be taken slowly enough. "Omnipresent tempo modification" is "a positive life principle in all our music." Emotional commitment dictates plasticity of pulse: different speeds for each passing image or mood. "Sustained tone," avoiding accented downbeats, is the basis for long-breathed phrasing. A deep subjectivity—Germanic *Innigkeit*—correlates with the ebb and flow of harmonic rhythm. In opera, the new conductor must equally be a man of the stage. In effect, the new conductor is Wagner himself—or Anton Seidl, whose interpretations espoused and perpetuated Wagner's own.

This impression, from written accounts, is reinforced by Seidl's own essay "On Conducting," published in 1895.[6] Seidl begins by asserting that conducting cannot be taught; it is "a gift of God with which few have been endowed in full measure." The only worthwhile readings on the subject are by Wagner and Berlioz. "Most of you," Seidl instructs gifted novices, are "too exclusively musicians." His detailed admonitions on "blending the scenic action with the music and song" remain discouragingly timely. Every contemporary Wagnerite can cite the abuses of stage directors who do not hear what the music says. Far more than is generally appreciated, Wagner's orchestra precisely dictates gesture and movement. Wagner once provided a performance manual for the Dutchman's monologue, "Die Frist ist um," including such instructions as:

—"During the deep trumpet notes . . . he has come off board . . . his rolling gait, proper to seafolk on first treading dry land after a long voyage, is accompanied by a wavelike figure for the violas and cellos: with the first quarter-note of the third bar he makes his second step."

—"With the tremolo of the violins at the fifth bar he raises his face to heaven, his body still bent low: with the entry of the muffled roll of the kettledrum at the ninth bar of the postlude he begins to shudder."

—"Only at the *piano* . . . does he gradually relax his attitude; his arms fall down; at the four bars of espressivo for the first violins he slowly sinks his head, and during the last eight bars of the postlude he totters to the rock wall at the side. . . . I have discussed this scene at such length in order to show how I wish the Dutchman to be portrayed, and what weight I place on the most careful adaptation of the action to the music."*[7]

Seidl, in "On Conducting," relates how Wagner rehearsed the movements of the Rhinemaidens, in the first scene of *Das Rheingold*, for six hours.

---

*I by no means suggest that every Dutchman must follow Wagner's directions. But deviations, empathetic or deconstructive, should proceed from comprehension, not ignorance.

I learned to know the meaning of every phrase, every violin figure, every sixteenth note. I learned, too, how it was possible with the help of the picture and action to transform an apparently insignificant violin passage into an incident, and to lift a simple horn call into a thing of stupendous significance by means of scenic emphasis. . . . The swimming of the Rhine-daughters is carried out very well at most of the larger theatres, but the movement of the nixies does not illustrate the accompanying music. Frequently the fair one rises while a descending violin passage is playing, and again to the music of hurried upward passages she sinks gently to the bottom of the river. Neither is it a matter of indifference whether the movements of the Rhine-daughters be fast or slow. At a majority of the theatres this is treated as a matter of no consequence, regardless of the fact that the public are utterly bewildered by such contradictions between what they see and what they hear. Wagner often said to me, "My dear friend, give your attention to the stage, following my scenic directions, and you will hit the right thing in the music without a question."

A second example:

In the first scene of *Die Walküre* between Siegmund, Sieglinde and afterward Hunding, there are a great number of little interludes—dainty, simple, and melodic in manner. Now, if the conductor is unable to explain the meaning of these little interludes to the singers, he cannot associate them with the requisite gestures, changes of facial expression and even steps, and the scene is bound to make a painfully monotonous impression. No effect is possible here with the music alone.

A related priority: in shaping the music, empathize with what the singers are expressing.

Look . . . to *Tristan und Isolde* for an example. A large space of time in the first act is occupied by Isolde and Brangaene, who are alone in the tent. A few motives are continually developed, but with what a variety must they be treated—surging up now stormily, impetuously; sinking back sadly, exhausted, anon threatening, then timid, now in eager haste, now reassuring! For such a variety of expression the few indications, ritardando, accelerando, and a tempo do not suffice; it is necessary to live through the action of the drama in order to make it all plain. The composer says, "With variety"—a meagre injunction for the conductor. Therefore I add, "Feel with the characters, ponder with them, experience with them all the devious outbursts of passion. . . ."

Seidl's ability to identify with his singers informs many pages of his essay. The orchestra must never overmatch the voices.* Wagner "was painfully anxious that every syllable of the singer should be heard." "How discouraging must be the effect upon an intelligent singer to feel that, in spite of every exertion, he is being drowned by the orchestra!" An orchestral forte is not the same as a vocal forte. For their part, the singers should not "scream." There is no such thing as a single "correct" tempo, Seidl maintains: different voices ask for different speeds. For that matter, there is no such thing as a single "correct" reading: different conductors differently experience the same overture or symphony. With the composer, as with the singer, the conductor strives for empathy. This will not always occur. Theaters demand of their music director that he "mount the funeral pyre tomorrow with Siegfried, and be incarcerated in a madhouse with Lucia the next day. I do not believe in such versatility; conductors are only human."

In closing, Seidl pays homage to "not only the mightiest of all musical geniuses, but also the greatest conductor that ever lived." Wagner conducted with his body immobile, "but his eyes glittered, glowed, pierced . . . and electric currents seemed to pass through the air to each individual musician." All "hung on his glance, and he seemed to see them all at once." Here is Huneker on Seidl: "[He possessed] the eye omniscient, for his tympanist, his contrabassist, his concertmaster will tell you that he seemed to watch each and every man throughout a performance." Here is Victor Herbert, Seidl's frequent principal cellist: "We always knew by a glance from his eye just what was expected of us."[8]

---

*It bears mentioning that, a century ago, instruments—and hence, orchestras—were softer and less brilliant than today.

Every iota of evidence—from Wagner's essay and Seidl's, from descriptions and reviews, from the recordings of turn-of-the-century conductors like Nikisch—suggests that Seidl was more mercurial, more prone to pervasive rubato than any conductor we are likely to encounter today. As New York's *Staats-Zeitung* reported, he was equally prone to *innerliche Empfindung*, and to "*Ur-Germanisch* liveliness and outwardness." "Tempo modification" was a principle with him. At the same time, he was, as Krehbiel put it, "an empiric." "He had no patience with theories, but a wondrous love for experiences. In him, impulse dominated reflection, emotion shamed logic. . . . With him in the chair, it was only the most case-hardened critic who could think of comparative tempi and discriminate between means of effect. As for the rest, professional and layman, dilettante and ignorant, their souls were his to play with."[9]

The Met's 1885–86 season, running from November 23 to April 10, began with a rush for subscription tickets that took Edmund Stanton by surprise. Ninety-five performances were given, including forty-one on tour in Philadelphia, Chicago, St. Louis, Cincinnati, and Cleveland. More than half of these—fifty-one—were of five Wagner operas: *Rienzi, Tannhäuser, Lohengrin, Die Walküre,* and *Die Meistersinger.* The remaining forty-three performances, all in German, were of *Carmen, Faust, Fidelio, Le Prophète,* and—a hugely successful American premiere—Carl Goldmark's *Die Königin von Saba,* whose fifteen New York performances averaged the highest paid attendance of any opera that season: 2,666.*[10]

---

*A second important non-Wagnerian American premiere during the seven German seasons was of Peter Cornelius's *Der Barbier von Bagdad*. Other recent works receiving their first American performances at the Met during this period included Ignaz Brüll's *Das goldene Kreuz*, the Duke of Saxe-Coburg-Gotha's *Diana von Solange* (a fiasco), Alberto Franchetti's *Asrael*, Goldmark's *Merlin*, Victor Nessler's *Der Trompeter von Sakkingen*, and Anton Smareglia's *Il vassallo di Szigeth*. Not until after World War I did the Met acquire its present hostility to contemporary opera.

Seidl conducted forty-five out of fifty-two New York performances, plus seven of the thirteen in Philadelphia. He opened the
season with *Lohengrin*, which (as we have learned) was said to have
"sounded differently" than on previous occasions. The principal
singers were Albert Stritt, Seidl-Kraus, Brandt, and Adolf Robinson.
Krehbiel, in the *Tribune*, called it "certainly the most artistic"
Lohengrin yet encountered in the United States. Seidl's reading—its
tempos and nuances, "poetical beauties" and "matchless technical
precision"—seemed "almost new." If Henry Finck is to be believed,
the performance ran an hour shorter than under other conductors.
"Yet [Seidl] never unduly hurried the tempi; he simply whipped up
his team in the proper places." There was another reason *Lohengrin*
sounded new: Seidl reportedly discovered 180 errors in the orchestral parts used by Leopold and Walter Damrosch.*[11]

Seidl's first *Tannhäuser*, on December 11, 1885, restored customary cuts (yet omitted the Bacchanale Wagner added for the Paris production of 1861). The finales to acts one and two were apparently
given complete for the first time in New York. The choral singing
was "perhaps the finest . . . ever heard in New York." As for Seidl—
"How he relieved declamatory parts of every suspicion of tedium by
his brilliant orchestral comments, how he made soloists, chorus, and
instrumentalists cooperate with machine-like precision, and how by
peculiar accents and gradual working up of a climax he brought out
the dramatic possibilities of the score—all this must be heard, for it
cannot be described." The principal singers were Eloi Sylva, Seidl-
Kraus, and Robinson.[12]

On January 4, 1886, came the season's centerpiece: the American
premiere of *Die Meistersinger*. Completed eleven years after *Die
Walküre*, it was by far the ripest Wagner drama yet staged in America.
High expectations had been whetted by concert hall performances

---

*According to another story, Seidl's first rehearsal of the *Lohengrin* Prelude was
interrupted by a carpenter sawing in the fly-gallery. Seidl stopped, as did the carpenter. The orchestra resumed, and so did the sawing. Seidl stepped onstage, looked
up, and shouted with hands cupped: "What *do* you? What *do* you?" The workman
shouted back, "What do I do? I'll do you, you fat-headed German, if I come down to
you!" Seidl replied, "Tank you. Now I go back." (See Francis Neilson, *My Life in
Two Worlds* [Appleton, Wis., 1953], vol. 1, p. 152.)

not only of the prelude, but also of Walther's trial and prize songs, Pogner's address, Sachs's cobbling song and *Wahnmonolog*, the quintet, the guild choruses and Dance of the Apprentices, and the chorus "Wach' auf." Emil Fischer was Seidl's Sachs (his most admired role); the other soloists included Seidl-Kraus, Stritt, and Brandt—all of whom were repeatedly recalled by the huge audience, packed with German-speakers and out-of-town delegations.

By Finck's count, eight months of sixty-six rehearsals had preceded the Munich premiere of *Die Meistersinger* under Bülow in 1868. Seidl's *Meistersinger* followed by only two days the company's Philadelphia tour, with twelve performances in thirteen days. Finck, who attended the final, eight-hour rehearsal on January 3, reported that "it revealed a number of weak points. But it also revealed another thing—Herr Seidl's extraordinary genius as an operatic conductor. Every weak point was 'spotted' on this occasion . . . so that when it came to the public performance . . . , the smoothness and animation of the ensemble was little short of a miracle. . . ."

Having attended *Die Meistersinger* more than a dozen times abroad, Finck found certain details of the New York performance less clear than in Vienna or Munich. But for "general animation," Seidl's reading was in his view unsurpassed. "This is in the first place due to Herr Seidl's thorough appreciation of Wagner's intentions. He put so much variety and 'go' into his tempi that the performance never dragged for a moment." Finck reported that Seidl's *Meistersinger*, whose "necessary cuts" were less extensive than those "in some German cities," lasted four hours and twenty minutes, including the two intermissions and a clumsy fifteen-minute delay for the final scene change midway through act 3. The closing scene itself (for which the Met chorus had been augmented with singvereiners participating without fee) he thought "too cramped and crowded," this being "the only serious shortcoming of the whole representation."

The bulk of Finck's sixteen-hundred-word *Post* review, however, was devoted to the work itself, which he predicted would prove Wagner's most popular. With the exception of *Tristan*, no other Wagner opera was "more characteristic of his genius and contains more of the reddest blood of the best period of his manhood"—typical Gilded Age metaphors, warding off effeminacy. The story—lovingly summarized along with the music—symbolizes "the Wagnerian cause itself." Walther's unfettered song stands for Wagner's "music of the future," Sachs for "enlightened public opinion."[13]

Krehbiel, a more sober, more intellectual critic, embodied the genteel perspective. Read as Walther, Wagner appears a rebel. For Krehbiel, *Die Meistersinger* is no allegory of artistic rebellion, but a masterpiece steeped in history: of medieval Nuremberg, of centuries of Western culture. Taking pains to define and justify why Wagner called *Die Meistersinger* a "comedy," he disputes "French and English critics" who equate comedy with wordplay or farce. (One cannot imagine him guffawing alongside Finck, who considered the cobbling scene in act 2 "exceedingly comic.") Rather, *Die Meistersinger* exemplifies "the classical definition of the purpose of comedy—Ridendo castigat mores." It restores "the ancient boundary between comedy and tragedy." It "deals with the manners and follies and vices of the masses; it aims primarily to amuse, and only ultimately to chastise."

Sniping at Finck and other "extreme admirers," Krehbiel finds no symbolism in the story; he even implausibly insists that Walther "nowhere discloses himself as the champion of a free expression of spontaneous, vital art." Instead, Walther is a young knight in love, and the work as a whole is nothing more nor less than a comic representation of "the social life of a quaint German city three centuries ago." As such, its vividness and truthfulness are validated by the most meticulous scholarship. Wagner has brought to life his archaic sources: the poetry and music of the singers' guild, the documentation of Johann Christoph Wagenseil's Nuremberg chronicle of 1697. Finally: "In its delineation of character [*Die Meistersinger*] is Shakespearean, and although its fun is a little brutal (as becomes the place and period with which the play deals), it is not at all malicious, and is always morally healthy."[14]

Is *Die Meistersinger* really so wholesome? The riot that ends act 2 is both funny and menacing; chaos, not harmony, is found to underlie human affairs. Sachs, reflecting on why Nuremberg came apart that night, on why "people torment one another in useless, foolish anger," exclaims: "Wahn! Wahn!"—for Wagner, a Schopenhauerean noun conveying illusion, madness, folly: the essential human condition. If such weary pessimism contradicted the earnest striving of genteel intellectual discourse, the opera's Germanic nationalism—an ideological backdrop arguably tainted by anti-Semitism[15]—would become its most notorious leitmotif. As early as 1924, the Bayreuth audience stood for Sachs's closing address, with its warning of foreign domination and admonition to "honor your German masters"; directly following the performance, the national anthem was sung and shouts of "Heil!" resounded. In honoring the opera's historical roots in sixteenth century Germany, Krehbiel managed to ignore its contemporaneous roots in Wagner's Germany, whose drive towards national unity was laced with chauvinism and xenophobia. These darker *Meistersinger* strains, conscious and unconscious, articulate the perils of mass emotional release, whether anarchic or patriotic. They violated the genteel agenda, with its confluence of truth, beauty, and morality. They went unheard.*

---

*To some present-day commentators—notably the cultural historian Jackson Lears—turn-of-the-century Wagnerism signified a revolt against modernity, a yearning for a romanticized medieval past. "The Wagnerian cult," writes Lears in *No Place of Grace* (New York, 1981), p. 171, "was of a piece with the fairy and fantasy vogues." With its frequently idyllic depiction of sixteenth century Nuremberg, *Die Meistersinger* superficially fits this interpretation. And Wagner did fulminate against science, technology, and other diseases of the modern world. But it bears stressing that Gilded Age commentaries on *Die Meistersinger* do not, to my knowledge, pursue this theme, nor are Gilded Age portrayals of Wagner much concerned with his antipathy to the industrial order. Wagner's most relevant writings, incidentally, postdate *Die Meistersinger*. His October 1879 open letter in support of the antivivisectionist movement, for instance, incorporates denunciations of his own "despiritualized age" and the "specter of science." After 1880, he criticized the dehumanizing implications of electricity and the phonograph. More important, the medieval past, as glimpsed in *Lohengrin, Tannhäuser, Tristan,* and *Parsifal,* is by no means necessarily wholesome or inspirational. Perhaps *Die Meistersinger* exerted a tacit appeal to Gilded Age intellectuals and aesthetes estranged from machines. (As will be seen in Chapter 15, Henry Krehbiel's resistance to modernism was accompanied by complaints against traffic noise and Einsteinian physics.) The spiritual needs addressed by the meliorist Wagner must have reflected the disruptive impact of industrialization, urbanization, and evolutionary science—yet did not depend on Wagner's tacit or explicit critique of these changes.

Following *Die Meistersinger*, New York's music critics gave a dinner for Anton Seidl. "The critics have agreed to confer the honor of their invitation only upon such artists as are absolutely above criticism," the *Musical Courier* explained. (Adelina Patti had been honored two years before.) Theodore Thomas was invited, but stayed away, pleading fatigue—whereupon the *Courier* commented that he should have at least written a letter expressing satisfaction that *Meistersinger* had been seen in New York.[16]

Seidl's arrival had placed Thomas's achievements in lowered perspective—and Thomas himself was obviously piqued by Seidl's success. As for Walter Damrosch—his continued presence in the Met pit, leading *Die Walküre*, exasperated the Wagnerites. According to the *Musical Courier*: "No more amusing sight can be imagined than this youthful Adonis sitting for a quarter of an hour between each rising of the curtain in the conductor's chair and leering at the ladies in the boxes and making the most of his opportunities for demonstrating his personal vanity."[17] Damrosch was defended by the socialites he charmed. Like Thomas's supporters, they perceived the critics and Seidl as a hostile pack. In fact, Seidl's close acquaintances did include Krehbiel and Finck. And he did not suffer Damrosch.*

For Seidl's first New York *Die Walküre*, on January 13, the singers were Lehmann, Seidl-Kraus, Brandt (Fricka doubling as Rossweisse), Stritt, and Fischer. Damrosch had previously led the same work in the same house eleven days before. "New life throbbed in the orchestra," reported the reviews. The singing was "freer, more intense, more virile than before." The Valkyries performed "with

---

*In a May 30, 1891, letter, preserved in the Anton Seidl archive at Columbia University (Butler Library: Rare Books), Henry Finck asks for Seidl's permission to dedicate his new Wagner biography "to Mr. Anton Seidl, the Greatest of Wagner's Interpreters." Finck continues, in German: "Kindly say yes, or I will dedicate it to— Walter Damrosch!" Seidl's antipathy to Damrosch is sometimes traced to Damrosch's decision, in 1886, to present the American concert premiere of *Parsifal*, a work Seidl considered his own. But Seidl doubtless appreciated Damrosch's artistic shortcomings.

such barbaric force that [the] audience was unable to restrain its enthusiasm." The climaxes were "developed with stupendous effect." The play of tempo—Damrosch's performance had lasted forty-five minutes longer—enlivened the play of feeling.[18]

On February 5, Seidl led the Metropolitan Opera premiere of *Rienzi*. Nearly forgotten today, it is Wagner's only French grand opera, five acts of spectacle and pomp. In his 1860 essay "Music of the Future," Wagner himself disavowed it: "there is not yet evident any important instance of the view of art which I later came to assert." But the 1842 Dresden premiere was a triumph. *Rienzi* succeeded elsewhere as well, delighting audiences acclimated to *William Tell* and *Les Huguenots*. In the United States, *Rienzi* only arrived in 1878—too late to matter. Bayreuth had already staged the *Ring*. Neuendorff had already led *Die Walküre*.

In fact, *Rienzi* lay dormant for the eight years preceding Seidl's 1886 revival. The Met furnished lavish sets and costumes (some borrowed from other operas). The cast included Sylva, Lehmann, Robinson, Brandt, and Fischer. In Krehbiel's opinion, the company had taken leave of lofty endeavors to exploit the sudden vogue for German opera. "There is no musical vice which Wagner was so merciless in condemning in Meyerbeer's operas," he grumbled, "which does not exist in this score in an exaggerated form."[19] *Rienzi* returned to the Met in 1886–87 and 1889–90, then disappeared for good.

More lasting was the impact, on February 25, of Seidl's American debut as a symphonic conductor. The occasion was a benefit concert for the Bayreuth Festival, hosted by the Metropolitan Opera. Seidl led an orchestra of 114 players drawn from the Met orchestra, the New York Philharmonic, and the New York Symphony. The program consisted of Beethoven's *Leonore* Overture No. 3 and *Eroica* Symphony, plus four Wagner extracts: from *Tristan*, the Prelude and *Liebestod* (with Lehmann); from *Götterdämmerung*, the Rhinemaidens' chorus and Siegfried's Death and Funeral Music (with Stritt); from *Parsifal*, the Good Friday Spell.

In Krehbiel's opinion, the *Liebestod* was "the finest interpretation this passionate outburst has ever received in New York," while Siegfried's Funeral Music, steeped in "Old Gothic grief," was "almost wholly transformed." But the evening's revelation was Seidl's Beethoven.

In an 1887 interview with Krehbiel, Seidl would have occasion to discuss his reading of the third *Leonore* Overture. "Those who have heard [it] under my direction will share with me the conviction that this jubilation over the reunited husband and wife can well stand a stormy Allegro. This tempestuous outbreak of conjugal love which sweeps before it all barriers can not be imagined in a moderate, circumspect tempo, chosen for the sake simply of sensuous tonal beauty." Seidl's performance of the same work, at his 1886 benefit concert, was notable—and controversial—for the slowness of its introduction and for the power of its coda, whose brassy flourish was said to sound Wagnerian. The *Eroica* was, according to Finck, vociferously applauded after every movement by "as critical and intelligent an audience as could be seen in New York," brought together by "the desire to see Herr Seidl as concert conductor." If not an altogether polished performance, it was singularly "emotional." It strove continually for climax. The funeral march was surprising quick—not grieving but "manly." The Scherzo was astonishingly fast—except for the Trio, which was unusually slow. Krehbiel was impressed, but too much the purist entirely to approve. Finck was enraptured. He argued: "At the time when Beethoven wrote the 'Eroica' symphony, it is probable that he would have conducted it himself more like Hiller or Mendelssohn; but after he had written the ninth symphony he would doubtless have leaned to the mode of conducting adopted by Wagner and Seidl." The *Musical Courier* announced that Seidl intended to give a series of symphonic programs the following season, in which his "great ability as a concert conductor" could be further assessed.[*20]

The final *Die Walküre* of the Met's New York season took place March 5. The conductor was to have been Damrosch.[†] Seidl took his place. During his second recall after act 2, he was handed an

---

[*] For more on Seidl as concert conductor, see Chapter 9.

[†] In the *Metropolitan Opera Annuals* and some other sources, Walter Damrosch is incorrectly identified as the conductor of this performance.

immense laurel wreath, with ribbons in red, white, and green—
Hungary's colors—and the names of the company's stockholders.
Damrosch next conducted Wagner for the Metropolitan Opera some
thirty-two months later.

In the visual arts, the period of the late Gilded Age is known as the
"American Renaissance." The term, coined in 1880,* reflected
raised consciousness regarding the arts generally, and the specific
aspiration to recapture for America something of the style and spirit
of the European Renaissance. Once despised, now positively re-
assessed, the American Renaissance proves more than nostalgic and
derivative. Like Renaissance Italians recollecting a mythical past,
"Renaissance" Americans aimed to synthesize old and new knowledge in pursuit of something better, in which the United States
could take pride. Like Renaissance Italians, again, American aristocrats sought both to put their wealth and prestige on display, and
to elevate and refine public taste.

Obviously, this agenda partook of the genteel. But, as the century
drew toward a close, the American Renaissance transcended Victorian inhibition. Intoxicated by the sensuous and exotic, delighting
in ornament for its own sake, American painters and sculptors,
designers and architects achieved a vivacity challenging their earlier
mistrust of immoral Europe. According to one recent authority, a
"period of intense interest and activity in all the arts" commenced in
the mid-1880s.[21] Despising the gauche pastiche designs of the
American Renaissance in its earliest phase, a new spirit of "scientific
eclecticism" emphasized scholarship and experimentation. Its practitioners included the sculptors Augustus Saint-Gaudens and Daniel
Chester French, the painters Kenyon Cox and Francis Millet, and
the architects Charles F. McKim and Stanford White—both of whom

---

*And not to be confused with the nineteenth-century "American Renaissance"
in literature identified by F. O. Matthiessen in 1941.

helped transform New York from a city of dark brownstones to one of spacious clubs, churches, and hotels of light stone, yellow brick, and terra-cotta.

One trademark of this renaissance was cosmopolitanism. "I've come to see Europe, to get the best out of it I can," says Christopher Newman in Henry James's *The American* (1877). "I want to see all the great things and do what the best people do. . . . I feel something under my ribs here . . . that I can't explain—a sort of strong yearning, a desire to stretch out and haul in."[22] Not only Europe, but the Orient, the South Seas, and the Near East exerted fascination. Americans grew emboldened to celebrate beauty wherever and however they found it. John La Farge, the discoverer of opalescent glass in 1879, pioneered in the decorative use of brilliantly tinted stained glass. Louis Tiffany's unprecedented experiments in glass, metal, and stone began around the same time. Candace Wheeler invented the "American tapestry" in 1883. Outside the American Renaissance, the painters Thomas Eakins, Albert Pinkham Ryder, and (in his sun-drenched, nearly impressionistic watercolors of Europe and Asia) John Singer Sargent were breaking out in different ways.

In an earlier chapter, I assigned Theodore Thomas to the Brown Decades of Lewis Mumford, for whom no refreshing American Renaissance took place. Earnest, sober, Thomas is a transitional, pre-renaissance figure: more cosmopolitan than the alcoholic Carl Bergmann, provincial beside the longer-haired and less scrutable Anton Seidl. Juxtaposed to Thomas's brownness, Seidl is an exotic Hungarian cloaked in romantic purples and reds, an Artist. His relationship to Europe, to Richard Wagner himself, was detailed and sophisticated; his interpretations of the Music of the Future were creative, almost improvisational. Thomas, who never performed abroad, was a cruder appropriator of new Old World music, more literal and methodical because more remote. Thomas "dignified" Wagner. Seidl candidly delivered the *Liebestod*.

6

Tristan und Isolde

hile composing *Tristan und Isolde*, Wagner wrote to Mathilde Wesendonck: "Child! This Tristan is turning into something *terrible*! . . . I fear the opera will be banned—unless the whole thing is parodied in a bad performance—only mediocre performances can save me! Perfectly *good* ones will be bound to drive people mad."[1]

The premiere was at one time planned for Vienna in 1861. Aloys Ander, the Tristan, repeatedly lost his voice, then his nerve. The press blamed the "impossible" work. The production was abandoned after dozens of rehearsals. *Tristan* was eventually scheduled for Munich in 1865, by which time Ander had died insane. To facilitate the use of Wagner's chosen conductor, Ludwig made Hans von Bülow "Court Kapellmeister for special services." Tristan and Isolde were Malvina and Ludwig Schnorr von Carolsfeld. Instrumental and vocal rehearsals were held daily under Wagner's supervision. Bülow, who fainted at one rehearsal, worked himself to a high pitch of nervous intensity. He managed to offend the press, which responded in kind. A dress rehearsal was attended by the king and some six hundred invited guests—most of whom, according to one account, were so mentally and physically exhausted they could not retain a single detail afterward. Malvina von Carolsfeld now became hoarse, postponing the premiere and igniting a new round of rumors: that Wagner had ruined her voice, that Bülow feared for his life, that the orchestra had quit. Rehearsals resumed, and, following two months of preparation, *Tristan* was finally unveiled June 10. Of its reception, Schnorr, an artist of supreme sensitivity and intelligence, wrote to his mother: "Perhaps about no other theatrical production has so much nonsense ever been written as about *Tristan und Isolde*. The poor lovers would not have let themselves be awakened in their graves had they known how maliciously the world would behave towards their awakener, and consequently to themselves. To the devil with these wretched notices!" Days later, Schnorr was dead at the age of twenty-nine. On his deathbed, delirious, he had cried out: "Farewell Siegfried! Console my Richard!" The newspapers, of course, blamed *Tristan*. Malvina communed spiritually with her dead spouse; eventually, she sought refuge in a mental institution. Wagner was driven from Munich. Bülow wrote:

> Yes, without any reproach to its mighty creator, *Tristan* has given me the *coup de grace*. . . . Poor Eberle, [Hans] Richter's pet repetiteur, was driven mad during the rehearsals by the opera itself (we tell the public it was an excess of beer); as for me, who confess always to have lacked the necessary courage in my very numerous arrangements for taking my life, I assure you I could not have resisted the temptation if anyone had offered me a few drops of prussic acid.[2]

The American premiere of *Tristan und Isolde* took place on December 1, 1886, at the Metropolitan Opera House. Anton Seidl conducted. The lovers were Albert Niemann and Lilli Lehmann. Seidl, who had led *Tannhäuser* on November 26 and *Aida* on November 29, had only five orchestral rehearsals, of which one was used to correct the parts. The house was sold out four days in advance. (James Huneker pawned his overcoat to buy a ticket.) The *Musical Courier* reported:

> The greatest triumph that the cause of Wagner, and with it the management of opera in German at the Metropolitan Opera House, has so far achieved here was gained last Wednesday night, when the master's undoubted *chef d'oeuvre*, "Tristan und Isolde," was performed for the first time in the United States. An audience that filled every available seat and the standing room of the vast building listened to the performance, which lasted till nearly midnight, with an attention and a genuine enthusiasm which had thus far not been equaled in the musical history of the land. After each of the three

acts there were numerous recalls for all of the artists, and especially also for Anton Seidl, our great conductor, whom the audience rightly insisted upon sharing the honors of the evening with the soloists. . . .

It must be seen to be believed with what an enthusiastic reception, for instance, among other climaxes, the magnificent finale of the first act meets. . . . Even those who had the tertium comparationis of last summer's Bayreuth performances in their mind did not unwillingly compare notes to the effect that on the whole our performance was as good, if not better, than were the model renderings at the Mecca of Wagnerism. . . . On Monday night of this week "Tristan und Isolde" had its second hearing, when the house again was sold out and the same scenes of frantic applause were enacted at the close of each of the three acts.

According to Krehbiel, "the tenseness of attention was almost painful." Given eight times in seven weeks, *Tristan* was the season's most popular offering.[3]

New York's critics rebuffed the irreverence of the Bavarian press twenty-one years before. Gustav Kobbé wrote in the *Mail and Express*:

A sense of personal triumph must have thrilled those in the audience who had recognized Wagner's genius long ago and at a time when it was the subject of misrepresentation and prejudiced attacks. Wagner himself believed that his works would find a warm place in the hearts of American audiences, whom he understood to be cosmopolitan in their tastes and, uninfluenced by tradition, ready to accept an art work on its merits. The success obtained by such of his music-dramas as have been heard here justifies his opinion.

Krehbiel, reviewing New York's *Tristan*, pertinently remarked: "Conservatism toward Wagner's music is much more likely to be found in communities with whom fixed tastes and prejudices are the result of a certain degree of artistic culture attained than in communities like ours where a work is listened to by unbiased hearers for its own sake." Vienna's reigning musical arbiter, Eduard Hanslick, had written of *Tristan*: "[We must] protest most emphatically against the idea of accepting this assassination of sense and language, this stuttering and stammering, these bombastic, artificial monologues and dialogues, void of all natural sentiment, as a poetic work of art." Schnorr von Carolsfeld, in Munich, had deplored critics who showed "not the faintest evidence" of even having read the libretto.[4] New York's critics found *Tristan* a supreme "poetic work of art." They studied the libretto's medieval sources. They wrote detailed synopses, cued to the leitmotifs. They pondered Wagner's harmonic language and orchestration. Finally, they considered an aspect of the drama with which few of its enthusiasts have ever seriously grappled: they asked themselves what it meant.

Compared to *Tannhäuser* or *Lohengrin*, *Die Walküre* or *Die Meistersinger*, *Tristan* is an opera with scant external action. Rather, the action in internal—and ambiguous. Are Tristan and Isolde heroic or selfish, tools of fate or scheming activists? Krehbiel, Finck, and W. J. Henderson undertook detailed answers. And, as Gilded Age intellectuals, they necessarily coped with the opera's tricky moral and erotic content.

Consider the drink Tristan and Isolde share in act 1—not a fatal poison, as they imagine, but a love potion. Finck, in his analysis, stresses that the tragedy is not therefore merely "chemical"—that, as Wagner repeatedly tells us, Tristan and Isolde loved one another before the fateful cup. "They both drank the potion heroically in the belief that it would end their life and suffering." The unexpected outcome "purifies the moral atmosphere of the drama." Without the drink, which compels him to express and fulfill his love, Tristan's behavior would be odious. Instead, we sympathize with his intention: he seeks oblivion rather than dishonoring his uncle the king, to whom Isolde is betrothed. Furthermore, Tristan is no adulterer—King Marke, Finck argues, at no point marries Isolde. "This is proved by his words at the close . . . when he tells Isolde that he has come not to punish, but to give her in marriage to Tristan. How could he have done this if she had been his wife?" In any event, Tristan obeys a law of nature: the Law of Love. Loveless marriage between Isolde and Marke would have been a "crime." "Love is the highest of all moral and hygienic laws, because it provides for the welfare of the next generation." In short, Tristan and Isolde are noble victims, neither puppets nor criminals.[5]

Krehbiel, typically, probes deeper—with even more tortuous results. In versions of the story by Gottfried von Strassburg, Matthew Arnold, and Algernon Swinburne, he begins, the potion is drunk accidentally and the lovers are not held responsible for the passion that destroys them. With Tennyson, there is no potion: "The passion is all guilty." Wagner falls in between: "The love exists before the potion, and the potion is less a maker of uncontrollable passion than a drink which causes the lovers to forget duty, honor, and the respect due to the laws of society."

Krehbiel's thoroughness—his refusal to gloss over what offends and troubles—makes his *Tristan* writings a case study in Gilded Age discomfort: in the thrill and alarm of emotional surrender. Listening to Wagner, he believes, should never become a sensual indulgence devoid of thought. Fortunately, it affords a distinctive intellectual task: "reflection and comparison" conditioned upon "a recognition of the themes and their uses." The Wagnerian pleasures, then, include the exercise of memory, the leitmotifs being not mere "footmen" or "ushers," but deeper symbols. That is: music may directly attack the emotions, "but it is chiefly by association of ideas that we recognize its expressiveness or significance."

In Krehbiel's discomfort we can recognize the mistrust of emotion once personified by John Sullivan Dwight, for whom morality was decency and truth intellectualized beauty. Nineteenth-century expressions of this viewpoint often seem merely silly—as in the writing of the Reverend Hugh Reginald Haweis, whose *Music and Morals* was printed twenty-five times between 1872 and 1934. But Krehbiel's warnings against surrendering to Wagnerian narcosis are not so different from Nietzsche's when he wrote of "Wagner as a Danger":

> One walks into the sea, gradually loses one's secure footing, and finally surrenders oneself to the elements without reservation: one must *swim*. In older music, what one had to do . . . was something quite different, namely, to *dance*. The measure required for this, the maintenance of certainly equally balanced units of time and force, demanded continual *wariness* of the listener's soul—and on the counterplay of this cooler breeze that came from wariness and the

warm breath of enthusiasm rested the magic of all *good* music. Richard Wagner wanted a different kind of movement; he overthrew the physiological presupposition of previous music. Swimming, floating—no longer walking and dancing.

Like Krehbiel, Nietzsche succumbed to Wagner. Like Krehbiel's, his second thoughts insisted upon wary intellect's discriminating check on unfettered feeling. More surely than Krehbiel, he sensed the danger of an emotional totalitarianism.

Krehbiel's cautionary interpolation of "memory" and "ideas" pays off in Siegfried's Funeral Music, where Wagner's recollection of Sieglinde's love song intensifies the pathos—at least for those listeners whose minds have not shut off. But *Tristan* is a different case— no longer a balanced *Gesamtkunstwerk* whose leitmotifs invite intellectual cognition, but an erotic floodtide whose oceanic undertow makes even swimming difficult. And Krehbiel knows this all too well. *Tristan*'s "tumultuous lava current," he writes, assaults "one's emotional part more than the intellect or the judgment." It disarms his insistence that a presiding intellect govern empathetic listening. He fully concedes that, compared to *Tannhäuser*, *Tristan und Isolde* does not embody the "beautiful ethical principle," running "like a golden thread" through Wagner's tragedies, of "erring man's salvation through the self-sacrificing love of a woman"—Tannhäuser is a loftier hero, inspired by a purer heroine. And yet Isolde's *Liebestod* incomparably demonstrates "the purifying and ennobling capacity of music"—its elevating power is not to be resisted: "While listening to this tonal beautification, it is difficult to hear the voice of reason pronouncing the judgment of outraged law." But then, again, Tristan and Isolde are unrepentant sinners: "It is right that that voice [of law] should be heard." Krehbiel never gives up. We must bear in mind, he now argues, that the story "is a picture of chivalry in its palmy days," when "the odor which assails our moral sense as the odor of death and decay was esteemed the sweetest incense." Conjugal codes denied the possibility of conjugal love; the object of knightly love was another man's spouse. If this line of argument tends to assuage Tristan's sin, elsewhere Krehbiel takes pains to emphasize Tristan's sinfulness. Not only does mutual passion precede the potion: Tristan craves power and glory. Isolde, with the potion, tries to commit murder and suicide. The lovers therefore retain a "taint of guilt"—as required in Greek tragedy, whose deep religious purpose demands that the pity we feel for heroic suffering will not overcome "the idea of justice in the catastrophe."[6]

Ultimately, if confusedly, both Finck and Krehbiel make something relatively wholesome of Wagner's disturbed psychodrama. The lovers, with whom Wagner has us identify, remain more admirable than not; we feel uplifted, not appalled. And the fatal love potion is not a metaphor suggesting the incompatibility of personal salvation and earthly life.* The message of resignation in *Tristan*—its seductive Schopenhauerean "Night," silencing unquenchable desire—is brightened or dismissed. Finck even appropriates Schopenhauer as a sunny influence: the "great law of love, which we all feel but which Schopenhauer was the first to formulate, is the moral key to Wagner's tragedy, and explains why every spectator sympathizes with the interrupted lovers and not with the king. It is here that the influence of Schopenhauer on Wagner may perhaps be traced, and not, as many of the commentators have fancied, in the longing of the lovers for a blending of their souls in death, which is a common pantheistic notion thousands of years older than Schopenhauer."[7]

More commonly, Schopenhauer was condemned by Gilded Age Wagnerites as a "pessimist." His brand of salvation through negation—not to mention the web of insatiable strivings he saw ensnaring the human condition—was found lacking in meliorist buoyancy. Krehbiel, in his *Tristan* account, acknowledges "the symbolism of pessimistic philosophy in which night and death and oblivion are glorified and day and life and memory are condemned"—but rather than pursue this strain, he criticizes it. "Pessimistic philosophy, transmitted through verbal plays which are carried far beyond the limits of reason, if not to the verge of childishness, is not good

---

* A metaphor, incidentally, in no way diminishing the lovers' responsibility for their behavior. In a crucial act 3 passage, Wagner has Tristan exclaim: "The terrible drink which brought this anguish on me I, myself did brew!"

dramatic matter, and half an hour of it is too much. . . . It is said that to understand the drama in its completeness one must sympathise, or, at least, know its philosophical undercurrent. There is some truth in the observation, but the necessity is lessened by the reduction of [the second act] duet."[8]

William J. Henderson—with Krehbiel New York's best turn-of-the-century Wagnerite writer—also navigates these murky waters.

If the lovers had sworn renunciation and had suffered from the enforcement of their vow, there would have been consistency in their desire to die. But in the midst of unbridled indulgence in their passion they would have wished to live, unless there had been sur-feit and the subsequent moral reaction. But of this we have no hint. The yearning for death, however, is an outcome of Wagner's absorp-tion of the philosophy of Arthur Schopenhauer. This writer was a subjective realist and regarded extant phenomena as the products of the will—that is, the world exists because man wishes to think so. The highest ethical destiny of man is the nullification of the will by the practice of an asceticism which shall remove from him all desire for the objects of sense. These, then, being but creations of the will, shall disappear, and the will, the only reality, shall quietly renounce itself and vanish into the infinite. The doctrine is closely allied to that of the Buddhist Nirvana. Wagner's endeavour to reconcile it with the dramatic ideas of "Tristan und Isolde" was not successful. Asceticism and adultery are not companions.

Still, Henderson is a *Tristan* addict. Whereas Krehbiel cautions emotionally susceptible listeners to keep their minds consciously engaged with the leitmotifs, Henderson counsels intuitive under-standing: "Learn their meaning . . . then let them alone, and they will do their work." Analysis frustrates him; he gladly surrenders to the music. "I find it difficult to proceed coolly and systematically. There is a witchery in this marvelous drama of fatal love that masters my mind. If the reader finds me wanting in the calm of judicious equipoise, let him forgive me, for I am dealing with that which lies next to my heart." He is notably engrossed by the frenzy of the opera's third act; he calls it "the most convincing piece of dramatic writing in the literature of the lyric stage."[9] Finck predictably prefers the more soothing ecstasies of the love duet and *Liebestod* (which even without the music he finds "divine"). Krehbiel confronts Tristan's third act agony and winces. Its length is a "mistake." Its suicidal culmination is "too horrible." This "is one of the grounds on which excisions are to be commended, for there were moments in the representations which the work received during the season when the emotional tension was great beyond the bounds of pleasure." Elsewhere, Krehbiel's discreet account of the opera's prelude suggests another problem area. It is, he tells us, a "mood picture" embodying "the passionate stress of the story and its profound melancholy . . . constructed out of the principal melodic elements of the score which are not scenic." Wagner, in his prose description of the same music, is franker: it is a poem of "desire without attainment, for each fruition sows the seeds of fresh desire"; a torment whose only escape is "quitting life."[10]

In the Gilded Age, Wagner was cleansed, Schopenhauer purged. These transformations were not, however, simplistic, but emotionally fraught and intellectually formidable. They fit a pattern of sanguine Americanization: generations later, Freud, also a Germanic philosopher of darkness, would also be reconstrued in America as an agent if not of uplift, of pragmatic improvement.*[11]

*Around the turn of the century, American abundance therapists preached the liberation of instinct as a pathway to more wholesome feelings. Here, for instance, is Elwood Worcester, in *Religion and Medicine* (1908): "The subconscious mind is a normal part of our spiritual nature . . . [and] what we observe in hypnosis is an elevation of the moral faculties, greater refinement of feeling, a higher sense of truth and honor, often a delicacy of mind, which the waking subject does not possess. In my opinion the reason for this is that the subconscious mind, which I believe is the most active in suggestion, is purer and freer from evil than our waking consciousness." (Quoted in T. J. Jackson Lears and Richard Wightman Fox, eds., *The Culture of Consumption* [New York, 1983], p. 16.)

The American impact of *Tristan und Isolde* also records the impact of its Tristan and Isolde: Albert Niemann and Lilli Lehmann. No other members of the Met's German ensemble left such galvanizing impressions.

In her memoirs, Lehmann wrote:

> In the whole world there was nothing that could free greater emotions in me than [my] Tristan performances in New York with Niemann, where the audience sat still for minutes, silent and motionless in their places, as though drunk or in a transport, without being conscious that the opera was over. . . . Seidl was in sympathy with us, carried his orchestra along in the wings of worship of his Master, and made every instrument proclaim what he had inherited, in teaching and knowledge, from the creator. Emil Fischer as Marke, Adolf Robinson as Kurwenal, Alvary as the Steersman were with us, united, in loving comprehension and glowing adoration, to do homage to the majesty of the Master. Every evening of Tristan with Niemann was a fresh event to me.[12]

Lehmann's New York seasons were a fresh event for another reason: previously, as the Berlin Opera's leading coloratura, she had been denied the heavier repertoire she sought. At Bayreuth in 1876, aged twenty-eight, she sang not Brünnhilde, but a Rhinemaiden, a Valkyrie, and the Forest Bird; Wagner was quite literally infatuated with her. She first sang Isolde at Covent Garden in 1884—an assignment she prepared with typical diligence, building her endurance by singing every phrase hundreds of times, then each act from beginning to end three and four times consecutively. Her 1885 New York debut, as a heroically sinister Carmen, confounded American preconceptions of the role. As the *Walküre* Brünnhilde five days later— a young goddess, radiant of face, trim of figure—she triumphed decisively. "It became clear," Henderson later recalled, "that she was possessed of that rare combination of traits and equipment which made it possible for her to delineate the divinity in womanhood and womanhood in divinity, the mingling of the unapproachable goddess and the melting pitying human being which no one else has ever portrayed on our stage as she did. Her 'Todesverkündigung' scene remains unrivaled. It was the perfection of awe-inspiring solemnity and underlying sympathy."[13]

Lehmann proceeded to appear 260 more times with the Met—an average of 37 appearances per season—in twenty-six roles ranging from Mozart (Donna Anna) and Beethoven (Leonore) to Gounod (Marguerite), Bellini (Norma), and Verdi (Aida, Amelia, Leonora). The overwhelming majority of her assignments were Wagnerian. Krehbiel wrote: "For zeal and unselfish devotion preparing an opera I have never met an artist who could be even remotely compared to her." In rehearsal, she always sang full voice; in free moments, she might rummage through the property room or rearrange the scenery.[14] On tour with the company in 1889, she sang eighteen Brünnhildes in less than seven weeks, plus Venus and Leonore.

No previous phase of her professional life had been so fulfilling. In fact, she sacrificed her European career, breaking her contract with Berlin. Krehbiel helped her opt for America, calculating that her New World fees would more than compensate for the Old World pension she would lose. Lehmann defended her decision as principled: "One grows weary after singing nothing but princesses for 15 years," she trumpeted in the Berlin press; as Germany had constrained her, America now let her grow. The remainder of her operatic career was based in New York; she also sang the three Brünnhildes at Bayreuth in 1896 (notwithstanding surgery on an egg-sized abscess that would have felled a less tenacious performer). She continued to appear in opera into her early sixties. By that time, her repertoire encompassed 170 roles in 119 operas.[15]

Though her early florid singing unquestionably extended her longevity, she was never a flawless vocalist, nor could she unleash such avalanches of tone as a Nordica, Flagstad, or Nilsson. Henderson, who knew about such things, nonetheless testifies that her voice "was a full-toned dramatic soprano, immense in volume and resonance, and of voluptuous quality. . . . She could always reach the high F and frequently did so in practice."[16] Lehmann's recordings, made when she was already in her late fifties, disclose a focused, steady, and powerful soprano voice, weakest in the middle register, and somewhat squeezed at the top. They also disclose an artist of magisterial temperament. Cursing her father's murderer, she is the most terrifying, most intimidating Donna Anna of my experience.

Photographs of Lehmann complement these impressions: she is severe, statuesque, regally handsome. And she was regal to her colleagues, most of whom she excluded from her own elite circle.* Henderson wrote:

> What seems to me most important to record was the impressive grandeur of her greatest operatic impersonations. This grandeur was inherent in the woman; she could not rid herself of it when she sang such parts as Filina. But in Brünnhilde and Isolde it fit her like a royal robe. . . . In moments of tragic fury her voice pealed like a trumpet and her action was that of a Boadicea. Scenes that can never leave my memory are those of Isolde's rage in the first act and the all-conquering wrath of her personification of violated justice when she hurled aside the retainers of Gunther, and, seizing the haft of Hagen's spear, pealed forth her "Helle Wehr, heil'ge Waffe."†[17]

Lehmann's autobiography puts the finishing touches on this portrait of independence and self-esteem. Of Seidl, she wrote that he was

> the most talented and earnest of the Bayreuth Guild of 1876. He has always been to me the best of all Wagner conductors, who . . . used the baton flexibly and unobtrusively, without seeking after sensational effects in conducting. I may say, indeed, that we were happy under his perfect leading, and he also, on the other hand, must be deemed fortunate that he needed only to follow, in an intellectual sense, so many artistic authorities, which made it

---

*Lehmann was allegedly the woman in a box who broke into raucous laughter during dialogue between Marianne Brandt, as Leonore, and Albert Niemann's Florestan on January 14, 1887. Brandt blamed the incident on Lehmann's jealousy; she subsequently quit the company.

†For another view, see George Bernard Shaw, quoted in Robert Hartford, ed., *Bayreuth: The Early Years* (New York, 1980), pp. 230, 234.

possible for both sides to give admirable renderings. We understood each other, and not the slightest discord ever arose.*

Of America, Lehmann wrote:

Whence comes the peculiar sense of freedom that is at once felt by
everyone in America? . . . There is a moral element in the natural
manner of life of the American people, even the poorest feels himself a gentleman, desires to be treated as such, and thereby deems
it worth his while to treat others so. . . . No policemen need inter-
fere. . . . Each man trains himself. It is compulsion that excites the
emotions and that calls forth defiance.

Of New York harbor:

Not another one of all the artists can have given it such devotion,
nor have gazed upon it and admired it again and again with such
grateful sentiments for a happy fate and all the love America gave
me.[18]

When Wagner wrote that *Tristan* was "turning into something dreadful," something that would "drive people crazy," he could have been
referring to the third act. It epitomizes the work's revolutionary psychological landscape, the black interiority whose musical expression
is a tortuous chromaticism, and whose dramatic scenario combines

*Lehmann felt differently about Cosima Wagner's 1896 Bayreuth Festival:
"Many roads lead to Rome but to the Bayreuth of today only one, that of slavish sub-
jection. There is also no clear conception there of how high a valuation is to be set
upon individual artistry. Without it nothing great can be created, and the audience,
no matter what nationalities it may represent, will not be moved nor transported. [In
1876] Richard Wagner . . . left to the artist, left to each his own; he stepped in only
when he came upon lack of understanding or dilettantism, and the harmony existing
between him and his artists, the artists and his work, was always guarded." (Lilli
Lehmann, *My Path Through Life* [New York, 1914], p. 433.)

two contradictory narratives, the one healing, the other lacerating. Tristan has suffered a breakdown; he is suicidal and amnesic. Dredging up his past, he succumbs to paroxysms of delirium and clairvoyance. He attains a state of illumination, but the catalyst is a fathomless descent. When Schnorr von Carolsfeld died, Wagner confided to this diary:

> "I drove you to the abyss! I was used to standing there: my head does not swim. But I cannot see anyone else standing on the brink: that fills me with frantic sympathy. I lay hold of him to check him, to draw him back, and I push him over, just as we kill the somnambulist when we cry out to him in our alarm. Thus I pushed him over. And myself? My head does not swim. I look down: it even delights me. But—the friend? Him I lose! My Tristan!"[19]

For Schnorr, the abyss was unbearable. And so did it seem to Henry Krehbiel in 1886, when he urged excisions where "the emotional tension was great beyond the bounds of pleasure." The embodiment of this tension was Schnorr's truest successor: Albert Niemann.

Every description of Niemann begins with his physical presence. He was a giant of a man, perhaps six and a half feet tall. Krehbiel recorded, and photographs confirm: "The figure is colossal, the head, like 'the front of Jove himself,' the eyes large and full of luminous light, that seems to dart from the tangle of matted [red] hair that conceals the greater part of his face." And Niemann, like Schnorr, was an artist of high emotion and intelligence who followed faithfully where Tristan led. When, in act 3, he tore the bandage from his bloody wound, it was too much. Krehbiel wrote: "An experienced actress who sat ... at my elbow grew faint and almost swooned. ... [Niemann] never again ventured to expose the wound in his breast, though the act is justified, if not demanded, by the text."[20]

Like others coached by Wagner, he shunned exaggeration and extravagance. His absorption insured that every gesture told. His Tristan was at once plotted and spontaneous: the descent from chivalric reserve to frenzied dissolution admitted no lapse or detour. A correspondent for the *Musical Courier* reported that, "from a histrionic point of view" it was "the finest portrayal . . . that can well be imagined," far outrivaling the European performances of Heinrich Vogl and Hermann Winkelmann. Lilli Lehmann called Niemann's Tristan "certainly the most sublime thing that has ever been achieved in the sphere of music drama."[21]

Incredibly, Niemann was already fifty-five years old. Like Lehmann, he was indomitable, a force of nature. Like Lehmann, again, he had never been a supreme vocalist. His New York Tristan was not beautifully sung. But his declamatory skill—his ability to color and shape the text—completed his physical portrayal.

Niemann sang Lohengrin in 1855, Rienzi in 1859, before Wagner chose him for his Paris *Tannhäuser* of 1861. He joined the Berlin Opera in 1866. Though his personal relations with Wagner were often inflamed, he triumphed as Siegmund in the first Bayreuth *Ring*. Saint-Saëns, who found German singers inferior generally, complained that Niemann's baritonal tenor was worn on top, nor could he sing piano or legato. Other witnesses seemed not to care. According to Edvard Grieg: "Niemann as Siegmund was overwhelmingly good, so successful in combining his vocal and acting abilities on the stage that he represents the very best I have seen. Even in passages where Wagner relies on the orchestra alone to express the inner sense of the drama Niemann acts with conviction and sensibility." According to Angelo Neumann: "I shall simply say that, great though my enthusiasm was for [the other] splendid artists, . . . Albert Niemann's performance of Siegmund transcended them all, and I was moved to the very depths of my being." According to Lehmann: "Never since have I heard or seen a Siegmund to compare with him; all the rest of them—they can resent what I am saying or not, as they please—may as well let themselves be buried. His intellectual power, his physical impressiveness, his incomparable expression were superb beyond words. . . . This Siegmund was unique; it will no more return than another Wagner will." She returned to Bayreuth in 1896 and reported of *Die Walküre*: "With the exception of Frau Sucher [Sieglinde], who acted beautifully, I saw and heard only wooden puppets and I thought, with sorrow, of 1876 when Niemann, with but one glance, set the seal on the whole first act."[22]

Siegmund was Niemann's debut role at the Metropolitan, under Seidl, on November 10, 1886. Lehmann, the Brünnhilde, reported that he received "an ovation such as Germany had scarcely ever given him." After act 1, the orchestra rose and joined in the applause. Krehbiel reported:

> The first claim to admiration which Herr Niemann puts forth is based on the intensely vivid and harmonious picture of the Volsung which he brings on the stage. There is scarcely one of the theatrical conventions which the public have been accustomed to accept that he employs. He takes possession of the stage like an elemental force. . . . His attitude and gestures all seem parts of Wagner's creation. They are not only instinct with life, but instinct with the sublimated life of the hero of the drama. . . . The fate for which [Siegmund] has been marked out has set its seal in the heroic melancholy which is never absent even in his finest frenzies.

Siegmund's first words—the first words of the opera—are "Wes Herd dies auch sei, / hier muss ich rasten." The vocal line is tellingly contoured: a brief, sharp exclamation starting on the E an octave above middle C ("Whoever's hearth this is . . ."); a weary statement of fact, on five descending notes ending a ninth below (". . . here must I rest"). Siegmund's explosive attack suggests breathlessness; his subsequent exhalation is faint with fatigue. And yet of how many present-day performances can it be said, as Krehbiel said of Niemann, that "When he staggers into Hunding's hut . . . a thrill passes through the observer. Part of his story is already told, and it is repeated with electrifying eloquence in the few words that he utters when his limbs refuse their office. The voice is as weary as the exhausted body." Of Niemann's *Winterstürme* Krehbiel wrote:

> It puts truthful declamation before beautiful tone production . . . and lifts dramatic color above what is generally considered essential musical color. That from this a new beauty results all those can testify who hear Herr Niemann sing the love song in the first act of "Die Walküre," which had previously in America been presented only as a lyrical effusion and given with more or less sweetness and sentimentality. Herr Niemann was the first representative of the

character who made this passage an eager, vital, and personal expression of a mood so ecstatic that it resorts to symbolism [of Spring], as if there was no other language for it. The charm with which he invests the poetry of this song (for this is poetry) can only be appreciated by one who is on intimate terms with the German language, but the dramatic effect attained by his use of tone color and his marvelous distinctness of enunciation all can feel.[23]

It speaks volumes that W. J. Henderson, a connoisseur of beautiful singing, was not put off. He reported:

It is gratifying to say that the newcomer at once revealed himself as an artist of rare intelligence and experience and that the uneasiness felt in some quarters as to the impaired condition of his vocal organs was promptly dispelled, partly through the evidence afforded that the German tenor is still in possession of a pretty robust voice, partly through the remarkable cleverness with which he contrived to *réparer des ans l'irréparable outrage.* . . . His Siegmund . . . was carried out . . . with extreme simplicity, directness, and consistency. . . . His love song, half sung, half declaimed, was rendered with the most delicate expression."*[24]

*On the vexing question of Wagner's own expectations, David Breckbill comments:

> Although he wrote appreciatively of singing that cultivated beautiful tone, Wagner's primary concern in his vocal writing was to develop a vehicle for flexibility and conviction of utterance that simulated heightened speech. . . . Even at the Bayreuth *Ring* production of 1876 his last advice to his singers included the words "Distinctness! The big notes will take care of themselves; the little notes and the text are the chief things." Wagner's hope was that, after mastering the notes and durations of his vocal lines, singers would "proceed with discretionary freedom, showing animation rather than reserve" in order to "produce the impression of an impassioned and poetical mode of delivery." . . . Albert Niemann, whose effect in Wagner roles made an impact on his contemporaries that could be compared to [Wilhelmine] Schröder-Devrient's on Wagner, even though he had a stormy relationship with Wagner both personally and on artistic grounds, demonstrates that the singing style Wagner sought could be conceived in different terms from those on which the composer insisted. Hanslick assigned to Niemann the same label with which Chorley branded Schröder-Devrient, "nature singer," but also described his singing as the "complete fusion of word and tone, of poem and composition." While Wagner's desire for tractable singers was perpetuated and made into a virtue at Bayreuth after his death, it was Niemann's singing and acting which exerted influence as the first long-lived model of a great Wagner singer. (Barry Millington, ed., *The Wagner Compendium* [New York, 1992], pp. 357–58.)

The following February, Niemann gave his apparent "farewell performance" opposite Lehmann in *Tristan und Isolde*. The house was sold out by speculators at prices six times the norm. The audience included groups from Boston, Philadelphia, and Cincinnati. Krehbiel wrote:

> Herr Niemann husbanded his vocal resources in the first act, but after that both he and Fräulein Lehmann threw themselves into the work with utter abandon. . . . After two recalls had followed the second fall of the curtain a third round was swelled by a fanfare from the orchestra. To acknowledge this round Herr Niemann came forward alone, and was greeted with cheers, while a laurel wreath, bearing on one of its ribbons the line from "Tannhäuser," "O, kehr zurück, du kühner Sänger," was handed up to him. The third act wrought the enthusiasm to a climax. After the curtain had been raised over and over again, Herr Niemann came forward and said, in German: "I regret exceedingly that I am not able to tell you in your own language how sincerely I appreciate your kindness toward me. I thank you heartily, and would like to say 'Auf Wiedersehen.'"[25]

In fact, Niemann returned to the Met the following season. His two New York years encompassed fifty-nine performances of nine roles, including Florestan, Eleazar (*La Juive*), Lohengrin, and Jean (*Le Prophète*). His Tannhäuser was recalled by Finck as "an exhibition of combined musical and dramatic genius which could not be duplicated on the stage today." His *Götterdämmerung* Siegfried, in Krehbiel's opinion, was "from a histrionic point of view . . . equalled only by his performance of Siegmund and Tannhäuser; nothing else has shown such stature that has been witnessed on the operatic stage of New York."[26]

This last role was new to Niemann. A dozen years before, he had hoped to sing it at Bayreuth, but Wagner did not want his Siegmund enacting another part. In New York, Niemann prepared the role with Seidl. Krehbiel, as ever, was there: "I chanced one evening to be a witness of his study hour—the strangest one I ever saw. It was at the conductor's lodgings in the opera house. There was a pianoforte in the room, but it was closed. The two men sat at a table with the open score before them. Seidl beat time to the inaudible orchestral music, and Niemann sang sans support of any kind. Then would come discussion of readings, markings of cues, etc., all with indescribable gravity, while Frau Seidl-Kraus . . . sat sewing in a corner."[27] And so Niemann was Seidl's Siegfried for the first American *Götterdämmerung*, on January 25, 1888. Lehmann was the Brünnhilde, Emil Fischer the Hagen. Brandt sang the Rhinemaiden Wellgunde.

*Carl Bergmann (top left), Theodore Thomas (top right),
Leopold Damrosch (bottom left), and Walter Damrosch
(bottom right) all played vital roles in introducing
Wagner to American audiences.*

Anton Seidl (above); Seidl's house in the
Catskills, with wife, Auguste, and dogs Wotan
and Mime (top right); his brownstone apartment
on East 62nd Street (bottom right).

The Metropolitan Opera House as it looked in the late nineteenth century. Henry Krehbiel of the New York Tribune *was the dean of America's turn-of-the-century music critics.*

The Brighton Beach program cover for 1889 shows the 3,000-seat seaside music pavilion.

A typical letter from Anton Seidl to Laura Langford,
founder of the Seidl Society. Brighton Beach, with
the hotel in the background.

For Anton Seidl's funeral, the Metropolitan Opera House was transformed into a mortuary chamber.

New York's critics considered Albert Niemann, here as Tannhäuser, the greatest singing actor of his time. His colleague Lilli Lehmann, here as Isolde, was an imperious stage personality.

Succeeding her teacher Lilli Lehmann, Olive Fremstad
was New York's leading Wagnerian soprano just after 1900.
As Kundry (above), Fremstad stained her skin a sulfurous brown.
Her freedom of movement, racing across the stage or thrashing
on the ground, paralleled developments in modern dance.

An actress of limitless resource and intensity, Olive Fremstad costumed her Isolde (top) in a Secession-style robe of deep green. With the passing of Wagnerism after World War I, the Wagner experience contracted to the vocal phenomenon Kirsten Flagstad, here as Isolde (bottom).

7

Der grosse Schweiger

The Metropolitan Opera's German seasons—normally from November to March, plus tours—lasted from 1884–85 to 1890–91. There were usually four performances a week, on Mondays, Wednesdays, and Fridays, and Saturday matinees. Of 589 opera performances, all in German, 329 (including 99 on tour) were of works by Wagner. In addition to *Die Meistersinger* and *Tristan und Isolde*, three *Ring* operas—*Das Rheingold, Siegfried,* and *Götterdämmerung*—received first American performances; also, the *Ring* cycle in its entirety was given in America for the first time.*

During the six seasons following his arrival in November 1885, Anton Seidl conducted nearly all of the Metropolitan's New York Wagner performances. He also coached the principal singers and worried over the stagings, which never pleased him; in this department Bayreuth's standard was higher, according to Henry Finck (who knew both houses, and who complained of "incompetent" and "careless" stage managers at the Met).[1] Otherwise, the company was at least as strong as any in Germany or Austria. Lilli Lehmann, as we have seen, was the resident Brünnhilde and Isolde. Of the

*See Chapter 8. The other Wagner operas given at the Met during the German seasons were *Rienzi, The Flying Dutchman, Tannhäuser, Lohengrin,* and *Die Walküre.* The non-Wagner list included works by Auber, Beethoven, Bellini, Bizet, Boïeldieu, Brüll, Cornelius, Ernst II, Franchetti, Gluck, Goldmark, Gounod, Halévy, Meyerbeer, Mozart, Nessler, Rossini, Smareglia, Spontini, Verdi, and Weber.

bass-baritones and basses, Emil Fischer—whom W. J. Henderson, among others, considered unsurpassed as Hans Sachs—participated in all six Seidl seasons.

Fischer's lengthy stay—he settled in New York—partly resulted from contractual problems resembling Lehmann's. The Dresden Court Opera objected to his prolonged Metropolitan commitments and curtailed his pension. In general, however, German singers were granted leaves of absence for the New York season: American fees were higher, and the German houses received a cut. These arrangements were negotiated by Edmund Stanton. But the Germans, not Stanton, oversaw artistic affairs. "The tradition of Italian opera seems to be dying out," observed a *Times* editorial in early 1886. Finck gloated in 1888: "There is no hope for the Italianissimi, who sigh for their macaronic arias and the 'Ernani' and 'Gazza ladra' soup." Eleven years later, he expounded: "German opera held the fort, and more and more did Wagner come to the front. In the season of 1889–90, for instance, the box-office receipts for Wagnerian performances were $121,565, while those for all other performances combined were only $83,982. As a matter of fact, the public got into such a state of mind that it practically refused to attend any operas but Wagner's in paying numbers." If Krehbiel is to be believed, New York heard only a single performance of an Italian opera in Italian during the season of 1888–89. Meanwhile, Seidl also became New York's most prominent concert conductor, with a repertoire stressing Wagner and other Germans, as well as Berlioz, Liszt, and Saint-Saëns.[2]

Seidl's American career might have been short-lived. In February 1887, a week after he had been toasted a second time by New York's critics, it was announced that he would leave New York for Berlin, where Albert Niemann had persuaded the Court Opera to make him chief conductor. At Seidl's penultimate operatic performance of the season—*Die Meistersinger*, on February 25—he was presented with a silver loving cup whose panels depicted scenes from three Wagner operas. The cup was carried down the aisle while the orchestra played a fanfare. When a speech was demanded, Seidl spoke in German: "From a full heart I thank you for the gracious and kind reception which I have had at your hands. I shall always remember with pleasure these two years of my New York sojourn and the splendid appreciation and inspiring public that I found here." On March 1, he gave a farewell concert at Steinway Hall, with a program of Beethoven, Schumann, Wagner, and Dvořák. The audience was large and effusive. Krehbiel, in the *Tribune*, saluted the departing conductor, "who in seasons of four months each has acquired an influence in the musical affairs of America second to that of no other man. The record is a remarkable one, but it has been made by honest labor in behalf of high ideals; by efforts in which it was patent to all that self-interest played a much smaller role than we are accustomed to find in the exertions of artists who come to us for brief seasons from abroad."[3]

In fact, Seidl would become a confirmed American. To date, his career had been transient. Some of his tours for Angelo Neumann had been planned to include the United States. Instead, Seidl reached America without Neumann—and now, in 1887, decided to remain. In years to come, he took American citizenship and bought a summer home in the Catskills. He acquired English, if imperfectly. He was "Tony" to his wife, and "Mr." Seidl—never "Herr"—to most others. He was fond of talking politics and kept himself informed. (According to Huneker: "He took the deepest interest in the row with Spain and actually seemed gleeful over the prospect of a fight.") He once told a reporter: "I like the [American] people; and I like the freedom they enjoy." According to his friend, the critic Albert Steinberg, he was finally "afflicted with 'Americamania' in its acutest form. Everything appealed to him—our democratic ways, our enthusiasm for the works of Wagner, our mixed drinks . . . our American clubs, our American scenery." As America had adopted Europe's musical high culture, Seidl adopted America. More than a cultural adornment, he increasingly proved a mentor, a friend, and an inspirational goad.[4]

As Seidl the musician became better known, something was learned of Seidl the man. But he did not reveal himself readily.

To the public at large, he was a picturesque and romantic figure, cloaked in sphinx-like self-possession. One trademark was his raven hair, long, flowing, and glossy, combed straight back from the forehead. His eyes, behind spectacles, nearly black, were contemplative or piercing. His skin was smooth. His sculpted features were nearly immobile: the nose formidable; the mouth grave or slightly curled, suggesting whimsy; the chin firm. His large head and torso belied his moderate stature. He dressed simply but carefully, in black or white suits. Many thought he resembled Liszt. Huneker called his Gothic appearance and composed bearing churchly—"involuntarily your eye looked for the Episcopal ring on his finger." Krehbiel wrote: "His face shows a singular combination of youth, perspicacity, calm and inflexible determination, and strength of character . . . a countenance which has behind it a huge reserve force." This was when Seidl was thirty-six years old.[5]

More remote than aloof, Seidl shunned society. In public, he ignored amenities and rarely spoke. In the opera pit, he did not smile when Lehmann or Niemann was cheered and applauded. On the concert stage, he never shook hands with a Paderewski, Joseffy, or Ysaÿe. His wife urged him "to show at least a pleasant countenance" when he was honored with flowers. "He promised to do so, but the effort proved too great for him, as it was very painful for him to become the focus of the public gaze. His modesty did not admit of his displaying any pleasure, although at heart he felt very happy."[6]

He slowly acquired a small group of close friends, including Finck, Krehbiel, and Niemann. To them he showed a different and more genial face. At a favorite restaurant or cafe, he shed his crust of indifference. He was fond of good food, especially if German, and also of good conversation. Though he could "hold his tongue in several languages"—he was dubbed *Der grosse Schweiger* (The Great Silent One)—his weighty and absorbent presence was felt by all. "When Seidl was silent you could almost hear him thinking," wrote Huneker. "He had the sort of personality that overpowered through sheer existing."[7]

Though he espoused a rounded education for musicians, he did not seem to care for literature or painting. He did not discuss details of music history or theory. If the gathering was small enough, he might disclose bits of personal history—that his parents intended him for the priesthood, that at the Leipzig Conservatory he planned to become a pianist. Instead, his religious and musical leanings fixed on Wagner and Bayreuth—constant topics, in praise of which he could be pedantic or naive. He believed that Wagner had "forever" established the highest form of opera, "the perfect expression of life through the union of the drama with music. . . . Other great composers are sure to come, but they will work according to the principles which Wagner has established." He even considered Wagner's literary ability of the "highest quality."[8] He also ardently described his native Hungary: its women, its landscape, its heroic history.

His speech, in German, was precise and laconic, not quick or fluent. He practiced a slow but scathing irony, embellished with sweet and damning smiles. Victor Herbert recounted how, in a conversation at Brighton Beach, Seidl offered the following observation:

> In the property room of the Metropolitan Opera House, gentlemen, there is a helmet. . . . If you were to hunt it up you would find that this specimen is much like other helmets save for the "Schwanritter" emblem which it bears. It was made for *Lohengrin*, and my dear friend Italo Campanini wore it in a truly magnificent performance of the role. Yet if you were to find that helmet to-day you would discover that in addition to the prescribed dimensions and insignia of this piece of knightly headgear Mr. Campanini had put on a blue plume, probably three feet in length. That, my dear gentlemen, is Italian opera.[9]

In contrast to the excitable Leopold Damrosch and the neurotic Gustav Mahler to come, Seidl seemed "manly." Huneker wrote: "He was pervious to the influences of good-fellowship, but let a stranger intrude and like some deep-sea organism Seidl shut up and looked grim things through you and over you. His face at such times was granitic; carved in implacable stone. He made enemies easily, friends slowly; his very failings were virile, his virtues masculine. He was a man to his ensphered soul!"[10]

To Finck, who knew him more intimately, and who revered him, the essential Seidl was nobility tempered by warmth. He was proud but not vain or ostentatious. In bad times, he toured his orchestra without salary for himself and even paid hotel bills out of his pocket. He often conducted charity concerts. According to his wife, on whom he showered gifts: "I had frequently to give away [clothes] to strangers when he could have quite well worn them himself a while longer; but he could not refuse the clothes to a poor man who said that, but for the want of decent clothes, he might get a good position. I was sometimes compelled, when all the half-used clothes had been disposed of, to give away even the new ones." His carelessness with money was such that he gave away more than his income comfortably allowed. His dedication to his work precluded all else. When rehearsing Wagner, he sometimes went twenty-four hours without food. Before performances, he was perfectly quiet; only initiates could sense his extreme excitement. Afterward, he lit a cigar and expounded on the opera until relaxed enough to sleep.[11]

Seidl's most frequent companion was a young Englishman named Francis Neilson; born in 1867, he was seventeen years Seidl's junior. Neilson wrote the libretto for Victor Herbert's first operetta, *Prince Ananias*, successfully produced in 1895, as well as the libretto for an Indianist opera Seidl intended to compose.* He was also an actor and journalist. In later life, he became stage manager for London's Covent Garden. "Entirely apart from the musical halo that [Seidl] seemed to wear, I grew to love him very dearly indeed," Neilson wrote in his 1953 autobiography. "I had never had a close companion, and, although he was many years older than I, he never patronized me or showed even the slightest inclination to take a fatherly interest in me; but foster-father he was to me." On one occasion, Neilson was taken to be Seidl's son; when Seidl heard, he roared with laughter and exclaimed, "I vish it vas true."

Neilson's Seidl anecdotes describe a good-natured personality. Once, spurning a lunch invitation, he shook his head and said, "No, I tank you, they have a band there, and when I eat, I cannot get my jaws to follow the beat." One of his favorite expressions was "That is a cream"—meaning "crime." Rehearsing one day, he complained to a horn player: "Nein, no! That is a cream." The player rose,

---

*See Chapter 9.

bowed, and said, "Thank you, Mr. Seidl." Seidl grew perturbed and said: "You tink I pay you compliment? *Nein, nein! Cream*, I say. Don't do it once more!" When, at Brighton Beach, he was prevailed upon to listen to the singing of a certain lady's daughter, he puffed his cigar following her painful rendition of a Rossini aria and offered, "I tink you let her grow." To his amazement, the mother turned severely to her daughter and said, "It serves you right! Now, will you forget that you have a voice?" Seidl was so pleased he invited them both to lunch. After hearing Seidl conduct Tchaikovsky's *Pathétique* Symphony, Neilson composed a series of sonnets, one for each movement. "I shall always remember the way he was affected when he read them. He folded the sheets up tenderly, and then, holding them up to me, kissed them and put them in his pocket. . . . There was a suavity of living in those days that is gone forever." In retrospect, Seidl's reverence for Wagner seems uncritical. In Neilson's view, however, Seidl was cognizant of "the faults and failings of the master." What is more:

> None of Seidl's acquaintances realized that he was a shrewd reader of character. Perhaps, because so many took advantage of him, found their way to his open purse, and sometimes used him in a shocking manner, they thought that he did not know the ways of the world. When I criticized him for being too generous, he said to me, "Never mind, they tink they fool me, but not so."
>
> One day I asked him if he liked to be taken in, and his great sense of humor bubbled over. He replied, "It is good. I learn sometimes, not often."[12]

Seidl's home life, at 38 East 62nd Street, was outwardly happy. His wife—whose singing career ended prematurely; the New York climate did not agree with her voice—was loving and vigilant; she cheerfully spoiled him. His friends were always about. The brownstone apartment was warmly appointed and decorated with rare portraits of Wagner; other pictures were of Bach, Beethoven, and Bismarck. During the off-season, when he was not touring or conducting at Coney Island, Seidl retreated to his Catskills cottage, known to friends as "Seidl Berg." Away from the prying eyes of the city, he enjoyed a morning of billiards at Fleischmann's resort, where he was a popular figure. He went for walks in the woods, whose trees and plants he could not name. His relaxation permitted more time at the piano than in Manhattan; he improvised and also composed pieces heard only by his wife. In the country, too, his childlike disposition emerged undisguised. He delighted in pranks. At a costume ball, he sang Hans Sachs's name-day song dressed as a curly-haired maiden in sleeveless dress and flowered straw hat.[13]

Though the Seidls were childless, their eight dogs were omnipresent. Seidl followed Wagner in his boundless affection for these creatures. The favorites were Mrs. Seidl's dachshund, Mime, and Seidl's St. Bernard, Wotan. Mime could "speak" and walk on his hind legs. When Seidl breakfasted in bed, Wotan struck the newspaper from his hand until offered a share of the meal. Both dogs slept in the same room with mistress and master. Once, when Seidl and Wotan traveled by train to the Catskills in chilly mid-May, the former lent the latter his overcoat as well as his company in the baggage car.

But Mime and Wotan were jealous of each other. Mime often growled at Wotan and attempted to bite his feet. One day, the Seidls heard Wotan bark peculiarly. He had murdered Mime. Wotan was banished to the top floor, where he refused all food. He later rejoined the family but was often found sniffing the spot where blood was shed and following the scent to the wash table where Mime had expired.[14]

Seidl had a third home as true as the other two: in front of an orchestra he was, as Huneker put it, "a baton incarnate." "Seidl was universally admired and loved by the members of his orchestra," according to Victor Herbert. "He never showed the faintest trace of false pride. His players were his companions, his helpers; he was simply one of them." For the audience, watching his back, Seidl with his spare gestures seemed the image of Alpine composure. For the orchestra, reading his face, the sleeping volcano of Seidl's personality sprang to life. In rehearsal, he was all energy, alert to the tiniest error. In performance, the bond to Wagner stripped him bare. Finck called him "the most emotional conductor that ever lived." According to Herbert: "Certain passages in *Siegfried* and the wonderful closing scene of *Tristan* always made him cry like a child, so that by the time the curtain had dropped he would be in a state of emotional collapse."

He returned the admiration of his musicians. After a Madison Square Garden benefit concert at which he led a double orchestra in excerpts from *Tannhäuser* and *Tristan*, he commented to the press: "If you were to tell a conductor in Europe that such a thing was possible in New York he would laugh in your face. In no city of the world are there so many orchestra musicians of the first class. In no other city of the world could such a huge orchestra be brought together at such short notice, and in no other city of the world could you have found musicians with such an advanced repertoire at their fingers' end."[15]

Events of this kind emphasized the startling popularity of both Wagner and Seidl. An audience of eight thousand, including hundreds of standees, heard Seidl conduct Wagner at a free concert at New York's Castle Garden in 1891. Seidl was greeted with such enthusiasm that, according to the *Morning Journal*, "it seemed almost as though he would never be allowed to begin the opening number." The same report called him "pre-eminently a man of the people, whose life is spent in educating the public to know what music is." In the same vein, the *Sun* remarked in 1898 that "no conductor was ever so popular with a mass of people in this city as Mr. Seidl was." "Whether he appeared before a large audience at the Metropolitan or at a concert of less importance he was certain to be greeted with applause. He was well known by sight to more New Yorkers than any other musician in this city, and he was recognized everywhere in public."[16]

If this populist imagery of Seidl seems incongruous applied to so private a man, we must bear in mind the period. One hundred years ago, New York was a smaller place. Its cultural community was more public and more compact than today. Face-to-face social relations were not discouraged by telephones, radios, or televisions.* As Francis Neilson recalled:

> In the nineties, when men would stroll down Broadway, people became better acquainted. There was time to stop and have a chat or to saunter into a bar to see who was about. News was spread by the press to its readers nearly as rapidly then as it is today. Gossip was just as interesting and amusing as it is now. A good story about a well-known person was all the better for being told by a first-class raconteur in the flesh. Life ambled along in that day, but people got things done. I daresay there was more real work crowded into the day then than there is now. . . . There has been a noticeable falling off in the cheerfulness and light-heartedness that were encountered day by day in such places of activity as the Strand and Broadway.

The outdoor intermingling of notable men of different classes and callings had its indoor equivalent. In New York, as in Paris, the cafe was, in Huneker's phrase, "the poor man's club. It is also a rendezvous for newspaper men, musicians, artists, Bohemians generally. It is the best stamping-ground for men of talent. Ideas circulate. Brain tilts with brain. Eccentricity must show cause or be jostled. If there is too much drinking, there is the compensation of contiguity with interesting personalities." In the best hotel restaurants, the "free-lunch counter" provided hearty meals, for a five-cent tip, to those who merely paid for a cocktail, a beer, or a milk-and-seltzer. According to Neilson: "Almost any day of the week, between the hours of eleven and one, a sprinkling of men connected with the drama, literature, journalism, and art might be found in the barrooms of Broadway's big hotels. . . . In those days the man of business, the scientist, the doctor and lawyer would be found in the company of

---

*In a memorable evocation of Paris in the twenties, Virgil Thomson once wrote: "Everything, literally everything, was different, even the food. . . . Joyce and Stein . . . Picasso and Braque, were simply around. They could be bitter about one another and refuse to meet, but they saw the same people, frequented the same galleries and bookstores, appeared in the same little mags. They were reputable artists and definitely worth knowing. But they were in no way publicity stars, as Hemingway and Picasso were to become." (*New York Review of Books*, Feb. 19, 1976.)

artists, glad to be in close touch with them and to dispense their quips and sallies to an ever-widening circle."

One hub of the city's cultural life was Union Square, at 14th Street and Broadway, among whose trees and fountains families would promenade at night. The neighborhood included Steinway Hall, the Academy of Music, and the National Conservatory of Music—plus such eating establishments as Lüchow's, Lienau's, and Mould's. All these were musicians' haunts, frequented by Antonín Dvořák, Victor Herbert, Rafael Joseffy, Lilli Lehmann, Moriz Rosenthal, Xaver Scharwenka, William Steinway, and Theodore Thomas. Albert Niemann—according to Huneker, a "drinker that would have pleased Pantagruel"—would down cocktails from a beer glass all night until noon the next day, then sing Wagner at the Met the same evening. As for Seidl, he would daily take the Fourth Avenue streetcar—whose drivers and brakemen called him "the Professor"—to Fleischmann's, near Grace Church at Tenth and Broadway, there to drink coffee and smoke cigars in a large upstairs room Neilson called "the most famous rendezvous in the world." Seidl's social regime also included Sunday night soirees given by patrons of the New York Philharmonic. Neilson remembered a night at the Lotus Club in 1897:

> Ysaÿe was there with his fiddle; Gregorovitch had brought his; Rafael Joseffy and several other pianists came. Joe Vanderburg was there, but not with his oboe. Before I could reach Seidl, someone had pushed him onto the piano stool, and he struck up Walther's "Prize Song"; a person whom I did not know and whose name I cannot remember sang. Evidently it was a free-for-all, for Ysaÿe took out his violin and gave Gregorovitch the nod to follow his example. Joseffy sat down at another piano; then other singers raised their voices. Before long, everything was going full blast. When the song was finished, with tremendous huzzas, Seidl banged into the overture. There had been good food and plenty of wine, and they were all in great spirits.

Huneker, writing around the time of World War I, complained of the noisiness and ugliness of turn-of-the-century New York, its tenements and paucity of trees. But he knew no city, with the possible exception of London, that compared with New York "for versatility in eating and drinking." He rhapsodized the champagne cocktails and morning bracers of twenty years before: "Men seemed more vigorous to us then, and seem more fidgety and nervous in this year of grace." Huneker imbibed, as well, the glow of 1890s summer afternoons, when from his tenth-floor apartment at Madison Avenue and 76th Street he could see the Hudson River to the west, the East River to the east, and the Statue of Liberty to the south. He thrilled to the bravado of the city's boulevardiers and intellectual hucksters, to the very "air of New York, that electric ozone which makes for optimism."[17]

Another Seidl acquaintance, whom we have already encountered as the author of a eulogy delivered at Seidl's funeral, was Robert Ingersoll. He was among the best-known Americans of his day, a touring orator of whom it has been said that he spoke to more people in person than anyone before or since. Ingersoll was a freethinker, "the Great Agnostic," who blamed the Bible for denigrating women and condoning slavery. "The woman is equal to the man," he preached. He espoused women's suffrage and called for birth control. He defended Jews, immigrants, and American Indians. He believed life should be lived to the hilt on this earth—a theology supporting artistic curiosity and personal sensuality. His close friends included Susan Anthony, Eugene Debs, and Walt Whitman. George Brandes, once the doyen of European criticism, wrote: "In Ingersoll's mind common sense rose to genius."

The case of Robert Ingersoll dramatizes the reach of Seidl and Wagner in Gilded Age America. A devotee of Shakespeare and Robert Burns, of Rembrandt and Corot, he had always been impervious to music. As he explained at an 1895 Lotus Club dinner speech in honor of Seidl:

> I always thought there must be some greater music somewhere. One day I heard it, and I was waiting for it. "Who wrote that?" I felt

it everywhere. I was cold. I was almost hysterical. It answered to my brain, my heart; not only to association, but all there was of hope and aspiration, all my future; and they said this is the music of Wagner. I . . . was utterly and absolutely ignorant of music until I heard Wagner interpreted by the greatest leader, in my judgment, in the world—Anton Seidl.

Ingersoll's understanding of Wagner is an intriguing variant on the meliorist Wagner Americans adored. For Christians, Wagner was a great Christian. For the atheistic Ingersoll, Wagner embodied a "wild and splendid independence." Wagner's music was not German—"Germany would not have it. Germany denied that it was music. The great German critics said it was nothing in the world but noise." Rather, Wagner was universal and "spiritual."

[Wagner] develops the brain, it gives the imagination wings; the little earth grows larger; the people grow up; and not only that, it civilizes the heart; and the man who understands that music can love better and with greater intensity than he ever did before. . . . The man who understands and appreciates that music becomes in the highest sense spiritual [as] when you feel that you know what there is of beauty, of sublimity, of heroism and honor and love in the human heart. [Wagner's is] the greatest music, in my judgment, that ever issued from the human brain. . . . No man will ever produce greater pictures in sound, greater music, than Wagner. Never! Never! And I don't believe he will ever have a better interpreter than Anton Seidl.

On Sunday evenings, the Ingersolls received guests at their New York home. No invitations were sent. Seidl sometimes visited and even played Wagner on the piano. A short list of other typical Sunday night visitors suggests the range of acquaintances Seidl made outside the German community, and also outside music: Debs, Andrew Carnegie, the actors Edwin Booth and Edwin Forrest, the feminist Helen Gardner, the wealthy radicals Courtland Palmer and Ella Wheeler Wilcox.[18]

In New York Seidl was part of a public community of culture, not an invisible celebrity.

8

Der Ring des Nibelungen

Wagner never pursued his fancy of starting a New World Wagner festival. Instead, Americans flocked to Bayreuth. They were mainly women: a subject of bemused observation by blasé Europeans. Joseph Bennett of London's *Daily Telegraph* discovered them "in chronic states of ecstasy about 'darling Liszt' whose shadow they hoped would fall upon them," and in "an aggravation of ecstasy" upon spying Wagner himself. Another Englishman, the artist Walter Crane, overheard an American remarking to her companion in the dark of the Festspielhaus: "Em'ly, this excitement is breaking me up fast." [*][1]

The first Bayreuth visitors from America also included Leopold Damrosch, who attended the premiere of the *Ring* in 1876—eight years prior to bringing Wagner's operas to the Metropolitan. He filed five copious reports for the *New York Sun*, all demonstrating the enthusiasm of a devout and knowledgeable disciple. Of Wagner himself Damrosch reported: "[He] is everywhere, urging, praising, directing, reviving . . . wearied souls with sparkling wit, and with eye and ear, with the magic of his whole nature, always guiding and inspiriting his obedient followers." And again: "The master . . . remains good-humored and unwearied in all his arrangements, great

---

[*]A more sympathetic glimpse of American women at Bayreuth is that of Willa Cather, who in her novel *The Song of the Lark* (New York, 1915; rpt. 1991, p. 244) describes "the group of young women who followed Wagner about in his old age, keeping at a respectful distance, but receiving now and then a gracious acknowledgement that he appreciated their homage."

or small, for the momentous event. It is a pleasant thing to see the great master, who has conquered the world, still restlessly at work, and by no means the smallest testimonial of his greatness is the unanimous zeal of all the executants to execute worthily their share of the duty." As for the performers: "Nothing could be finer than the inspiration with which the singers and musicians go about their duties, all urged on by the sole desire of satisfying the illustrious creator of the 'Ring of the Nibelungen.'" As for the work itself: "The listener feels that once in his life he has heard colossal music." "No description can give any notion of the boldness and loftiness of style, the dramatic life and impressiveness, the depth of tragedy.... Doubtless here, as so often before, Wagner's opponents will attack him bitterly, but with the rage of impotence. If Wagner has ever triumphed . . . certainly this time the triumph must be decisive. . . . A new epoch in art has arisen." "It seems to be conceded by friend and foe alike, that Wagner stands first among musical artists. . . . The performance of the 'Ring of the Nibelungen' has surpassed any previous production of dramatic art the world has ever witnessed." Damrosch also expressed pride, "as an American," that his adopted country was "both in quantity and quality so well represented among the audience."[2]

Another correspondent attending the first *Ring* was John R. G. Hassard, the critic of the *New York Tribune* in the years before Krehbiel took over. His reports were as detailed as Damrosch's and hardly less enthusiastic. Hassard declared the *Ring* "the greatest of Wagner's creations." He called the festival "the most remarkable [experiment] that has ever been made either in music or in any of its sister arts."

> The theory of Wagner has been accepted within a few years by so many of the best musicians and by such a large proportion of the unlearned public that there has been little doubt of its ultimate recognition, at least in its main points, by all the world of art. The only serious question to be solved here at Bayreuth was as to Wagner's own application of the theory. . . . Let me satisfy doubtful inquirers at once: the performance is one of the most stupendous successes the stage has ever witnessed. . . . Familiar as we deem

ourselves in New-York with Wagner's music, I must confess after this that we do not begin to know it. I do not express my own opinion only; I reflect the judgment of every man and woman I have seen—and I have talked with those of many nations and of various musical tastes—when I say that nothing in the remotest degree approaching the grandeur or effectiveness of what we are now hearing has ever been presented on the lyric stage. The victory of Wagner is overwhelming.

Hassard's reports of the first *Ring* cycle were followed in the *Tribune* by summaries of cycles two and three by the twenty-two-year-old Henry Finck, who also managed to exchange words with his hero, "the greatest operatic genius the world has ever known."[3]

Back in Boston, John Sullivan Dwight dutifully reprinted Hassard's dispatches, and also some from the *New York Times* that evolved from skepticism to fervent approval. Dwight himself, though he had only heard excerpts from the *Ring*, disapproved. "Can anyone easily believe that an audience can really be interested in the Nibelungen plot as such?" he asked his readers.

> Has it meaning? has it human interest? does it touch deep emotions, the very end and aim of music? . . . There is nothing but recitative, one only speaking at a time. . . . [The music] keeps formlessly and vaguely on, a slightly musical modification of mere talking. . . . Time only can decide the full intrinsic worth and power of Wagnerism. To judge from these Cable rhapsodies, it is all over with the old art of Music. . . . Bach and Handel, Mozart and Beethoven, and all that sat upon high thrones, are superseded. . . . Yet we dare believe upon the other hand, that musical humanity will still hail with more delight than ever "the large utterance of the elder gods."[4]

Dwight cautioned that Hassard, among other "Cable rhapsodists," had arrived in Bayreuth "a thoroughly committed Wagnerite beforehand." He predicted that other Americans would file more tempered reports once the zealots had been heard. Apparently, no such reports crossed his desk. Only by resorting to clippings from France, Italy, and Britain was Dwight able to present views buttressing his own. Finally, triumphantly, he reprinted the dispatches of Wagner's arch nemesis, Vienna's Eduard Hanslick, who wrote:

> Never have human beings spoken to one another in this fashion, probably not even gods. Jumping here and there in awkward intervals, always slow, always glum, exaggerated, one dialogue is essentially like another! . . . The people involved are not distinguished from one another by the character of the vocal melodies assigned them, as in the old-fashioned opera . . . but are identical in the physiognomy of their *sprechton*. . . . In the *Ring* there may be two, three or six persons standing together on the stage, but, aside from insignificant and fleeting exceptions, they never sing together; they speak, instead, as in court proceedings, one after the other. Only he who has experienced it can fully appreciate what a torture it is to follow this musical goose-step set-up for a whole evening. . . . I shall waste no words on the indigestible German stammered in *Rheingold* and offered as poetry. . . . The second act is an abyss of boredom. . . . This utterly tuneless, plodding narrative, in a slow tempo, engulfs us like an inconsolable broad sea from which only the meagre crumbs of a few leitmotifs come floating towards us out of the orchestra. Scenes like this recall the medieval torture of waking a sleeping prisoner by stabbing him with a needle at every nod.[5]

I cite Hanslick at length to stress that no such fulminations issued from any prominent American pen. Dwight himself may have been the closest thing to a New World Hanslick—and yet was insufficiently informed or resourceful. His best hope was that someone else could do the job. *Dwight's Journal* ceased publication in 1881.

The Ring of the Nibelung came to the United States in installments. First, as we have seen, there were Adolf Neuendorff's *Die Walküre* of 1877 and Leopold Damrosch's of 1885. Anton Seidl, at the Met, led the first American *Siegfried* on November 9, 1887, the first American *Götterdämmerung* on January 25, 1888, the first American *Das Rheingold* on January 4, 1889. The first American *Ring* cycles were mounted in 1888–89, when *Das Rheingold, Die Walküre, Siegfried,* and *Götterdämmerung* were staged sixteen, ten, thirteen, and eleven times, respectively. That spring, Seidl and the Met gave complete cycles in Philadelphia, Boston, Milwaukee, Chicago, and St. Louis, on tour continuously from March 25 to May 11. This heroic enterprise, with a company of 164, demonstrated the far-flung reach of the Wagner cause. As in New York, newspaper reviews were detailed and perceptive (critics in Philadelphia, Boston, and Milwaukee had attended the 1876 Bayreuth *Ring*). In St. Louis (where the *Ring* was advertised as "THE GREATEST OPERATIC ATTRAC-TION IN THE WORLD"), four thousand crammed the thirty-five-hundred-seat Music Hall. In Milwaukee, where some patrons stood in the aisles, the Met's set for *Die Walküre,* act 1, would not fit on stage; its improvised replacement included a table "which might do in a nineteenth century frontier scene [but] would have been structurally impossible in a Teutonic log-house of that time."[6] The following season, the four operas were given three, three, two, and five times, respectively, at the Metropolitan Opera House; the tour included a single Boston *Die Walküre.*

The modest size of the Met's roster—in 1886–87, there were only eleven female soloists—testifies to the company's dedication. Lehmann was the usual Brünnhilde. Fischer's twenty-eight roles included Wotan and Hagen. In addition to Niemann, the Siegmunds and Siegfrieds included Max Alvary, Paul Kalisch, and Heinrich Vogl. Brandt, the leading mezzo during her four seasons, sang Erda and Fricka. Theodor Reichmann, who created Amfortas at Bayreuth, was heard as all three Wotans.

Cast lists for the first American *Ring* performances show no Norns for *Götterdämmerung*—because the Norns scene was cut. So was Waltraute's narrative and the scene between Alberich and Hagen at the start of act 2. Seidl deferred to his New York public by trimming Wagner's operas to four hours. He once commented: "I did this really with a heavy heart. The public may believe me when I say that any cut, no matter how short, does not save as much time as will compensate for the less thorough understanding of the opera therefrom resulting." And yet, in earlier years, Seidl had trimmed Wagner for Angelo Neumann with Wagner's authorization. At the Met,

Seidl's cuts were accepted even by Krehbiel, who considered them appropriate in an American house where many in the audience knew no German; it was "better to achieve success for the representations by adapting the drama to the capacity of the public," he wrote, "than to sacrifice it bodily on the altar of integrity."[7] (At today's Met, the operas are given uncut for an audience that knows incomparably less German than a century ago.)

Other, more prevalent, causes for dissatisfaction were the Met's costumes and scenery. Generally, these were modeled after Bayreuth. In retrospect, Wagner's eye for decor was lamentably conventional. And the Met's sets, moreover, were often shabby, flimsy, or both. The lighting effects were poor. The magic fire disappointed. The Immolation tableau was considered inept. In *Das Rheingold*, a fifteen-minute interval was needed to reset the stage between scenes 2 and 3. And yet the dramas told. When Huneker attended the *Ring* in Bayreuth in 1896, he reported back to New York that Richter's conducting was "tame and colorless," that the singing was "not superior." Seidl's readings at the Met had been "much more powerful, virile, and passionate."[8]

Met audiences of the German seasons completed Seidl's shrine. Their attention, comprehension, and appreciation—at times bordering on frenzy—were regularly acknowledged in the press. They militantly silenced every disturbance from the boxes. Their ranks were fortified with pilgrims from other cities, who came equipped with librettos and handbooks. "One could hardly listen to 'Götterdämmerung' among throngs of intensely young enthusiasts, without paroxysms of nervous excitement," reported Henry Adams. One such enthusiast, the youthful composer Sidney Homer, exclaimed on hearing his first *Ring*: "A new world burst forth! Life would never be the same again, the commonplace was banished from our . . . lives forever!"[9]

The quintessential Wagner plot is the quest for redemption. Earthly life is oppressive. Its victims seek routes of transcendent escape. Do they succeed? Overtly or implicitly, complexly or confusedly, Wagner's endings are ambiguous.

According to the musicologist Carl Dahlhaus: "The truly fundamental dramatic motive, with which any interpretation must begin, is not . . . the redemption that Wagner sought and longed for but the entanglement that he felt reality to be. . . . His genius lay in the tying . . . of the dramatic knot and not in its untying."[10] Wagner's trapped protagonists and irresolute endings speak to twentieth-century sensibilities; we identify with his ambivalence about redemption. For the Gilded Age, life's torture seemed more remediable. In fact, Wagner's ambivalence was not even acknowledged.

Wagner's most ambivalent, most ambiguous ending closes the *Ring*. He changed the text for it at least six times. Does the Immolation Scene signify a terminal catastrophe or a new beginning? Is Brünnhilde's leavetaking purgative redemption or fatalistic destruction? Certainly Wagner's changes tend toward the second interpretation; in earlier variants, Wotan survives in a healing conflagration that also frees humanity. Following his reading of Schopenhauer in 1854, Wagner grew morbid and disillusioned; he had Brünnhilde say: "I saw the world end." George Bernard Shaw, writing in 1889, viewed the *Ring* as a mordant Fabian allegory of capitalist greed; for him, *Götterdämmerung* was a vapid non sequitur whose final "love panacea," a "romantic nostrum for all human ills," lacked conviction. For Hassard, reviewing the first *Ring* in the *New York Tribune*, *Götterdämmerung* was the sublime and necessary capstone to a drama of edification. "The Gods have perished, and the powers of darkness in the recovery of the 'Ring' are broken. A new era opens—the era of free impulse and of heroic endeavor, unrestrained by the machinations of sorcerers or subdued to a desire for gold."[11] (Hassard, not so incidentally, was a respected Catholic scholar of formidable moral authority.)

If *Tristan und Isolde* posed problems for a smiling Gilded Age reading, the *Ring* yielded a consummate meliorist tract. According to W. J. Henderson, the Immolation Scene showed the gods dying in solemn atonement for their sins; "Brünnhilde perfects and completes [Wotan's] plan. The ethical plot of the drama is finished."

Krehbiel echoed: "Wagner's ethical conception seems to be that the era of selfishness and greed of power and gold gives place to an era of the dominion of love." The end of the gods is "a vast and righteous necessity," "a stupendous deed of morality." For Freda Winworth, whose 1898 *The Epic of Sounds* proposed an "ethical exegesis" of the *Ring* cycle, the end of *Götterdämmerung* saw the beginning of a "reign of love"; "the ethereal tones fade away into silence, leaving in the heart of the listener a sublime sense of perfect peace." Equally upbeat is Henry Finck's version of Brünnhilde's Immolation:

> Here, all the pertinent leading motives of the whole Tetralogy are once more recalled and combined, with an astounding art of construction at which Bach himself would have opened wide his eyes in wonder, and with an overwhelming emotional effect at which he would have bowed his head in awe and admiration. It is an ocean of sound to which each of the dramas contributes its rivers and rivulets. How exultingly Loge's fire-motive seizes upon the burg of the gods! Once more Siegfried's motive is heard, but the sounds which have presaged the end of the gods smother it. But neither Loge nor this gloomy Götterdämmerung motive have the last word. The new melody, symbolizing the redemption through love, rises on the violins, upheld by the harps, proclaiming that the curse of Alberich's Ring has been expiated.*[12]

If a hundred years later this reading seems impossibly anachronistic, it is partly because Siegfried and Brünnhilde seem so much less attractive than the more complex, more flawed characters they supersede. I am thinking of the depressive Siegmund, who commits incest and threatens suicide; of his sister, Sieglinde, whose vulnerability drives her toward madness; of the young Brünnhilde, whose reckless compassion rules her judgment; of Wotan, whose ego undermines his authority; of Loge, whose intellect makes him devious.

---

*This theme, first heard in *Die Walküre*, act 3, actually signifies "the glorification of Brünnhilde," according to an unpublished letter (September 6, 1875) written by Cosima. (Cited by John Deathridge in *19th-Century Music*, vol. 5 [1981], p. 84.)

Even the evil dwarfs Mime and Alberich prove poignant victims in such recent productions as Patrice Chéreau's 1976 centenary *Ring*.

To Gilded Age commentators, Wagner's dwarfs were repulsive. Loge defamed intellect. Wotan desecrated divinity. Siegmund's depression was ignoble, and his incest—a transgression endlessly worried about and rationalized—was unseemly. *Götterdämmerung*, in Chéreau's influential staging, is all decadence: a sordid melodrama populated by monsters. For the Gilded Age, the *Ring*'s decadents were the sinful gods; carefree Siegfried, righteous Brünnhilde seemed the less vulnerable, the more wholesome, the more "human." It bears stressing that Seidl's excisions—of the Norns, of Waltraute's speech, of Alberich's scene with Hagen, all fraught with foreboding—streamlined the narrative toward a succession of robust set pieces, beginning with Dawn, the love duet, and the Rhine Journey, culminating with the Funeral March and Immolation. How telling—how astonishing—is Finck's analogy from Wagner's finale to the religious contrapuntist Bach, epitomizing joyful fervor and moral rectitude. As for Siegfried's threnody, according to Krehbiel it registered an ideal manly grief untainted by "tears of hopeless mourning"; according to Finck, it surpassed everything else "in the whole range of dramatic composition, with or without music."[13]

What these drastically shifting *Ring* interpretations ultimately document is a demise of faith in the perfectibility of mankind. Thoughtful present-day productions can do little with Siegfried, whose innocence is intended to make him strong and autonomous; he seems simplistic, a cartoon hero whose once mighty Funeral Music echoes in a void. For smiling Henry Finck, little detained by the *Ring*'s darker episodes, Siegfried was the "grandest role for tenors of the future. What life, what buoyancy, what melody, what humor pervade these songs!"[14] I have already cited William Dean Howells's famous 1886 advice that America's writers "concern themselves with the more smiling aspects of life, which are the more American." A century ago, Siegfried *did* seem American: his high spirits, his physical strength, his instinctive intelligence—he understands the Forest Bird and befriends a bear—evoked the Frontier.

As we have seen, Wagner and Seidl had predicted a triumphant United States mission; we have also seen that they were right. The first American *Ring* cycle, in 1889, more than ever persuaded Americans that they were Wagner's sons and heirs. The New World now identified with Wagner not only because there were no Hanslicks to defend outraged tradition; experiencing *Siegfried* and *Götterdämmerung*, Americans identified with Wagner's characters. Unlike Tristan and Isolde, unlike Hans Sachs, Siegfried and Brünnhilde championed a new world, a realm of experience unencumbered by tortured needs or thoughts. "There is something peculiarly sympathetic to our people in the character of the chief personages of the drama," Krehbiel wrote of *Siegfried*. "In their rude forcefulness and freedom from restrictive conventions they might be said to be representative of the American people. They are so full of that vital energy which made us a nation. . . . Siegfried is a prototype, too, of the American people in being an unspoiled nature. He looks at the world through glowing eyes that have not grown accustomed to the false and meretricious."[15]

In his popular 1893 "frontier thesis," Frederick Jackson Turner argued that the pioneer's arduous westward route forged an American character type: "that coarseness and strength combined with acuteness and inquisitiveness; that practical inventive turn of mind, quick to find expedients; that masterful grasp of material things, lacking in the artistic but powerful to effect great ends; that restless, nervous energy; that dominant individualism, working for good and for evil, and withal that buoyancy and exuberance which comes from freedom." If Turner's frontiersman did not exist in fact, neither did Wagner's Siegfried, whose inquisitiveness leads him to Fafner's cave; whose inventive mind intuits how to forge Siegmund's sword; whose exuberance and dominating individualism overcome Brünnhilde's shyness and fear. The frontiersman and Siegfried both bravely explore a mythic world without borders or constraints. Both serve to define a cultural belief—in untutored instinct, in self-made success, in "America." Call Siegfried Davy Crockett, who fought and rejected his tyrannical father; who refused education; who roamed the wilderness; who selected and courted his future wife without adult guidance. Henderson, among others, explicitly portrayed Siegfried as a pioneer, confronting the "mystic powers of nature" as he scaled Brünnhilde's rock.*[16]

Mark Twain, America's late-nineteenth-century Everyman, was also a frontiersman of sorts. He also happens to have left the best-known American account of early Bayreuth: "At the Shrine of St. Wagner."

As ever, he is an innocent abroad—a posture half-feigned, half-authentic. Like America itself, with its impressive yet borrowed musical high culture, he is a rambunctious offspring of European parents: initiate and outsider, sophisticate and provincial. In Venice, on the grand tour two decades before, he had called his gondola "an inky old canoe" and yet was seduced by "the gentlest, pleasantest locomotion we have ever known." In Rome, he had compared St. Peter's unfavorably to the United States Capitol; yet he found the Milan Cathedral "the princeliest creation that ever brain of man conceived." In Bayreuth, in 1891, he ridiculed devotees come "to worship their prophet in his own Ka'aba in his own Mecca"—and yet confessed that *Tannhäuser* was "the only operatic favorite I have ever had"; he was introduced to it as a youth, and had last heard it the preceding season at the Met, led by Anton Seidl.

The Bayreuth *Tannhäuser* left Mark Twain "drunk with pleasure"; it was "music to make one take scrip and staff and beg his way round the globe." Attending *Parsifal*, he enjoyed act 1 "in spite of the singing" but concluded that "seven hours at five dollars a ticket is almost too much for the money." Attending *Tristan und Isolde*—like *Parsifal*, new to him—he was chiefly impressed by the audience.

> I have seen all sorts of audiences—at theatres, operas, concerts, lectures, sermons, funerals—but none which was twin to the Wagner

---

*Or call Siegfried Old Shatterhand, the frontiersman created by Karl May (1842–1912), whose adventure novels, set in the American West, were phenomenally popular in Germany. Like countless other Germans, May envisioned a New World wilderness untainted by the anomie and materialism of modern civilization.

audience of Bayreuth for fixed and reverential attention. . . . You seem to sit with the dead in the gloom of a tomb. You know that they are being stirred to their profoundest depths; that there are times when they want to rise and wave their handkerchiefs and shout their approbation, and times when tears are running down their faces, and it would be a relief to free their pent emotions in sobs or screams; yet you hear not one utterance till the curtain swings together and the closing strains have slowly faded out and died: then the dead rise with one impulse and shake the building with their applause.

Mark Twain's fascinated response to the Festspielhaus patrons should not surprise us. The American in him identified with the crowd, with the demos. He prickled when the gathering was elite. Old World privilege and ostentation offended and disconcerted him; an upstart Yankee, he felt both proud and insecure. To his relief, Bayreuth Wagnerites did not overdress. Unlike boxholders at the Met, they did not squeak their fans, titter, or gabble. And the theater itself was a model of functional simplicity. "There is no occasion for color and decoration, since the people sit in the dark." At the same time, this Old World egalitarianism was almost too good; it usurped his very pedigree. When an "imperial princess" turned up, and the petrified Wagnerites "began to gaze in a stupor," Mark Twain was aggrieved and gratified—in a long and cathartic tirade, he protests too much: "The standing multitude . . . gaze mutely and longingly and adoringly and regretfully like sinners looking up into heaven. . . . There is no spectacle anywhere that is more pathetic than this. It is worth crossing many oceans to see." Ultimately, he regains his ambivalence: "I feel strongly out of place here. Sometimes I feel like the sane person in a community of the mad. . . . But by no means do I ever overlook or minify the fact that this is one of the most extraordinary experiences of my life. . . . I have never seen anything so great and fine and real as this devotion."[17]

Self-made man, autodidact, Yankee pragmatist, violator of taboos, archenemy of aristocrats, a tornado of energy prone to gusts of depression, an atheist susceptible to the holiness of art, an artist insufficiently esteemed in his homeland yet never at home anyplace else—all this describes Mark Twain, whom an authorized biographical sketch called "characteristically American in every fiber."[18] It also describes Richard Wagner as seen through American eyes. As they recognized something of themselves in Siegfried, Americans thought they recognized Wagner the man. Even before they knew his music, they had remarked upon his democratic zeal, his entrepreneurial acumen, his uplifting spiritual agenda. Now, having acquired the *Ring*, they drew fresh and fuller portraits, of which the fullest was penned by Henry Finck in his two-volume *Wagner and His Works*, published in 1893.

Wagner was in so many respects an unlikely exemplar of Gilded Age rectitude, of personal "character," that we may marvel that writers like Finck felt called upon to redeem this difficult candidate. They did so not merely because, in Wagner's case, man and artist so obviously interlock; half a century before the "new criticism," it was a dual article of faith that great music was a moral force and great composers were moral men. "Music is an expression of character, of the moods, the spirit, the meaning of the man that makes it," wrote John Sullivan Dwight. "His words can only tell the meaning of his thoughts; his actions, the meaning of his present purpose; his music tells the meaning of *him*."[19] Wholesome readings of *Tristan und Isolde*, meliorist interpretations of the *Ring*—themselves exercises in sophistry and censorship—dictated special pleadings on behalf of Wagner's irascibility and egocentricity.

Finck's brief begins: "Never was a man more lied about, by envious colleagues and common gossip, than Wagner." Granted, Wagner was far from flawless. But "great mountains throw deep shadows"— his faults were "the inevitable shadows of his virtues." The artist in him demanded solitude and self-absorption. The Horatio Alger in him—his passion for hard work, his crushing disappointments— made him unsociable and inaccessible; "could he have curbed this eagerness for work, he might have lived longer." In his countenance, moreover, "you will discover the other side of his character"—his kindness, refinement, and serenity, qualities little glimpsed by the world at large. In fact, "he was the most amiable and cordial man to his friends." In this regard, he was a genuine democrat: he took everybody, servant and king, at their own merits. He adored dogs. "His heart was overflowing with tender love."[20]

Finck's Wagner portrait seems not to have been controversial. William Foster Apthorp, a critic of intellect and discrimination, whose own perceptions of Wagner the man are typically subtle, called it "probably the best and most lifelike that has yet been given to the public." Another portraitist, W. J. Henderson, similarly insisted on the prerogatives of genius, and on a "second Wagner" known best to intimates. Henderson conceded that Wagner's luxurious taste in fabrics and perfumes was "unmanly," that his "extremities of depression" were "pathetic" and "pitiable." But—in a maneuver that both gauges the pressure of the genteel agenda, and of the even greater pressure to excuse Wagner's lapses from genteel norms—he added that:

> In such a man as Wagner the artistic traits are dominant. They rule the personality. The conviction of this man that he had in him the conception of epoch-making works, and his recognition of the fact that the world was his artistic enemy, were the moving forces of his life. Without constantly keeping this in mind, it is quite impossible to comprehend the character of Wagner. It explains at once its weakness and its strength. It accounts even for his domestic history, while it does not justify it. His first wife was a good woman, and in a way he loved her. But she was never able to become an essential part of his life, because she could not enter into his artistic thoughts and purposes. Hence she was unable to control his impulses to wander. Cosima von Bülow understood him. . . . To her Wagner was constant in spite of the fact that temperamentally he was an inconstant man. She controlled his desires, and they needed control.[21]

Other writers, of course, turned a blind eye to Wagner's infidelities, just as they smoothed away Sieglinde's. Here is how Freda Winworth neutralized the incest of the Volsung twins: "Such unions, in the case of gods and goddesses, are common to the legends of both Egyptian, classical, and Scandinavian mythology. . . . The divine origin of [Siegmund and Sieglinde] is meant to set their action on a different light from that in which it would appear, had they been the offspring of human parents."[22] But Wagner, who flaunted marital conventions in his own life, purposefully depicted heroes and heroines intolerant of bourgeois mores.

Perhaps the most disingenuous evasion of Wagner's promiscuity was fashioned by the Bayreuth apostle Houston Stewart Chamberlain for the October and November 1898 issues of *Ladies Home Journal*. Addressing "The Personal Side of Richard Wagner," Chamberlain stressed Wagner's domesticity. He "never spent an evening outside his home." He was "moderate in all his habits." His "fortress was his home." He "could not live without the love and companionship of a noble-hearted woman." He married a beautiful woman who, unfortunately, gave him no children—"which somewhat marred their happiness, for he adored children." She died in 1866, "after almost 30 years of married life." Shortly afterward, Wagner wed Cosima. Thus were readers of the *Journal* spared hearing that Cosima had lived with Wagner since 1864, and that their first child was born the following year.

For Chamberlain, an Englishman turned German, Wagner was not the tenacious entrepreneur he seemed to some admiring Americans. Rather, his Old World image of the Artist dictated that "Wagner was not what we should call a businessman. For this a considerable store of healthy egoism is requisite, and Wagner possessed none at all. I know of no single act of his whole life which could be interpreted as a wish to do himself a good turn, amass riches, or to seek honorary distinctions."

As ever, Wagner beheld reveals the eye of the beholder. Chamberlain—whose Wagner portrait is as cynically manipulative as American worshipers like Finck were ingenuous—supported Hitler's National Socialists until his death in 1927.

The Met's German seasons enthralled New York's German population. That (as we have seen) local *Singvereine* participated onstage in *Die Meistersinger* supports the reasonable assumption that this German American Wagner constituency—like the Italian American audience for Italian opera—included the plain as well as the pedigreed. And there were non-Germans—on some Wagner nights, comprising half the audience—who cherished Wagner. Even the boxholders included gentlemen like George Washington Vanderbilt, who spoke six languages and cultivated the company of artists.

Still, over time, the boxholders were bound to rebel. For many of them, Wagner was always an expedience—his operas sold tickets. They arrived late and left early. They objected to the German policy, new in its day, of darkening the auditorium. They claimed the prerogative to converse as they pleased. The Wagner diet also inflamed the city's Italians, tired of Germanophile jibes against "hurdy gurdy" Donizetti and Bellini (a style of derision conveying class bias against immigrant street culture).

Lilli Lehmann, who always knew best, claimed in her memoirs to have warned Seidl and Edmund Stanton in 1889 that the repertoire "was made up of too much . . . Wagner, which would become an excessive amount in the long run."[23] This concern was taken to heart in the fall of 1890. The new season included two Italian premieres (sung in German, of course): Alberto Franchetti's *Asrael*, which opened the season on November 2 with Seidl in the pit, and Anton Smareglia's *Il vassallo di Szigeth*, also led by Seidl, on December 12. A third premiere, conducted by Seidl on January 9, was *Diana von Solange* by Ernst II, Duke of Saxe-Coburg-Gotha. The Wagner repertoire, meanwhile, was trimmed to *The Flying Dutchman*, *Tannhäuser*, and *Lohengrin*. These concessions backfired. The new operas pleased no one. To sell tickets, Stanton abandoned his schedule and reverted to the usual Wagner list, beginning with *Die Meistersinger*. *Siegfried*, *Die Walküre*, *Götterdämmerung*, and *Tristan und Isolde* followed, as did a concert of excerpts from *Parsifal*. But the axe had already fallen. On January 14—the night *Die Meistersinger* returned—the directors announced a plan secretly conceived the previous summer: that, beginning in 1891–92, the house would be turned over to Henry Abbey, who would present performances in Italian and French only.

To Germans and other Wagnerites, the edict seemed incredible. For the remainder of the season, Seidl's every appearance unleashed a demonstration in favor of the outgoing management. For the penultimate performance, of *Tristan* on March 20, tickets sold for as much as fifteen dollars, and hundreds were turned away. The orchestra greeted Seidl with a *Tusch*—a fanfare—when he appeared to lead the third act. After the *Liebestod* the audience would not leave. The following afternoon the season closed with *Die Meistersinger*. W. J. Henderson reported in the *Times*: "After the performance the scene was wonderful. For fully half an hour the people stayed in the house, applauding, cheering, stamping, and waving handkerchiefs." Fischer, who was making his farewell appearance in his greatest role, was showered with flowers and wreaths. He briefly spoke in English: "Ladies and gentlemen, it is impossible for me to express what I feel for your kindness and love; and I hope it is not the last time that I shall sing for you here, on this stage, in German." Seidl was presented with flowers by every member of the chorus. Eventually, inevitably, he was compelled to appear alone. The crowd's enthusiasm now grew to an avalanche of sound, a combination of celebration and dismay. Seidl gestured for quiet and managed to stammer: "Believe me, ladies and gentlemen, I understand the meaning of this great demonstration. For myself, the orchestra, and the other members of the company, I thank you." Then, overcome, he hastily left the stage. Only the appearance of workmen breaking down the sets persuaded the crowd that the last German season had ended.[24]

According to advocates of the new regime, the novelty of the German seasons had diminished, and so had the financial advantages. The assessments per box had grown to $3,200. The floating debt now totaled more than $4,000. According to defenders of the old regime, German opera retained its popularity, and the debt was partly caused by more than $46,000 in unpaid assessments to box-holders. Krehbiel, in the *Tribune*, produced a table showing that Wagner performances averaged $3,209.46 in receipts for 1890–91—somewhat lower than previous years. The average for non-Wagner performances during the same period dropped from $3,056.71 to $2,605.37. The average audience for Wagner was twenty-seven hundred, versus two thousand for *Asreal*, *Il Vassalo*, and *Diana*.*[25]

---

* I will not attempt to sort out whether the German seasons continued to make financial sense. Paul E. Eisler, in *The Metropolitan Opera: The First Twenty-five Years, 1883–1908* (Croton-on-Hudson, N.Y., 1984), summarizes: "The complete figures will

Abbey, who had managed the house during its first and only non-German season of 1883–84, pledged to limit losses to the costs of operating the building. He would share responsibility with Maurice Grau, who had previously worked with Abbey and with Clara Louise Kellogg, among others. (A third partner, John Schoeffel of Boston, was silent.) Legions of famous vocalists—a list including Campanini, Lehmann, Patti, and the de Reszke brothers—would be engaged. Ticket prices would be raised. The repertoire would include *Lohengrin*, *The Flying Dutchman*, and *Die Meistersinger*—but in Italian. The credibility of the new plan was enhanced by Abbey's experience at the Met in the spring of 1887, when his touring company, including Patti, took in $70,000 for six performances—compared to $137,000 in receipts for the entire German subscription season.[26]

In Krehbiel's opinion, the directors had sold out. Echoing the *Staats-Zeitung*, for which the German seasons had fulfilled "a great educational mission," he deplored the forfeiture of a serious and reformist audience "with intelligent tastes and warm affections." The Met, he believed, had condemned opera to remain an exotic diversion for a privileged elite. Discouragingly timely a century later is the denunciation he flung at the house's new operators: "The

---

almost certainly never be known. The available evidence, however, confirms that for at least the majority of its years, the German opera period was as financially successful as unsponsored opera on a grand scale might be expected to be" (p. 170). Also see Henry Krehbiel, *Chapters of Opera* (New York, 1909; rpt. 1980), p. 212; and Martin Mayer, *The Met: One Hundred Years of Grand Opera* (New York, 1983), p. 64. In any event, the burden on the shareholders must be placed in perspective. John Diziges, in *Opera in America: A Cultural History* (New Haven, 1993), writes:

> Wall Street millionaires like to think of themselves as Fifth Avenue Medicis, princely patrons of the arts. The actual extent of their patronage, as opposed to their self-congratulation about it, was niggardly. The annual operatic assessment for *all* thirty-five shareholders was less, for an entire decade, than what Morgan paid for one Old Master. The Breakers, the Vanderbilt palace in Newport, cost $2.5 million in 1895. Mrs. Pembroke Jones set aside $300,000 annually for her Newport summer entertainment. Many dinner parties cost more than the opera's season subscription. Balls and costume parties were fabulously expensive. The Bradley Martin ball of 1897, so extravagant that even the rich were impressed, cost $369,000. By comparison, operatic expenditure was a trifle. (pp. 290–91.)

fickleness of public taste, the popular craving for sensation, the ego-
tism and rapacity of the artists, the lack of high purpose in the pro-
moters, the domination of fashion instead of love for art, the lack of
real artistic culture—all these things have stood from the beginning,
as they still stand, in the way of a permanent foundation of opera in
New York."[27]

In 1888, as we have seen, Henry Finck had exulted: "There is no
hope for the Italianissimi, who sigh for their macaronic arias and the
'Ernani' and 'Gazza ladra' soup." In fact, there was no hope for the
Wagnerization Finck believed had occurred. That the future of opera
was wholly German, that the symphony, too, was a German preserve,
were potent ideas in fin-de-siècle America. The former idea, especially, could never have endured. But it altered the future all the
same. In 1873, John Knowles Paine could portray the fierce "war of
opinion" that "divided the musical world into two hostile camps,"
pro and contra Wagner. A mere generation later, the war of opinion
was forgotten. Wagner, if no longer dominant at the Met, was
entrenched. New York would soon discover that it could no more
exist without opera in German than with opera in German only.

Partial Eclipse

"Radiant with happiness Dr. Antonin Dvorak listened to the second concert of the Philharmonic Society in Carnegie Music Hall last evening," wrote the *New York Herald* on December 17, 1893, reviewing one of the most significant concerts ever given by the New York Philharmonic.

The famous Bohemian composer is indeed difficult to please if he was not gratified with the enthusiasm created in the immense audience by his new fifth symphony in E minor, "From the New World."

He received a genuine ovation after the second movement—the larghetto [*sic*]. The applause swelled to a perfect tumult. Every face was turned in the direction in which Anton Seidl was looking. Every neck was craned so that it might be discovered to whom he was motioning so energetically. Whoever it was, he seemed modestly to wish to remain at the back of the box on the second tier.

At last a broad shouldered individual of medium height, and as straight as one of the pines in the forests of which his music whispered so eloquently, is descried by the eager watchers. A murmur sweeps through the hall. "Dvorak! Dvorak!" is the word that passes from mouth to mouth. . . .

With hands trembling with emotion Dr. Dvorak waves an acknowledgement of his indebtedness to Anton Seidl, to the orchestra, to the audience, and then disappears into the background while the remainder of the work goes on. . . .

As Dr. Dvorak has said the symphony has been inspired by a close study of the native melodies of the North American Indians and the negro race of this country.

This study resulted in the discovery that in all essential particulars the national music of the two races is identical. The scale is characterized by the absence of the fourth and the seventh tones. The minor scale also has its own individual peculiarities. Instead of the seventh being omitted, in the minor it is the sixth tone which is lacking. . . .

[At the close of the performance,] the composer was loudly called for. Again and again he bowed his acknowledgements, and again and again the applause burst forth.

Even after he had left his box and was walking about in the corridor the applause continued. And finally he returned to the gallery railing, and then what a reception he received! The musicians, led by Mr. Seidl, applauded until the place rang again.

Three aspects of this review—all typical of the times, atypical today—bear stressing. The first is its extraordinary length: about two thousand words. The second is the focus on music rather than the performance, about which the writer—probably Albert Steinberg—only remarks that it "was a most poetical one." The third—which our extract briefly samples—is the detailed description and appreciation of a symphony by a living composer: twelve meaty paragraphs, accounting structure and harmony, method and effect. The remainder of the program, including the star soloist, is allotted a single sentence: "The orchestra played the 'Midsummer Night's Dream' music, and Henri Marteau played Brahms' violin concerto with an original cadenza by himself." As with Seidl's Wagner performances, new music was the compelling first topic for music-lovers and critics alike.* The *New World* Symphony premiere encapsulates a moment, a century ago, when audience and composer were one.

*According to the musicologist Michael Beckerman, at least ten major articles in the New York press, including two with musical notation, devoted serious consideration to the *New World* Symphony on the occasion of its premiere.

With the demise of the Metropolitan Opera's German seasons in 1891, Seidl's New World mission lost its central vehicle. Fortuitously, 1890–91 was also Theodore Thomas's final season as conductor of the New York Philharmonic.

Thomas had led the Philharmonic since 1877, presiding over what had been the orchestra's most successful seasons artistically and financially. But the Philharmonic remained a part-time ensemble, giving only six pairs of concerts a year. As I have earlier noted, Thomas longed for a full-time, fully endowed orchestra such as the Boston Symphony, and he found one in Chicago, for which he departed with sixty musicians in tow.

There was a second reason Thomas left New York: he had been displaced. Henry Finck came upon him one evening and innocently inquired: "Hello! Are you still alive?" Thomas bristled: "Yes, and more than ever!" Finck later commented: "I had simply meant by my question that I had not seen him for a long time, whereas he, with his abnormal sensitiveness, twisted it into an indication that I had thought him musically dead and buried."[1]

And so the Philharmonic hired Seidl. Under Thomas, its musicians and repertoire were already predominantly German. Seidl brought with him the disenfranchised audience for German opera. Given the diverse Wagner constituency he served, he also sustained the Philharmonic's increasing attractiveness to the richest and most prominent New Yorkers.

During Thomas's last season, receipts had totaled $28,246—more than ever before. Under Seidl, receipts began at $29,306, and grew steadily to $34,323. In 1897, two more pairs of concerts were added, and receipts rose to almost $50,000. Even the depression of 1893 did not slow the Philharmonic's progress toward higher sales and dividends. Celebrity soloists became affordable as never before. It was under Seidl, too, that the Philharmonic moved into the new Music Hall built by Andrew Carnegie.*[2]

---

*In his *Autobiography* (London, 1920), pp. 48–50, Carnegie would describe his first encounter with the *Lohengrin* Prelude, which "thrilled me as a new revelation. Here was a genius, indeed, different from all before, a new leader on which to climb upward."

In terms of repertoire, Seidl programmed more Beethoven and less Wagner than elsewhere—the Philharmonic had its traditions. But the Philharmonic programs represented a fraction of Seidl's symphonic concerts during this period. He commanded the services of dozens of fine free-lance musicians variously constituting the "Metropolitan Orchestra," "Seidl Orchestra," or "Seidl Society Orchestra." He and his men also toured. In Utica and Rochester, Boston and Philadelphia, Baltimore and Pittsburgh, Cleveland and Dayton, St. Louis and Cincinnati, his fame preceded him. And Wagner was his calling card.[3]

Like Theodore Thomas before him, Seidl became New York's leading symphonic conductor. Like Thomas, he craved a permanent orchestra such as Boston's. He wanted stable personnel, adequate rehearsal time, a consistent venue. Still, his impact, as Thomas's antipode, was great.

In the concert room no less than in the opera pit, Seidl was the embodiment of Wagner: his music, his conducting, his manual "On Conducting." His espousal of Wagnerian license ensured unusual results.

Seidl's Beethoven crystallized his new approach. Wagner the heaven-storming conductor had identified with Beethoven the heaven-storming composer—as in this passage, from "On Conducting," on the fermata ending the four-note motto beginning the Fifth Symphony:

> Our conductors hardly make use of this fermata for anything. . . . In most cases the note . . . is not held any longer than a forte produced with a careless stroke of the bow will last upon the stringed instruments. Now, suppose the voice of Beethoven were heard from the grave admonishing a conductor: "Hold my fermata firmly, terribly! I did not write fermatas in jest, or because I was at a loss how to proceed; I indulge in the fullest, the most sustained tone to express emotions in my Adagio; and I use this full and firm tone when I

want it in a passionate Allegro as a rapturous or terrible spasm. Then the very life blood of the tone shall be extracted to the last drop."

In a more analytical vein, Wagner argued that, compared to the "absolute" or "naive" sonata-allegro movements of Mozart and Haydn—an early species, propelled at a steady pace—Beethoven's "sentimental" allegros, emotionally varied structures infused with song, require "modification of tempo" as a "sine qua non." In the first movement of the *Eroica*, for instance, Wagner specifically cites the modulating bridge at measure 83 and the development's new tune at measure 284 as moments requiring extra time and special attention. The finale, again, transforms a traditional form: the theme-with-variations. Compared to earlier variation sets, it traverses a broader range of feeling and more cunningly organizes the whole; "accordingly it should be interpreted with as much variety as possible." An example from the variations movement of the *Kreutzer* Sonata illustrates one thing Wagner has in mind: accelerating or retarding the end of one variation gradually to approach the tempo of the next. Wagner's ultimate Beethoven interpretation was of the Ninth Symphony, a significant inspiration for his own operas. Its slow movement was for him the apex of Germanic *Innigkeit*.

> In a certain delicate sense it may be said of the pure Adagio that it cannot be taken too slowly. A rapt confidence in the sufficiency of pure musical speech should reign here; the languor of feeling grows to ecstasy. . . . None of our conductors are courageous enough to take an Adagio in this manner. . . . I am, perhaps, the only conductor who has ventured to take the Adagio section of the third movement of the Ninth Symphony at the pace proper to its peculiar character. This character is distinctly contrasted with that of the alternating Andante in triple time; but our conductors invariably contrive to obliterate the difference, leaving only the rhythmical change between square and triple time.[4]

Seidl heard Wagner discuss Beethoven interpretation on hundreds of occasions. He heard Wagner conduct Beethoven. In an interview in the *New York Tribune*, he said:

I am convinced that Beethoven never made any metronome music and that consequently his symphonies are not to be played according to the metronome. We have too many proofs of his manner of conducting not to have firm ground for believing that although Beethoven put many more marks of expression in his music than Mozart, for instance, he nevertheless left the greater part of the question of interpretation with the conductor. Naturally to play "in tempo" is the simplest way to get along with Beethoven, but a conductor who has grown up under the musico-educational influences of to-day would be ashamed to stand before an intelligent orchestra as a wooden time beater.[5]

When Seidl conducted the *Eroica* in New York, the Funeral March, as I have noted, was faster than under other conductors, as was the Scherzo—albeit with a slower Trio. His plasticity of pulse in the outer movements was considered an innovation; like Wagner, he read both with maximum expressive variety. His *Pastorale* eschewed the polished breadth and serenity of Thomas's; he made the storm cataclysmic. The accompanying table shows metronome markings Krehbiel recorded for Seidl and Thomas in the Seventh Symphony. The most startling tempo here is for Seidl's finale; he adheres to Wagner's advice in "On Conducting" that "it is . . . impossible to take [this movement] too quickly." In the Eighth Symphony, following Wagner's instructions, Seidl accelerated the second movement and slowed down the third.* [6]

Wagner's principles of interpretation—which his essay applies to Bach and Weber as well as to the *Eroica* and *Die Meistersinger*—have the effect of Wagnerizing all the music he touches. This was Seidl's way. His Bach and Mozart were formidably, zealously Romantic. The former he played in his own transcriptions for modern orchestra. Of Mozart, he gravitated to *Don Giovanni*, which he led only

---

*Seidl was repeatedly found to take less time in a symphony or opera than the norm—not because he slighted the slow passages but because of the alacrity with which he sped up. A careless reading of Wagner's "On Conducting" suggests a penchant for slow tempos, contradicting the brisk Mendelssohn. Actually, Wagner reports dispatching the *Tannhäuser* Overture in twelve minutes—versus the "20-minute" versions of less competent conductors. In the *Meistersinger* Prelude, he prescribes, as a basic tempo, a "true animated Allegro." Tellingly, he beats the shortened

Metronome Markings for Beethoven's Seventh Symphony

	Beethoven	Seidl	Thomas
Poco sostenuto, quarter notes	69	60	60
Vivace, [dotted] quarter notes	104	110	104
Allegretto, quarter notes	76	64	60
Presto, dotted half notes	132	128	100
Assai meno presto, dotted half notes	84	60	60
Allegro con brio, half notes	72	92	82

three times at the Met, yet liberally sampled in concert. An illuminating review once reported:

> It was worth while to learn how Mozart's music would [fare when put] through the Wagnerian sieve. . . . The overture alone took on a new physiognomy from Mr. Seidl's drastic methods which we consider worthy of praise. The opening chords best reflected the good in his principles of interpretation. They were held with adamantine firmness for the full time indicated (and a little more) without loss in quantity or quality of sound, and exemplified strikingly the value of sustained tone which Wagner in his book "On Conducting" asserts is the basis of all expression. In the allegro and portions of the finale, [and] most flagrantly in the buffo air "Madamina," however, we missed the lightness and humor which are as essential an ingredient of Mozart's score as the tragic element.

Equally suggestive is this 1892 review of Seidl's Schubert Ninth.

> It was a subjective yet sympathetic performance, and if it was not exactly Schubert that he gave . . . it was felt to be just as good and to be more enjoyable and interesting than a coldly correct and analytical performance of the work. He gave it an oriental opulence of color, a dramatic emphasis of expression, a variety in shading, and

---

version of the main theme at measure 122 in two, not four. The close of the prelude is not distended (as in many present-day performances) but essentially resumes the initial allegro. Seidl was sometimes favorably compared to Bayreuth conductors who, allegedly under Cosima's baneful influence, slowed down Wagner's tempos. Timings of *Parsifal* kept at Bayreuth, however, clock Seidl at 259 minutes for *Parsifal*—four minutes *longer* than Felix Mottl in 1888, only seven minutes shorter than Karl Muck in 1901. Hermann Levi's 1882 performance, coached by Wagner, lasted 244 minutes.

he played it with a great amount of energy. There was a steady increase in tempo through the first movement and the finale was taken at express speed, being rendered presto throughout.[7]

After Wagner, Liszt may have been the composer Seidl conducted the most in concert. Of his contemporaries, he also especially championed Rubinstein, Dvořák, and Saint-Saëns. He gave the American premiere of Bruckner's Fourth. He followed Wagner in his antipathy for Brahms—though, according to Krehbiel, he excelled in the finale from the Fourth Symphony. His huge orchestral library included hundreds of miniatures, many transcribed from piano originals by Seidl himself. He frequently programmed Mendelssohn's *Midsummer Night's Dream* music and Grieg's *Peer Gynt*. In addition to Berlioz, whom he honored as a precursor to Wagner, he performed quantities of French music by Bizet, Delibes, and Massenet. His favorite Italian instrumental numbers seem to have been the Intermezzos from *Cavalleria rusticana* and *Pagliacci*. In Russian repertoire, Tchaikovsky's *Pathétique* Symphony uniquely appealed to Seidl's temperament.* He wept when conducting it. Finck called the *Pathétique* Seidl's "last love . . . , which he conducted with more

---

*When Tchaikovsky visited New York in 1891 for the opening of Carnegie Hall, he was amazed to discover himself "ten times better known in America than in Europe"—testimony both to America's affinity for Tchaikovsky and to the sophistication of its symphonic culture. For the *New York Morning Journal* of May 3, he wrote an article in which he claimed that "Wagner was a great symphonist, but not a composer of opera." He also complained that the dogma of Wagnerism precluded true appreciation of other composers. Seidl (who of course met Tchaikovsky in New York) replied seven days later in the same newspaper. Wagner, he maintained, was necessarily and essentially a "composer of opera." He continued:

> Much as been written lately about the "Wagner craze," the burning of incense at Wagner's shrine, about how Wagner is over-estimated, concerning the intolerance of Wagnerites and their delusion that he is the only great one, etc. All this belongs in the realm of imagination. . . . No honest musician would idolize one composer and condemn all the rest. Some people endeavor to make it appear that I myself have a weakness in this respect, but I would declare once for all that this is wrong.
>
> If there was too much Wagner in the Metropolitan Opera House, it was not my fault at all, but Wagner's as he had composed those operas the New York public liked best.

(See Elkhonon Yoffe, *Tchaikovsky in America* [New York, 1986], pp. 71–72, 125–127.)

overwhelming passion at every repetition." The *Musical Courier* ranked his performance of the symphony's *Adagio lamentoso* among his "most masterful. . . . He displayed an emotional stress and imagination seldom equalled."* [8]

Seidl's core affinities—for Wagner, for Liszt, for Wagnerized Beethoven—demonstrate that, like all nineteenth-century performers, he specialized in the music of his own time and place. It follows that he eventually took a particular interest in the new music of America's composers.

When Seidl led the premiere of the *New World* Symphony at Carnegie Music Hall, no aspect of the work was more discussed than its "American" accent. Dvořák himself had commented in the *New York Herald* six months earlier:

> I am now satisfied that the future of music in this country must be founded upon what are called the Negro melodies. This must be the real foundation of any serious and original school of composition to be developed in the United States. When I came here last year I was impressed with this idea and it has developed into a settled conviction. These beautiful and varied themes are the product of the soil. . . . There is nothing in the whole range of composition that cannot be supplied with themes from this source.

In New York, the young African American composer Harry T. Burleigh had sung spirituals for Dvořák. Dvořák was also intrigued by the *Song of Hiawatha*, which he had first read in a Czech translation years before. The middle movements of the *New World*

---

*The last conductor to champion something like Seidl's interpretive predilections was Wilhelm Furtwängler, who was thirty-six years Seidl's junior and who outlived him by fifty-six years. Furtwängler's massive *Brandenburg* concertos and *Don Giovanni*, his Dionysian moldings of the Ninth Symphonies of Beethoven and Schubert, his turbulently Germanic *Pathétique*, made Wagner the measure of all things. Furtwängler was a throwback; by the time he died, in 1954, a new chameleon species of performance specialists, of versatile eclecticists, had taken over.

Symphony, it was known, were partly inspired by passages from Longfellow's poem. In fact, the symphony was said to have been generally influenced by Dvořák's examinations of American Indian and African American melodies. According to the *Herald*: "He created original themes which partook of the characteristics which he had discovered in the native music. These themes he employed as the subjects, the backbone of his composition, developing, harmonizing and accompanying them in every manner which musical science and modern theories of harmony could suggest. The result is a great work of art." Some American reviewers likened the symphony's "tremendous energy and vivacity" to American life. In the opinion of Krehbiel, among others, Dvořák himself, born a butcher's son, was especially drawn to America because his life had been "a study of manifest destiny, of signal triumph over obstacle and discouraging environment."[9]

The *New World* Symphony was sensationally popular, an instantaneous source of American pride. But not everyone agreed that Dvořák's method was propitious for American music. The concentrated cultural community into which the symphony was thrust included America's own composers. Some, like Edward MacDowell in his *Indian* Suite, had preceded Dvořák along a similar path. Others, in nuanced and compelling commentaries, rejected self-conscious Americanisms. John Knowles Paine wrote: "The time is past when composers are to be classed according to geographical limits. It is not a question of nationality, but individuality, and individuality of style is not the result of imitation—whether of folk songs, negro melodies, the tunes of the heathen Chinese or Digger Indians, but of personal character and inborn originality. During the present century musical art has overstepped all national limits." In the same vein, William Foster Apthorp argued that the ineffable essence of language, folksong, and temperament, rather than folk or folk-derived tunes, would ultimately infuse American music with Americanness.[10]

A central figure in this quest for an indigenous musical culture was Jeannette Thurber, whom we have already encountered as a champion of opera in English. Her National Conservatory of Music was conceived as a breeding ground for American composers and performers, American symphony and song. Thurber strategized that an eminent nationalist composer from abroad would both confer status on her enterprise and show the way toward an American idiom. In a triumph of persistence, she persuaded Dvořák to become the second director of the new school. She hired Seidl to teach conducting. In New York, Dvořák and Seidl were fast friends. Seidl's friend Krehbiel also befriended Dvořák. We can only guess how these individuals—Thurber, Dvořák, Seidl, Krehbiel—interacted in pursuit of common aims.[11]

No less than Dvořák, Seidl—who became the *New World* Symphony's central exponent—greeted the United States with inquisitive interest rather than Old World arrogance. It became well known that he considered MacDowell, whose successful career had begun in Germany, a greater composer than Brahms. He conducted MacDowell's Second Piano Concerto both in Brooklyn and with the Philharmonic, and also led the Philharmonic in the *Indian* Suite. He championed the music of his friend and protégé Victor Herbert, most notably the Second Cello Concerto—an important Philharmonic premiere, with the composer as soloist. As notable was his patient interest in lesser Americans, such as Henry Waller, who studied with Dvořák at Thurber's conservatory, and whose *Cleopatra* Prelude he performed. Waller later wrote:

> The first time I met Mr. Seidl was . . . when I had just finished the score of my first opera, *The Ogalallas*. I shall never forget his kindness to me when I presented myself to him, a complete stranger and with a very bulky manuscript under my arm. I believe the servants of most conductors have standing orders to admit no one carrying any sort of a parcel which looks as if a manuscript might be concealed in it. Mr. Seidl, though, was kind to everyone who went to him for his advice or assistance; whether he knew them or not did not matter. As an example of this I may mention that he examined carefully the score of my opera . . . , suggested many alterations, and took a great amount of trouble for one he had never seen before. This was the beginning of my acquaintance with him, and he always showed the same kindness and interest.

According to Henry Holden Huss:

> Few musicians would have bothered themselves as he did . . . to listen to a violin concerto, to go into the pros and cons of the instrumentation, whether the solo instrument was allowed due prominence, etc., in all displaying a discriminating musicianship and keen appreciation of musical perspective which is, alas, so often lacking in otherwise great conductors. Although boasting at the time of but a very slight acquaintance with him, this was but the first of many conferences about this and other of my compositions, and it mattered not whether his criticisms were laudatory or otherwise, I never left him without being stirred and inspired to fresh endeavor. A number of my colleagues can testify in the same way of the generous and painstaking interest manifested in their compositions.

The list of the American composers Seidl played also includes Howard Brockway, Dudley Buck, George Whitefield Chadwick, Arthur Farwell, Arthur Foote, and George Templeton Strong. His commitment to American music strengthened over time; as of 1897, it was his enunciated policy to perform it as frequently as possible—a policy frustrated on at least one occasion by the Philharmonic Society.[12]

It is scarcely irrelevant or unsurprising that Wagner's influence on America's composers peaked before World War I. Seidl's admiration for MacDowell reflected MacDowell's admiration for Liszt and Wagner—obvious influences on his symphonic and keyboard pieces. Walter Damrosch, while no friend of Seidl's, composed a couple of Wagnerian American operas: *The Scarlet Letter*, which Seidl chidingly termed "a New England Nibelung trilogy,"* and which Damrosch's own company mounted in 1896; and *Cyrano*, staged by the Met in 1913. Horatio Parker's *Mona* (1910), a cross between *Norma* and

---

*According to Henry Krehbiel: "The nixies of the Rhine peeped out of the sun-flecked coverts in the forest around Hester Prynne's hut, as if they had become dryads for her sake; ever and anon the sinister Hunding was heard muttering in the ear of Chillingworth, and Hester wore the badge of her shame on the robes of Elsa, washed in innocency." (*Chapters of Opera*, [New York, 1909; rpt. 1980], p. 262.)

Parsifal, won a Metropolitan Opera competition; produced there in 1912, it received four performances and respectful reviews. A fourth American opera with Wagnerian features was Victor Herbert's *Natoma*, a succès d'estime in Philadelphia in 1911. Among the more obscure Wagnerian operas by Americans were Eduard de Sobolewski's *Mohega, The Flower of the Forest*, produced in Milwaukee in 1859; Silas G. Pratt's *Zenobia* and *The Triumph of Columbus*, presented in New York and Chicago; Homer Moore's *Ring*-inspired *American Trilogy*, which was never staged; and Arthur Nevin's *Poia*, given in Berlin in 1910.[13]

Seidl himself embarked on an American Indianist opera on the same subject that Dvořák hoped to use for an opera or oratorio: Hiawatha. He started not with Longfellow's version, but with the Iroquois legend connecting Hiawatha with the founding of the Confederacy of the Five Nations. The result would be an operatic trilogy, an "American *Nibelungenlied*." Seidl procured examples of Indian music from Krehbiel and MacDowell. He engaged as his librettist Francis Neilson,* who had already worked on a Hiawatha libretto for Dvořák's abortive cantata (sketches for which supplied themes for the *New World* Symphony). Though he often improvised at the piano and had prepared many transcriptions for his concert programs, Seidl had never before composed ambitiously. At the time of Seidl's death, Neilson had completed the first two acts of the initial three-act opera, *Manabozo*, and Seidl had sketched all of act 1. Neilson subsequently finished and published the *Manabozo* libretto. According to a 1906 newspaper account:

> It has all the mysticism—almost vagueness—that characterize both the Wagnerian conception of music-drama and Ojibway tradition. It deals, as does the "Ring," with personages who have human passions and magic powers, and who seem to work with an illogical but fascinating mixture of free will and fatalism for the ultimate advancement of the human race. And "Nanabozho" [*sic*] is dramatic. There are moments in it when a silent reading of the text stirs the blood and fires the imagination, and the climax, the

*See page 130.

invisible chorus of Nature announcing the birth of the prophet, is remarkably poetic.[14]

In other words, Seidl's version of American opera combined American myth, Wagnerian technique, and the Indian tunes that stirred Dvořák.* He believed in the civilizing influence of New World music dramas—as a source of national and not merely musical identity. On one occasion, he proposed William Dean Howells as a likely librettist. Addressing "The Development of Music in America" in 1892, he maintained that the future of music would necessarily derive from Wagnerian theory and practice. Americans, he continued, "are a musical people. Their taste is still unformed, but it is naturally a good one and is sure to grow in the right direction." But proper cultivation was required. This meant, firstly, opera in the vernacular. "No satisfactory artistic results can be achieved here, nor can America produce any national music, until opera is given in English. I look forward to the time when American composers shall produce great operatic works of a distinctly original character written in the vernacular; but until that time comes I believe that such foreign works as are performed here should be translated into English. . . . The singers whom America imports in such large numbers from abroad do undoubtedly a great deal of good, but they also do harm, for they bring influences which are essentially un-American."[15]

Seidl also stressed the need for more systematic musical training. In particular, America needed a sophisticated school of opera, sup-

---

*Seidl's article, "Wagner's Influence on Present-Day Composers," in the January 1894 *North American Review*, expresses a different point of view. Here he calls Indian musical sources "pretty thin" and "lacking in those majestic elements which Wagner found in the norse legends." He also surmises that the "negro melodies" cited by Dvořák came originally from Europe, although it was "quite possible that the servitude of the negroes, or the laziness of their dispositions, gave to the melodies the melancholy cadence, the slow movement, that is characteristic of them"—all this serving to illustrate the point "that America has no national music, and is not likely to produce music free from European traditions. This fact, however, cannot be considered in the least as a discouragement to American composers. . . . There is every reason why they should rejoice that thus far they have not been enslaved by Wagner's influence, as their brother-workers in Germany have been."

planting study abroad. Not only singers, but orchestral players and conductors would enroll. Three or four operas would be publicly produced every year. "Such a plan . . . may seem impracticable, but I am convinced that if it were carried out under the best auspices, that is, controlled by persons who had the interest of music at heart, it would surely be a success. But if it were controlled simply by the rich who regarded music as a mere diversion, it would surely be a failure." On another occasion, Seidl wrote: "The musical bent of the Americans is retarded in its development partly by social conditions, partly by the need of premature money-earning. Here is a field of activity for wealthy philanthropists. America does not need gorgeous halls and concert rooms for its musical development, but music schools with competent teachers, and many, very many, free scholarships for talented young disciples who are unable to pay the expense of study."[16]

Though the Seidl articles I have cited appeared in English, it is perfectly plausible that Krehbiel, who sometimes quoted Seidl in English-language "interviews" that could only have been conducted in German, had a hand in writing them. Krehbiel, too, happened to believe that Wagnerian music drama pointed the way toward a significant American operatic tradition, and that only once opera in the vernacular was practiced and supported would the great American opera be composed.*

Wagnerism was not a mere import cultivated by imported Germans. America influenced the meliorism of the New World Wagner cult. The Wagner cult influenced American aspirations toward an independent cultural identity.

---

*Joseph Mussulman, in *Music in the Cultured Generation: A Social History of Music in America, 1880 to 1900* (Evanston, Ill., 1971), amplifies: "The majority of the [genteel] Culture-guardians . . . were unalterably in favor of opera in the vernacular." Unfortunately, Mussulman continues, only "great stars," singing in foreign tongues, could draw money from the "Barbarians"—by which he means persons of wealth for whom opera was a necessary social ritual (p. 140).

The story of Wagner and Seidl at the Metropolitan Opera after 1891 is a story of gradual re-engagement. The story begins with gusts of bitterness from the exiled Wagnerites, and stoic silence from their leader. In *Harper's*, George Curtis seethed sarcastically:

> The axiom . . . that men are queer, has been strongly confirmed recently by a decision of the authorities of the Metropolitan Opera-House in New York. That important body, producing the figures, has announced in effect that as it is clear from the accounts that the presentation of German opera is more profitable than that of Italian and French opera combined, it is evident that the public desires to hear Italian and French opera, and therefore for the present the German opera will be discontinued. . . . It is a striking illustration of the superiority of man to money, and in the mad struggle for a mere material advantage, this devotion to pure art, condemning the expense, is a notable tribute to the unselfishness of human nature.[17]

Wagner was still given, but in Italian, and conducted by Luigi Mancinelli and Auguste Vianesi—renditions of which Henry Finck later wrote: "Future generations will read with amazement that New York listened for years to second and third rate performances of Wagner's great works while Anton Seidl was looking on idle, neglected and despondent." Finck and others complained, as well, that orchestral and choral standards declined under the new regime. Seidl returned to the Met at the end of the 1891–92 season to lead four performances in Italian of *Die Meistersinger* and one of *The Flying Dutchman*. The company also gave *Fidelio* in Italian, conducted by Louis Saar. Krehbiel remarked of these three offerings:

> Curious questionings were raised by the production of "Fidelio" and "Die Meistersinger" in Italian. It was generally recognized that Mr. Abbey offered them as sops to Cerberus; but the German element in the population, which they were designed to appease, plainly were lacking in that peculiar bent of mind necessary to understand why Beethoven's opera done in Italian with a cast one-half good was supposed by the management to be worth two-thirds

more than the same opera done in a language which it could understand with a cast all good (two of the principals, Mme. Lehmann and Mr. Kalisch, being the same), during the preceding seven years. Was the Italian language sixty-seven per cent. more valuable than the German in an opera conceived in German, written in German, and composed in the German spirit by a German? The public thought not, and "Fidelio" had only two performances. A more kindly view was taken of the Italian "Meistersinger," which enabled the Germans to give expression to their feelings by making demonstrations over Mr. Seidl. There was much to admire, moreover, in the singing and acting of Jean de Reszke as Walther, and [Jean] Lassalle as Hans Sachs. There was nothing of the conventional operatic marionette in these men.[18]

In fact, the arrivals of Edouard and Jean de Reszke, and of Lassalle, proved a boon to Wagner. A fire gutted the stage and auditorium of the Met on August 27, 1892, canceling the 1892–93 season. The season after, the German list comprised seventeen performances of *Tannhäuser, Lohengrin,* and *Die Meistersinger,* all in Italian. In 1894–95, there were thirteen performances of *Lohengrin* and *Die Meistersinger.* The Met's astonishing casts for its Wagner-in-Italian performances disclosed new possibilities for vocal splendor: Jean de Reszke as Lohengrin, Nellie Melba as Elisabeth and Elsa, Emma Eames as Elsa and Eva, Lillian Nordica as Elsa and Venus, Victor Maurel as Telramund, Pol Plançon as Landgraf Hermann, King Heinrich, and Pogner, Edouard de Reszke as Sachs. Equally astonishing was that Seidl conducted no Wagner operas at the Met during these two seasons. He was instead given a weekly Saturday night concert, frequently shared with Louis Saar. Onstage with the Met orchestra, he performed programs of overtures, orchestral miniatures, and opera excerpts. His Wagner soloists included Plançon, whose Wotan's Farewell, given twice in February 1894, must have been a model of refinement. And yet the undoubted sensation of these years was Emma Calvé's uninhibited Carmen, first seen on December 20, 1893, and partnered by Jean de Reszke, Lassalle, and Eames. And the outstanding American premiere was of Verdi's *Falstaff*, on February 4, 1895, with Maurel (who had created the title role), Eames, Giuseppe Campanari, and Sofia Scalchi.

Wagnerites did not fail to appreciate the achievements of these seasons—after their fashion. Krehbiel's reaction to *Falstaff*, for example, was typically Germanophile:

> The last vestige of the old subserviency of the text to the music has disappeared. From the first to the last the play is now the dominant factor. There are no "numbers" in "Falstaff"; there can be no repetition of a portion of the music without interruption and dislocation of the action. . . .
>
> And how has this play been set to music? It has been plunged into a perfect sea of melodic champagne. All the dialogue, crisp and sparkling, full of humor in itself, is made crisper, more sparkling, more amusing by the music on which, and in which, it floats, we are almost tempted to say more buoyantly than comedy dialogue has floated since Mozart wrote "Le Nozze di Figaro." The orchestra is bearer of everything, just as completely as it is in the latter-day dramas of Richard Wagner. . . .
>
> The declamation is managed with extraordinary skill, and though it frequently grows out of the instrumental part, it has yet independent melodic value as the vocal parts of Wagner's "Die Meistersinger" have. . . .
>
> The finales of "Falstaff" have been built up with all of Verdi's old-time skill, and sometimes sound like Mozart rubbed through the Wagnerian sieve.

But Krehbiel bristled at suggestions that the new regime was more popular and profitable than the unforgotten German seasons had been. True, the subscription for 1893–94 was ten thousand dollars more than for any German season. But with ticket prices up, total attendance was down. Dvořák, who joined his friends Krehbiel, Seidl, and Thurber in favoring opera in English, refused to patronize the Met; he considered it a rich man's preserve, where "only the upper classes can hear or understand." As for Seidl, he was now privately enduring what Finck called "the years of his eclipse." In a letter of April 2, 1894, Seidl confided his eagerness to retreat to his

Catskills summer home "and forget one of the very unpleasantest seasons of working in art"—a season further complicated by the depressed national economy.[19]

The eclipse began lifting on November 27, 1895, when *Tristan und Isolde* returned to the Metropolitan Opera. For the first time since 1891, Wagner was sung in German. Seidl was the conductor, Nordica the Isolde, Jean and Edouard de Reszke the Tristan and Marke. All three singers worked assiduously with Seidl. In fact, their important Wagnerian careers depended on Seidl's inspiration and instruction. Nordica, who was born Lillian Norton in Farmington, Maine, and whose triumphs surpassed those of all other American singers of the time, was a prodigious worker and striver in the Lilli Lehmann mold. With her Yankee upbringing, she had to struggle to acquire Old World tradition and finesse. Of Seidl, she once wrote:

> One day after devoting three hours of his time to me, going over the score of *Tristan*, we went to a Broadway store to buy a veil for Isolde in the second act. He asked for samples of various kinds of tulle, and, when they came, he seized one after another at one end and flirted the other rapidly through the air, to the great astonishment of the shoppers and shop-girls, who were not quite sure whether he was in his right mind. But he knew just what he wanted.
>
> With the quenching of the torch he was just as insistent that it should be thrust into water and not sand to prevent the spreading of the flames from escaping alcohol. His devotion to his work in these details was inexhaustible. When matters of importance claimed his attention there seemed room in his mind for nothing else. In encouragement he was always ready with those earnest in their striving and his knowledge was at their disposal, a knowledge that meant to so many a help to advancement in their art. Even in the days when my voice was light he used often to say to me: "Wait, you will sing Wagner one of these days."
>
> When I did, and began to study the role of Venus, it was Mr. Seidl who taught it to me. Again it was Mr. Seidl who aided me in the first study of Elsa for Bayreuth [where Nordica appeared in 1892], an aid of such authority, enthusiasm and assurance that it laid a foundation of future purpose and determination.

Of de Reszke's and Nordica's *Tristan and Isolde*, Krehbiel wrote:

> Let one fact be pondered: "Tristan und Isolde" was sung in tune
> throughout. Never before have we had a Tristan able to sing the
> declamatory music of the first and last acts with correct intonation,
> to say nothing of the duet of the second act. Never since Mme.
> Lehmann left us have we had an Isolde capable of the same feat.
> But Mme. Nordica and M. de Reszke not only sang in tune, they
> gave the text with a distinctness of enunciation and a truthfulness of
> expression that enabled those familiar with the German tongue to
> follow the play and appreciate its dramatic value and even its philo-
> sophical purport. It is wonderful how Mme. Nordica rose to the
> opportunity which Wagner's drama opened to her. The greater the
> demand the larger her capacity. In the climaxes of the first act, in
> which Isolde rages like a tempest, her voice rang out with thrilling
> clearness, power and brilliancy. . . . As for M. Jean de Reszke, his
> voice was warm and every note he sang a heart-throb.[20]

Krehbiel also wrote of de Reszke: "He will be no more famous
with the general public, nor will he be any the greater tenor, for having sung Tristan. It is not essential to greatness to be a Wagnerian
artist. But M. de Reszke has proved that by adding a new role to his
repertoire—and in a language new to him—he had the insatiable
hunger of the genuine artist to achieve the one grand and noble
thing that was left to him to achieve."[21] De Reszke was already a
popular idol, the signature artist for the Met's Golden Age. With his
aristocratic features and polished mustache, his refined manner and
intellect, he was elegantly handsome. If his voice was no trumpet,
his vocal technique, in Henderson's opinion, was the most perfect of
any male singer except Plançon. And he was an artist, Henderson
continued, whose "searching analysis of every phrase" plumbed
"the innermost significance of the text." He excelled as Don José, as
Radames, as des Grieux, as Raoul in *Les Huguenots*, as Lohengrin and
Walther von Stolzing. All these roles he sang in French and Italian.
He undertook Tristan, in German, as the supreme challenge of his
career. In addition to working with Seidl, he and Edouard spoke
German to one another for two years in preparation. Some among
the Met's German Wagnerites considered the result inauthentic.

They remembered Albert Niemann. Henderson disagreed: "I am confident," he wrote, "that [de Reszke's] Tristan was closer to Wagner's ideal than that of any German singer after Schnorr [von Carolsfeld] except possibly Heinrich Vogl, whom the Germans regarded as a mediocre Tristan." *[22]

On December 30, 1896, de Reszke added the title role in *Siegfried* to his German-language Wagner repertoire. Edouard was the Wanderer, Melba the miscast Brünnhilde—a role she never repeated. Seidl conducted. Krehbiel wrote: "The accomplishment of M. Jean de Reszke was little short of a miracle. His every word, every tone, every pose, every action, was brimming over with youthful energy, vigor, enthusiasm. His Siegfried proved to be a worthy companion-piece to his Tristan . . . an artistic creation . . . even more amazing, more bewildering." Henderson wrote: "M. Jean de Reszke's Siegfried must go into the annals of opera as one of the master creations of the century." De Reszke even sacrificed his mustache.[23]

In their determination to undertake Wagner the de Reszkes were determined that Seidl would coach and conduct them. Behind the scenes, they pressured Grau and Abbey to restore the Wagner canon. According to Henry Finck, Jean de Reszke made Grau and Seidl sign a contract assuring Seidl's return to the pit.†[24] And this was not the only such pressure. The public clamored for Wagner.

Walter Damrosch proved it. Though he had not led Wagner at the Met since 1886, he performed extracts with his New York Symphony—as did Seidl with his Philharmonic. Then, on February 17, 1894, Damrosch staged *Die Walküre* in Carnegie Hall with Materna, Schott, and Fischer. The performance was slipshod, but New York had not seen a *Ring* opera since 1891, and the hall was

---

*For a different view, see David Breckbill, footnote to page 122.

†Luigi Mancinelli, having led Wagner in Italy and New York, refused to return to the Met because of Seidl's re-engagement as a Wagner conductor.

mobbed. Encouraged, Damrosch rented the Metropolitan Opera House in March and gave another *Die Walküre* performance and two of *Götterdämmerung*. He next moved to organize a Wagner company of his own. At the same time, Seidl sought backers for a similar troupe. But Damrosch's social connections and easy charm—his capacity for "Yankee push" so lacking in Seidl—insured superior access to wealth. He offered to share the conducting with Seidl. Seidl of course said no.

Supported by a Wagner Society led by women, the Damrosch Opera Company secured an army of subscribers. Damrosch again rented the Met—for eight weeks beginning in February 1895, followed by a five-week tour traveling as far west as Kansas City. The company offered *Tannhäuser*, *Lohengrin*, *Die Walküre*, *Siegfried*, *Götterdämmerung*, *Tristan*, and *Die Meistersinger*, plus two concert performances of *Parsifal*. Damrosch's workload was astonishing: up to six performances in four days. His company included Fischer, Max Alvary, and Johanna Gadski. It finished the season with a $53,000 profit. Even Krehbiel, though he continued to fault Damrosch the musician, was amazed by his efficiency and zeal. Damrosch himself remarked: "To re-enter the Metropolitan on such a Wagnerian wave after German opera had been so ignominiously snuffed out five years before, was a great triumph and satisfaction for me, especially because my father had laid the foundation." In a letter to Krehbiel, he added: "I was [driven] by an irresistible impulse which, so far, seems to have led me right."[25]

It was in the wake of Damrosch's popular success that Seidl was again invited to conduct opera in German at the Met: a new Thursday night series, beginning November 1895. One result was de Reszke's Tristan. The Met now refused to rent its auditorium to Damrosch. He performed instead in the Academy of Music, which had not hosted opera since 1888. Damrosch added two important sopranos to his strong roster: Katherina Klafsky and Milka Ternina. To his repertoire, he added *Fidelio*, *Der Freischütz*, and his own *The Scarlet Letter*. Though an ill-considered southern tour disclosed little interest in Wagner, the New York season again revealed a Wagner hunger not remotely satisfied by the Met's offerings.

A truce ensued. As Damrosch had discovered the desirability of a more balanced repertoire outside New York, Abbey now offered him some of his French and Italian singers, including Calvé. In exchange, the Met would avail itself of some of Damrosch's Germans. And Abbey agreed again to rent to the Damrosch Opera Company. In 1897–98, when the Met housed no resident company, Damrosch presented opera there—including six Wagner operas—in partnership with Charles A. Ellis, who managed Melba. His company now presented opera in French, German, and Italian. And Damrosch toured with the German repertoire to such cities as Cleveland, Buffalo, and Detroit. Meanwhile, he buttressed his efforts with Wagner clubs and Wagner lecture-recitals. Then, at the age of thirty-seven, he resigned his "duties as an opera impresario."

For five years, Damrosch had sustained a homeless company. The company had begun when the Met abandoned Damrosch and Wagner both. By the time it ended, the Met had returned to Wagner with notable artistic success—and failure. The de Reszke–Nordica *Tristan* was a supreme achievement. Seidl also led important performances of Boito's *Mefistofele*, with Calvé and Edouard de Reszke, and Berlioz's *Damnation of Faust*, with Plançon. But singers like Lola Beeth (as Elisabeth, Elsa, Eva, and Sieglinde), Adolph Wallnöfer (Siegmund, Tannhäuser, Tristan), Giuseppe Cremonini (Lohengrin), and Giuseppe Kaschmann (Kurwenal, Telramund, Wolfram, Wotan) were not to be compared with the casts of the German seasons, or with the Damrosch company's Gadsky, Klafsky, and Ternina. Except for Nordica, Marie Brema, and the brothers de Reszke, according to Krehbiel, "the German singers of 1895–96 were woefully inefficient, and the German season was an indubitable failure."[26] If de Reszke's Siegfried set the standard for 1896–97, standards of another sort were set by the November 20 *Tannhäuser*, for which some of the principals sang in French, some in Italian, and the Tannhäuser switched from one language to the other.

In fact, like Damrosch's opera company, the Met was in rapid transition to the modern status quo: French opera in French, Italian opera in Italian, German opera in German. There was even a separate Wagner orchestra, brought in by Seidl. Much was gained: a new respect for the language and spirit of the composer. Much was lost: the concentrated rapport between singers and audiences sharing a common tongue and a sustained cultural inheritance. Never again could a single artist unify the ideals of the entire company as Seidl had when the Met was a Wagner shrine.

In New York, Seidl's eclipse had lifted, but never entirely. Meanwhile, he had discovered new opportunities for Wagner—in Brooklyn.

The *Parsifal* Entertainment

For the Palm Sunday evening of March 31, 1890, the Brooklyn Academy of Music was transformed. From the carriage canopy to the Montague Street entrance (this was the old Academy in Brooklyn Heights, not the present one on Lafayette Avenue), carpets were laid between banks of flowers and plants. A temporary archway led to the foyer, itself remade as a series of drawing rooms hung with watercolors and engravings. In the auditorium itself, the boxes were decorated in green, red, and white. Green and white streamers looped from the ceiling to the walls. A white and silver cathedral scene—"the costliest scenery yet produced in the United States," according to Henry Hoyt of the Metropolitan Opera, who designed it—set the stage. An eighty-four-piece orchestra, also on stage, was partly concealed by a garden array of fan palms, geraniums, and lilies. A banner upon the proscenium arch carried the word PARSIFAL in flowered green letters, and also a medieval "S"— the insignia of the Seidl Society, which had conceived and sponsored the event and adorned the space.

The huge audience (every seat and standing place was taken) was considered the most distinguished—in bearing, in attire, in pedigree—in the building's twenty-nine-year history. Reporters took note of "the number of eager, intelligent faces, especially of the ladies," and "the interest with which the listeners followed the performance, many of them with scores on their knees." Ex-President Grover Cleveland was spotted, his wife at his side and a libretto in his lap.* Others in the boxes included Brooklyn Mayor Alfred C. Chapin and his wife, Dr. and Mrs. Lymon Abbott, and Mr. and Mrs. J. Pierpont Morgan. Distinction of another kind was lent by the ladies of the Seidl Society, who had prepared themselves with books and lectures—most recently, a talk on "*Parsifal,* the Finding of Christ through Art." In fact, local libraries could not keep their Wagner books on the shelves. Music stores in New York and Brooklyn were specially stocked with *Parsifal* scores and Wagner treatises. A milliner named a new spring style the *Parsifal* toque.[1]

The music began at 5 P.M., with an abridged concert performance of *Parsifal* act 1 and part of act 2. Then, at 6:30, came a ninety-minute dinner break—incongruously catered by an Italian, who ran out of food. The performance resumed at 8 and lasted until 10, after which a reception was held for Anton Seidl, his wife, and the principal singers.

The significance of the "*Parsifal* Entertainment" was threefold. It was a milestone in introducing Wagner's final opus to the United States. It stirred dreams of a New World Bayreuth in Brooklyn—a separate city of nearly one million people prior to its annexation to Manhattan in 1898. It was a high culture/High Society hybrid peculiar to the late Gilded Age, when Wagner reigned supreme: a concert as devoutly serious as its trappings were glamorous.

The first *Parsifal* performances, at Bayreuth, took place the summer of 1882. Angelo Neumann, who was there, was one of many who experienced "a lofty ecstasy," as if he had taken part in "a sacred ser-

---

*At Cleveland's 1885 inauguration, a Marine band performed Wagner excerpts on the White House lawn. At his 1893 inauguration, Seidl led excerpts from *Die Meistersinger, Tristan, Götterdämmerung,* and *Parsifal*. According to John Philip Sousa, Cleveland's wife, Frances, called the *Tannhäuser* Overture her favorite selection. Cleveland himself was a close friend both of the piano manufacturer William Steinway (a powerful force in the Democratic party) and of Edmund Stanton, who held high administrative posts at the Metropolitan Opera and at Jeannette Thurber's National Conservatory of Music. (See Elise Kirk, *Music at the White House* [Urbana, Ill., 1986], pp. 143–44.)

vice." The British clergyman H. R. Haweis, whom we have briefly encountered as an influential Wagnerite on both sides of the Atlantic, testified:

> I shall never forget the indescribable emotion which seized the whole assembly on the first representation of [the Grail scene]. . . . The light fades out of the golden dome, a holy twilight falls, and strange melodies float down from above, till, in the deepening gloom, the goblet slowly glows and reddens like a ruby flame, and the knights fall prostrate in an ecstasy of devotion; a moment only, the crimson fades out, the crystal is dark, the Grail has passed. I looked round upon the silent audience while this astonishing celebration was taking place. The whole assembly was motionless; all seemed to be solemnized by the august spectacle—seemed almost to share in the devout contemplation and trance-like worship of the holy knights. Every thought of the stage had vanished. Nothing was further from my own thoughts than play-acting. I was sitting in devout and rapt contemplation. Before my eyes had passed a symbolic vision of prayer and ecstasy, flooding the soul with overpowering thoughts of the divine sacrifice and the mystery of unfathomable love.
>
> The people seemed spellbound. Some wept, some gazed entranced with wide-open eyes, some heads were bowed as in prayer.[2]

The prominent American art critic Mariana Van Rensselaer was also a pilgrim that July. In an article for *Harper's* the following March, she called *Parsifal* "the deepest in theme and completest in execution" of Wagner's works. Of the performance, she reported that "the transcendental mood of the drama was preserved in every detail." She found the staging awesome and bewildering, the hall of the grail knights being the "most splendid and artistic" interior she had ever encountered in a theater. Another American at the 1882 festival was the writer Charles Dudley Warner, who had collaborated with his friend Mark Twain on *The Gilded Age* and so nicknamed an epoch. He called *Parsifal* "a modern miracle play" and added: "It is of course possible that the crowds of Bayreuth were victims of a delusion, and of skillful contrivance. I can answer for many of them that they would like to be deluded again in just that way."[3]

Wagner conceived *Parsifal* as a *Bühnenweihfestspiel*—a festival play for the consecration of a stage—to consecrate his Festspielhaus much as church festivals were celebrated with feasts. He composed it with the Bayreuth auditorium—its acoustic, its hidden orchestra, its committed audience and ascetic decor—in mind. The Wagner family intended to disallow staged *Parsifal* performances outside Bayreuth. A concert performance took place in London in 1884. Two years later, Walter Damrosch led two concert performances in New York with Emil Fischer, Marianne Brandt, and the tenor Felix Krämer, whose light voice proved inadequate. The orchestra was underprepared. Finck summarized: "it was a task that [Damrosch] should never have undertaken."[4]

It seems that Cosima Wagner did not learn of the first American *Parsifal*—for which Damrosch had orchestral parts copied from a miniature conductor's score he had purchased in London—until 1903. But Seidl was upset. This was the Wagner work he felt closer to than any other—the music Wagner was composing during Seidl's Wahnfried years. He had copied it, and sung and performed it at the piano with and for the composer. He considered it Wagner's masterpiece.*

According to Lilli Lehmann, Edmund Stanton considered staging *Parsifal* in 1887, and she dissuaded him. Stanton also, in Lehmann's opinion, "dreaded" rebuilding the stage equipment for the necessary special effects. In any event, Seidl was unlikely to have profaned the *Parsifal* embargo. Brooklyn's abridged concert performance in 1890, and three more abridged concert *Parsifal*s presented by the Seidl Society in New York and Boston in 1891, were the only Seidl *Parsifal*s prior to 1897, when he conducted it at Bayreuth. The Gurnemanz and Kundry for Brooklyn's *Parsifal* Entertainment were Fischer and Lilli Lehmann. Lehmann's husband, Paul Kalisch, was the Parsifal. Theodor Reichmann, the Amfortas, had sung the part at Bayreuth. As there was no possibility of adequately preparing a chorus, none took part. The Flower Maidens were also omitted.

---

*Seidl ranked Wagner's music dramas in the following order: *Parsifal, Tristan und Isolde, Siegfried, Götterdämmerung, Die Meistersinger, Die Walküre, Das Rheingold, Tannhäuser, Lohengrin, The Flying Dutchman, Rienzi.*

According to Finck, about three-quarters of the score was heard. Act 3, whose Good Friday music was already well-known to many in the audience, made a spellbinding impression. Other passages—in particular, Gurnemanz's act 1 narrations—proved ill adapted to concert use. Conversely, the absence of the choruses was much regretted. Krehbiel wrote: "It was evident that the music had been studied with great care and reverence, for the distinctness of enunciation, truthfulness of declamation and intensity of dramatic expression which marked the singing of the principals were greater than the audiences at the Metropolitan Opera House were privileged to hear during the season lately ended." According to Lehmann: "There was a Good Friday atmosphere. The place was transformed into a temple. . . . That the performance did not lack in devotion and dignity I can vouch for heartily." Seidl was transported, and transported his players. Nothing he had previously done in New York was more effusively praised.[5]

On another occasion, Krehbiel pertinently observed of Seidl: "In him, impulse dominated reflection, emotion shamed logic. It was much to his advantage that he came among an impressionable people with the prestige of a Wagnerian oracle and archon, and much to the advantage of the cult to which he was devoted that he made that people 'experience' the lyric dramas of his master in the same sense that a good Methodist 'experiences' religion, rather than to 'like' them."[6]

With *Tristan und Isolde, Parsifal* posed—or should have posed—the trickiest obstacles to genteel appropriation. It populates its rituals of religious uplift with a cast of neurotic misfits. It combines Christian symbolism with pagan, Buddhist, and Schopenhauerean motifs collected by a composer who had judged Christianity "incompatible with living art," called hypocrisy its "salient feature," and accounted the life-on-earth it sanctions a "loathsome dungeon." Could *Parsifal* be purged of decadence and sacrilege?

Its contradictions permit an array of contradictory readings. In Europe (but not America), present-day *Parsifal* productions explore such themes as fascism, misogyny, homosexuality, and racism. Nineteenth-century European interpretations were already varied and violent. The apostate Nietzsche considered *Parsifal* a contemptible sellout whose romantic aroma and posturing asceticism concealed a decadent despair, "helpless and broken, before the Christian cross." Hanslick, rather like Nietzsche, conceded the powerful spell *Parsifal* cast yet decried its "false religious-philosophical pretensions" and the "decaying mentality" that applied the Holy Grail and sacred miracles to the modern "mission of German art, and propose[d] therewith to effect the regeneration of humanity." And Hanslick attacked the "repulsive idolatry" that reserved *Parsifal* for Bayreuth alone.[7]

In Gilded Age America, the gamut of response was predictably more compressed. One centrist interpretation was that *Parsifal* crystallized religious exaltation without the burden of dogma, that its allegorical meaning, compatible with Christianity, was not exclusively Christian. Wagner, according to Henry Finck, had committed no sin when in the Grail rites he evoked the Last Supper; through transferring Biblical imagery to "the mystic regions of mythology," he made them "available for theatric purposes." Finck mainly appreciated the ritual power of *Parsifal*. W. J. Henderson, more the philosopher, wrote:

> [Wagner] has preached a sermon on the necessity of personal purity in the service of God, on the beauty of renunciation of sensual delight, on the depth of the curse of self-indulgence, and on the nature of repentance. . . . He has put before us a tremendous play of the inner life of man's soul when struggling with its most formidable problems, its own most irresistible passions. "Parsifal" is a religious drama, but it is one for the same reason that the "Prometheus" of Aeschylus was. It is a problem play also, and for the same reason as any modern French social drama is. Its boldness lies in the fact that it readopts the stage as the medium for the publication of tenets of religious belief and for the exhibition of the naked soul besieged by lust and tried by the moral law. That use was common in the time of the Greek tragedians.[8]

For Henry Krehbiel, however, the self-denial preached and practiced by *Parsifal* and the Grail knights was problematic. Nietzsche never permitted himself actually to hear and see *Parsifal*. Hanslick appeared moved upon leaving the Festspielhaus, but regained his opprobrium when it came time to write. Finck and Henderson pleasurably succumbed. Krehbiel struggled manfully against narcosis. The "effectiveness of 'Parsifal' as an artistic entertainment" he did not question. "But when one has escaped the sweet thraldom of the representation, and reflection takes the place of experience, there arise a multitude of doubts touching the essential merit of the drama." For Krehbiel, *Parsifal* seemed essentially a Christian play about redemption through suffering and compassion—and yet "more in harmony with the feeling of Buddhistic, or medieval asceticism than with the sentiments of modern Christianity." Krehbiel's own modern Christianity distanced him from Parsifal, whose redemptive path alluded to scenes from Christ's life, and who was invariably dressed and bearded even to *look* like the New Testament Savior. Krehbiel—a married man and, presumably, no ascetic—considered Parsifal's celibacy a relic of "medieval fanatics" and "crazed monks." The ethical idea he embraced in Wagner was the one "at the basis of all the really beautiful mythologies and religions of the world"—that "salvation comes to humanity through the redeeming love of woman." Parsifal, who rejects womanly love and keeps company only with men, glorified "a conception of sanctity which grew out of a monstrous perversion of womanhood, and a wicked degradation of womankind."*[9]

Other Gilded Age critics took Krehbiel's squeamishness a step further. Amid touchy Victorian distinctions between religious and

---

*Hanslick, in a similar vein, argued: "What is the Grail to us? A legendary curiosity, a long-forgotten superstition, foreign both to popular and enlightened consciousness." The late Carl Dahlhaus, in a 1972 commentary, turns this argument on its head. The archaism of *Parsifal*'s religious imagery—its patina of nostalgia—is precisely what makes it acceptable:

> It is on the sensation of being led back into the past by the music that the significance of the religious element in *Parsifal* depends. Christianity—seen as sacramental religion and not diluted and reduced to the condition of a philosophical abstraction—belongs to the past, according to the belief which Wagner gives expression to in the

profane ritual, sacred and secular music, some writers argued that *Parsifal* would be unfit for staging in America even if Cosima approved. Anticipating the *Parsifal* Entertainment, the *New York World* commented: "There are many scenes . . . that are too strikingly like the events of Christ's life to be treated in costume [in the United States] or in any other way except in oratorio fashion; especially the last supper, the descent of the Grail, the baptism, anointment and foot-washing of Parsifal by Gurnemanz and Kundry."[10] A more dominant New World reading, however, conceived *Parsifal* as not merely compatible with sanctioned ritual and belief, but specifically and commendably Christian—a view, already embodied in such accounts of the 1882 premiere as the Reverend Haweis's, as reassuring as it was naive.

In fact, Christian readings of Wagner extended even to the *Ring*, whose meliorism attracted Anglicans, Catholics, and Presbyterians alike. For such Wagnerites, *Parsifal* was Wagner's magnum opus in Christian edification, preaching lessons in charity, pity, and pure love. The liberal American theologian Washington Gladden, stirred by *Parsifal* in Bayreuth, counted Wagner among such "witnesses of the light" as Dante, Michelangelo, Fichte, Hugo, and Ruskin. Wagner had elevated opera into "a source of refinement and moral invigoration. . . . Its function was therefore an exalted and even a sacred one. . . . Deep ethical laws are found working themselves out; sin and its consequences—the retributions of violated law, and redemption through suffering and sacrifice—these great religious ideas are presented over and over, with tremendous power." Haweis believed that *Parsifal* foretold a "sacred musical drama of the

---

music. This is why the Last Supper celebrated on the stage during the Grail episodes of *Parsifal* is less a re-enaction—which would be in questionable taste—than a memory transformed into a picture. Wagner's *Bühnenweihfestspiel* does not absorb the rite it evokes by making it real and living, a religious ceremony presented through the medium of art, but by revealing it as belonging to the past, as a form that no longer carries any substance, a vision called up from the depths of memory.

The Wagner scholar Lucy Beckett comments: "Here the frequent aim of consigning the religious elements in *Parsifal* to a safe aesthetic distance has been particularly attractively achieved." (All three quotations from Lucy Beckett, ed., *Parsifal* [New York, 1981], pp. 106, 125–26.)

future," a "new eclectic art epoch" renewing the tradition of the Oberammergau passion play.[11]

The Americanization of *Parsifal*—its appropriation as a Christian drama, or as a religious drama compatible with Christianity—illuminates a drama of late-nineteenth-century religious need. Industrial capitalism, political corruption, positivism and Darwinian science— these were symptoms of a perceived moral decline that upset both intellectuals and clergymen. Intellectuals inclined to socialism and rejected religion in pursuit of remedies to class and industrial strife. Clergymen inclined to Christian socialism and other activist alternatives to orthodox dogma. While fatalistic Calvinism prevailed in America's towns, city preachers became new theologians, liberal or radical Christians. But the decline of orthodoxy, of orthodox intensity of conviction, remained worrisome to modern Christians adrift in a spiritual void.

Wagner's eclectic social vision appealed to these intellectual and religious needs. His utopia was classless. Founded in love, it shunned the curse of gold. His eclectic spiritual vision, buttressed not by scripture but by myth, offered redemption from bourgeois materialism without explicitly denying the findings of science. Lyman Abbott, whom we have glimpsed at the *Parsifal* Entertainment, and who succeeded Henry Ward Beecher at Brooklyn's influential Plymouth Congregational Church,* wrote in 1885 that "up to a recent date, industrial competition, even when producing suffering and death, was the best condition which existing circumstances would permit." Now, however, with capital accumulating among a few powerful and often unscrupulous men, "new principles" of cooperation and equitable distribution were needed. Abbott's own efforts included the Church Association for the Advancement of

---

*Abbott must have known Seidl, judging from the condolence note he wrote Seidl's widow in 1898 (preserved in the Anton Seidl archive, Columbia University [Butler Library: Rare Books]).

the Interests of Labor. Washington Gladden, whom we have heard praising *Parsifal*, also espoused applied Christianity. He criticized capitalism for its emphasis on egoism and competition, and wholeheartedly supported the labor movement. The meliorist Wagner, moreover, resonated with an American religious dynamic long predating the Gilded Age. Pondering the lightning popularity of Henry George's *Progress and Poverty* in the 1880s, the historian Page Smith has written:

> The fact was that Americans had lived, from the beginning, in the hope of universal redemption. It was the energizing principle, the motive power, that drove the strange, crude, unwieldy vehicle that became the United States on its dangerously accelerating course. . . . The notion of life on earth—animal and human—as a ruthless and bloody struggle for survival was profoundly alien to America and its deepest traditions. . . . [Americans] turned as the thirsty to water, the starving to food to the trumpet tones of the new prophet.[12]

Parsifal, too, pealed trumpet tones of redemption. It more buttressed than challenged the liberal Christian cause. As with the *Ring* cycle, its drama of regeneration enacted a ritualistic extermination of commercialism and materialism, of the bosses and robber barons whom clerics and genteel critics feared and loathed. Its narcotic music was both escapist and cathartic.

How would Wagner have reacted to these uses? For him, *Parsifal* absorbed Schopenhauer primarily and Christianity—for Schopenhauer, a source of one "great fundamental truth" in common with Brahminism and Buddhism—only secondarily. The great truth was that salvation from life's vale of tears resided in denial of the will. *Parsifal*, following Schopenhauer, preaches compassion; but it also exudes resignation and withdrawal. Christian activism is arguably not part of its implied agenda.[13]

Born in Tennessee in 1848, educated at the Nashville Female Academy, Laura Holloway was the daughter of a prominent country gentleman whose way of life was devastated by the Civil War. With her mother, a Quaker of Huguenot ancestry, she prevailed on him to take the family north. Early widowed, she lived for a time at the White House; President Andrew Johnson was a relative and close friend. While in Washington, she worked as a newspaper correspondent to help support her family. She spent some time abroad regaining her health. She returned to the United States to settle in Brooklyn, where she became well known both as a socialite and as an industrious journalist and author. She supported women's suffrage, and was corresponding secretary for the Brontë Society of England. She was admired for her cordial manner, for her rich and cultivated voice, and for her intrepid spirit. The *Brooklyn Daily Eagle*—for which she served as associate editor for more than a decade before leaving the paper in 1884—testified: "What she does is done with all her might. She is not easily daunted by difficulties and ordinary obstacles have no terrors for her." Colonel E. L. Langford, whom she married in 1890, was a well-preserved Civil War hero and former deputy police commissioner, secretary and treasurer of the Brooklyn Brighton and Coney Island Railroad Company.[14]

Anton Seidl was indispensable to the *Parsifal* Entertainment, but—quite unlike his mentor Wagner—was not the type to initiate it. He was "too modest," wrote Henry Finck. "He lacked the quality of Yankee 'push,' so necessary in this country." The push was supplied by Laura Holloway. It was she who founded the Seidl Society in May 1889. According to its constitution, it was "organized for the purpose of securing to its members and to the public increased musical culture and of promoting musical interest among women particularly. It aims to reach all classes of women and children and by its efforts in their behalf to prove the potent influence of harmony over individual life and character."[15]

Only women could join. At first, about two hundred signed on. Their initial goal was to undertake excursions to Seidl's summer concerts at Coney Island's Brighton Beach, then in their second season. Dues were five dollars. All members were furnished with concert tickets at twenty-five cents each—about one-quarter the minimum price of admission for comparable events in New York City. Rail transportation to Coney Island cost an additional fifty cents.

These outings, previously inaccessible to women without escorts, proved highly attractive once special cars were reserved for the Seidl Society. During the summer of 1889, as well, several thousand working girls, and poor or orphaned children, visited Coney Island's seashore, and seashore concerts, at the society's expense. The group also organized lunches, dinners, and receptions. It taught its members to sing. It aspired to build a Wagner opera house in Brooklyn to house a permanent Wagner festival.

Henry Krehbiel lectured for the Seidl Society at least five times in 1889. That Seidl furnished musical illustrations at the piano documents both his imperfect English, which prevented him from lecturing himself, and his missionary spirit (what present-day "great conductor" would undertake such work?). One of Krehbiel's talks, on *Parsifal*, led to the *Parsifal* Entertainment the following March. Its success, in turn, launched a series of ten Seidl Society concerts at the Brooklyn Academy of Music—after which the society's Academy concerts became a mainstay of the Brooklyn concert calendar. At Coney Island, the society's support ensured Seidl's re-engagement; as of 1894, the society took over sponsorship and administration of the Brighton Beach concerts.

In short: Laura Holloway, later Laura Langford, became a leading entrepreneur, responsible for the vast majority of Seidl's American concert engagements. She effectively promoted the Music of the Future for an expanding audience at inexpensive prices. She dreamed of establishing an American Bayreuth.

A final detail completes this overview: Brooklyn was known as a city of churches. Its skyline, unlike that of New York, was a modest plateau interrupted by steeples and spires. Its parks were bucolic. Its better homes fronted quiet, tree-lined streets. Though its 800,000 residents included 260,000 foreign-born, its neighborhoods mainly escaped the Calcutta turmoil of New York's Lower East Side. The Reverend Henry Ward Beecher—the "Hercules of American Protestantism," the *Eagle* called him—presided in Brooklyn Heights from 1847 to 1887. His message resonated with the aspirations of his affluent Anglican parishioners—and with the meliorism of Wagner and of the Seidl Society, which organized Sunday morning services at Brighton Beach and reserved Sunday nights for church and home life. Especially after the Metropolitan abandoned German opera in 1891, Wagner found a Brooklyn haven from immigrant chaos. Quipped the *New York World* of the *Parsifal* Entertainment:

> When Richard Wagner was looking for an ideal town wherein to demonstrate his harmonic ideals he selected Bayreuth as a city that had not been contaminated by the songs of vulgar Italian melodists. So in these degenerate days the members of the Seidl Society, intellectual descendants of Wagner, let their eyes rest upon Brooklyn . . . whose virgin senses were still unsullied by the low Italians who dealt in mere concourse of sweet sounds. Therefore it was that in the Brooklyn Academy of Music was held yesterday afternoon and evening the first real Festspiel of The Devoted Wagnerites of America.

The same article observed:

> One cannot but regret . . . that the beautiful churchly choruses had to be omitted because of the lack of time in which to train the singers. Whose fault this was we do not know. Probably it lies in the inability of the members of the society to sing the work in German. But English would, after all, have been the preferable language for the interpretation of the work to such a purely and characteristically American, intelligent musical audience as that of last night at the Academy.[16]

The writer exaggerates. In fact, Brooklyn's German-born population of 95,000, its largest non-native constituency,[17] must have known the Academy of Music. But the Academy was essentially a Heights venue, a place for uplifting lectures and charity balls. Juxtaposed with New York, Brooklyn was more "purely American," more a refuge for genteel Yankee Wagnerites, versus the world of *Singvereine* and *Bierstuben* that enveloped Seidl across the river. It was no coincidence that the Seidl Society began with *Parsifal*: the "Christian" Wagner.

The Seidl Society opened its first "winter" season at the Academy of Music on October 30, 1890, with an all-Wagner program: the *Lohengrin* Prelude, the Ride of the Valkyries, Forest Murmurs from *Siegfried*, the *Tannhäuser* Overture, Wotan's Farewell, excerpts from *Die Meistersinger* ("In Eva's Praise"), the *Götterdämmerung* Funeral Music, and the *Tristan* Prelude, "Love Song," and *Liebestod*. The second concert, November 6, was all-Liszt: *Les Préludes*, the First Piano Concerto (with Franz Rummel, who also played a set of solo pieces), *Tasso*, *Orpheus*, and the First Hungarian Rhapsody. The repertoire for the ten-concert series eventually included much more Wagner and Liszt, including a second all-Wagner night and a "Grand *Parsifal* concert." Grieg's *Peer Gynt* music was heard, as were *Omphale's Spinning Wheel* by Saint-Saëns and Strauss's *Don Juan*. Of earlier composers, Seidl programmed two Beethoven symphonies and excerpts from *Fidelio* but only a smattering of Bach, Mozart, Schubert, and Schumann, There was no Handel, and hardly any Haydn. Conspicuously absent, as well, were celebrity soloists; they cost money, and would have diminished Seidl's emphasis on the Music of the Future. "Speaking in all earnestness," commented the *Daily Eagle* of the season's final event, "it ought to be said in dignity, in beauty, in loftiness of aim and fullness of fulfillment the concert had not had its equal in either New York of Brooklyn this season. . . . The 10 concerts of the Seidl Society have been phenomenally successful. . . . They have also demonstrated most strikingly the capacity of women to labor in larger and nobler fields than ordinarily occupy their attention in the department of art."[18]

Subsequent Seidl Society seasons at the Academy offered, in addition to the main subscription concerts, young people's matinees and working people's concerts for which tickets were distributed at churches, asylums, and hospitals. A "popular concert" at the Claremont Avenue Rink attracted nearly four thousand listeners at fifty cents a head. The orchestra for all these events, usually called the "Seidl Orchestra" or "Metropolitan Orchestra," included members of the New York Philharmonic and of the Metropolitan Opera's Wagner orchestra. The conductor was always Seidl.

Democratic zeal was a constant motif. The *Daily Eagle* wrote of Laura Langford that she never "tolerated anything that savored of class or social distinctions." In fact, her fund-raising drives, which helped keep tickets prices low, stressed donations of twenty-five cents to a dollar. "Large contributions will of course be accepted, but if the desired sum should be raised by the donation of small amounts the society feels that it had accomplished a great work in reaching so many people."[19]

As a matter of policy, the Seidl Society never published a list of members. But membership conferred prestige on socialites who joined—and many did. Banquets and receptions in fashionable rooms were a part of the agenda. One of these, on April 21, 1894, was a fifth-anniversary dinner—the occasion for what may have been Seidl's first speech in English. According to the *Daily Eagle*: "Anything more quaint than Mr. Seidl's imperfect pronunciation of our tongue, and his little translations of German idioms into English, it would be difficult to imagine. Almost every sentence was enthusiastically applauded, and a vast deal of unpreventable laughter mingled with the applause."[20]

The honeymoon between the Seidlites and their hero was a long and harmonious one, interrupted by a single, informative crisis. The society's ambitious artistic mission inevitably invited rivalry with New York. In particular, its aspiration—never fulfilled—to stage German opera potentially challenged the Metropolitan Opera, where German opera was a diminished priority. Seidl himself felt frustrated in Manhattan, where Wagner was conducted by Vianesi, Mancinelli, and Walter Damrosch. Then, in late 1895, Maurice Grau—as we have seen—offered him a substantial series of engagements with the Met. Coincidentally or not, these new responsibilities in both New York and Brooklyn conflicted with Seidl Society concerts at the Academy of Music. Seidl now reneged on his commitments to Laura Langford. The ladies of the society seemed stunned into inaction. The *Daily Eagle* goaded: "It would be a strange thing if a body of women, who have kept Mr. Seidl in bread and butter for several years should go on doing it after he had repudiated his contract. If they were men there would be but one answer to the question." Other articles inferred that Seidl had merely used the Seidl Society while pursuing his main interests elsewhere, and that the women had in effect been duped. Langford had no comments for the press. Seidl was reported asserting: "I will not answer any question. But I will say that I do not ask any women for my bread."[21]

Rubbing salt into every wound, the *Eagle* now proposed that the Seidlites engage Theodore Thomas to lead the concerts Seidl would not. Thomas was "the best musician in America," "a man who inspires confidence." His success was "certain; it would be greater than that of Mr. Seidl." He would attract "a larger number of the public than the Seidl concerts, as Mr. Thomas had been known longer here and has a larger and better orchestra." In an agonizing move, the Seidl Society agreed there was no better alternative. It changed its name to the "Brooklyn Symphony Society" and booked Thomas and his Chicago Orchestra. They would give two concerts at the Academy of Music. The program for the first, on March 20, 1896, listed Beethoven's *Leonore* Overture No. 3, Schubert's *Unfinished* Symphony, Liszt's Second Piano Concerto (with Rafael Joseffy), Tchaikovsky's *Romeo and Juliet*, Goldmark's Scherzo Op. 45, and the Chopin/Thomas Polonaise in A-flat. The second concert, six days later, offered Goldmark's Overture to *Sappho*, the Romance from Berlioz's *Damnation of Faust*, Beethoven's Seventh Symphony, Strauss's *Till Eulenspiegel*, and, by Wagner, two Wesendonck songs, the *Siegfried Idyll*, and the *Tannhäuser* Bacchanale.

The critic of the *Daily Eagle* considered Thomas unsurpassed "as a concert conductor pure and simple." His readings were clear and uneccentric, strong and delicate, smooth and disciplined. The public evidently disagreed. The first Thomas concert nearly sold out. Attendance dropped for concert number two. The Seidl Society was reportedly left with a four-figure deficit. Seidl, declaring himself a "victim of circumstance," patched up his differences with Langford. The Seidl Society reverted to its original name. Surveying these events, the *Musical Courier* wickedly observed: "I suppose you know that we have gone back to our old Seidolatry. There was this winter an effort to convert [Brooklyn] from false gods to a worship of music as divorced from any personality whatever. The attempt has failed."[22]

Seidl's private correspondence reveals the behind-the-scenes agonies inflicted by this episode. The Seidl Society, which, far from being duped, had played a role in Seidl's resurrection at the Met, understood his passion to return to the opera pit. But, as Seidl explained to Langford on October 30, he could not get specific dates from Grau, and confirm or switch dates for the Academy concerts, until Grau returned from abroad in November. Exasperated, he exclaimed: "I wish I had never spoken to Grau about opera dates, and we had now our concert dates." On November 25, he denied that he had ever said that he "did not ask any woman for my bread." A reporter, he related, had visited his home and read to him the *Eagle*'s provocative characterization of "a body of women, who have kept Mr. Seidl in bread and butter for several years." This upset Seidl. "Then I said, *to him*, I never asked anybody for bread and butter; and then left him alone. Now I see in the evening paper of the Eagle this misrepresented in a very impertinent manner, and I beg you take this as a rectification. I think, you will hardly believe, that I can use such language toward women or the Seidl Society." To the public, the society may have seemed timidly indecisive. Seidl's letters to Langford, however, suggest no high-handedness on his part.[23]

In any event, rapprochement was sealed by a benefit concert for the society's summer music fund. Lillian Nordica was the soloist in excerpts from *Tristan und Isolde*. The remainder of the program included the *Siegfried Idyll*, *Les Préludes*, and an aria from Goldmark's *Königin von Saba*. Seidl began with the third *Leonore* overture—the same work with which Thomas had commenced his two Brooklyn concerts, but à la Wagner, dramatizing Beethoven's extremes of repose and agitation. The orchestra, of fifty men, was less polished than Chicago's had been, and the brasses overbalanced the strings. It hardly mattered. Seidl's mere appearance raised the roof. "It was well that he struck into the third Leonore overture with some precipitation, or the reception might have advanced to hysterics," reported the *Musical Courier*. After the Liszt, an usher presented the conductor with a laurel wreath. According to the *Daily Eagle*: "The [audience's] smoldering affection leaped into flame again when the object of it appeared in his jovian impassiveness and suffered himself to be decorated." In the *Courier*'s version, the wreath was "accepted with that lack of frantic delight which makes you wonder whether, after all, he will take it home or give it to some barefoot boy, who needs it more."[24]

No turn of events could more neatly have confirmed the sea change in musical taste that had overtaken New York and Brooklyn in a mere decade. Theodore Thomas's classical restraint seemed boring. His judicious Beethoven was passé. The hunger for "modern German music" was acute. The Wagner cult raged unchecked.

Wagner Nights

hree thousand people applauded, and the orchestra played a fanfare, as Anton Seidl left the stage to fetch Mrs. Laura Langford and escort her to the front of the Brighton Beach music pavilion. He then mounted the podium and closed his concert, the last of the 1894 season, with Liszt's *Les Préludes*, of which Langford was especially fond. As she listened to the enraptured nature music of Seidl's orchestra, her eyes swept the wooden auditorium, which was filled to capacity. To the sides, she could see the moonlit Coney Island sands, to the rear, the Atlantic sky. The ushers, all earnest-faced women, wore silver "S" pins on their dresses. Their job was to discipline smokers, talkers, and latecomers. But the stirring music, the sea breeze, and the whisper of the breakers cast a spell stronger than any enforced decorum.

This was the fruit of Laura Langford's "mission work." Her Seidl Society had disbursed $34,000 for the nine-week, June-to-September season. Tickets were sold for as little as a quarter, and yet she had finished the summer with her books balanced—"a remarkable feat of managerial skill," in the opinion of the *Brooklyn Daily Eagle*.

When the music stopped, the applause would not. After many bows, Seidl stepped to the front of the stage. The crowd hushed. He said: "I thank you very much for this evidence of your appreciation, and it is very gratifying. There is one thing, however, which I do not want you to forget and that is that this effort to raise the standard of music would not have been possible without the Seidl Society and the women who are its members. To them more than anyone else your thanks are due."[1]

Coney Island is a sandy peninsula at the foot of Brooklyn, eight miles southeast of Manhattan. In 1894, it was not yet the home of Steeplechase, its most famous and longest-lived amusement park, built in 1897. But it was already a notorious city of enticements, "Sodom by the Sea," a playground of beer gardens, shooting galleries and sideshows, con men and whores. Its Iron Tower, equipped with two steam elevators, was the tallest structure in the country. Its Sea Beach Palace could serve fifteen thousand diners at a time and house ten thousand guests overnight. Its Elephant Hotel was an immense tin-skinned structure with a cigar store in one leg, a diorama in another, and rooms available in the hip, shoulder, trunk, and thigh.

Coney Island was a metaphor for democracy. People from every walk of life mingled on Surf Avenue. And the surf itself was a common denominator, where men and women, boys and girls, donned revealing attire—arms and calves were fully exposed—to frolic in the waves.

If Coney's hot dogs and roller coasters catered to New York's toiling classes, fleeing their tenements, respectable families and their servants gravitated to the Island's east end, there to enjoy the vast Oriental, Manhattan Beach, and Brighton Beach hotels. These were patrolled by private detectives and supplied with fresh water piped from the mainland. They featured manicured lawns, elegant porches, fine restaurants, celebrated racetracks, and—on the model of comparable European watering holes—outdoor concerts.

Manhattan Beach's circular music pavilion, fronting the ornate verandas of the turreted hotel, boasted America's most famous bandmaster: Patrick Gilmore. The Brighton Beach Association, scrambling to catch up, built a second such pavilion and offered it to Johann Strauss, to England's Coldstream Guards, and to France's Republican Guard Band. When all said no, the association settled for Anton Seidl, who inaugurated the premises in June 1888 with members of the Metropolitan Opera Orchestra.

But the Brighton concerts were a bust. Patrons of the hotel and racetrack expected to hear marches and waltzes, not excerpts from symphonies and operas led by the sober "Hair Seedle." And the orchestra, performing twice a day, seven days a week, claimed illness and fatigue. Musicians griped to the press about Seidl's unreasonable demands. Seidl himself said:

"I will confess frankly . . . that I do not content myself with the approval of the fashionable musical public; my chief aim is, rather to attract to the concerts . . . the music-loving masses who wish to cultivate their taste, and who, lacking both time and means to attend the classical concerts given during the winter season, will now be afforded the opportunity of listening . . . at an outlay which lies within the reach of all. . . . I feel convinced that I have not been mistaken in the musical demands and progressiveness of the American people. . . . Why retard [that] progress . . . simply because Brighton Beach is a summer resort?"[2]

The solution to this impasse began with the formation of the Seidl Society in 1889. Its train loads of women rescued Seidl's seashore orchestra. Attendance increased by 50 percent. Seidl was emboldened to give entire symphonies, including Beethoven's Third, Fifth, Sixth, Seventh, and Eighth. But the project still seemed implausible. The music had to compete with bad weather and noisy railroad trains. Even when the elements and trains were quiet, the venue, so near rowdy crowds and roisterous amusements, seemed incongruous. It was assumed that the concerts had no future.

Early the next summer, when the concerts in fact resumed, Seidl blamed poor ticket sales on inadequate advertising by the Brighton Beach Association—whose president blamed Seidl's "too classical" repertoire. The weekly *Spirit of the Times* proclaimed: "The Seidl Society is in mourning."

As an iridescent dream, nothing could have been lovelier than a continuous, all year round season of Wagner, beginning at the Metropolitan; transferred to Coney Island; resumed at the Metropolitan, next autumn. Divested of their diamonds, free from the trappings of fashion, enjoying Wagner and clam fritters, Wagner and soft-shell crabs, Wagner and fish chowder, Wagner and bathing-suits, the worshipers of the Seidl cult could pass a summer of bliss-ful harmony, and Pat Gilmore and his military band would be ban-ished, for want of patronage, from the happy island. It was a dream worthy of the late king of Bavaria. But alas! it has not been realized. Herr Seidl went to Brighton Beach, and his orchestra and a full score of the Master's most intricate and diabolically difficult compo-sitions. But, except a few curious members of the Seidl Society, nobody else would come, and the concerts for a few members did not pay.

Advertise yourself! Play popular music! Appeal to the general public! This was the brusque advice of the soulless, practical spec-tators who put up their unaesthetical money to pay the salaries of Herr Seidl and his band. It was a bitter Seidlitz powder to swallow; but necessity and empty benches know no law. . . .

Here is the light, airy, popular program which is expected to attract crowds to hear Seidl's concert, this evening: "1. Overture to the *Flying Dutchman*; 2. *Waldweben*; 3. *Lohengrin*; 4. *Siegfried Idyll*; 5. Intermission of ten minutes; 6. Overture to *Tannhäuser*; 7. Song from *The Meistersinger*; 8. Good Friday, from *Parsifal*." If these selec-tions do not bring the multitudes, nothing can. In anticipation of the result, the Iron Steamboats are running every hour; trains are start-ing on the Long Island, Bay Ridge, and other routes; the Brooklyn Bridge is open, and an annex boat connects Jersey City with the Coney Island lines. It is now 8 P.M. and the streets of New York seem deserted. Evidently everybody has gone to hear the tri-umphant Seidl's almost too trivial, amusing and blithesome concert. Yet there were rude skeptics who offer to bet that the ten minute intermission will prove the most popular part of the affair.[3]

The Seidl Society proved the rude skeptics wrong. Brighton con-tinued to host concerts twice daily, with Seidl sharing the baton with his assistant Victor Herbert.* Attendance steadily increased. Some Seidl Society lecturers, such as W. J. Henderson, were assisted

---

*As a conductor, Herbert may be considered a Seidl protégé. We have already encountered him as a member of Seidl's Metropolitan Opera orchestra, beginning in 1886—the year he moved to New York from Stuttgart; as the composer of an impor-

by Seidl and his entire sixty-piece ensemble—an innovation considered unique in the United States and Europe. The repertoire intensified its emphasis on new music—a gamut running from Chabrier, Massenet, Mascagni, and Saint-Saëns to Borodin, Dvořák, and Richard Strauss. "The Americans must learn to know music better and to see the beauty of Beethoven and the great composers," Seidl intoned. "To that end I give concerts here and in New York. . . . I am not doubtful about the acceptance in America of the great German music—Wagner is already popular." Some Brighton regulars still grumbled. Others "disposed at first to scoff" remained—in the opinion of a letter-writer to the *New York Mirror*—"to pray."[4]

The grumblers prevailed in 1893 and 1894—the Brighton Beach Association withdrew sponsorship of orchestral concerts, and there were none. After that, the Seidl Society took over, and Seidl's concerts—now the Seidl *Society* Concerts—thrived as never before. Transportation improvements, including direct trains from Brooklyn Bridge and Fulton Ferry, made Brighton Beach more swiftly and cheaply accessible. Improvements to the pavilion increased protection against the weather. Seidl's evening concert was the event of the day. If one of his assistants led the opening numbers, his arrival was dutifully awaited. Then at last, unannounced, he swiftly picked his way to the podium through the stands of violins. He did not even nod acknowledgement of the surging applause before lifting his baton and launching his music. The moment was electric.

---

tant cello concerto and other works performed under Seidl's baton; and as the composer, as well, of the Wagnerian *Natoma*, his one full-length opera. Though Herbert had already conducted a small orchestra of his own in New York and Boston, his experience as Seidl's assistant conductor at Brighton Beach helped to mold his eventual success leading mixed programs for mixed audiences with the famous Victor Herbert Orchestra. A turning point in his career was his 1893 debut as leader of the Twenty-second Regiment band, following the death of Patrick Gilmore. His close friends Anton and Auguste Seidl were in the audience; the opening work was the *Tannhäuser* Overture. As conductor of the Pittsburgh Symphony, form 1898 to 1904, Herbert closed his inaugural concert with the *Meistersinger* Overture. His Wagner repertoire in Pittsburgh was enormous, including not only the standard overtures and extracts but vocal selections from *The Flying Dutchman*, *Tannhäuser*, *Lohengrin*, and the *Ring*.

According to the *Musical Courier*, Seidl's Coney Island audiences were quieter than those in New York's winter concert rooms. Smokers were banished to the back row and talkers subdued or excluded. The seashore locale, with its fresh air, was a tonic; audiences experienced no compulsion "to assume an expression or impression of restraint while listening." The crash of the breakers, which had once seemed a distraction, now seemingly enhanced Wagner's orchestral storms. The cheapest seats still cost only fifteen to twenty-five cents—"ridiculously" little, in the opinion of the *Musical Courier*. This, plus inclement days, plus the hotel's withdrawal of its former subsidy, plus the national depression, insured that the society lost money at Brighton Beach. Its deficits were covered by individual members.[5]

The 1896 season was the longest ever—nine weeks and five days—and drew the biggest audiences. Seidl had effectively silenced calls for lighter programing. In fact, he was perceived to influence John Philip Sousa—who had taken Gilmore's place at Manhattan Beach (hence his famous *Manhattan Beach* March)—toward programing more "seriously." Then, on October 12, a "monster wave" struck. The highest tidal incursion in Coney Island's history, it split the storm-proof iron pier at West Brighton. Bathing pavilions, boardwalks, and shooting galleries were swept out to sea. Even before the storm had fully subsided, tear-stricken women rushed to the site. Where the Brighton Beach music pavilion once stood, the wreckage looked like a lumberyard.

The Brighton Beach Association notwithstanding, Seidl's Coney Island programs were distinctly lighter than the programs he gave with the New York Philharmonic at Carnegie Hall. But they also included a higher proportion of new and recent music. As at the Brooklyn Academy, Wagner was scheduled in limitless quantities. A summary in the *Brooklyn Daily Eagle* showed that, for the 1895 summer season, Wagner selections were performed, on average, more than twice daily. The following selective statistics—representing the number of performances per composer at Brighton Beach that year—tell an amazing story.*[6]

Wagner	156	Berlioz	19
Liszt	50	Weber	17
Saint-Saëns	46	Schumann	15
Grieg	37	Haydn	15
Mendelssohn	33	Schubert	14
Beethoven	29	Bach	10
Dvořák	27	Mozart	6
Tchaikovsky	21	Handel	3
Johann Strauss	21	Brahms	2

Most of the works were miniatures. But Seidl did include six Beethoven symphonies, three by Haydn, two by Mozart, and one by Schubert. Italian music was notably neglected (on one occasion, he passed his baton to an assistant rather than lead the *William Tell* Overture.) His neglect of Brahms correlated with his allegiance to Wagner. But the most startling neglect was that suffered by the old German masters Bach, Handel, Haydn, and Mozart—composers already canonized, if less frequently performed than in the century to come.

According to the *Daily Eagle*, Seidl's Brighton Beach orchestra had "the largest repertoire in America"—more than five hundred works by more than one hundred composers. The *Musical Courier* urged music students to attend the seashore concerts—they could hear as much good music in ten weeks as they could hear in ten years in Europe. The press also plausibly claimed that nowhere else in the United States was so much music so well played. In fact, with each passing week, with each passing summer, orchestra and conductor refined their rapport until maximum results could be achieved with minimal preparation. That Seidl was one of the leading conductors

---

*Some of these selections—there is no telling how many—were led by Seidl's assistants.

of his time was assumed. And Brooklynites understood that, in Europe, Nikisch and Richter were not known to conduct twice daily at the seashore.

But the chief distinction of Seidl's Brooklyn programming, summer and winter, was never remarked upon. It was taken for granted. Nowhere else—nowhere in America, nowhere, by all odds, abroad—was the Music of the Future so relentlessly pursued. Even Beethoven received five times fewer performances than Wagner, half as many as Liszt or Saint-Saëns. All the numbers on Seidl's 1894 "Liszt Night," for instance, were—thanks to Seidl—already familiar at Brighton Beach. These included not only *Les Préludes*, *Mazeppa*, and the *Spanish* Rhapsody (the latter in Seidl's own orchestration), but a march from *The Legend of St. Elisabeth* and the Benedictus from the *Hungarian* Coronation Mass.

The biggest draw, always, was Wagner. Here is the Wagner night program for Thursday, August 23, 1894—a concert that broke attendance records at the Brighton Beach pavilion, and so excited its listeners that, according to reviews, they urged the repeat of every number.

> *Tannhäuser* March [Entrance of the Guests]
> "Dich teure Halle" from *Tannhäuser* (with Ida Klein)
> *Tannhäuser* Overture and Bacchanale (Paris version)
> *Die Meistersinger* Prelude to act 3, Dance of the Apprentices, and
>   Procession of the Mastersingers
> *Fliedermonolog* and *Wahnmonolog* from *Die Meistersinger* (with Emil
>   Fischer)
> Walther's Prize Song from *Die Meistersinger* (with William Rieger)
> *Die Meistersinger* Quintet
> *Tristan* Prelude and *Liebestod* (orchestral version)

The *Daily Eagle* wrote of Seidl's Wagner audiences: "All the social and intellectual factors of Brooklyn life are present . . . and the crowd there is unlike any gathered anywhere outside of Bayreuth. The Seidl concerts are the attraction. . . . When [they] are underway the grounds are deserted and the place wears a quiet Sunday afternoon aspect, amazing to strangers whose ideas of Coney Island have been gathered from accounts of the West End."[7]

Today, our orchestras are museums. They curate the canonized masters. Audiences are trained to respond appreciatively, and shun the new. Seidl's audiences shunned the old. He was a contemporary music specialist.

As early as 1889, Seidl at Brighton Beach had himself become a cult. A New York newspaper recorded these vivid impressions:

> It is on the quiet days, the days when the week is new and all the Philistines and the madding crowd are gone, leaving only a wake of picnic litter behind them, that . . . the Seidl devotees are out in force. Perhaps Herr Seidl knows that he is adored. At all events his daily promenade about five in the afternoon in an event to see. With his white hat set well back on his head and the tails of his frock coat held at a meditative tilt by his right hand placed under them he paces deliberately along the paved walk which divides the hotel veranda from the pretty sweep of trim lawn which stretches away to the water's edge from the hotel. It is just barely possible that the gifted musician knows that hundreds of adoring eyes from hundreds of pretty faces are then bent upon him. I say it is barely possible he knows this, that his soul is not so bent upon heaven soaring symphonies or in searching the key to the intricate knots which tie the hidden soul of harmony, but he knows that there, all in a row on the veranda, is a ravishing line of summer costumes and that each costume holds an adorer more ravishing than the costume itself. My impression is he does know it. But that may be blasphemy.
>
> At all events the Herr is not so wrapt in soulful reverie but that he catches the eyes of some one among the throng he recognizes, and then off goes the high hat and down goes the Professor's head in the great sweep of an Oriental salaam, and thus he goes by leaving a row of eyes bent heavenward only to come to earth again to follow his form farther, farther away to the beaten sands of the much-sounding sea where he stands in graceful pose with head

uncovered to the mists of the mighty Atlantic and the vagrant, spiced breezes from Barren Island which toy with his ambrosial locks.[8]

Not all Seidl's adorers, the article continued, were "of the gushing type"—by which the writer meant women. Others were "serious and earnest lovers of music," who would "take their dinners solemnly" and "smoke a sentimental cigar"—in other words: cultivated gentlemen. Then, later in the week, the "true Seidlites" were swallowed up by gradually larger and noisier multitudes—many of whose number found their way either into the music pavilion or onto the nearby verandas and promenades, from which Seidl's orchestra was readily (and romantically) audible.

Obviously, workers who escaped New York to ride the Steeplechase with wives and children were unlikely to wander east to the Brighton and Manhattan Beach preserves. Still, newspaper and magazine accounts leave no doubt that Seidl's Coney Island audience was notably diversified. And the same accounts stress that Laura Langford's commitment to class diversity was no lip service—that her society's roughly five hundred members encompassed a gamut of backgrounds and lifestyles.

A rough breakdown would have to include at least five categories of Brighton Beach listeners—all seated side by side in a circular structure unfitted with boxes and other signatures of status. Especially after the Seidl Society undertook sponsorship in 1894, the best families of both Brooklyn and New York regularly attended Seidl's concerts—as they might the Metropolitan Opera, the New York Philharmonic, or the Brooklyn Academy. Some husbands came willingly on the weekend, joining wives and children who summered at the seashore; others were "overawed and somewhat sheepish looking."[9] The intellectual gentlemen who took solemn dinners comprised a second Seidl constituency. Third, there were the ladies of many degrees. For toiling women, the Seidl Society provided not only free or inexpensive railroad and concert tickets, but child care; as I have mentioned, special arrangements were made, as well, for ladies without escorts. Germans were a fourth distinct constituency, the only one to which symphonic resort concerts were not a novelty.

Finally, there were the incidental patrons who had come to Coney Island mainly to swim or stroll along Surf Avenue.

It goes without saying that many upon whom Seidl cast his spell were newcomers to the music he conducted. The *Daily Eagle* observed:[10] "Hundreds of Brooklyn people got their first taste of fine music . . . dropping in because [it was] cheap, and became regular patrons of the pavilion." Langford and Seidl testified alike that progress in musical taste was tangible in Brooklyn—that listeners who once considered a parlor ballad or a Strauss waltz "classical music" now stated their preference for this Beethoven symphony or that Wagner overture.

The Brighton Beach phenomenon amplified the singularity of what was taking place across the river in Manhattan. Gilded Age stereotypes notwithstanding, the Wagner cult gripped both Yankees and Germans, natives and immigrants. Startled observers repeatedly emphasized Seidl's appeal to all classes of Americans. And nothing startled more than the role women played in Brooklyn as initiators and administrators. Langford called the Seidl Society a "new departure in the history of women's clubs." No American resort had ever offered a symphonic orchestra with any but—as *Scribner's* magazine once put it—"the rheumatic instruments which a dancing master marshalled for his nightly dances in the hotel parlors." And the Seidl Society concerts were an American landmark in providing outstanding performances of important new music at low prices. The experiment was initially ridiculed as quixotic. Then, summer by summer, admiration gave way to amazement. "The capacity of the members of this society to hustle and sell concert tickets is what baseball managers call phenomenal," wrote the *Daily Eagle* in 1891. Three years later, the same newspaper marveled that the Seidl Society had

> maintained itself . . . with a perseverance almost of the Calvinistic saints until its name is everywhere known and famous. Businessmen would not assume such responsibility in the hope of accumulated wealth. They can scarcely be blamed, for business is business. But an organization of women will sometimes courageously assume risks from which mere men will shrink. . . . They were prepared to accept [Seidl's] most advanced notions and were inclined to advise

him to go a step further. After some seasons of experience in New York, he learns in Brooklyn the worth of a woman constituency as contrasted with the disappointing worthlessness of a faint-hearted following of men.

In 1896, regarding what would be the Seidl Society's final summer season, the *Musical Courier* exclaimed: "Goodness knows what they do it for. Ordinary women would rather put the energy into new bonnets and send the money to the missionary Huyler. But these women are extraordinary, and some time after they are all dead the town will be putting up a monument to them as public benefactors, perhaps with a bas-relief representing Herr Seidl waving his baton and a chorus of adoring angels about him."[11]

Today, even books about Coney Island make no mention of Anton Seidl. But he was no marginal player at America's most famous playground. In the mid-1890s, Theodore Dreiser saw Broadway's first electric sign. Its fifteen hundred lights flashed seven messages, first in sequence, then all at once in a blaze of green, white, red, blue, and yellow. The sign read:

SWEPT BY OCEAN BREEZES

THREE GREAT HOTELS

PAIN'S FIREWORKS

SOUSA'S BEST

SEIDL'S GREAT ORCHESTRA

THE RACES

NOW—MANHATTAN BEACH—NOW[12]

The Seidl Society papers, at the Brooklyn Historical Society, include a speech in Seidl's clear hand, painstakingly composed in English, with many words crossed out and revised. It was delivered at Brighton Beach; no year is given. I cannot resist reproducing it in full:

Wagner Nights

Now we are again on work, to play good music for good men and women. Those who are good, they like the music and go to the places, where the good music can be heard. Those, who like only the airs as "Jonny get your gun" find places on this shore very many. We will play only good music; we know, the people *need* it, and this is the cause, that the noble ladies of the Seidl Society dont spare the large expenses and the terrible difficult and heavy work to give the *good* people, what he needs, and what he must have. It is not only right, to give the poor free music at the different parks, but the Bands must play *good* music. The people not understand it first, but later he will whistle it with more dash and vigor, as the rich, who sits in his box and—chatter, because—he does not understand it. But the low kind of music demoralizes the people. One of the many good works of the Seidl Society is to give good music for the less rich, for the poor, and in the same time enjoys and educates himself. This is a grand and glorious mission! And a point to which of must direct the eyes of the whole world, is, that this society works not for money, as the socalled managers of nearly all the musical organizations do, but the noble ladies of this society brings many thousands and thousands dollars together, to enable themselfs to give good music for 25 cents to the poor and music needing people. This only women can do. The men must stand still and be astonished before such a grand work! We dont ask for kind criticism of our performances, if you dont like it; but our missionary work is worth of your support; and if you remember always, that this concerts are not grand Symphonic Concerts of the Winter-Season, but popular Concerts to popularize good music in the big heart of the American people, then you will find very easy the way, in which you take part in this very needed missionary work, and you will say with me: Hats off before these noble women! How Wagner, Beethoven, Schumann, Schubert, Liszt, and all the great men of musical art admired the women and her mission in life and art, you need only to luck at the different operas, songs, oratorios, what they have written about women. Take Tannhäuser, Lohengrin, Flying Dutchman, Götterdämmerung, Saint Elisabeth, Fidelio, the various songs of Schumann and Schubert, and you will have the ideas of the great men about the eternal woman and her glorification in the music art,—and all this glorious works shall be never heard by the great mass of poor people? That man, who asks for not playing some classical works at the popular concerts, is not a democrat, is not a republican, not an—American. He is a despot, and shall be enclosed in that place, where the despots are living in our time.

12

Protofeminism

Attempting to account for the "curious" fact that newcomers to symphonic music at Brighton Beach became, first and foremost, enthusiastic Wagnerites, the *Brooklyn Daily Eagle* surmised: "The pictorial and dramatic qualities of [Wagner's] music appealed to them more quickly than did the purely musical quality of other composers."[1] But this is a mere starting point. What were the pictures and dramas that appealed so quickly?

We begin with the overture to *Tannhäuser*, because this was Wagner's signature tune. At Brighton Beach, it was "the most widely liked piece of music," heard ten times a season and more. Elsewhere, too, the *Tannhäuser* Overture was Wagner's most frequently performed composition—possibly the most frequently performed symphonic composition by any composer. Today, this music remains rousing and familiar. In Gilded Age America, where even bands played it, it was galvanizingly new—and not only for its sensuous chromaticism and technicolored orchestration.

When *Tannhäuser* was first performed in New York in 1859, the *Post* commented (as the reader may recall): "The general idea is the struggle between the pleasure of the senses and the conviction of duty." This struggle—"but a romanticized epitome of the similar trials in every day real life"—is equally the idea of the *Tannhäuser* Overture. It begins with a prayer: the Pilgrim's Chorus. The prayer's antithesis, the second polarity in a musical dialectic, is the Venusberg music, whose erotic maelstrom—including phallic lunges no previous composer had dared describe—stunned its first listeners. One 1890 New York review called the *Tannhäuser* Bacchanale "beyond comparison the most intoxicating piece ... ever composed. . . . If an abstainer wants to realize the voluptuous dreams of an oriental opium-smoker, he may have the experience without bad after-effects by simply listening to this ballet music."[2] The story of the Overture is the story of pilgrims and intoxicants locked in mortal combat—until a final, triumphant reprise promulgates virtue's victory.*

This was one microcosm of the whole. Wagnerism in America did not, as in Europe, herald an iconoclastic modernism. Rather, to a remarkable degree, America's Wagner cult was absorbed within the dominant genteel tradition. Like the *Tannhäuser* Overture, Wagner was meaningful, titillating, and, mainly, reassuring. He evoked the "trials of real life," stirred powerful and neglected feelings, and yet in many cases left no "bad after-effects." He was found not to challenge but to reinforce the intellectual mainstream.

No less than the "Christian Wagner" of the *Parsifal* Entertainment, the *Tannhäuser* Overture speaks to Wagner's role as a timely inspirational bulwark, buttressing faith, banishing looming twentieth-century doubt. And Tannhäuser himself seemed the embodiment of noble perseverance, a flawed hero whose deserved salvation, Henry Krehbiel wrote, "no one can ... doubt when ... as impersonated by Herr Niemann, [he] sinks lifeless beside the bier of the atoning saint [Elisabeth] and Venus's cries of woe are swallowed up by the pious canticle of the Pilgrims."[3]

But what, then, of Tristan? Notwithstanding ingenious meliorist readings, he was a less lofty, less redeemable sinner. The later

---

*As Wagner himself remarked in an 1852 "programmatic commentary": "The whirring and whispering sounds, which had been like the eerie lament of the damned, are now transformed into ever brighter waves of elation ... [which] swell into a joyous tumult of sublime ecstasy. It is the Venusberg triumphant, redeemed from its unholy curse. . . . Every living pulse springs in with this song, and the two sundered elements—the spirit and the senses, God and nature—embrace in the holy, unifying kiss of love." (And yet Baudelaire, in his essay on the *Tannhäuser* Overture, discovered decadent narcotic and aphrodisiac qualities. See Baudelaire, "R. W. et Tannhäuser à Paris," in vol. 2 of *Oeuvres complètes* [Paris, 1925]. I am indebted to Thomas Grey, whose unpublished article, "Sickness or Redemption? 'Wagnerism' and the Consequences," brought Baudelaire's description to my attention. And I use Grey's translation of Wagner's commentary on the *Tannhäuser* Overture.)

Wagner, which he exemplifies, possessed "pictorial and dramatic qualities" equally bearing on America's Wagner hunger. But it occupied libidinal realms more menacing than any Venusberg, and furnished opportunities for emotional release surpassing mere opium dreams. It spoke to the women of the Gilded Age.

Even if the *Daily Eagle* had never remarked that the husbands of the Seidlites were jealous; even if the *Musical Courier* had never recorded that, when Seidl conducted, middle-aged women stood and screamed; even had nine-tenths of the downstairs mourners at Seidl's funeral not been women, it would remain obvious that many members of the Seidl Society were excited in ways their husbands could neither understand nor displace.[4] The explanation transcends Seidl's charisma and Wagner's sensuality. The Seidl Society included Gilded Age housewives whose professional opportunities were shackled by genteel breeding and decorum. It included women of passionate sensibility for whom Wagner represented a consuming alternative to a world of marriage and men.

Especially in the middle-class households of the Northeast, women had been relieved of spinning, quilting, and other vital domestic duties. And yet women were expected to shun the male contagion of money-making. They were no longer welcomed as midwives, printers, or proprietors of small businesses. In school, they were seldom asked to undertake such "masculine" subjects as mathematics or the natural sciences. They were meant to wear corsets, to deny their sexual urges, to preserve their virginity; and intercourse was imperiled by disease and unwanted pregnancy. Henry Adams, eying the resulting limbo, called American women "still a study."

Their plight was reinforced by a larger pattern of fin-de-siècle transition and malaise. The anomie and enforced passivity of modern urban life, the decline of religion, the sustained economic depression beginning in 1873—these were late Gilded Age currents eroding personal identity. Nietzsche termed the result "weightlessness." The American cultural historian Jackson Lears has commented on the American condition circa 1880: "A weightless culture of material comfort and spiritual blandness was breeding weightless persons who hoped for intense experience to give some definition, some distinct outline and substance to their vaporous lives."[5]

Coney Island's Steeplechase Park offered a form of "intense experience" to workers whose factory jobs produced another kind of weightlessness. For weightless housewives of the Gilded Age, however, the conventional spiritual outlets were, in Lears's view, anything but intense. Religion meant the genteel ministry. Culture meant sentimental fiction or the parlor piano. The costs of emotional and sexual repression are suggested by epidemic ill health. Nervous prostration was the disorder of the day. When Catharine Beecher polled her female friends, she found that "habitual invalids" and "delicate or diseased" outnumbered the "strong and healthy" from four to one to ten to one.[6]

Lears, in *No Place of Grace*, has catalogued the therapies with which Americans attempted to heal their nerves. "Intense experience" was the core prescription. One such cure—which he briefly considers in the context of "the turn toward medieval irrationality"—an effort to recover a collective unconscious of myths and fantasies—was Wagner. He concludes: "Though devoted Wagnerians complained that the mass of visitors to Bayreuth were simply fashion-mongers, [Wagnerism] was more than an aesthetic fad."[7]

Merely to glimpse the pilgrims is to amplify this understatement beyond recognition. At the Met, at the Brooklyn Academy, at Brighton Beach, they were transfixed and transformed. They lived for Wagner. No less than the roller coaster or revival meetings that serviced the lower classes, Wagner was a necessary source of violent excitation. And Seidl, with his irresistible gift for climax, was the necessary medium. At the Met, Isolde's death-song, thrusting toward regions of oceanic wholeness, of womb-like security, of pre-pubescent play, was consummated by the hypnotic and statuesque Lilli Lehmann. The bad effects of husband and bedroom were silenced by a musical-dramatic orgasm as explicit and complete as any mortal intercourse. And Isolde's second-act duet with Tristan— their clandestine Love-Night, shutting out the world, beckoning dissolution—was a secret pact, a shared conspiracy with Wagner, with Seidl, with the dissolving Seidlites. For the moment, the parlor spinet, the neurasthenia of the bedroom, were banished and forgotten. The Wagner pilgrims were addicted, body and soul.

Clare Benedict, of Philadelphia, felt impelled to document her Bayreuth impressions in a pamphlet, *The Divine Spark*.

> This Richard Wagner . . . what was this power that he possessed? Was it not a greater Power working through him? . . . In every case that one has heard of, the influence has ennobled by producing complete forgetfulness of self, the master's true followers having always been distinguished by one marked common quality—disinterested devotion. . . .
>
> Thank God for music, for Richard Wagner; thank Him besides for having kindled so many sparks of love and faithfulness at the divine spark of one man's genius for is not human genius a gift of God?

The poet Ella Wheeler Wilcox attended *Tristan* and wrote:

> . . . in the flood of music swelling clear
> And high and strong, all things save love were drowned.
> A clamorous sea of chords swept o'er my soul,
> Submerging reason. Mutinous desire
> Stood at the helm; the stars were in eclipse:
> I heard wild billows beat, and thunders roll;
> And as the universe flamed into fire,
> I swooned upon the reef of coral lips.

Charlotte Teller, in her novel *The Cage*, described the impact of a Wagner concert on Frederica, whose boyfriend, Harden, cautions her: "This is your wine . . . be careful!"

> There was only a moment's silence, and the orchestra began to play the "Ride of the Valkyries." At first the accent was without excitement, but little by little it grew more impetuous and carried her with it. She felt herself, struggling, breathless, to get higher and higher, and feeling that his hand was in hers, that he, too, was being swept upward. . . . She felt herself strong and vital, astride a horse of Walhalla. But the man was not dead that she carried; there was hope for him if she could take one long deep breath instead of breathing harder and harder, as though it were breath that was motion. . . .

The end came, and it was as though she had been thrust back and down just before she had reached the summit. Her nostrils were tense, and she did not relax, even though she sat with her hands folded in her lap, a most unusual attitude of quiescence for her. "Wotan's Farewell" and the "Fire-music" came to an end, too, and there was another intermission. As the audience stirred in its place and began to move about the aisles, Harden rose.

"You must not stay longer," he said, bending over Frederica. "If you are too long away from the real world you will *never* go back to it."

Mabel Dodge Luhan, the influential *bohémienne*, attended the Bayreuth Festival with her mother and girlfriends. The girls sat holding hands in the darkness. "We . . . were keyed up to the moment. My heart was beating and my hands were hot." Listening to the invisible orchestra, she experienced an

energy that was bound together and flowing, an ultimate and vital unison of sound that I have never heard surpassed. And it was not alone from the orchestra that one got the sense of being enveloped and lifted higher into areas of intense feeling. . . . There existed between the musicians and the audience a rapport that was creative to them both. They were polarized. . . . The great audience at Bayreuth was not the same after it had left the music festival as before it had participated. . . . When people listened to [Wagner] they were only listening to their own impatient souls, weary at last of the restraint that had held them.

Luhan left Bayreuth mired in "a colorless depression." "Everything in life seemed flat and hopeless. . . . My body was like an engine whose fuel has given out. Even my skin changed in two or three days."[8]

The most poignant, most dispassionate account of Wagner jarring awake dormant feeling is Willa Cather's, in her 1904 short story "A Wagner Matinee." Aunt Georgiana, who once taught music at the Boston Conservatory, returns to Boston to collect a small inheritance. As a girl, she had eloped to Nebraska with a farm boy, there to settle a rugged homestead. To her Boston nephew, Clark, who greets her at the station, she seems "at once pathetic and grotesque" in her soiled duster, lumpy dress, and sooty bonnet. Her shoulders sag over her sunken chest. Her false teeth don't fit. Her skin is yellowed by wind and water. With trepidation—she "seemed not to realize that she was in the city where she had spent her youth"—he takes her to a Wagner concert.

> I asked her whether she had ever heard any of the Wagnerian operas, and found that she had not, though she was perfectly familiar with their respective situations, and had once possessed the piano score of *The Flying Dutchman*. . . .
>
> We sat at the extreme left of the first balcony. . . . The matinee audience was made up chiefly of women.
>
> When the musicians came out and took their places, [Aunt Georgiana] gave a little stir of anticipation, and looked with quickening interest down over the rail. . . .
>
> The first number was the *Tannhäuser* overture. When the horns drew out the first strain of the Pilgrim's chorus, my Aunt Georgiana clutched my coat sleeve. Then it was I first realized that for her this broke a silence of thirty years; the inconceivable silence of the plains. With the battle between the two motives, with the frenzy of the Venusberg theme and its ripping of strings, there came to me an overwhelming sense of the waste and wear we are so powerless to combat; and I saw again the tall, naked house on the prairie, black and grim as a wooden fortress; the black pond where I had learned to swim, its margin pitted with sun-dried cattle tracks. . . .
>
> I watched her closely through the prelude to *Tristan and Isolde*, trying vainly to conjecture what that seething turmoil of strings and winds might mean to her; but she sat mutely staring. . . . She preserved this utter immobility throughout the number from *The Flying Dutchman*, though her fingers worked mechanically upon her black dress, as though, of themselves, they were recalling the piano score they had once played. . . .
>
> Soon after the tenor began the "Prize Song" [from *Die Meistersinger*], I heard a quick drawn breath and turned to my aunt. Her eyes were closed, but the tears were glistening on her cheeks, and I think, in a moment more, they were in my eyes as well. It never really died, then—the soul that can suffer so excruciatingly and so interminably; it withers to the outward eye only; like that

strange moss which can lie on a dusty shelf half a century and yet, if placed in water, grows green again. . . .

The second half of the programme consisted of four numbers from the *Ring*, and closed with Siegfried's funeral march. My aunt wept quietly, but almost continuously, as a shallow vessel overflows in a rain-storm. . . .

The deluge of sound poured on and on; I never knew what she found in the shining current of it; I never knew how far it bore her, or past what happy islands. From the trembling of her face I could well believe that before the last numbers she had been carried out where the myriad graves are, into the gray, nameless burying grounds of the sea. . . .

The concert was over. . . . I spoke to my aunt. She burst into tears and sobbed pleadingly, "I don't want to go, Clark, I don't want to go!"* [9]

When rehearsing his operas, Wagner would enact the various roles on stage. His histrionic powers amazed. Angelo Neumann, in his

*Among Cather's prominent contemporaries, Kate Chopin more obliquely betrays Wagnerian input, as in *The Awakening* (1899), when a Chopin impromptu glides into "the quivering love-notes of Isolde's song," music "turbulent, insistent, plaintive and soft with entreaty." Kate Wiggin, the author of *Rebecca of Sunnybrook Farm*, wrote a popular spoof, *Bluebeard* (1896), about an unpublished Wagner opera discovered in a hatbox identified by a halo. The story also parodies the lecture-recitals of Walter Damrosch, attended mostly by women "through whom in course of time a certain amount of information percolated and reached the husbands." Edith Wharton, abroad in 1911, immersed herself in Wagner's autobiography and reported: "I don't know what I shall do when it's done. Everything will seem insipid—even Nietzsche!" To Bernard Berenson, she wrote that Wagner's *Mein Leben*, "the only thing that rouses me," was "incomparable" and "inexhaustible"; were it not for his terrible jargon—"I never read worse—not even in German!"—he could have produced an "immortal" book. Two years later, Wharton accompanied Berenson to the *Ring* in Berlin. (R. W. B. Lewis and Nancy Lewis, eds., *The Letters of Edith Wharton* [New York, 1988], pp. 18, 237, 240.) Inspired by Wagner, another important turn-of-the-century writer, Sidney Lanier (who also composed and played the flute), undertook a systematic study of the relationship between music and poetic verse. His poems include "To Richard Wagner" (1877). For more on Wagner and literature, see Chapter 15 and the Postlude.

memoirs, writes of Wagner's stage rehearsals for *Lohengrin* and *Tannhäuser* in Vienna in 1875: "[After] thirty long years I can still distinctly recall certain incidents of his wonderful mimetic powers."

> How wonderfully he took the part of Tannhäuser finding himself at the crossways in the forest after his release from the enchantments of Venusberg. Riveted to the spot, he stood like a graven image, with arms upraised; then gradually, at the entrance of the pilgrims, came to life with a tremendous shuddering start, and finally, overcome with emotion, sank to the ground as the chorus proceeded; to break out at the end in his great cry—"Ach, schwer drückt mich der Sünden Last!"

But Wagner's most startling impersonations were of women. Of Wagner's Elsa, Neumann says: "How well he simulated [her] rapture as she throws herself into Lohengrin's arms. . . . No one who had not seen Wagner playing the role could believe how marvelously it was done." In the bridal procession

> with arms outstretched, the palms turned toward the audience, with uplifted countenance and radiant eyes—and never a glance at the steps he was to traverse—Wagner moved serenely down in stately progress. . . . Up to the instant when Elsa is about to mount the first stair and Ortrud rushes to bar her way, Wagner maintained that wonderful look of radiant exaltation, his whole progress a triumph of histrionic art.[10]

In fact, Wagner's was a strikingly androgynous personality. He once wrote: "The true human being is both man and woman." He loved silks and perfumes. He wept freely. And he created a gallery of women as prepossessing as his men. Their marginality, which he sympathetically understood, reflected his own experience as a political exile, social iconoclast, and artistic pariah. "It is so hard to find a place for myself in this world," he told Mathilde Wesendonck. Siegmund, who stirred his full compassion, sings:

> What I thought right, others found bad;
> what seemed wrong to me,

others approved.
I encountered feuds wherever I found myself,
Disfavor tracked me wherever I went;
if I longed for happiness, I only provoked misery.*[11]

To some female Wagnerites, Senta and Elisabeth, Sieglinde and Brünnhilde must have seemed—as they did to Houston Stewart Chamberlain in the 1898 *Ladies Home Journal*—models of exalted purity. To others, what mattered was that, like Siegmund, Wagner's women are oppressed. They are driven to flaunt convention. Their fathers cannot read them. Their husbands are brutes. Senta, in *The Flying Dutchman*, is already a *locus classicus*. With the other village maids—husband-fodder, peripheral to a man's world of activity and excitement—she sits and spins. She is regarded as odd and unruly. Lacking any healthy outlet, her intensity—like that of "overly active" Gilded Age neurasthenics—more than verges on hysteria. Erik, who "loves" her, is a dullard. Her father, a materialist, tries to understand but cannot. The visionary Elisabeth, in *Tannhäuser*, is cut from the same mold. Fricka and Isolde are victimized by unsuitable actual or potential spouses; they become scourges. Sieglinde, whose father abandons her, has a monster of a husband; upon eloping with her twin brother, she is traumatized by guilt; she sinks into halluci-

---

*According to Thomas Mann: "Before the foundation of the Reich and before he made his home in Bayreuth, Wagner's relationship to his fatherland was that of a man isolated, misunderstood and rejected, full of hostile criticism and contempt. . . . The longing for Germany that so consumed him in his exile was replaced by bitter disappointment at the reality he found when he did return home." ("The Sorrows and Grandeur of Richard Wagner," translated by Allan Blunden, in Thomas Mann, *Pro and Contra Wagner* [Chicago, 1985], p. 142.) The significance of Wagner's marginality is underestimated. He is hollowest, it seems to me, as a ranting nationalist (e.g., at the end of *Die Meistersinger*—a passage Cosima urged on him). The ironic Loge, who stands apart, is closer to Wagner's own persona than the Germanic *Übermensch*, Siegfried—a cardboard figure beside such pariahs as the Dutchman, Tannhäuser, Siegmund, Alberich, Mime, the Wanderer, and Tristan. Wagner's protagonists puzzle over their origins. More the Wandering Jew than the rooted German, Wagner himself suspected that the actor Ludwig Geyer, not the police actuary Friedrich Wagner, might have been his father. And there was a suggestion (which we now know to have been false) that Geyer had Jewish blood. Wagner's marginality is also one source of his appeal to Jews. For more on Wagner and Judaism, see the Postlude.

natory derangement. Brünnhilde's father, who frustrates her exemplary intuitive gift, condemns her to Senta's condition: to "sit and spin by the fire." Though he changes his mind, she finds herself being married off to Gunther, who is no better than Senta's Erik. Finally, there is Kundry: a study in schizophrenia, an analysis of sociological dislocation. Kundry's is the pathology of the Wagner heroine heightened and exposed. She is the woman without a place, whose only compelling roles are imbalanced: the domineering temptress, the submissive servant.

Around the time of Kundry, Strindberg and Ibsen fashioned victimized women in some ways comparable, in some ways not. Compared to Senta and company, Miss Julie and Hedda Gabler are modernist heroines, condemned to a bitter uselessness. Notwithstanding their varieties of entrapment, Wagner's heroines are juicier, more robust, more consummated. One essential function is oldfashioned. They are versions of the muse. They redeem men. As selfsacrificing lovers and wives, they—no less than Marx's workers—are the agents of teleological progress. Thus Senta saves the Dutchman and Elisabeth rescues Tannhäuser. In more complicated ways, Isolde and Brünnhilde also offer and experience redemption through love. Fricka, who redeems no one, is at least revenged. Kundry is at least redeemed. Sieglinde, who cannot save Siegmund, saves his son. When Brünnhilde intuits that Siegfried lies asleep in her womb, Sieglinde's ecstatic response ("O hehrstes Wunder! /Herrlichste Maid!") registers as a signature moment in *Die Walküre*. It happened to resonate with the Gilded Age's cult of motherhood as woman's highest and noblest calling. It also happens to furnish the music with which the *Ring* ends—the soaring leitmotif Wagner identified as the "glorification of Brünnhilde." In fact, Brünnhilde proves stronger and truer than that strongest of heroes and truest of lovers, Siegfried.*

In sum, Wagner's powerfully and compassionately drawn women—muses and helpmates, scourges and heroines, victims and saviors—

---

*William Foster Apthorp, in "Some of Wagner's Heroes and Heroines" (*Scribner's* magazine, 1889, pp. 346–48), writes:

As a concrete character, Brünnhilde is Woman, *the* Woman, *das Ewigweibliche*, in the fullest sense. At the time when Wagner was at work on the text of the "Nibelungen," conflate aspects of Romantic sentimentality with intimations of the new modernism. That this fosters confusion is most obviously the case with the two Brünnhildes: the first (in *Die Walküre*) a penetrating study in healthy, unrepressed adolescent ardor and rebellion, the second (in *Götterdämmerung*) interpolating the melodrama of revenge, and culminating in a paean to the witless Siegfried.* More significant for the late Gilded Age: as up-to-date images of the victim, Wagner's bipolar heroines consoled. As old-fashioned images of the redemptress, they inspired fantasies of heroic utility. They were supportive but not (like Ibsen's Hedda and Strindberg's Julie) explicitly subversive.

In Europe, art saturated life. As read by George Bernard Shaw, Wagner espoused new political awareness: heightened class consciousness, social reform. Read by Baudelaire, Wagner embodied a drugged world of feeling altering every cranny of existence, a potential madness. In America, art and life remained distinct. Or did they?

It is significant that the Wagner pilgrims of today are no longer predominantly women, that the imagery of American Wagnerites is no longer female. To be sure, wives and sisters of the late Gilded Age

---

he wrote to Liszt: "Never has such a tribute been paid to Woman as in this last work of mine!" Indeed, the picture of womanhood Wagner has painted in Brünnhilde is at once as exalted, poetic, and complete as any that I know of. Of course, it is a picture of women *as man sees her*—that absolute completeness which would have come from a double and converging point of view was out of the question; but there is nothing mean nor puny in the likeness, every stroke is large, noble, and heroic.... Brünnhilde first appears as the virgin-goddess, the Valkyr, in all the joyous pride of her own power, and conscious—or half-conscious—that her power lies in her maidenhood....

Nowhere, in all dramatic poetry, have I seen [the] gradual transition in woman from virginity to muliebrity, from the maiden to the wife, and the acute moral wrench it involves, so vigorously, largely, poetically, and truthfully portrayed as in this Brünnhilde of Wagner's.

*Carolyn Abbate, in *Unsung Voices: Opera and Musical Narrative in the Nineteenth Century* (Princeton, 1991), ingeniously attempts to reconcile these conflicting portraits.

were in general more likely to be "music lovers" than husbands or brothers. But the Wagnerite phenomenon was something more. What accounts for its special intensity? Jackson Lears's imagery of a "therapeutic" culture beginning in this period suggests an avenue of explanation.

One Wagner signature is the restless void out of which the *Tristan* Prelude emerges with its message of insatiable erotic yearning. Wagner "knows a sound for those quiet, disturbing midnights of the soul, when cause and effect seem to be out of joint and where at any moment something might originate out of nothing," wrote Nietzsche. He also termed Wagner "the Orpheus of all secret misery." Thomas Mann, in a similar vein, called Wagner's orchestra "the kingdom of subliminal knowledge." Mann identified "two forces" that combine to elevate Wagner's work "far above the intellectual level of all previous forms of musical drama." The forces are psychology and myth—the subject matter of Freud and Jung.[12]

Wagner's is the psychic world of Siegfried rejecting his father and discovering his sexuality—and crying out for his mother; of Parsifal, whom Kundry seduces by instilling guilt for his mother's death. He is the analyst of concealed sexual drives, of incest, homosexuality, and Oedipal unrest. The submerged pedal points at the start of *Das Rheingold*, or of Wotan's monologue, or of Isolde's *Liebestod*—these are nothing if not musical representations of a protean subconscious landscape. Wagner gives expression to that which is repressed.

One result is a form of therapy—not least for Wagner himself, whose nervous condition could be pertinently diagnosed as "neurasthenia." He suffered constipation, melancholia, insomnia, exhaustion. He would sit and cry for fifteen minutes at a time. He experienced art as a narcotic escape. "For me the 'enjoyment of life, of *love*' is merely something to be imagined, not experienced," he wrote at the age of thirty-nine. "So my heart was forced to enter my brain, and my life became a wholly artificial affair: only as an 'art-ist' can I live my life henceforth, now that my 'person-ality' has been wholly subsumed into that function."[13]

For some Wagnerites, too, life can become "a wholly artificial affair." Only in contact with the charged psychological substratum Wagner reveals do they make contact with themselves. It is, the

British critic Bryan Magee continues, "like being in love. . . . It is the abandoned utterance of what has been in some way forbidden. . . . [It] seems to have a special appeal for the emotionally isolated or repressed. . . . It makes possible a passionate warmth and fullness of emotion without personal relationships."[14] For Gilded Age women in love with Seidl, in love with Wagner, the impact of *Tristan*, the *Ring*, and *Parsifal* gauged the emotional repression they suffered.

Recent scholarship has usefully proposed other, more flattering readings of Gilded Age women, stressing progress toward liberated lives. Though the fundamental reality of oppression remains undeniable—men dominated the public sphere—certain private lives suggest a different explanation of Wagnerism's magnetic appeal a century ago. The prescriptive literature that enforced public codes of postmarital restraint may conceal a much different private reality—an eroticism behind closed doors. In particular, American women of the late nineteenth century formed passionately intimate ties with other women, not excluding intensely sensual love avowals and uninhibited physical contact. Carroll Smith-Rosenberg, in a landmark 1975 essay, argues that, in a society whose men and women inhabited distinct, emotionally segregated spheres, women did not necessarily become an oppressed subcategory of male society. Rather, a "female world of love and ritual" nourished a fulfilling life of feeling. Whether or not these women had genital contact and can be termed "homosexual" is less significant than that their husbands and families found their behavior socially acceptable. Subsequent mores, by comparison, welcomed fuller heterosexual relations but imposed taboos on homosocial ties. In other words: "The supposedly repressive and restrictive Victorian sexual ethos may have been more flexible and responsive to the needs of particular individuals than those of the mid-twentieth century."[15]

Exploring this realm of female companionship, another contemporary historian, Helen Horowitz, infers that certain women were enabled to understand themselves in new ways as a result of mutual encounters with Romantic art. She studies the case of M. Carey Thomas, who was the founding dean and, in 1894, second president of Bryn Mawr College. As a young adult, Thomas studied in Leipzig and Zurich. This European sojourn liberated impulses that had been building up before she left. By the time she returned to the United States, at the age of twenty-six in 1883, she was a confirmed agnostic and an ardent reader of Gautier and Swinburne. Also, to safeguard her future autonomy, she had throttled her heterosexuality in favor of passionate alliances with other women. In later life, as a public figure, Thomas necessarily "sheathed herself in the conventions of her era." But her personal life remained fixed. She read the new medical literature which described women as sexual beings. She never married. She retained a private identity, a "passionate" sensibility.[16]

We should not be amazed that one of Thomas's passions was Wagner. Upon hearing Seidl conduct *Tristan* at the Met in 1891, she wrote to her intimate friend Mary Garrett:

> If I say it seemed to me the most glorious of all Wagner's operas, flawless from first to last, the most triumphant rhapsody of love ever th't, rapturous, soaring, heavenly high, winging thro. the Empyrean, without a touch of earth, all human emotion sublimated into godlike passion & longing panting & throbbing thro. thousands of memories of the splendid things of seas & stars and plains and marble & pictures & poetry until all together are blended into one in the rapture & fire of the music—I never imagined Wagner so great. During the bridal night of Tristam [*sic*] & Iseult as she lies in his arms while this glorious chant rises & falls one thinks passion has said its last word, but when the dying Tristam hears of Iseult's approach & tears open his wound in the wildest excitement it rises higher & over his dead body in the death song of Iseult so high that one fairly breaks down under its weight of splendour. I never in a public place came so near to losing my self control and I never cared so much for an opera of Wagner's.

Later the same year, when Mary Garrett attended *Parsifal*, Thomas wrote: "I am so delighted you were carried away. I cannot tell you how glad I am. It is so much worthwhile to be carried away and you know the twice I have heard Tristram [*sic*], the nearest in time to Parzival [*sic*], I have been utterly lost to everything else. . . . I think I should be capable of any thing mad and impulsive after a week of Tristam—& there wd be the rest of one's life unlit with Wagner to repent in." Two years later, Thomas wrote that a performance of *Lohengrin* had made her "feel a little like my real self."[17]

Like Mabel Dodge Luhan and Willa Cather—like Isabella Stewart Gardner of Boston, the "millionaire *bohémienne*," an inveterate Bayreuth pilgrim as well as a leading art collector and concert-giver*—M. Carey Thomas was at once a woman of strong personality, of "passionate sensibility," and a Wagnerite. The Swinburne poems she avidly read aloud linked love and pain. They celebrated sexual ambiguity, homoeroticism, and paganism.

> That I could drink thy veins as wine, and eat
> Thy breasts like honey! . . .
> . . . oh that I
> Durst crush thee out of life with love, and die,—
> Die of thy pain and my delight, and be
> Mixed with thy blood and molten into thee!

This, from Swinburne's *Songs and Ballads*, published in 1866, scans the emotional world of *Tristan*. I have already speculated that Wagner's characters fulfilled fantasies of liberation and violated taboo: oppressed at home, Sieglinde elopes with her brother Siegmund. But there is more to be read between the lines. An encoded homosexuality envelops Parsifal, Amfortas, and the Knights of the Grail. Equally subversive is the emotional imagery of Brünnhilde's awakening, during which the onetime goddess becomes wife—and so loses her wisdom, her strength, her independence, her entire previous persona.

---

*Mrs. Gardner annually undertook an impressive schedule of formal semipublic concerts (with printed tickets) in her Fenway Park music room, which could accommodate a small orchestra. The programs for 1888–89, for instance, included the *Siegfried Idyll* and the Prelude to *Die Meistersinger*, act 3, with Wilhelm Gericke conducting members of his Boston Symphony. Jean and Edouard de Reszke also performed at Mrs. Gardner's concerts. Her friends included Amalie Materna and Karl Muck. Lilli Lehmann and Walter Damrosch are known to have performed in other distinguished Boston homes. This private Wagner precinct, which doubtless flourished in New York as well, is little documented.

Alas, the shame
and disgrace of my plight!
I have been wounded by the man who awakened me. . . .
I am Brünnhilde no longer. . . .
My senses reel.
My knowledge falls silent
Must my wisdom vanish . . .
My eyes grow dim,
their light extinguished. . . .
From mist and gloom
emerges a raging
fear and confusion.[18]

Like other Wagner heroines, Brünnhilde is ultimately conceived in contingent relationship to a man. But the "reader" need not agree with Wagner's reading that this relationship signifies an acceptable trade-off. Rather, M. Carey Thomas reading Wagner, like Thomas reading Swinburne, was able to forge an impassioned, and passionately autonomous, personal identity.

In sum: the genteel complexion of American Wagnerism, its explicit and overt face, correlates with intellectual conformity, with the sanguine *Tannhäuser* Overture and no "bad after-effects." A second face, correlating with *Tristan* and the later Wagner, is both more hidden and more subversive. For women of the Gilded Age, the ephemeral titillation of the Venusberg, experienced by some, contradicted the mature feminine subjectivity activated or reinforced in others; Thomas's letters to Garrett describe not a correct meliorist sermon but an emotional blasphemy, a truthful heresy "with the rest of one's life to repent in." The result was a dialectic, so typical of Wagner's impact, of submission and liberation.[19]

The Gilded Age was a special time for women. Especially in the last decades of the century, women emerged—energetically, even aggressively—from shadows of anonymity. The interior, passionate sensibility of an M. Carey Thomas complemented new public leadership roles as reformers and culture-bearers.

Dated conventional wisdom holds that an eviscerated "feminized" culture pervaded the parlors, libraries, and churches of the Gilded Age. The domain of prim women and effete clergymen, it inflicted piety and parochialism. In *The Feminization of American Culture* (1977), Ann Douglas writes of "the active middle-class Protestant women" who shaped literary affairs:

> [They] did not hold offices or own businesses. They had little formal status in their culture, nor apparently did they seek it. They were not usually declared feminists or radical reformers. Increasingly exempt from the responsibilities of domestic industry, they were in a state of sociological transition. They comprised the bulk of educated churchgoers and the vast majority of the dependable reading public; in ever greater numbers, they edited magazines and wrote books for other women like themselves. They were becoming the prime consumers of American culture.[20]

One does not have to appeal to the heresy of an M. Carey Thomas to challenge this view of women confined to "a claustrophobic private world of over-responsive sensibility." The Seidl Society suggests a genteel tradition more resilient and complex than Santayana or Douglas allow. Granted, the Seidlites were not "radical reformers." They did consume culture. Their sensibility could perhaps be called "claustrophobic" and "over-responsive." And yet Douglas's portrait gets them wrong.

The feminine culture-bearers undertook "holy causes," according to Douglas. Culture was a surrogate religion, a "redemptive mission." So it was for the Seidlites. But did their Wagner mission also "propagate the potentially matriarchal virtues of nurture, generosity, and acceptance"? The liberal minister, Douglas says, "shaped his female parishioners' taste and fantasies." So did Seidl, the high priest of Wagnerism, mold his flock. But did his tastes and fantasies, like the liberal minister's, embody indecisive, emasculated authority?[21]

In short: Does Wagner ever stand in for Douglas's feminized culture? Is he, for instance, part of the parlor repertoire—a vehicle for the spinet to which Gilded Age daughters and wives gravitated from their abandoned spinning wheels? It is true that Seidl Society programs included advertisements for pianos and sheet music, and that English-language versions of the "Bridal Chorus" from *Lohengrin* and "To the Evening Star" from *Tannhäuser* both enjoyed some currency as sheet music, and that a 1903 *Parsifal* craze generated domestic renditions of "Parsifal and the Flower Maidens," the "Good Friday Spell," and the like. But these were exceptions, not typical instances. Essentially, Wagner was too big and complex for parlor dimensions, too nourishing for parlor diets.[22] Of the novels that feminized culture, Douglas writes that they confused literature with religion—which fits the Wagner case. But she also writes of their "small scale," "intimate scenes," and "chatty tone"—none of which fit at all. The heroines of these books "did not act or observe; they *felt*." Senta, Fricka, Brünnhilde, Isolde, Kundry—these are creations as remote from Martha Finley's once-famous Elsie Dinsmore as Electra or Medea. "The triumph of sentimentalism in nineteenth century America is never clearer," Douglas concludes, "than when one realizes the relatively small number of romantic writers and theologians, male or female, this country produced."

> For, however one defines the romantic impulse ... it clearly involves a genuinely political and historical sense, a spirit of critical protest alien to the sentimentalism so often confused with it. Romantics such as Goethe, Schiller, Keats, Shelley, Coleridge, or even Byron never lost touch with ethical concerns as the mainspring of their inspiration. ... The unmistakable exaltation of the self found in the works of the romantics was a desperate effort to find in private resources an antidote and an alternative to the forces of modernising society; it was not, like sentimentalist self-absorption, a commercialization of the inner life.[23]

To this list of Romantics we may add the important American painter Albert Pinkham Ryder, who attended Seidl's *Götterdämmerung* at the Met in 1888, then (as he once told a friend) returned home and worked for two days without sleep or food. The eventual result was "Siegfried and the Rhine Maidens"—with its writhing trees and moonlit shadows, a memorable study in fierce enchantment.* Wagner himself was a Romantic not produced by America, and yet meaningfully appropriated. Did Americans recon-strue Wagner? Of course. Did these reconstructions transform him into an anti-intellectual sentimentalist out of touch with "ethical concerns"? Of course not.

Especially for the antebellum and early postbellum decades, Douglas's insights remain valuable. But she ignores the fin-de-siècle ferment of which the Seidl Society was part. Challenging Douglas, Kathleen McCarthy, in *Women's Culture* (1991), portrays women play-ing marginal or ambiguous roles as culture custodians, not fully at home in male houses of power, but seeking to live there. Truer authority, she argues, resided in "cadres of male professionals and elites" who founded and managed the great Gilded Age museums. Late in the century, when women emerged as influential cultural philanthropists, they tended to sponsor "new aesthetic priorities." Bypassing the mainstream museums, foundations, and universities, women sponsored their own voluntary associations. They were spe-cialized non-profit entrepreneurs, who relied on infusions of volun-teer time and often made do with limited financial resources.[24]

Though McCarthy concentrates on the visual arts, she glancingly observes that the Philadelphia Orchestra formed a women's auxiliary to promote out-of-town concerts and find new subscribers through women's groups in other cities and states, and that the Chicago Symphony similarly organized tours through women's clubs in other cities. In fact, women founded the Cincinnati Symphony in 1895. Anna Millar managed the Chicago Orchestra from 1895 to 1899. Jeannette Thurber (as we have seen) helped support Theodore Thomas's Wagner tour in 1884, and founded the American Opera Company and the National Conservatory in 1885. According to Thomas, Midwestern advances in musical understanding were due "almost wholly to women. They have more time to study and

---

*Ryder's "The Flying Dutchman" is not inspired by Wagner but by another ver-sion of the myth. A second notable, if less singular American painter of Wagner was Maxfield Parrish, whose chromolithographs of scenes from the *Ring* appeared in the December 1898 *Scribner's* magazine.

perfect themselves in all the arts. They come together in their great clubs and gain ideas."[25] These clubs were part of a vast and varied network espousing a variety of causes, including Christianity and temperance, music and literature, equality of suffrage and education. In effect, they empowered women who possessed scant power as individuals. Typically, they invoked the language of religion—of women's moral suasion—in advocating culture and reform. At the same time, they advocated intellectual self-improvement, presenting classes and lectures for the clubwomen themselves. They tapped into previously dormant creative energies. After 1880, legions of dynamic clubwomen, of whom Jane Addams is today the most remembered, burst into national prominence. The sum total, writes Anne Firor Scott in her 1991 history of women's associations, was a formidable social movement, long hidden from view because it lacked the public edifice of a Metropolitan Museum.

> Since the early days of the Republic women have organized to achieve goals that seemed to them important. In retrospect it is clear that such women, constrained by law and custom, and denied access to most of the major institutions by which the society governed itself and created its culture, used voluntary associations to evade some of these constraints and to redefine "woman's place" by giving the concept a public dimension. Many years later a participant summed up the matter succinctly: "Suddenly they . . . realized that they possessed influence; that as organizations they could ask and gain, where as women they received no attention.

Addressing the vexing issue of "social control"—the argument that one abiding, if unstated, purpose of the reform movement was to keep the underclass in line—Scott writes:

> I think the evidence does not support any simple hypothesis. The [clubwomen], though often, perhaps nearly always, conscious of the difference between "our own people" and other people, did not always draw distinctions in terms of economic or social class. Their world might be divided into the saved and the lost, the abstemious

and the intemperate, the chaste and the licentious, native born and immigrants, workers and loafers, those who cared about children and those who exploited them, the worthy and the unworthy—and they did not assume that these categories were necessarily connected to class. There is a difference, too, between trying to promote social order by keeping people "in their place," as the phrase went, and trying to help them develop characteristics that—if accomplished—might admit them to the middle class.[26]

Though, like McCarthy, Scott barely mentions music, the relevance of their findings to the Seidl Society is obvious. With its public concerts, and lectures and singing classes for members, the Seidl Society was a voluntary association dedicated both to cultural reform and self-improvement. As a nonprofit entrepreneur, it espoused new music, not the canonized masters. Perhaps, in subconscious ways, its workers' concerts imposed symphonies and other upper-class refinements to civilize the moody and disordered masses. On the surface, it cheerfully aspired to reach women of all classes. There can be no doubt that New York's musical high culture would have been tangibly less progressive, tangibly more insular, had no Seidl Society existed. And the Wagner cult as a whole, with its additional immigrant constituency—with Albert Niemann, with Lilli Lehmann, with Coney Island's Wagner nights emblazoned on Broadway's first electric sign—more contradicted than reinforced the notorious parlor culture of the Gilded Age.

Laura Langford herself clinches this perspective. What was she like? Her books and letters provide answers whose contradictions define her transitional fin-de-siècle role.

The books genteel women wrote occupied two principal genres. One was sentimental fiction. The other was sentimental biography— a hortatory genre innocent of the larger play of history. Langford's books are entirely of this second type. Her sixty-page *Adelaide Neilsen: A Souvenir* (1885), for instance, is a "labor of love" whose purposes include revealing "the degree to which [Neilsen] possessed the power of recuperation." That is, Neilsen was an illegitimate child. She ran away from home and worked as a barmaid prior to her regeneration as a famous actress. Offstage, she was "a very lovable and loving woman," "sweet and reverent; strong and earnest of soul." Of her early death—she was only thirty-two—Langford remarks that "doubtless it was best" for her to expire "in the fullness of her prime."[27]

Langford's *Ladies of the White House* (1884) is a seven-hundred-page survey of every first lady from Martha Washington to Lucretia Rudolph Garfield—"short and simple annals of virtuous and exemplary women, who occupied the highest social and semi-official position known to their country, one replete with matter to point a moral or adorn a tale." Andrew Johnson's invalid wife, whom Langford knew personally, is portrayed with intense affection as a model of tenacious self-improvement. Another heroine of the book is Mrs. Rutherford Hayes, who was college-educated and took an interest in issues outside the family. "Her strong, healthful influence gives the world assurances of what the next century's woman will be." And yet Lucy Hayes's feminist contemporaries rejected her docility and her deference to her husband's career.

Langford's other major volumes include her six-hundred-fifty-page *The Mothers of Great Men and Women, and Some Wives of Great Men* (1883) and the seven-hundred-eighty-page *Famous American Fortunes and the Men Who Made Them* (1885). She was also the author of shorter books about Charlotte Brontë and General O. O. Howard, the latter a Christian soldier friendly to freedmen and American Indians. She was the editor of the letters of General Charles George Gordon, of portraits of twenty notable American women, and of a volume of religious poetry. One aspect of this output disturbs its prevailing complacency of tone and outlook: the advocacy of greater roles for women. Langford even betrays annoyance with her noble first ladies: "Not a few strong, gifted natures have been content to lead automaton lives in that famous old mansion." Especially in the United States, she observes, wives of "public men" are "left behind" and "doomed to slavery of the most repulsive kind during perhaps the best years of life."[28]

It is in her letters to Anton Seidl, however, that another Langford completely emerges. The very antithesis of "automaton" or "slave," she sheds her florid style and stands behind no man. In every sense, she is all business, ascertaining how much to pay the musicians, how to transport music and instruments, what arrangements are needed for rooms and meals at the hotel. Back salary is due. The scheduled soloist has canceled. Inevitably, these practical issues broach artistic issues. "I swear that this is the only time that this will happen," Seidl writes on November 8, 1893, apologizing for the necessity of an extra rehearsal. On May 15, 1894, Seidl counsels as follows regarding a possible violin soloist: "I think Miss Maude Powell can be had, she wrot [sic] to me, and will be very moderate in salary. *Shall I write to her?* Otherwise let out her name and put in Liszt's Preludes." Sometimes Seidl instructs Langford to choose a soloist herself.[29]

A particularly revealing episode in their relationship occurred in 1896 when the Brighton Beach orchestra engaged its first and only female member, a harpist identified as Miss Casuri. Some in the orchestra objected that she was not a member of the union—which, as a woman, she could not be. Miss Casuri complained that she was being paid much less than her male predecessor. Samuel (or Siegmund or Sigismund) Bernstein, who contracted the players on Langford's behalf, reportedly threatened to fire the new harpist if she refused to keep quiet. But she spoke to Langford, who instantly and publicly took her side. Langford told the press she had put the matter in Seidl's hands: "I trust him." The affair died down as quickly as it had erupted: Miss Casuri stayed.

Langford's surviving correspondence with Seidl is at all times brisk and unadorned. She addresses her letters "Dear Mr. Seidl" and signs them "Sincerely." Seidl, who always writes in creditable English, calls her "Mrs. Langford." What personal relations lay behind the formal surface of these exchanges we can only guess. Langford unquestionably stood on equal footing in Seidl's world of art and artists. Lilli Lehmann, in a letter to Langford, signs herself "Lilli." Auguste Seidl, writing to "Mrs. Langford," calls her "my best friend. . . . You have my love for ever."

Well-bred females of the Gilded Age wrote romantic biographies like Langford's. They espoused Christianity, women's suffrage, and uplift through art much as she did. Hypersensitive, rarified, they were held in awe by their husbands and other male admirers. Langford was a businesswoman, a nonprofit impresario without whom no Seidl Society concerts could have existed. She did not shrink from the public gaze when Seidl acknowledged her with bows and bouquets, and the Brighton Beach audience "applauded wildly." Once, in 1893, Seidl proposed to Langford that his New York Philharmonic perform regularly under the auspices of the Seidl Society. "You will be then the Queen of the musical world in Brooklyn."[30] It never happened, but Langford must have seemed to many a queen. That is one possible explanation for the abuse the *Musical Courier* hurled at the Seidl Society on October 28, 1896:

> There has always been lax management, the press has not been treated with the courtesy that insures attention, the whole scheme has been retained and carried on for the effort at personal aggrandizement of a few enterprising people, and the endeavor to establish popular classical orchestral concerts at a low price of admission has been defeated because of the internecine struggles of its adopters, because of the inaccessibility of the place in which they were given, and because of the narrow-minded policy which dictated the display of the names of a few women who sought social supremacy as the total object of their efforts. . . .
>
> Never before in America has there been such a series of programs as those at the Brighton Beach Musical Hall, considering the fact that these were summer concerts. Never before has there been spent so large a sum of money . . . with so little net results to the good of art.

Nothing ever published in the *Brooklyn Daily Eagle* supports such an attack—but then the *Eagle* was for many years Langford's employer. It bears considering that denunciations of women who violated the genteel code were far from uncommon by 1896.

One signature fin-de-siècle phenomenon was the New American Woman. University-educated, sexually independent, she denied that fulfillment dictated marriage. She spoke of sexual desire as a beautiful and pleasurable impulse. She advocated a future world of sexual equality: of access to the "masculine" professions, of level camaraderie between men and women.

Ultimately, after 1900, the New Woman discovered a place within the modernist movement. In particular, dance, shedding the stigma of degeneracy, became an outlet for spirituality and self-expression. Modern dance, America's first native high art form, knocked culture off its pedestal. For Ruth St. Denis and other dance pioneers, art became praxis.*

In this revolutionary context, Laura Langford seems a diligent worker on the sidelines of art, the New Woman's mother. She no more resembled St. Denis, born in 1880, than the Wagner cult embodied modernism, whose delayed American arrival awaited the turn of the century. But Langford's protofeminist Seidl Society defies stereotypes of "Lady Bountiful" and "feminized culture." On Wagner nights, the ocean breezes at Brighton Beach swept aside musty parlor memories.

The legacy of the parlor lingered, of course. Eleven years after Anton Seidl's death, Gustav Mahler became Seidl's most distinguished successor at the head of the New York Philharmonic. Concomitantly, the Philharmonic was reorganized by a group of philanthropic socialites. These "guarantors," headed by Mrs. George R. Sheldon, pledged to cover the orchestra's deficits in conjunction with expanding its activities. Mrs. Sheldon was no Mrs. Langford. When Philharmonic audiences dwindled, the lady guarantors began bickering with Mahler over his salary. They may have tried to supervise his programming. In the eyes of Mahler's wife, "he had ten ladies ordering him about like a puppet."[31] Mahler was already an ill man. His condition worsened. He died two years after his New York appointment.

*See the Postlude.

If Mrs. Mahler is to be believed, the Philharmonic guarantors were meddlesome, ignorant ladies. They notoriously fulfilled caricatures of the idle rich. In America, where the state stands aside, the affluent arts patroness plays a special role. Had Mahler enjoyed the services of a Laura Langford, of a "Mahler Society," the New World would have taken fuller advantage of his gifts, and he of ours.

13

Trauermusik

In two cities outside New York, the local Wagner cause enlisted figures of world importance: the conductor Arthur Nikisch, in Boston, and the architect Louis Sullivan, in Chicago.

For most of the nineteenth century, Boston was considered the most musical American city. But, with tastemakers like John Sullivan Dwight, it was also notably conservative. An eminent Wagnerian visitor, Hans von Bülow, tartly summarized in 1876:

> There are two types of musical cultivation; for want of better termi-
> nology, I might call them in-breadth and in-depth. In the latter
> respect, I would consider Boston the most cultivated; but the peo-
> ple are narrow and too pretentious for the measure of their knowl-
> edge. Puritanism has frozen art in New England; it's a miracle that
> it hasn't killed it altogether in the last 100 years.
>
> The Bostonians feel their indifference not only to an extreme
> degree: they even display it openly with pride. Presumably they
> reckon it as one of the Fine Arts. But that it is not. It is simply a
> form of paralysis.[1]

German opera, including Wagner, was heard in Boston as early as 1864. Two prominent local Wagnerites were the pianist-conductor-composer Benjamin Lang, who was a personal friend of Wagner's and helped to organize Seidl's Boston *Parsifal* concert of 1891; and the conductor Carl Zerrahn, who arrived in the United States with the Germania Orchestra and gave important Boston performances of the *Lohengrin* finale (1856) and Prelude (1860), the *Faust* Overture

(1857), and the *Siegfried Idyll* (1878). The Met brought Wagner to Boston beginning in 1884, with *Lohengrin* in Italian, and 1885, with *Tannhäuser*, *Lohengrin*, and *Die Walküre*, all led by Walter Damrosch. In 1889, the company returned with two complete *Ring* cycles; Alvary, Lehmann, and Fischer were among the principal singers; Seidl conducted. Wagner was also performed in Boston during the Met tours of 1890, 1892, 1894, 1895, 1896, and 1897 and was so popular with students at Harvard that Maurice Grau could charge them fifty cents per performance for the privilege of being supernumeraries. But Bostonians considered opera a "showy hybrid," a "breathless, exotic, passing excitement."[2] The symphony concert was their dignified ideal. The Boston Symphony became America's first and finest permanent concert orchestra. Nikisch, from 1889 to 1893, was its most famous conductor. His predecessors were George Henschel (1881–84) and Wilhelm Gericke (1884–89), his successors Emil Paur (1893–98) and Gericke (1898–1906).

Already famous at thirty-four, Nikisch was a certified Wagnerite. He had performed under Wagner's baton, and as a young conductor was a colleague of Seidl's in Leipzig. His romantic extravagance was not appreciated in dour New England; Henschel, Gericke, and Paur were more restrained. All four programmed quantities of Wagner. During their combined tenure, and including tour performances (the orchestra traveled widely and frequently in the northeastern states), the overture to *Tannhäuser* and the *Meistersinger* Prelude were each given more than one hundred times.*

If Boston retained its cultural pedigree, it shrunk in relative size. By 1890, Chicago, with 1.1 million people, rivaled Philadelphia as the nation's second largest city; Boston's population totaled 448,477. Most of Chicago's new immigrants were Germans; they comprised

---

*Other popular Wagner extracts included the *Tristan* Prelude (84 performances), the *Liebestod* (72), the *Rienzi* Overture (54), *Waldweben*, from *Siegfried* (53), the *Siegfried Idyll* (51), the *Faust* Overture (48), a Hans Richter conflation of Siegfried's penetration of the Magic Fire, from *Siegfried*, plus Dawn, the Rhine Journey, and Brünnhilde's Immolation, all from *Götterdämmerung* (37), "Dich teure Halle," from *Tannhäuser*, as sung by Melba, Nordica, and Gadski, among others (36), the Prize Song from *Die Meistersinger* (35), the *Flying Dutchman* Overture (34), the *Lohengrin* Prelude (34), and, surprisingly, the since forgotten *Kaisermarsch* (33).

over 15 percent of the population. Hans Balatka, born in Moravia, was—as in Cincinnati, Cleveland, Detroit, and Milwaukee—an influential local conductor whose programs included Wagner. Like Bergmann, he fled Europe following the mid-century revolts, arriving in Chicago in 1849. Eleven years later, he led what is believed to be the first local Wagner performance—of the Pilgrims' Chorus from *Tannhäuser*. Around the same time, Louis Moreau Gottschalk took part in a five-piano performance of music from *Tannhäuser*. The whole of *Tannhäuser* received its first Chicago performance in 1864— five years after the American premiere in New York. As in New York, the audience was essentially German, and by no means elite. A German company gave Wagner at Hooley's Theater in 1877. Theodore Thomas, who began visiting Chicago regularly in 1872, introduced higher performance standards, and more Wagner. An all-Wagner matinee at his 1882 Chicago festival attracted more than six thousand listeners. During his twelve seasons as founding conductor of the Chicago Orchestra (later the Chicago Symphony), beginning in 1891, Thomas led forty-two performances of the *Tannhäuser* Overture and thirty-six performances each of the preludes to *Lohengrin* and *Die Meistersinger* and of the Ride of the Valkyries.[*][3]

The Met first brought Wagner in German to Chicago in 1885. The opening performance, on February 23, was of *Tannhäuser*. A snowstorm delayed the curtain by two hours, but the audience stayed until 1:30 in the morning to cheer. The company extended its visit from two weeks to three, giving two more performances of *Tannhäuser*, and three each of *Lohengrin* and *Die Walküre*, all led by Walter Damrosch. The house was thronged with Germans, including the working classes; the Potter Palmers, the Marshall Fields, and other notables also attended. The Met returned in 1886 with a repertoire including *Rienzi*, *Lohengrin*, and *Tannhäuser*. As in Boston, Milwaukee, and St. Louis, the Met came with Seidl, Lehmann,

---

*Other popular Wagner selections included the Prelude and *Liebestod* from *Tristan* (30 performances), Siegfried's Funeral Music (26), *Waldweben* (26), the *Tannhäuser* Bacchanale (24), Siegfried's Rhine Journey (20), the *Kaisermarsch* (22), the *Siegfried Idyll* (20), and the Good Friday Spell from *Parsifal* (20). These figures cover the subscription concerts from October 1891 to December 1904. The orchestra does not currently have a repertoire index for its early tours.

Fischer, and the *Ring* in 1889; *Tannhäuser*, *Lohengrin*, and *Die Meistersinger* were also given. In 1890, 1891, 1894, and 1895, the Met's Chicago offerings included *The Flying Dutchman*, *Tannhäuser*, *Lohengrin*, and *Die Meistersinger*, led by Mancinelli, Vianesi and Damrosch. In 1896 and 1897, it gave *Lohengrin*, *Tristan*, and *Siegfried* under Seidl. The last of these visits, commencing with *Carmen* on February 22, was at first so poorly attended that Grau considered canceling the remaining dates. Instead, he dropped ticket prices, and business picked up. For *Lohengrin*, on March 10, the Germans came out in force. According to the *Chicago Dispatch*:

> Enthusiastic Teutons with score books in their laps and the sacred scars of Heidelberg glowing from their beards or creeping into their hair sat beside queer-looking Americans with bronzed faces and red hands and puzzled eyes or sweet-faced matrons in new silks and cloth gloves and continually performing opera glasses. It was the first legitimate night for curious philistines to come in contact with enthusiasts.

Two nights later, Jean de Reszke sang Siegfried, drawing the largest crowd of the season. Walter Damrosch's company also toured Wagner to Chicago during the 1890s, drawing Germans who hissed down noise from the boxes. When Damrosch led the Chicago premiere of *Tristan* in 1895, ladies and gentlemen of fashion were conspicuously absent.[4]

One famous Chicagoan who became an ardent Wagnerite was Louis Sullivan, who had frequently heard Balatka perform Wagner in concert. Sullivan later wrote in his third-person autobiography:

> Louis needed no interpreter. It was all plain to him. He saw it all. It was all as though addressed to himself alone. And as piece after piece was deployed before his open mind, he saw arise a Mighty Personality—a great Free Spirit, a Poet, a Master Craftsman, striding in power through a vast domain that was his own, that imagination and will had bodied forth out of himself.... Here, indeed, had been lifted a great veil, revealing anew, refreshing as dawn, the enormous power of man to build, as a mirage, the fabric of his dreams, and with his want of toil to make them real.[5]

Like Walt Whitman, whom he considered "the greatest of poets,"* Sullivan discovered in Wagner a commanding personality, an encompassing vision, a creative idealism stressing organic wholeness and binding art and religion. Fortuitously, Sullivan and his partner Dankmar Adler were in 1886 commissioned to build a new opera house for Chicago. Sullivan in turn engaged, to assist with the interior decoration, one Frank Lloyd Wright—who later described Sullivan in these years attaining a force of expression "as complete as Wagner's."†

Finished in 1889, the ten-story Auditorium Building was the tallest in the city, the heaviest in the world. It incorporated a 400-room hotel and 136 offices—illustrating, in Adler's words, "how the versatile Western American can combine sentiment with thrift,

---

*Many writers sensed a strong connection between *Leaves of Grass* and Wagner. Thus, H. R. Haweis, whom we have encountered extolling Wagner in England and the United States, paralleled Whitman's and Wagner's "revolt against rigid form." (Haweis, "A Visit with Walt Whitman," *Pall Mall Gazette*, Jan. 13, 1886.) Whitman himself was of course a great lover of Italian opera. His 1881 article, "The Poetry of the Future" (*North American Review*, February 1881, p. 202) lists Wagner among other "music of the future" composers tending "toward this free expression of poetic emotion." According to Huneker, Whitman "once confessed to me his love for Wagner; 'it makes my old bones sweeter,' he said" (Huneker, *Overtones* [New York, 1904; rpt. 1970], p. 330). Whitman's Boswell, Horace Traubel, urged Wagner on the old man. On August 10, 1888, Traubel records Whitman recalling once having heard bits of Wagner at concerts "which have astonished, ravished me, like the discovery of a new world." The following January 29, Whitman was heard to regret never having heard a Wagner opera. "I feel they are constructed on my lines." In March 1889, Traubel gave Whitman the libretto for *Die Walküre*. Whitman read about half of it and reported: "No doubt Wagner is our man—the man for us." To which Traubel replied: "He has done for music what you have done for poetry: freed it, disclosed its unity with life, set aside its harassing traditions" (Traubel, *With Walt Whitman in Camden* [Boston, 1906], vol. 2, p. 116; vol. 3, pp. 48, 506).

†Another turn-of-the-century American architect influenced by Wagner, as conservative as Sullivan was innovative, was Ralph Adams Cram. Cram, whose buildings include such Gothic monuments as New York's vast Cathedral of St. John the Divine, attended the Bayreuth Festival in 1886, where he heard *Parsifal* and *Tristan* three times apiece. He was also crucially inspired by the *Ring*. For Cram, Wagner signified an anti-modern, anti-modernist retrenchment toward the Middle Ages, dictating an architecture rooted in religious community. (See T. J. Jackson Lears, *No Place of Grace: Antimodernism and the Transformation of American Culture, 1880–1920* [New York, 1981], pp. 203–09.)

and . . . how he can endeavor to cultivate the service of Mammon simultaneously with an effort to attain his higher artistic ideals."[6] The auditorium itself, a vast sweeping space that—like Wagner's Bayreuth theater—flared outward and upward from the stage, sat forty-two hundred. As at Bayreuth, boxes were included but de-emphasized: only forty were provided, and they were not enclosed. The orchestra pit, if not—as in Bayreuth—hidden beneath the stage, was low and deep. The acoustics were considered ideal for opera. The decor included murals on mythic themes and soaring arches spanning the interior and suggesting, in the words of one recent writer, "one of the great themes of Wagnerian music drama, the transcendence of our mortality . . . a bridge by which the spirit crossed from this world to a Valhalla for heroes."[7]

The grand opening of the Auditorium Building, on December 9, 1889, was attended by President Benjamin Harrison. Adelina Patti sang "Home Sweet Home." The following evening, Patti appeared in Gounod's *Romeo and Juliet*. Wagner arrived the same season with the Damrosch troupe.

But Chicago had no resident opera company until 1910. The first Boston Opera Company did not begin until 1909. Outside New York, Wagner enjoyed no steady venue. Exposure to his staged music dramas was sporadic. The appeal of visiting Wagner productions partly depended on local Germans, partly on the local fashionability of opera generally. We have already taken note of Damrosch's tours, of the Italian companies that appropriated *Lohengrin*, of the opera-in-English crusades of Clara Louise Kellogg, whose own best roles included Senta, and of Jeannette Thurber's American Opera Company, with its lavish mountings of *Lohengrin* and *The Flying Dutchman*. More modest than Thurber's troupe, but more enduring, were the companies of Henry W. Savage, whose English-language productions commenced in 1895; in Chicago in 1900, for instance, Savage successfully offered *The Flying Dutchman*, *Tannhäuser*, and *Lohengrin* at twenty-five cents to a dollar per seat.[8]

And there was Seidl. In addition to touring with his own orchestra, he led the vast majority of the Wagner performances the Metropolitan Opera gave on tour between 1885 and 1897. Beyond the Boston and Chicago visits already mentioned, the Met presented Wagner during these dozen years in Brooklyn, Cincinnati, Cleveland, Louisville, Milwaukee, Philadelphia, St. Louis, and Washington, D.C.

By 1896–97, Seidl was on the rebound from his 1891 eclipse. At the Met, he led fourteen opera performances and took part in the same number of concerts; on tour, he conducted the company twelve times in six cities. His offstage rapport with Campanini, the de Reszkes, Eames, Lassalle, Nordica, and Plançon compensated for the departed Brandt, Lehmann, and Niemann. But 1897–98 was the season no resident company occupied the Metropolitan Opera House. Since the destruction of the Brighton Beach Music Pavilion in 1896, Seidl also lacked regular summer employment. He considered resettling in Europe.

He had returned to Covent Garden and Bayreuth during the summer of 1897. In London, where he had not conducted since his tours with Angelo Neumann, he was said by a correspondent for the *New York Sun* to have enjoyed a triumph "greater than that of any other foreign conductor, nearly all of the critics admitting that his interpretation of Wagner has been a fresh revelation of the great composer's work, and the best ever given to the English public." London's own newspapers reported: "Once again was a potent influence of this great conductor made manifest in the remarkably subdued and refined playing of the orchestra, which brought home to the ear all the beauties of Wagner's instrumentation, and yet never overwhelmed the voices of the singers." "Anton Seidl has proved himself the best orchestral conductor we have had up to now." "Wagner should have been present himself to hear justice done, almost for the first time, to some of his exquisite phrases." "[Seidl] has that power which so few conductors possess, of making the player feel exactly what he wants. In moments of danger, he displays the utmost coolness." "The Covent Garden band has never played so smoothly, so softly, or with such spirit. And yet Seidl is a quiet man, with an immovable face and very little action. The way he waits for the singers must make them adore him."[9]

At Bayreuth, where he was intimately remembered yet had never conducted, Seidl for the first and only time led staged performances of the Wagner work he held supreme, and whose composition he had daily observed and assisted: *Parsifal.* Siegfried Wagner introduced him to the orchestra as a too-long absent Knight of the Grail. The orchestra applauded not only these words, but the rehearsal itself. Cosima wept; she told Seidl his face and gestures reminded her of her father Liszt. And yet Seidl visited neither Wahnfried nor Wagner's grave. He kept his distance from Cosima and her coterie. They remarked upon his independence, inscrutability, and contempt for hypocrisy. He gave an impression of "carelessness," one of the devout later wrote; he seemed to have come to fame and fortune "as if by accident." The composer Arthur Farwell, drawn to Bayreuth by Seidl's presence, called his *Parsifal* performances "a profoundly moving and unforgettable experience for those so fortunate as to have attended them." Another American visitor, Natalie Curtis, later reported: "At the close of the first performance of 'Parsifal,' we waited for Seidl at the doorway that led from the orchestra. We were eager to tell him of his triumph, but when at last he came, the rapt and tear-stained face silenced us. We knew that he had, indeed, beheld the Grail."[10]

Seidl returned to New York pursued by offers: from London, Bremen, Berlin, Munich, Pest, Warsaw, St. Petersburg, Moscow. With no engagements to be had at the Met, he greatly increased his symphonic activity. To his New York Philharmonic concerts, expanded from twelve to sixteen, and those at the Brooklyn Academy, he added concerts at the Astoria Hotel and Chickering Hall—more than sixty in all. Only the Philharmonic engagements insured adequate rehearsal; most of the others were compromised by hasty preparation and shifting personnel. Beginning in early 1898, stories in the New York press claimed that Seidl's departure—for Hamburg, according to some reports, for Berlin, according to others—was imminent.

Seidl had often dreamed of presiding over an American company of his own in pursuit of stagings more fastidiously designed, directed, and costumed than conditions at the Met permitted. Now, his dream was of a permanent orchestra—like Emil Paur's in Boston and Thomas's in Chicago, or Walter Damrosch's New York Symphony, or Frank Van der Stucken's Cincinnati Orchestra, founded in 1894, or Victor Herbert's Pittsburgh Orchestra, begun in 1895. This second dream almost came true.

The threat of losing Seidl mobilized a response. More than one hundred people met at the home of W. H. Draper to plan for a permanent Seidl orchestra. The meeting was called to order by Richard Watson Gilder, who noted: "To build up great works of architecture or sculpture requires many years of waiting, but the art of instrumental musical reproduction can be had in perfection at once. We have a leader of genius, and plenty of first-class players; all we need, therefore, is to hold these together by financial support, and the thing is accomplished. To see any city of the world purveying for itself finer orchestral music than we might make permanently ours is something not to be endured. A city dedicated primarily to trade needs especially the detachment of spirit that comes through hearing the noblest music, nobly rendered."[11] Subscriptions for a guarantee fund were solicited, with each guarantor to pay a share of any deficit during the five years beginning May 1, 1898. Over fifty thousand dollars was swiftly pledged. Maurice Grau announced he would engage the Seidl Permanent Orchestra for his 1898–99 season, insuring six months employment; he also offered the Metropolitan Opera House free of charge for all rehearsals and concerts. As of March, the subscription lacked seventy-five thousand dollars—a sum considered attainable in a few weeks time.

According to Henry Finck, "Seidl was wonderfully elated at the prospect which thus suddenly opened before him. He gave up all thought of accepting the offers from Berlin and other German cities, and began making plans for the season."[12] No matter that the orchestra's opera duties would initially permit no more than a dozen concerts. Seidl's reinstatement at the Met seemed complete. His concertmaster would be Eugene Ysaÿe, one of the ranking instrumentalists of his time, who would also do some conducting. And Seidl would remain conductor of the New York Philharmonic. He planned, as well, to return to London and Bayreuth. He had even reconciled with Theodore Thomas, who had cordially complimented him when the Met was on tour in Chicago. When Thomas visited New York, the compliment had been returned. These exchanges could only have been sincere; neither man suffered flatterers.

But this career upturn coincided with sharply declining health. Seidl—who lived for music, neglected meals, and never exercised—had almost died of pneumonia in 1896. Subsequently, according to Henry Finck, he seemed to have aged ten years. "He looked tired and careworn, and was no longer the strikingly handsome man everyone had admired for his splendid head no less than for his interpretative genius."[13] Mrs. Seidl was alarmed by her husband's appearance upon his return from Europe in September 1898. His rehearsal itinerary had forced him to shuttle between London and Bayreuth. He had caught a severe cold and had not eaten for twelve days.

Seidl's heavy concert schedule the following winter further taxed his constitution. Auguste begged him to conduct less—"but he always managed to comfort me and appease my anxiety." He fretted that, with no pension such as he would enjoy in Europe, he might die a pauper if he did not work and save. The prospect of a permanent orchestra, as it materialized that spring, soothed his worries. "Now at last I shall be able to show what I can do!" he told Auguste, according to the brief memoir she later wrote for Finck. "I am sure that in the very first year I shall surprise everybody, and after three years I shall not fear comparison with the best orchestra in the world."[14]

The morning of Monday, March 28, Seidl arose in good spirits. At six that evening, he would host a dinner in honor of the pianist Raoul Pugno, who was leaving for Europe in two days. Auguste had urged him to postpone the party. "My principal reason was that my husband would be kept unusually busy during the week by the Philharmonic rehearsals for [Beethoven's] Ninth Symphony, besides other rehearsals; feeling that this would be too much for him in his enfeebled condition, I begged him to give his dinner later on . . . but he insisted on giving it on Monday, because Pugno had to be present and my dear husband had to attend a rehearsal of the chorus on Tuesday." At 11 A.M., Seidl rehearsed at home with Henry Holden Huss, whose *Cleopatra's Death* he was scheduled to conduct. Upon leaving, the composer inquired how Seidl was feeling. He replied that he was in tolerable health only. Another rehearsal followed, after which he lunched with his wife on shad roe, of which he was especially fond. At 2 P.M. he left for Fleischmann's restaurant, at Broadway and Tenth. He next walked to the home of his orchestra manager, Samuel Bernstein, at 312 East 19th Street. Suddenly, he fell terribly ill. He took some whiskey at Bernstein's suggestion, but his condition worsened. He lost consciousness. Meanwhile, Mrs. Seidl awaited his arrival for dinner. Among the guests was Ysaÿe, expecting to discuss his imminent New York duties. Mrs. Seidl inquired what time it was. "Six-fifteen," said Ysaÿe. "Then Tony may be here any minute," she replied. The doorbell rang; it was Bernstein's brother, who advised Auguste that her husband was suffering from a gastric disturbance, that he had vomited and passed out, but that he was now feeling better and would come when he was able. Auguste took a cab to Bernstein's house, praying for Seidl's safety. She found him in bed, attended by a doctor. He could neither open his eyes nor speak, but could slowly move his hands and feet. The family physician arrived and sent for a stomach pump; blood-letting was tried, all in vain. Seidl died at 10:15 P.M. He was forty-seven years old.[15]

At midnight, the body was removed to the Seidls' brownstone apartment on East 62nd Street. There were many callers the next morning. Mrs. Seidl remained in her room. It was initially thought that Seidl had been poisoned by the fish he had eaten for lunch. An autopsy revealed serious gallstone and liver ailments. He could never have undertaken the strenuous responsibilities he had anticipated.

A committee organized the March 31 funeral service. Tickets were distributed at Schubert's music store, for New York Philharmonic subscribers; at Lowenstein's, for subscribers to Seidl's Astoria concerts; at the Metropolitan Opera, for opera subscribers; and at the Brooklyn residence of Laura Langford, for members of the Seidl Society. The demand far exceeded the supply. I have already described the overcast day and flower-strewn coffin; the procession down Fifth Avenue to 40th Street, where the cortege was met by a hundred-piece band led by Victor Herbert and Nahan Franco; the smothering crush of women in the vestibule of the Metropolitan Opera House; the solemn procession toward the sad, candle-lit stage, with its blankets of flowers and cathedral setting; the wreath of four thousand violets sent by Jean and Edouard de Reszke; the eulogy spoken by Henry Krehbiel, whose trembling voice set many sobbing; the performance of Siegfried's Funeral Music, which transformed the mortuary ambience with visions of brave energy and doomed exploits; the four thousand mourners, to whom Seidl's loss seemed an American calamity.

Though he was reportedly born a Roman Catholic and was said to have studied for the priesthood, Seidl was no churchgoer, and no priest was summoned to his deathbed. According to his wishes, his body was cremated at Fresh Pond Cemetery. An organist played Siegfried's Funeral Music and Elsa's prayer. A floral tribute from the Seidl Society bound two large *S*'s with a fringed sash on the ends of which were painted the words "Seidl Society" and "Les Préludes." A photograph was taken for inclusion in a documentary volume the society planned to publish, but no such book survives, and the society itself disbanded. Plans for the Seidl Permanent Orchestra were terminated. Ysaÿe was offered the New York Philharmonic, but refused. Auguste retired to the Catskills.

Seidl had died in his artistic prime. His onetime mentor Hans Richter, seven years his senior, survived him by eighteen years. His stalwart soprano Lilli Lehmann, two years his senior, survived him by thirty-one. Given a normal lifespan, he would have made recordings and consolidated a reputation in Europe commensurate with his American fame. New York's Philharmonic and Metropolitan Opera would have differently evolved after 1900. Nikisch, Muck, and Weingartner, among others, were mentioned as possible replacements; none came. The *New York Staats-Zeitung*, whose Seidl obituary was the page-one lead story, called Seidl "almost irreplaceable." "That he will be missed, unendingly missed, is a sad, irrevocable truth," summarized the *Musical Courier*. "A short time ago we learned that Europe had tempted him to leave us; then at least we could have said, as alas! we now cannot—'O kehr zurück du kühner Sänger!' "*[16]

In the decades to follow, Seidl was too soon forgotten. One who remembered was Arthur Farwell, whose long and intriguing career included writing, publishing, and composing, and whose vision of democratic musical pageantry was tangibly influenced by Wagner and Seidl.† Seidl's early sponsorship of Farwell the composer enabled him to study in Europe. He began by attending the 1897 Bayreuth festival in order to seek counsel from Seidl. This meeting and its aftermath, recounted by Farwell in a 1944 article for the *Musical Quarterly*,[17] add a remarkable pendant to the Seidl story.

In Bayreuth, Farwell discovered Seidl strolling on the outskirts of town. The two men walked to a bridge spanning a small stream. Seidl seemed sad. He was homesick for New York, especially for his dogs. He did not mention Auguste. He spoke of *Parsifal*, but expressed no happiness at being in Bayreuth. He advised Farwell to study with Engelbert Humperdinck, then in Bayreuth. "No incident of my wanderings has impressed itself more deeply upon my memory than this privileged moment, when the soul of this silent man so simply, no nobly revealed itself," Farwell later wrote.[18]

Humperdinck agreed to teach Farwell the following fall in Boppard-on-the-Rhine, where he lived. Through Humperdinck,

*An obituary in the *Bayreuther Blätter*, 1898, *Stück* 6, p. 138, summarized Seidl's American career as "spiritual colonization."

†In, for instance, his article "The Struggle Toward a National Music" (*North American Review*, December 1907), Farwell blends Wagner and America as follows: "Music which most deeply touches America must rise up from our own soil. Wagner understood the spirit of America. . . . He was more of an American than many of our own composers, for he worked with the primal forces of man and nature, and not with the over-refined and predigested delicacies of a decadent culture" (p. 566).

Farwell met Wagner's stepdaughter, Daniela Thode, daughter of Cosima and Hans von Bülow. She proved a woman of great charm, "with that added grace which a high degree of culture so subtly confers. The absence of color in her olive-toned face lent a peculiar emphasis to her eyes, which I remember as her most striking feature. These were memorable for the somewhat drooping contour of their lids and for the evidence they gave in a marked degree of that depth and richness of nature which mark those whom the Germans designate as *geistreich*, or rich in spirit." When Frau Thode learned that Farwell knew Seidl, she eagerly inquired about his life in New York. Her tone conveyed affection as well as admiration. Later, discussing this conversation with Frau Humperdinck, Farwell was told: "It was on Daniela Thode's account that Seidl left Europe and went to America." Daniela's marriage, to the art historian Henry Thode, was unhappy. Her past infatuation with Seidl was well known at Bayreuth.

When Seidl died, Frau Thode worshipfully paid tribute to him in the *Bayreuther Blätter*. In 1899, Farwell saw her in Paris, and perceived a "shadow of sadness that now lay beneath her natural graciousness." In 1900, he was engaged by Auguste to make conductor's scores of Seidl's arrangements of Wagner extracts, for which only orchestral parts existed. He later discovered that this work had actually been commissioned by Daniela Thode.

Forty-four years later, in his *Musical Quarterly* article, Farwell set out to unravel the full story of "America's Gain from a Bayreuth Romance"—a story, to his knowledge, never told in America. Daniela, born in 1860, was a child when Seidl lived at Wahnfried as a young man. With his marriage to Auguste in February 1884—one year after Wagner's death—Seidl may have "thrust the entire Bayreuth scene somewhat into the distance, the marriage now entering as a compensatory experience." Prior to his departure for America in the fall of 1885, however, he apparently re-encountered Daniela, now twenty-four, beautiful, and refined. She must have powerfully reanimated Seidl's memories of his watershed years: his second home at Wahnfried; of Wagner, of Cosima, of Daniela herself. He fell in love with her, and the love was returned. But these developments "could not reduce the moral fortress of this deep and noble soul. He would countenance no wrong to Auguste. Europe would present too close quarters; he must get as far away, in his career of Wagnerian conductor, as opportunity would permit. And so America was immensely enriched by this hidden tragedy of love." Farwell adds: "It is significant that Mrs. Seidl appears at no time to have urged her husband to return and follow up his European triumphs."

In Farwell's opinion, Seidl's silence, "the reserve and depth of soul for which he was noted in his American life, as well as . . . his unceasing and reverent devotion to his art," may have been rooted in his tragic love affair. Huneker once wrote of Seidl: "He never seemed a happy man to me." In Europe, Seidl could have had a permanent ensemble, unlimited rehearsal, financial security, assured pre-eminence. In America, he suffered the vagaries of a musical market economy. Farwell's tale helps explain why Seidl came and stayed.*

But it in no way denies Seidl's affection for the United States. Farwell himself testifies of Seidl and Wahnfried that "he refused to enter into any of the politics and prejudices of that mentally polar-

---

*In his autobiography (*My Life in Two Worlds* [Appleton, Wis., 1953]), Francis Neilson, who was with Seidl in Bayreuth, remembers Seidl confiding an early infatuation with Wagner's daughter Eva. Following a dinner party with Eva and her friends, which Seidl had attended with great ambivalence, he "was buried in deep reflection. . . . At last he confessed that, while he was working for Wagner, he had fallen in love with Eva, and she had reciprocated the feeling. Both were afraid of Cosima. Wagner knew what was taking place. The young pair had seldom been alone more than a moment or two, and only a few words had passed between them. . . . Something occurred, however, which caused Cosima to become suspicious. From that day Seidl seldom set eyes on Eva. What Wagner and Cosima thought, Seidl could not say, but he guessed that his presence in the house was not looked upon with favor. This happened just at the time when Angelo Neumann was negotiating with Wagner to perform *Tristan* and *The Ring* in the leading cities of Europe" (p. 164). But Eva, born in 1867, would have been only twelve years old when Seidl left Bayreuth for Neumann and Leipzig in 1879. Remembering his conversation with Seidl half a century later, Neilson may well have misremembered which member of Wagner's family Seidl had mentioned. As for Cosima, it may be pertinent that, when Henry Finck asked her to contribute to his *Anton Seidl: In Memoriam*, she "replied curtly that she was no authoress" (*New York Post*, Jan. 19, 1904).

ized and self-centered circle," that Seidl preferred to room on the outskirts of Bayreuth, that he missed New York, that he "had come to love" America.

He was a first-generation immigrant in many ways unsuited to assimilation. He spoke German with his German wife, he habituated German restaurants, his friends were mainly German or German-speaking. He could not slap backs or trade small talk. Theodore Thomas, who arrived in America at the age of ten, eventually married an American and turned his back on his German American beginnings. He was the embodiment of "Yankee push." So was Walter Damrosch, whose wife was the daughter of the onetime presidential candidate James G. Blaine. Compared to his immigrant father, who seemed both German and Jewish, Walter meshed with the likes of Carnegie and Flagler. He both entertained at home and plied the domestic concert circuit, conducting in the living rooms of Vanderbilts. His accent—like Thomas, he left Germany as a youngster—conveyed cultural pedigree; his fluent English and social aplomb conveyed privilege.

Seidl, by comparison, was a relative outsider, an innocent to whom entrepreneurial savvy was as alien as Bellini. Things had to be done for him. And yet they were. The names of the men and women who helped initiate the Seidl Permanent Orchestra tell the story of Seidl's assimilation. Civic and political leaders, writers and businessmen, Germans and Anglo-Americans united to prevent his departure. Reform-minded Republicans were strongly represented*— American Wagnerism, after all, was meliorist—as were prominent banks, law firms, and cultural and educational institutions. Among those who organized on his behalf were Richard Watson Gilder and Robert Ingersoll, both of whom we have already encountered, and both of whose homes were magnets for artists and intellectuals. The others, all highly prominent, included:

*Reform Republicans such as Seidl's friend Carl Schurz bolted the party in 1885 rather than back James G. Blaine—who happened to be Walter Damrosch's father-in-law. They instead supported Grover Cleveland—who (as we have seen) attended Seidl's 1890 *Parsifal* Entertainment.

Arthur von Briesen, a German-born lawyer who was president of the Legal Aid Society.

Mrs. Henry Clews, whose husband, an associate of J. P. Morgan, was a leading Wall Street financier, a close friend of Grover Cleveland, and a leading reformer.

W. Bayard Cutting, of the Knickerbocker aristocracy, a reform-minded corporation lawyer who was also a trustee of Columbia University.

Robert W. DeForest, a lawyer and philanthropist who would shortly help found the Russell Sage Foundation and chair New York State's historic Tenement House Commission.

Dr. William H. Draper, who was one of the city's distinguished physicians and medical educators.

Charles F. McKim, the famous architect, who frequented the highest social and political circles.

Henry W. Poor, who made a fortune in the railroad business and also as a securities dealer.

Whitelaw Reid, editor of the *New York Tribune*, who had been the Republican nominee for vice president in 1892.

Gustav Schwab, whose father was born in Bremen, of the North German Lloyd Steamship Company.

Mrs. James Speyer, whose husband, from a distinguished German family, was a banker, philanthropist, and former officer of the German-American Reform Union.

Mrs. Henry Villard, whose German-born husband was a railroad promoter and financier as well as principal owner of the *New York Evening Post*, and who herself, the daughter of the abolitionist William Lloyd Garrison, would become a leading women's suffragist and pacifist.

This list offers confirmation, if confirmation were needed, of the breadth of the Wagner movement in America in the year of Seidl's death. It retained powerful ties to the German community in which it began. It emotionally enfranchised the housewives and mothers of the late Gilded Age. It was a vital component of genteel intellectual life. It made traitors of many "barbarians" for whom opera had meant warbling and jewels. Even Wagner, when he considered moving to Minnesota, could not have envisioned that he would matter so much.

Other European musical luminaries had collected their dollars and retreated to France, Germany, Italy. Seidl was by far the most luminous European to come and stay. Expensive imports like Nikisch, expensive visitors like Anton Rubinstein and Peter Tchaikovsky, not to mention flocks of extravagantly priced sopranos, beginning with Jenny Lind—these temporary accoutrements paradoxically reinforced a cultural inferiority complex: the guilty knowledge that America's glamorous musical culture was borrowed. Seidl's commitment to the New World made Americans feel confident, not insecure. When the *Musical Courier* announced his appointment to the Berlin opera in 1887, dismay was tempered by resigned understanding: with revealing facetiousness, the *Courier* reckoned that the new position would prove "a trifle more important and satisfying" than working at the three-year-old Metropolitan Opera.[19] A decade later, New Yorkers well understood that their opera was at least as distinguished as Berlin's.

The visits of Lind, Rubinstein, and Tchaikovsky had made Americans feel good about Lind, Rubinstein, and Tchaikovsky. Seidl, pedigreed by Richter and Wagner, Bayreuth and Leipzig, made Americans feel good about themselves. And so his contributions did not inspire reverence so much as—the keynote of innumerable memorial tributes—gratitude. Half a century later, in the time of Toscanini and Stokowski, Arthur Farwell looked back and wrote:

> For all those in any degree sensitive to the spirit of music and romance, the presence of Anton Seidl, famous alike for the depth of his silence and the height of his art, tinged the atmosphere and the consciousness of the city with a peculiarly individual and glowing quality of feeling such as it has not known before or since. Seidl was among the last of the typical nineteenth-century conductors, immediately preceding the advent of the more dazzling, but, as many hold, less sympathetic virtuoso-conductor. What one felt, in Seidl's

evocation of orchestral or operatic masterpieces, was his reverential love for the nobly beautiful in music and his complete self-
effacement, which made it possible for this beauty to go forth to his
hearers unaffected by any slightest intrusion of his own personality.
And because of this, and of his known love for New York, it was
downright affection, rather than admiration or awe, that New York
returned to him.[20]

14

Parsifal Revisited

In the decades after Seidl's death, America's great Wagner event was the first staging of *Parsifal* at the Metropolitan Opera House in December 1903. But this was an event great in new ways.

Concert performances of *Parsifal*, as we have learned, took place in New York and Boston in 1886, 1890, and 1891. King Ludwig had witnessed eight private performances at the Munich Court Opera in 1884 and 1885. Only at Bayreuth could the public see *Parsifal* enacted in addition to hearing it played and sung. This restriction was stipulated by Wagner and enforced by Cosima following his death.

It took Heinrich Conried to flout the Wagners. He was the manager of the Metropolitan Opera of whom it was once said that he knew no more about opera than an ordinary chauffeur knows about airplanes. Born in Austria, a former actor, Conried ran a small German theater and several operetta companies before taking over the Met in 1903—an appointment sponsored by Henry Finck, who feared that Walter Damrosch might otherwise get the job. His brief regime was distinguished by its combination of business cunning and clownish ignorance, of incidental boldness and retrenchment. The quick-buck artist in Conried cherished his tenor sensation, Enrico Caruso, whom he claimed to have discovered but had not. Caruso sang more than fifty times a season—as many as one-third of all performances. Conried's contract entitled him to a share of the company's profits; Caruso was his prime investment. But his pièce de résistance was *Parsifal*, which he wrested from the composer's widow and her Bayreuth shrine.

In Cosima, Conried discovered a worthy adversary. Her devotion to her husband's memory was as single-minded as Conried's to his pocketbook. She jealously guarded certain Bayreuth traditions and invented others; she made the shrine a mausoleum impervious to necessary change. Her *Parsifal* ties were boundlessly proprietary. Wagner had inscribed the score to her as a birthday and Christmas present. He had many times told her that he intended it for Bayreuth only. When, following Ludwig's death in 1886, Munich claimed performance rights to *Parsifal*, Cosima swooned, threatened, negotiated, and won. With the copyright on Wagner's works due to expire in 1913, she mounted a campaign to safeguard *Parsifal* for all time from defilement on unconsecrated stages. In *Parsifal*, Conried gleaned a singularly profitable operatic property. And the United States was party to no international copyright agreement.

There followed a public relations crescendo unparalleled in operatic history, with every move and countermove copiously reported in the New York press. Early in 1903—with Maurice Grau still in charge of the Met—Conried was already denying rumors he would mount *Parsifal* during his first season. The ruination of Bayreuth was predicted: only the drawing power of *Parsifal*, it was argued, ensured the festival's survival. Conried confirmed the rumors: he would satisfy the prerogative of American Wagnerites to see *Parsifal* for themselves. Felix Weingartner was among those who agreed that Cosima deserved no *Parsifal* monopoly. Cosima's early supporters included Humperdinck and Scharwenka, Prince Ludwig Ferdinand of Bavaria, and, reportedly, the German Embassy in Washington. Conried now alleged he had planned a *Parsifal* production with Anton Seidl—which Seidl's scattered ashes could neither confirm nor deny. Meanwhile, according to the *Telegraph*, "'classy' people and those who hover on the fringe" began to debate whether evening dress would be appropriate for the scheduled 5 P.M. curtain. At this, Conried "laughed shrewdly" and advised evening dress because the sun sets early in winter.[1]

Cosima was reported threatening to stage a rival *Parsifal* in New York with Bayreuth's singers, orchestra, chorus, costumes, scenery, and stage equipment. "Mme. Wagner Will Cross Ocean to Fight Conried" trumpeted the *Journal*. Was it a bluff? Conried, according to the *Telegraph*, "chuckled audibly."[2] By September, the clergy had noisily entered the fray. *Parsifal* must not inhabit a "common playhouse," said the Passion Play Society, which asked the Mayor to intervene and prevent "a public scandal." According to a supportive attorney, unseemly applause and "bejeweled women of fashion" would defile Our Lord were *Parsifal*, with its Christian ceremonies, to take to the stage. Hans Richter declared the proposed performance the "scandal of the century." He urged European artists to boycott the United States. To which Cosima added that all participants in Conried's adventure were traitors to Wagner.

Many newspapers—including the *Evening Post*, which remembered that Wagner himself had once considered reserving *Parsifal* for the United States—resented Cosima's possessiveness. The *Musical Courier*, however, took her side. Denying allegations of Bayreuth greed, the *Courier* attested that "there is no money making scheme in Bayreuth." Deferring to Wagner's mandate was a purely moral issue; law and religion were peripheral. Conried's "literary piracy" would damage America's world prestige.[3] Cosima even more indignantly denied commercial motives. "The commands of the Master" were her one and only beacon.

In October, Felix Mottl arrived in New York. He was a pedigreed Wagnerite, in 1888 and 1897 a *Parsifal* conductor in Bayreuth. He had come to lead Wagner at the Met. This interesting bombshell was defused by Conried, who advised Mottl not to discuss *Parsifal*— "and I agree with him," Mottl told reporters. Conried's *Parsifal* conductor would be Alfred Hertz, who had joined the company in 1902. The cast was distinguished: Alois Burgstaller in the title role, Ternina as Kundry, Anton van Rooy as Amfortas, Robert Blass as Gurnemanz. Anton Fuchs and Carl Lautenschläger had been brought over from Munich to supervise the staging. Conried spent lavishly on scenery and rehearsals. He knew that for *Parsifal* to pay off it had to be done well—"better than Bayreuth," he boasted. At the same time, as later became known, he spurned Jean de Reszke, who expressed interest in ending his retirement to sing Parsifal in New York. In the opinion of Charles Henry Meltzer, a Conried scout in Europe, "that shortsighted manager killed all hopes of our hearing Jean again in opera." As one historian of the Met has commented: "Conried, of course, was not being shortsighted, merely practical, in his own way. He knew he could sell out *Parsifal* without having to pay a de Reszke fee."[4]

Conried announced *Parsifal* for December 24, a date bound to excite the clergy, for whom it was Christmas Eve, and Cosima, for whom it was the night preceding her birthday. He doubled prices in the parquette, first balcony, and boxes. There was controversy over the allotment of tickets to subscribers, who expected access at reduced rates. The box office opened at 9 A.M. November 9, by which time several women, in line since before daybreak, had fainted. "The most remarkable advance sale of tickets ever seen in New York" netted $60,000 by 6 P.M., when the window was shut with hundreds still on queue.

The swelling chorus of outraged clergy, led by George L. Shearer of the American Tract Society and including at least one rabbi, was by now—as in 1890—answered by an equally vocal pro-*Parsifal* contingent. Was *Parsifal* "sacrilegious"? Was it "ennobling"? Conried called it "moral." But then Conried, the *Musical Courier* pointed out, was Jewish. In fact, according to the *Courier*, German and Jewish business interests supported Conried's adventure. "This is not a time for Jews to be employed in any kind of business transaction for which the Saviour of mankind is to be a drawing card," *Harper's* chimed in, worried that anti-Semites would use Conried's *Parsifal* as a worldwide weapon. On November 11, the *Courier* invoked American foreign policy in arguing: "We steal Panama to get the canal through, and we steal *Parsifal* to get the opera through"—and yet, the *Courier* continued, the *Post* and *Times* favored the second and condemned the first. The *Daily News* predicted: "It is probable that the Mayor will be requested to stop the performance if it is not killed by the overwhelming public opinion which Dr. Shearer and his associates expect to arouse."[5]

On November 22, Walter Damrosch led four *Parsifal* excerpts with his New York Symphony at Carnegie Hall. In a preconcert speech, he condemned the work's impending profanation. The *Parsifal* Prelude, he explained, should be heard at Bayreuth, "where it is played by an invisible orchestra led by an invisible conductor." He then, as the *Telegraph* remarked, "stood up in full view of the audience and conducted it." Other press reports recalled that Damrosch had hoped that he, not Conried, would succeed Grau at the Met, and that he, not Hertz, would lead *Parsifal* there. The *Courier* added:

> Like a good commercial drummer [Damrosch] used his opportunity to express his sentiments on *Parsifal*, of which extracts were performed under his direction. Because of these extracts considerable money was extracted from the public, which went to Carnegie Hall not to hear the concert but to hear *Parsifal*, the best advertised musical proposition that has been in the United States for some years, much of the advertising having been done by this paper free of charge.... *The Musical Courier* always lauds and commends Mr. Damrosch ... for his magnificent skill in the line of commercialism, something which must not be disregarded and disdained in the United States of America.... Mr. Conried should now get out on the stage ... and give his opinion that *Parsifal* as a production in mutilated form on a concert stage [contradicts] the wishes and desires of Richard Wagner.[6]

All this sparring formed the backdrop to "a motion for an injunction pendente lite"; Cosima had sued. Her lengthy affidavit included the publishing history of the score, which was issued in limited numbers by B. Schott of Mainz for private circulation only, imprinted with the words "performing right reserved." Rudolph Schirmer, as Schott's American agent, had received three copies, not to be sold without compelling the purchaser to sign an agreement not to let the same be used for any stage performance. Conried's affidavit argued a different publication history, in which Wagner relinquished his rights before the family had second thoughts. *Parsifal*, he asserted, was public property in the United States. He also denied it was "religious." On November 24—the day after the opera season began—Judge Lacombe of the United States Circuit Court refused to grant the injunction sought by the Wagners. The verdict, reported on the front page of the *Tribune*, ignited a storm of condemnation in Germany. But Ternina, arriving in New York, told the

Times: "It is only the kinsmen and very intimate friends of Frau Wagner that think [*Parsifal*] ought to be kept in [Bayreuth] forever." She also denied that *Parsifal* was "religious," or that Wagner "intended the hero and Kundry to represent Christ and Mary Magdalen."[7] A petition to the mayor asked that the license of the Metropolitan Opera House temporarily be revoked. It was not.

The performance itself was no anticlimax, but the climax was tainted. Mesmerized by the build-up, the audience froze to attention. The Grail pageantry, painstakingly prepared, told. Two curiosities reported in the press were that the wife of one of the ushers had given birth to a son and called him Parsifal, and that Damrosch had volunteered that Hertz's tempos were "unduly restless and hasty" in the Good Friday Spell. But Damrosch was in the minority. The majority opinion was given by Richard Aldrich in the *Times*:

> "Parsifal" was presented in a manner wholly befitting its distinctive character as a work of art—a manner that recognized and gave a full exposition of the solemnity and dignity of its theme, the lofty eloquence of its treatment, the overpowering impressiveness of the drama. . . . The artistic value of the "Parsifal" production was of the very highest. It was in many respects equal to anything that has ever been done at Baireuth, and in some much superior. It was without doubt the most perfect production ever made on the American lyric stage.

Accompanying Aldrich's review was a half-page of themes in musical notation, two and one-half pages of pictures, reports on audience composition and attire, and tributes to Conried.[8]

But even Aldrich sensed that something was not right. "'Parsifal,' in truth, is calculated for a different environment than New York," he worried following the Met performance, "and after the excitement has subsided, the curiosity been appeased, the strain and tension have been relaxed, it is possible that it may be found to present difficulties as human nature's weekly, if not daily, food. The substance of the drama, its motive, and the lessons it seeks to enforce cannot make an appeal to modern sympathies and understanding. These need the beguilement of Bayreuth, the withdrawal from other interests, the special pilgrimage, the unaccustomed attitude of mind. Wagner knew well what he was doing when he calculated these surroundings for 'Parsifal.'" Krehbiel, nine years Aldrich's senior, amplified these reservations. Weary with experience, he recalled Seidl's performances. The *Parsifal* Entertainment of 1890, if not lacking in social éclat, was a pilgrim's affair for which the Brooklyn Academy was redecorated. The discourse it invited, if not without rancor, sympathetically explored Wagner's intentions; the thrills of public controversy and illicit pleasure were not vital to its appeal. As for Bayreuth's *Parsifal*, which Krehbiel also knew, it was more thoroughly prepared and better lit, if less successful in its stage effects. In particular, the scene with the Flower Maidens had never been as magically realized as in New York. Krehbiel perceived Conried and his audience as cynical or goggle-eyed parvenus.

The music of the drama was familiar to New Yorkers from many a concert performance. . . . Only the action and the pictures were new. . . . Nevertheless the interest on the part of the public was stupendous. The first five representations were over on January 21st, but before then Mr. Conried had already announced five more, besides a special day performance on Washington's Birthday, February 22d. After the eleventh performance, on February 25th, Mr. Conried gave out the statement to the public press that the receipts had been $186,308; that is, an average of $16,937.17. But this was not the end. Under Mr. Grau the custom had grown up in the Metropolitan Opera House of a special performance, the proceeds of which were the personal perquisites of the director. In all the contracts between the director and his artists there was a clause which bound the latter to sing for nothing at one performance. Before his retirement Mr. Grau grew ashamed of appearing in the light of an eleemosynary beneficiary under such circumstances, and explained to the newspapers that the arrangement between himself and the singers was purely a business one. Nevertheless he continued to avail himself of the rich advantage which the arrangement brought him, and in the spring closed the supplementary season with a performance of an olla podrida character, in which all of the artists took part. Mr. Conried continued the custom throughout his administration, but varied the programme in his first year by giving a representation of "Parsifal" instead of the customary mixed pick-les. The act was wholly commercial.[9]

In the wake of Conried's triumph, the Henry Savage Grand Opera Company toured *Parsifal* throughout the United States for nearly a year in a distinguished English-language production. A Yiddish version was given on the Lower East Side. *Parsifal* pastiches and parodies also materialized. Excerpts from the opera, with titles like "The Sacred Relics," "The Swan," and "Amfortas's Lament," were arranged for piano solo and piano duet. Thomas Edison, an opera-lover, made a 1904 *Parsifal* film in which scenes from the work were enacted for some thirty minutes; intended for lecture presen-tations with piano accompaniment, it was a commercial failure.* More successful, remarkably enough, were presentations of *Parsifal* as a spoken play with music. One such 1904 production, at Brook-lyn's Lee Avenue theater, gave a two-week sold-out run at fifty cents a ticket. The entire libretto was delivered in a blank-verse English translation, the orchestra numbered eighteen, the chorus was hired from the Met, and the Met's sets and costumes were faithfully copied.[10] At the Met itself, Conried continued to double prices for *Parsifal* in 1904–5 (twenty-seven performances, including tours) and 1905–6 (four performances). By 1906–7, as a regular subscription opera, its drawing power had ebbed: only two performances were possible.

Compared to 1903's *Parsifal*, the Met's initial post-Seidl seasons were both more distinguished and less sensational. This was, in fact, the house's "Golden Age." Grau was a shrewd manager, keenly respon-sive to the dual dictates of commerce and art. Imperturbably calm, invariably urbane, he was, Krehbiel testified, "neither communi-

---

*But Wagner subsequently became an important source for silent-movie music. See Chapter 15.

cative nor secretive." His company included Calvé, Campanini, Eames, Homer, Journet, Maurel, Melba, Plançon, Scotti, Sembrich. For Wagner (whose operas were not among his personal favorites) he imported Franz Schalk, later director of the Vienna Opera and a founder of the Salzburg Festival. Schalk led the Met's first unabridged *Ring* cycle and also took it on tour. And he led *Tristan und Isolde* with de Reszke and—returning after six years' absence—Lehmann. Henderson remembered one 1899 performance as the greatest *Tristan* of his experience; Lehmann remembered it as the *Tristan* performance of her life.[11] Schalk and Lehmann left the next season, but Grau retained Nordica for his Wagner ensemble. The Wagner singers he brought to the Met included Gadski and Ternina, already known to New York; van Rooy, considered the finest Wotan and Sachs of his time; and Ernestine Schumann-Heink, the most famous of all Erdas.

Tannhäuser, *Lohengrin*, *Tristan*, *Die Meistersinger*, and the *Ring* were regularly given with stellar casts. On March 19, 1900, Sembrich sang Eva—her only Wagner appearance at the Met, excepting an 1899 memorial concert for Seidl, at which she took part in *Die Meistersinger*, act 3, under Schalk. Henderson wrote: "It is out of the common order that the perfect Rosina and Violetta of our time should also place herself on record as one of the most admirable Evas. But after all is said and done, there is nothing so victorious in opera as art; and to the tips of her fingers Mme. Sembrich is an artist." On December 31 of the same year, Jean de Reszke returned after a season's absence, singing Lohengrin; Henderson wrote: "The story that the greatest male singer of our time had reached the end of his career proved to be untrue." On March 25, 1901, de Reszke gave his final full performance at the Met and drew the largest house of the season; Henderson wrote: "Mr. Jean de Reszke was in splendid voice and sang Lohengrin as well as he ever did in his life. He was an ideal Knight of the Grail. Miss Ternina gave a lovely and sympathetic interpretation of Elsa. . . . Mme. Schumann-Heink won hearty applause for her familiar Ortrud, and Mr. Edouard de Reszke was the orotund king of old. The audience was out with the intention of being enthusiastic, and it had every reason for its demonstrations."

On April 29, de Reszke sang once more at a gala, joining Nordica, Schumann-Heink and brother Edouard in *Tristan*, act 2; according to Henderson, the combination of heat and excitement caused sixteen women to faint, a house record. The ovation "was little short of frantic."[12]

We can eavesdrop on the Golden Age with Lionel Mapleson's cylinders, documenting actual Metropolitan Opera performances of 1901–4. The noise and distortion of these recordings are discouraging, but music can be heard. The Wagner excerpts are distinguished by the utter security of the brass playing, and by Nordica's stentorian Brünnhilde and Isolde—like the horns and trombones, her thrusting soprano penetrates the sonic grit. The great disappointment is de Reszke, none of whose other recordings survive: he is barely audible. Still, something like the "searching analyses of every phrase" Henderson described can almost—or, perhaps, actually—be discerned, especially in passages from *Lohengrin* and *L'Africaine*. The notion of such a singer interpreting Siegfried really is, as Krehbiel reported, "bewildering."

With the advent of the Conried Metropolitan Opera Company, Wagner at the Met went into a tailspin. Lehmann and the de Reszkes were gone for good. Mottl, discouraged by Conried's crudity, stayed for a single season only. According to Krehbiel, Fuchs and Lautenschläger, whose contributions to *Parsifal* were so admired, returned to Germany "feeling something akin to humiliation." Nordica and Schumann-Heink were more absent than present. Blass, Burgstaller, and van Rooy remained. The most important newcomers, as far as Wagner was concerned, were the tenor Carl Burrian and the beauteous Olive Fremstad, who had studied with Lilli Lehmann and performed under Anton Seidl; Carl Van Vechten called her *Götterdämmerung* Brünnhilde a "wild creature, a figure of Greek tragedy, a Norse Electra."[13]

Disorganization and dispirit were the more pronounced in contrast to the sudden success of a rival operatic venture: the Manhattan Opera, founded in 1906 by the picturesque Oscar Hammerstein. The inventor of a revolutionary cigar-making machine, Hammerstein combined Conried's promotional flair with Grau's sagacity. He was also a trained musician and a cultural democrat. He built a three-thousand-seat opera house better in every way than the oversized, overstuffed Met. Its acoustics and sight lines were excellent. Its forty-two boxes faced the stage (the Met's Diamond Horseshoe, by comparison, invited bejeweled boxholders to admire one another). Third-tier seats were modestly priced at one dollar. There were no grand entrances. "It is society in the broad sense that I hope to attract and to please," Hammerstein said. He sailed to Europe and signed Alessandro Bonci, Mary Garden, John McCormack, Maurice Renaud, and Luisa Tetrazzini. His principal conductor, Cleofonte Campanini, was more admired than any of the Italians on Conried's staff. The opening-night audience, including women in orchestra seats wearing ordinary clothes, shushed the slightest disturbance.[14] Krehbiel, in the *Tribune*, compared Bonci favorably to Caruso. By the time the Met bought off Hammerstein for a fabulous sum in 1910, he had startled and provoked New York with *Salome*, *Elektra*, and *Pelléas et Mélisande*, and proved that opera could flourish without the lures of fad and fashion. Not since the Met's German seasons had opera been so liberated from social trivialities.

Hammerstein's success hastened Conried's departure. His health failing, his sins mounting, he quit in February 1908. It seems his job was offered to Gustav Mahler, who turned it down. Mahler had arrived in New York the previous December at Conried's invitation. He had resigned as director of the Vienna Opera seven months before. In Vienna, Mahler's reign had been stormy, historic, and draining: he came to New York weakened by a diseased heart. For three months' work, Conried paid him three times what he earned year-round in Europe. Alma Mahler later wrote of Mahler's first visit to Conried's garish apartment: "Our host's utter innocence of culture kept us in concealed mirth until we were in the street again and could burst out laughing."[15]

Mahler's first New York opera was *Tristan*, with Fremstad and Heinrich Knote. His impact was electrifying. Implicitly comparing Mahler to Mottl, the *Times* commented:

> The influence of the new conductor was felt and heard in the whole spirit of the performance. He is clearly not one of the modern conductors, upon whom the ban of [Bayreuth] of the present day

rests, with the result of dragging the tempo and weighting the performance of Wagner's works with lead. His tempos were frequently somewhat more rapid than we have been lately accustomed to; and they were always such as to fill the music with dramatic fire.[16]

The Mahlers found the Met's physical production farcical in comparison with Alfred Roller's art nouveau sets and costumes in Vienna. The company's singers amazed them.

Mahler subsequently led seven more operas in New York, including *Die Walküre* and *Siegfried*. But his contribution was overshadowed by that of another newcomer: Arturo Toscanini. As Mahler had intransigently reformed opera in Vienna and left, Toscanini had tyrannized La Scala, instilling new standards of preparation and commitment. He resigned in February 1908—the same month he accepted employment at the Met, whose new director, replacing Conried, would be La Scala's Giulio Gatti-Casazza. The huge Met was now too small to house its two leading conductors. They quarreled over *Tristan und Isolde*, which Mahler considered his exclusive property in New York. Toscanini annexed *Tristan* on November 27, 1909. Mahler left to take over the New York Philharmonic. In the course of seven seasons, Toscanini led 479 Metropolitan Opera performances. Naturally, the new regime favored Italian composers, not excluding Catalani, Franchetti, Giordano, Leoni, and Wolf-Ferrari. But Toscanini was also a Wagnerite. At the Met, he led *Tristan*, *Die Meistersinger*, and *Götterdämmerung*. His singers included Burrian, Fremstad, Gadski, Louise Homer, and Leo Slezak.

Looking back, the thought of Wagner led by a Mahler or Toscanini is an awesome thing; today's Metropolitan Opera offers nothing remotely comparable. But as of 1908, when Toscanini arrived, Met audiences had heard Wagner under Seidl, Schalk, and Mottl. The New York Philharmonic and New York Symphony had performed Wagner under Thomas, Seidl, and Weingartner. On New York visits, the Boston Symphony had played Wagner under Nikisch and Karl Muck. Critics like Henderson and Krehbiel took new Wagner conductors in stride. Toscanini, they agreed, was a godsend for Verdi. In Wagner, he completely surpassed Mancinelli and Vianesi: Toscanini's was the finest Italianate Wagner New York had heard. Here, for instance, is Henderson on Toscanini's *Götterdämmerung*:

> At the outset it may be said that taking into account the temperament and acquired tastes of an Italian musician the interpretation of the score by Mr. Toscanini was thoroughly commendable. It would be injustice to others and flattery to this conductor to say that it was a great reading. It would be equally unjust to deny that, granting its emotional outlook (which is by no means indefensible), it was a good reading.
>
> Mr. Toscanini naturally feels above all the sensuous quality of Wagner's melody, and it is this in all its ebb and flow that he seeks and exposes. Whenever the sensuous beauty of the melody is such as to tempt a conductor to dwell unduly on the phrase, to exaggerate the rhetorical pause, to smooth out all the rugged edges of the instrumental declamation Mr. Toscanini yields to it with avidity and spreads the syrup on the bread as thin as possible. . . .

Further evidence of Toscanini's catholicity was his performance of Beethoven's Ninth with the Metropolitan Opera orchestra on April 13, 1913. It was thrillingly crisp, marvelously vital. Krehbiel wrote:

> His tempi . . . seemed to indicate that he was laboring under a somewhat abnormal nervous strain. . . . He did wonderful things [in the] finale. . . . The scherzo last night was taken at a quicker speed than Beethoven prescribed, and the effectiveness of the trio, in particular, was marred and some passages were blurred. Nor was the flight to the empyrean in the variations quite so transfiguring as it might have been. But the music held the listeners in an irresistible grip, nevertheless.*[17]

If Krehbiel more than tolerated Toscanini's Wagner and Beethoven, he suffered Mahler with mounting aggravation. He approved of

---

*These reviews are only partly relevant to the Toscanini Americans came to know after World War I. (See Joseph Horowitz, *Understanding Toscanini: How He Became an American Culture-God and Helped Create a New Audience for Old Music* [New York, 1987], pp. 321–72.)

Mahler's Wagner with the proviso that Mahler was no more a messiah than New York was a backwater. "Herr Mahler," his first Mahler review began, "is a newcomer whose appearance here, while full of significance, is not likely to excite one-half the interest in New York that his departure from Europe did at the other side of the water."[18] Krehbiel objected to Mahler's vigorous retouchings of Beethoven's scoring, and Mozart's, and Schubert's. He disliked Mahler's own music; he called him "a prophet of the ugly."

Krehbiel's arrogance, while not pretty, had been unmasked by Mahler's own. "It will be my aim to educate the public," Mahler announced upon arriving at the Savoy Hotel, "and that education will be made gradually and in a manner which will enable those who may not now have a taste for the best later to appreciate it." He pledged to make the New York Philharmonic "equal to any [orchestra] in the world." Listing the world's great orchestras, he named those of Vienna, Munich, Dresden, Berlin, and Paris. He did not think to mention Boston.[19] During his first season with the Philharmonic, his forty-five concerts—crammed, incidentally, with Wagner—included not a single American work (his record the next season was better).

Everything about Mahler—his programming, his rescorings, his interpretive machinations—struck Krehbiel as objectionably didactic. When Mahler died, on May 18, 1911, Krehbiel responded with a withering fifty-inch postmortem. It read in part:

> It is a fatuous notion of foreigners that Americans know nothing about music in its highest forms. Only of late years have the European newspapers begun to inform their readers that the opera in New York has some significance. Had their writers on music been students they would have known that for nearly a century New Yorkers have listened to singers of the highest class—singers that the people of the musical centers of the European continent were never permitted to hear. Mr. Mahler . . . never discovered that there were Philharmonic subscribers who had inherited not only their seats from their parents and grandparents, but also their appreciation of good music. He never knew, of if he knew he was never willing to acknowledge, that the Philharmonic audience would be as

quick to resent an outrage on the musical classics as a corruption of the Bible or Shakespeare.*

And yet one may doubt that the Philharmonic's audience was as sophisticated as Krehbiel claimed. For one thing, Mahler's expanded seasons attracted some of the tiniest houses in Philharmonic history. For another, the orchestra, no longer viable as a musicians' cooperative, had been taken over by millionaires some of whom knew much less about music than Heinrich Conried did. In some ways, Krehbiel was as alienated by these developments as Mahler. As he grew older, he longed for the past. The present seemed summarized by Conried and *Parsifal*, by the Philharmonic guarantors who, according to one anecdote, accused Mahler of a work stoppage when in rehearsal he interrupted the orchestra to discuss a point with his piano soloist. Here is Carl Burrian, a distinguished New York Siegmund, Siegfried, and Tristan under Mahler and Toscanini, writing in 1908:

> The Wagner performances are the least patronized by the public. The whole business apparently bores the audiences to death. If one of these performances does interest the public, how do the most conspicuous—that is, the richest—express their feelings? The beginning of the performance is announced for 8 o'clock. "They," however, come after 9. An usher with an electric light in his hand enters the box and shows the guests their seats. There is a constant coming and going. . . . The principal thing is the long intermission during which the gentlemen and ladies of society promenade about arm in arm to show their toilets and diamonds in their greatest beauty. After the long intermission one need only to glance in the boxes to see that by a few minutes after 11 there is a packing up of

---

*In a similar vein, W. J. Henderson wrote in the March 22, 1908, *New York Sun*:

It is most instructive to study the logic of the European intellect when it is engaged in its favorite amusement, that of demonstrating that the American is the product of a distinctly inferior order of the dust of the earth. In one sentence it writes us down a nation of moneymaking merchants and in the next it charges us with business methods fit only for the ravings of an asylum. . . .

It is always instructive to read European newspapers on American affairs. It gives us the much needed opportunity to see ourselves as others see us—with their eyes shut.

opera glasses in reticules and the start for home. What may happen on the stage after that interests nobody. It is true that in *Tannhäuser* the audience rises and flees from the opera house after Wolfram's song to the "Evening Star." The tenor who appears after Wolfram's song sings the closing music of his part to the baritone on the stage or the conductor. He might as well play cards with them so far as the public is concerned. I would like to bet that the fewest possible number of subscribers to the Metropolitan Opera House have the least idea how the story of Tannhäuser and poor Elisabeth ends.[20]

And Krehbiel was alienated by his own colleagues in the press, who trivialized the *Parsifal* debate and noisily billed both Mahler and Toscanini "world's most famous." Toscanini, in particular, became the beneficiary of a public relations juggernaut. "In New York, Toscanini has conducted twenty-two operas," ran one typical item.

The number of pages in the full scores of those works . . . is approximately ten thousand. Yet that does not nearly represent the prodigious amount of material that he has filed away in his mind, ready for immediate use. In countries outside of the United States he has conducted by heart not only seventy other operas, thus bringing the number of operatic scores he has committed to memory to the stupendous figure of ninety-two, but has also produced various oratorios, symphonies, and tone-poems.[21]

Ballyhoo had been the keynote of Jenny Lind's tours for P. T. Barnum sixty years before. It had flavored the American visits of famous and not-so-famous violin and piano virtuosos. But only after 1900 did it invade the Germanic citadel of Beethoven and Wagner. Surveying New York's operatic affairs between 1908 and 1918, Krehbiel groaned:

Even in journals of dignity and scholarly repute the gossip of the foyer and the dressing rooms of the chorus and ballet stood in higher esteem with the news editors than the comments of conscientious critics. . . . If in this [the newspapers] reflect the taste of their readers, it is a taste which they have instilled and cultivated, for it did not exist before the days of photo-engraving, illustrated supplements and press agents. . . . The phenomenon . . . marked the operatic history of the decade of which I am writing more emphatically than any period within a generation.[22]

Krehbiel's discriminating response to Mahler and Toscanini, his contempt for Conried and the gossiping press, his insistence on a New World of sophisticated music-making unrecognized in Europe—all this testifies to the legacy of fading Wagnerism. He could not abide that the Viennese—and, too obviously, many New Yorkers—knew nothing of what the Metropolitan and New York Philharmonic had stood for a mere generation before. His diatribe against the dead Mahler, which has perplexed and offended ever since, can only be understood once his relationship to Anton Seidl is considered. As man and musician, Seidl signified to Krehbiel everything Gustav Mahler was not. Mahler, emotionally undone by the meddlesome guarantors, was neurotic and high-strung; Seidl was "manly" and composed. Mahler mistrusted his New York Philharmonic players: he employed a "spy" to report on malcontents; of Seidl, Victor Herbert said: "It was through [a] strong bond of fraternity that he came to acquire a powerful personal influence over the instrumentalists which was entirely distinct from the musical magnetism exerted in rehearsals and public performances." Though he achieved magnificent results, Mahler called his Philharmonic "a real American orchestra—untalented and phlegmatic."[23] Seidl called New York's pool of orchestral musicians the finest in the world. Mahler's New York income allowed him to spend summers in Europe composing; Seidl, who summered in the Catskills, was an "Americamaniac." Seidl's Metropolitan Opera, whose devoted Wagnerites came to sing, play, watch, and listen, had been a shrine; Mahler's and Conried's, with its expensive singers and inattentive crowds, seemed a circus. Its vulgarity cast a shadow on the twilit cult of Wagner.

15

Enter Modernism

The commercialization of *Parsifal* was a dramatic detail in Wagnerism's decline, but not a necessary cause. In Europe, where *Parsifal* remained exclusively enshrined at Bayreuth, the cult of Wagner was equally on the wane. In fact, the history of the Wagner movement in Europe sheds vital perspective on its New World fate.[1]

In certain respects, France furnished Wagnerism's most prominent and influential model. Unlike pious Bayreuth, the Parisian avant-garde made *wagnérisme* a heady cause célèbre, propagated by such artist-intellectuals as Baudelaire and Mallarmé. An 1850 performance of the *Tannhäuser* Overture was one early stimulus. Though no more Wagner was heard in Paris for eight years, his writing kept him controversial. In the enemy camp, including the important critic/musicologist François-Joseph Fétis, Wagner was labeled the "Courbet of music," an outrageous "realist"; in advanced circles, he dictated fashion. Wagner himself arrived in 1859, to be hailed and denounced as a democrat and revolutionary. His varied political appeal did not preclude the support of the liberal statesman (and eventual prime minister) Emile Ollivier, or of Napoleon III, who ordered the Imperial Opera to stage *Tannhäuser* partly to court Austria, partly to conciliate the left. The resulting performance, on March 13, 1861, is famous—the one the Jockey Club disrupted with dog whistles because the second act included no "grand ballet." In subsequent years literary *wagnérisme* was taken up by the idealistic *Revue wagnérienne* (1885–88). Another circle of *wagnéristes* included art critics and painters, of whom Renoir frequently heard Wagner performed in concert. A symbolist Wagner faction included Karl Huysmans and the mystical/hedonistic aesthetics of decadence. Meanwhile, the orchestral Wagner was championed by Pasdeloup, Colonne, and Lamoreux; it had become an integral part of the repertoire. Wagner's operas were staged with fair frequency beginning in the 1890s. By then, Wagnerism was losing its élan; anyway, its symbolists and decadents more offended than pleased more purely musical adherents. An American historian summarizes: "No matter how much French artists used Wagner's music and ideas to suit their own purposes, they maintained a consistent commitment to 'progressive' taste. To say that all of them belonged to the artistic avant-garde would be an exaggeration, since that implies rather more self-conscious modernism than many of them . . . were willing to admit. But . . . French Wagnerians were committed to furthering the cause of forward-looking trends in French culture. The movement indeed played a central role as a catalyst for the concept of the avant-garde in France."[2]

As in France, Wagnerism in Italy emerged against a background of political ferment; as in Germany, the polity itself was in formation. A special circumstance was the legacy of Italian opera, which seemed challenged or revitalized by Wagner. In an early phase, the bohemian *scapigliati* (or "disheveled ones"), many of whom were Mazzinian republicans, used Wagner as a club to beat bourgeois philistines. One of the *scapigliati* was Arrigo Boito, whose *Mefistofele*, introduced in 1868 (and later championed by Anton Seidl at the Metropolitan Opera), was criticized as Wagnerian. Three years later *Lohengrin* in Bologna became the first Italian Wagner production. *Tannhäuser*, *The Flying Dutchman*, and *Tristan* followed in the same house in 1872, 1877, and 1888. Also in Bologna, the *Cronaca wagneriana* (1893–95) kept the flame for Riccardo Wagner. In rival Milan, however, the first *Lohengrin*, in 1873, was disrupted by nationalists; Wagner did not return to La Scala until *Lohengrin* came back in 1888. Giovanni Papini, later a futurist, was jailed as a martyr to Wagner when he and his friends expressed their ecstasy too fervently. Wagner also volatilized discontent with liberal Italy in the person of Gabriele D'Annunzio. Novelist and statesman, apostle of decadence and heroic egoism, he embedded Wagner the poet/politician in his

1898 novel *Il fuoco*. The constitution of D'Annunzio's 1919 Republic of Canaro established music as a "social and religious institution." Variously appropriated by socialists and elitists, Wagnerism helped define Italian culture for the dissident young and their leaders.

Even compared to Mallarmé's France or D'Annunzio's Italy, Russian Wagnerism was extravagant and arcane. Its advent was delayed by delayed economic and political maturity, by the delayed strains of industrialization. Its impact was untempered by the liberalism and rationalism of the more secular West. Russia's "Silver Age," 1890 to 1917, was centrally influenced by Wagner. The *Ballets russes* of Diaghilev and Benois russified the *Gesamtkunstwerk* ideal. Even Stravinsky's *The Rite of Spring*, musically antithetical to Wagner, produced integrated music theater—a Diaghilev ballet— refurbishing national myths. Alexandr Blok, the emblematic Silver Age symbolist poet, called his dacha "Valhalla." His imagination was fired by the Dionysian ecstasy and religious rapture of *Tristan* and *Parsifal*. After 1917, Anatoli Lunacharsky, the Marxist head of the Commissariat of Enlightenment, invoked Wagnerian ideals of social transformation through art. The Wagner operas themselves came late to Russia. When Angelo Neumann arrived with the *Ring* in 1889, only *Tannhäuser* and *Lohengrin* had been given. Beginning in 1907, however, St. Petersburg's Mariinsky Theater produced an annual *Ring* cycle. Two years later, Vsevolod Meyerhold directed a stylized *Tristan*. As late as 1940, Meyerhold's protégé Sergei Eisenstein mounted a *Walküre*, for the Bolshoi, in which a pantomime chorus was employed to amplify the characters' thoughts and feelings.

Milder by far was the British context, with its legacy of stable governance and Enlightened rationality. Still, industrialization produced a potent Wagnerian backlash, rejecting materialism and scientism, striving toward a transformative spiritualism. Here, the Christian motif was pronounced; even pious clergymen espoused the *Ring* and *Parsifal*. Wagner was also hailed as a prophet of the occult. Wagnerian theosophists included not only Kandinsky and Scriabin, in Russia, but William Ashton Ellis, today remembered for this translations of Wagner's prose, and William Butler Yeats, for whom Wagner contributed to "the new sacred book that all the arts were seeking to create." At an opposite extreme, the irreligious George Bernard Shaw, in his famous *The Perfect Wagnerite* (1889), read the *Ring* as a Fabian rebuke to rapacious Capitalists. Another prominent British Wagnerite, the Scotsman David Irvine, preached a liberalism compounded of "radical politics, Protestantism, and rationalism." And, as in France, Italy, and Russia, there were Wagnerian decadents and modernists: Aubrey Beardsley, Oscar Wilde, Arthur Symons. D. H. Lawrence, Virginia Woolf, James Joyce, and T. S. Eliot also reveal the influence of Wagner.

If Bayreuth's petrification rites narrowed Wagnerism's range in Bayreuth, elsewhere in German-speaking lands more progressive Wagnerian modes prevailed. In Vienna, Schopenhauer and Nietzsche were invoked to propel renewal—a movement prominently including Mahler, who vitalized the Opera, Victor Adler, a frequent opera-goer before becoming Austria's leading socialist, and the prescient city planner Camillo Sitte, who formulated new visions of integrated urban life. In Germany, Thomas Mann loved Wagner, but "without believing"—passionately yet skeptically, and mindful of newer, cooler aesthetic currents.

Quite predictably, the sum total of these European Wagnerisms is a patchwork: not a system of thought, but a heuristic impetus. Still, three linked yet contradictory tendencies may be extrapolated, beginning with the most obvious and general: the Wagner movement challenged the status quo. It baited the bourgeoisie. It repudiated philistines and materialists, positivists and utilitarians. In complaining that science, industry, and commerce were corruptive, it responded to new needs. Political-minded Wagnerites often railed against liberal moderation, and yet—generations before Hitler—the movement can by no means be called protofascist; more often than not, Wagnerian nationalists veered toward the left. The utopian search for regeneration also conveyed strong religious overtones. Music, especially at Bayreuth, was sacred and transformative, never frivolous.

Some Wagnerites were devout Christians. And yet organized religion was sorely tested by rapid industrial and urban growth. A pervasive spiritual search led to Christian Science and theosophy. Wagner offered not only uplift, but—and we may call this a second general attribute—ecstatic emotional release. Sexuality and eroticism, sublimated and not so sublimated, were frank Wagnerian motifs, challenging moral conventions, satisfying libidinal cravings aggravated by crowded, sedentary, fractured city life. Perhaps no previous music—perhaps no previous art in any form—had promoted such orgasmic catharsis.

The Wagnerian impulse to *épater* the bourgeois promoted a third, aesthetic tendency: Wagnerism was avant-garde. Contradicting other, Romantic aspects of itself, it was modernist. It was not only sensual, but arcane, or "realistic," or amoral. Its aesthetes, decadents, and symbolists encompassed an array of modernist prophets. Unlike that of meliorist Wagnerites, their repudiation of the mainstream took the form of acute withdrawal: into troubled realms of the nonlogical and unconscious; into art for art's sake. And this was no distortion of Wagner, but a selective fixation on themes of disease and psychic disturbance other Wagnerites preferred to ignore.

Finally, it is possible to generalize about the timetable for Wagnerism in Europe. It began around the time of the revolutions of 1848–49—coinciding with Wagner's essays of 1849 to 1851, which became more widely known than his music. The music began catching up in the two decades that followed. The first complete *Ring* cycle, inaugurating the Bayreuth Festival in 1876, was of course a landmark event. The movement maintained strength during the seventeen years from Wagner's death to the turn of the century. Except in Russia, where it came late, Wagnerism subsided during the early twentieth century. Its relevance to the avant-garde diminished. Befriended by the new, cruder Germany of Wilhelm II, it grew alien to French, British, and Russian tastes and interests. By World War I, Wagnerism as a pervasive ideology, as opposed to a personal and primarily aesthetic enthusiasm, had substantially ceased.

All this illuminates the American experience of Wagner, with its emphasis on uplift. The genteel culture-bearers who absorbed and interpreted Wagner's essays and operas were nothing if not embodiments of the socio-cultural critique that galvanized Wagnerism in Europe. Barbarian politicians and bankers made them cringe. They yearned for sweetness and light. John Sullivan Dwight excoriated prima donnas and virtuosos. Theodore Thomas preached sermons in tones. Anton Seidl lamented that "the need for premature money-earning" had retarded America's musical aptitudes. Henry Krehbiel denounced the commercialization of *Parsifal*. Meliorist interpretations of the *Ring* and *Tristan*, purged of pessimism and psychosis, exuded an American wholesomeness, a curative moralizing power.

In fact, as in England, reassuring Christian readings were popular among American Wagnerites. Equally evident—sometimes half-concealed by genteel manners, sometimes not—was the thrill of sublimated sexuality, transcending more orthodox modes of release. For Gilded Age women, Wagner fever—no less than wholesome understandings of Wagnerian immolation and love-death—could be a form of self-affirmation or therapy.

In an earlier chapter, I mentioned Jackson Lears's emphasis on the hunger for "intense experience" in Gilded Age America—in which context Lears locates Wagnerism. The larger sweep of his analysis postulates a "therapeutic ethos," an urgent preoccupation with psychic and physical health generated by "a weightless culture of material comfort and spiritual blandness." Of late-nineteenth-century America, he observes that the erosion of traditional communal and religious structures transformed the search for health into a "self-referential project, rooted in peculiarly modern emotional needs." To heal the fragmented self, Americans turned to depth psychology, mysticism, and mind cure, to roller coasters, exotic dancers, and hootchy-kootchy girls. The hunger for "real life" encompassed Jane Addams's settlement house movement, Randolph Bourne's call for "education through living," and Van Wyck Brooks's diagnosis of cultural anemia. Even American raids on European art, according to Lears, were at times less greedy than medicinal; William James compared Isabella Stewart Gardner's private museum to a clinic. Mrs. Gardner was also a Wagnerite.

And yet all this was somewhat less than it seemed. The intense experience afforded by Coney Island, by Rembrandt, by occultism was partly illusory. Its outcome, according to Lears, was not liberation but a controlling consumer culture mired in apolitical narcissism and passivity. The "abundance therapies" of the period—the injunction to "let go"—promised rapturous self-realization. But, in seeking to liberate instinct, they denied instinct's darker side. Like Krehbiel reading *Tristan*, they understated the conflict between eros and civilization; they dismissed the rage and longing of the insatiable libido. This insistence on inherent health was unhealthy; it resulted in a condition of anxious self-absorption.

However far one wishes to follow Lears's argument, it fits aspects of America's Wagner cult. Like other turn-of-the-century cures Lears documents, Wagnerism in America reveals a quest for meaning and purpose that belies stereotypes of Gilded Age complacency. Yet, like those same therapies, Wagner in many instances subverted complacency less than it thought or seemed to. It realized voluptuous dreams and intoxicating pleasures, but "without bad after-effects."

In the United States, rampant Wagnerism signified more than fashion, more than entertainment. It registered real emotional tumult. For a Mabel Dodge Luhan or M. Carey Thomas, it resonated with profound issues of interior identity; its "after-effects" *were* subversive. At the same time—to restate its contradictory trajectory another way—it was undeniably contained in comparison to Wagnerism abroad. Its social agenda was milder than in countries where questions of national identity seemed more perplexing or urgent, less potent than where artists and intellectuals were more politically empowered. Relative to Europe, its ecstasies were—at least in public—inhibited by the Victorian codes they stretched. There were no Wagner riots, as in Paris or Milan. There were no poetic flights half as rarified as a Mallarmé's or Blok's.

If America therefore generally muted Wagnerian attributes of social criticism and ecstatic release, it altogether ignored the third and last general trait we have extracted from our European survey. American Wagnerites had nothing to do with modernism. From the vantage point of Krehbiel, Wagnerism was not—as it seemed to Seidl and other European advocates of Music of the Future—suddenly progressive; rather, Wagner sustained a grand lineage connecting to Bach, Mozart, and Beethoven. The modernist agenda was inexplicable, obnoxious, or unknown. Modernism aggressively distorted reality. It craved change for the sake of change: new ways of seeing, new possibilities of expression. It denied the therapeutic function of art.

Nothing more discloses this distinctively American dissociation of Wagnerism from modernism than the careers of New York's leading Wagnerite critics after 1900. The new music and art coming out of Europe antagonized them. It did not have to be Joyce, or Picasso, or Schoenberg and Stravinsky. Strauss's post-Romantic *Salome* seemed the acme of modernist nihilism when Heinrich Conried mounted its American premiere in 1907. Conried was banking on scandal and publicity: a commercial killing, a second *Parsifal*. But many in the audience, in the words of one newspaper report, experienced "a strange horror or disgust." They exited when Olive Fremstad, a mesmerizing Salome, received the head of John the Baptist. J. P. Morgan called a special stockholders' meeting at which further performances of the offensive work were forbidden. With this decision, Henry Krehbiel agreed: "Decent men did not want to have their house polluted with the stench with which Oscar Wilde's play had filled the nostrils of humanity. Having the power to prevent the pollution they exercised it."

Krehbiel's account of Strauss's handiwork is a classic of critical opprobrium which I cannot resist quoting at length. It begins:

> A reviewer ought to be equipped with a dual nature, both intellectually and morally, in order to pronounce fully and fairly upon the qualities of this drama by Oscar Wilde and Richard Strauss. He should be an embodied conscience stung into righteous fury by the moral stench exhaled by the decadent and pestiferous work, but, though it make him retch, he should be sufficiently judicial in his temperament calmly to look at the drama in all its aspects and determine whether or not as a whole it is an instructive note on the life and culture of the times and whether or not this exudation from the diseased and polluted will and imagination of the authors marks

a real advance in artistic expression, irrespective of its contents or their fitness for dramatic representation.

To this query, Krehbiel answered no. Of special interest is his distinction between Strauss's method and Wagner's. Isolde's erotic suicide, after all, is first cousin to Salome's orgasmic apostrophe to the severed head. The manic, neurasthenic Herod bears musical comparison with the ranting Mime, moral comparison with the self-castrated Klingsor. Krehbiel's case is shrewdly argued:

> It would be wholly justifiable to characterize "Salome" as a symphonic poem for which the play supplies the program. The parallelism of which we hear between Strauss and Wagner exists only in part—only in the application of the principle of characterization by means of musical symbols or typical phrases. Otherwise the men work in diametrically opposite lines. With all his musical affluence, Wagner aimed, at least, to make his orchestra only the bearer and servant of the dramatic word. Nothing can be plainer (it did not need that he should himself have confessed it) than that Strauss looks upon the words as necessary evils. . . . It is amazing how indifferent the listener is to both vocal quality and intervallic accuracy in "Salome." Wilde's stylistic efforts are lost in the flood of instrumental sound; only the mood which they were designed to produce remains. Jochanaan sings phrases, which are frequently tuneful, and when they are not denunciatory are set in harmonies agreeable to the ear. But by reason of that fact Jochanaan comes perilously near being an old-fashioned operatic figure—an ascetic Marcel, with little else to differentiate him from his Meyerbeerian prototype than his "raiment of camel's hair and a leathern girdle about his loins."

The caliber of Krehbiel's outraged intelligence is no less evident in such passages as:

> Startling effects are obtained by a confusion of keys, confusion of rhythms, sudden contrasts from an overpowering tutti to the stridulous whirring of empty fifths on the violins, a trill on the flutes, or a dissonant mutter of the basses. The celesta, an instrument with

keyboard and bell tone, contributes fascinating effects, and the xylophone is used;—utterances that are lascivious as well as others that are macabre. Dissonance runs riot and frequently carries the imagination away completely captive. The score is unquestionably the greatest triumph of reflection and ingenuity of contrivance that the literature of music can show. The invention that has been expended on the themes seems less admirable. Only the pompous proclamation of the theme which is dominant in Jochanaan's music saves it from being called commonplace.

The nub of Krehbiel's argument, finally, is this: Even if we concede—a reluctant concession, a sign of the times—that truth is not always beautiful, that ugliness is entitled to be raised to a valid principle in opera, who can justify that Strauss lends his loveliest strains "to the apotheosis of that which is indescribably, yes, inconceivably gross and abominable"? Salome's steamy adoration of the dismembered head, one of the score's "supremely beautiful musical moments," can "only be conceived as rising from the uttermost pit of degradation."

> Strauss has striven to outdo [Isolde's *Liebestod*], and there are those who think that in this episode he actually raised music to a higher power. He has not only gone with the dramatist and outraged every sacred instinct of humanity by calling the lust for flesh, alive or dead, love, but he has celebrated her ghoulish passion as if he would perforce make her an object of . . . "redemption."[3]

Krehbiel rejected *Salome* as meretricious. It lacked the moral fervor that, however erratically, buoyed the Wagner canon. A year later, he rejected Debussy's *Pelléas et Mélisande*—also a symbol or harbinger of modernism—on the grounds that "nine-tenths of the music is a dreary monotony," bereft of "musical thought."[4] It is worth adding that Krehbiel's antipathy to Mahler had more than a little to do with new aesthetic fashion. He objected to Mahler's way, in his symphonies, of juxtaposing the sublime and quotidian. Here, again, Krehbiel's conservatism was never blind; all his judgments were considered, precise, articulate. His knowledge was vast.

Krehbiel embodies the genteel tradition at its best. His swan song for the *Tribune*, on February 11, 1923, was "The Curse of Affectation and Modernism in Music"—an essay also bemused by the noise of traffic and machines, and by Albert Einstein's revelation that there was "no such thing as a straight line in the universe." The pallbearers at Krehbiel's funeral, a month later, included his fellow Wagnerites Richard Aldrich, Henry Finck, and W. J. Henderson. That spring, Aldrich resigned from the *New York Times*. In a retrospective column, he remarked that "disinterested critics of New York from abroad say that New York is very conservative in music matters. . . . Perhaps there has been in some quarters too much eagerness to feed popular things to docile listeners. . . . [But] it is a task to listen to new things at best; and when the result seems to be that the new things are poor stuff, discouragement comes too easily." Finck quit the *Post* the following season, and wrote:

> Richard Aldrich [retired] chiefly because, as he himself told me, he could no longer endure the torture of listening to the preposterous cacophonies of the so-called futurists or modernists in music and because of the boredom of writing about them. . . . I may as well say it now as later—one of the chief reasons why I gave up writing criticisms for a daily paper was the same as Aldrich's.[5]

The last of the critical Old Guard to go was Henderson—with Krehbiel, New York's most discerning Wagnerite critic. Stylistically, Henderson's terse, epigrammatic prose made him Krehbiel's antithesis. Aesthetically, he and Krehbiel were one. Like other genteel writers, Henderson believed in progress—as a continuation of past endeavor, not a revolutionary leap. In *What Is Good Music?* (1898), he rejected the tenets of modernism. "The fleeting nature of a musical thought demands that it be repeated in order that the mind may become acquainted with it." "Music is a romantic art, and . . . it must be tinged with emotion which is generated by the fire of high imagination." "The first obligation of music and its final achievement is to be beautiful." Henderson's conviction that art should uplift never degenerated into prattle. His 1897 condemnation of *Tod und Verklärung* and *Also sprach Zarathustra* bears comparison with Krehbiel's *Salome* diatribe.

> I challenge any living man to say honestly that he ever came away from the performance of a symphonic poem by Richard Strauss with any finer impulse of his nature quickened, with any high emotion warmed, or with any sweeter sensibility touched. . . . To prod the dying man to more gasps and record them with phonograph and metronome for future reproduction on trombones in syncopated rhythms; to turn the face of the convalescent to the light and read in it wild dreams of the fever-drained mind that they may be hereafter voiced in the stentorious pantings of stopped horns or the sepulchral moanings of violas; to read the vision of a world-wreck in the mind of a drunken man hearing the tolling of the midnight hour that it may afterward be hurled at an amazed audience in a stunning clangor of tympani, bass drum, cymbals, and gong—these seem to be worthy objects for the art of music, according to the gospel of Richard Strauss, prince royal of tonal decadents.[6]

Like Krehbiel, Henderson lived to become an anachronism—except that he lived much longer: to 1937. Both his old-fashioned opinions and his old-fashioned acuity set him apart from younger colleagues who knew and said less. Faced with a new composition, he typically studied the score and attended rehearsals before casting judgment. Of Schoenberg's *Die glückliche Hand*, he wrote: "[It is] the last word in merciless ingenuity. There is not an instant of apparent spontaneity in the score." He preferred the same composer's *Pierrot lunaire*: "The machinery is simple; the method novel. But there is life in the creation." Berg's *Wozzeck*, in Henderson's opinion, contained "not a flash of wholesome beauty"—and yet "The score is free from the uncertain gropings [of] many modernist works. . . . Berg goes to his mark with a fine certainty." Of Stravinsky, Henderson considered *The Rite of Spring* "undoubtedly a masterpiece of modernistic music. . . . Nothing apparently is done for the sake of sensationalism. . . . Much of it is very beautiful even to ears trained [in] the old melodic and harmonic formulae. Some of it is ugly, but the purpose of the ugliness is unmistakable." Of the

Symphonies of Wind Instruments, Henderson wrote: "To understand it, you must think about nothing at all. . . . It is not a composition. It is not even a tone painting of externals. It is merely a shameless public exposition of a tone painter's method of setting his palette. . . . It is a singular experiment, an almost swaggering piece of effrontery." An exception to this and other condemnations of the neo-classical Stravinsky was Henderson's response to *Apollo*: "chaste, dignified, restful and . . . genuinely beautiful."[7]

Henderson joined Krehbiel in lamenting the commercialization of high art. He disliked popular music, and mistrusted the vox populi. The cult of celebrity promoting Toscanini after World War I offended him. In 1926 he wrote:

> These are days when the plain workaday utterance of music will not suffice for a populace incessantly demanding new ways of saying old truths and ready to sink into apathy unless mental stimulants are liberally administered. In such conditions the true merits of such a temperamental conductor as this famous Italian are likely to be obscured behind a red screen of what those who hear with their eyes believe to be inspiration of the moment and sorcery of the baton.[8]

Early in 1937 Henderson, at the age of eighty-one, was weakened by the flu. On July 4, while writing an article about Josef Hofmann, he put a gun to his head and pulled the trigger. His friend Richard Aldrich, a last link to the past, had died a few days before. The fates of Krehbiel and Henderson—the forms of estrangement they experienced—help us understand the fate of Wagnerism in the United States.[9]

Alongside Krehbiel and Henderson, James Gibbons Huneker—a precise contemporary—singularly rejected Gilded Age gentility. His protégé H. L. Mencken called him "a divine mongrel." He campaigned for Cézanne, Hauptmann, Joyce, Mallarmé, Matisse,

Munch, Strindberg, and Wedekind. As a music critic (he had studied to become a pianist), he was, again, progressive and eclectic. Unlike his colleagues, who took their cues from Germany, Huneker was itinerant, the complete cosmopolite. It was Paris, he wrote, that "had lent me aplomb, had rubbed off my salad greenness." The flamboyant and cynical Huysmans, in particular, inspired Huneker's risqué verdicts and dense, polysyllabic prose. And Huneker had also been schooled by the rambunctious German intellectuals and anarchists of New York's Lower East Side—a community, intermingling with more respectable Union Square types six blocks to the west, that included Ambrose Bierce and Emma Goldman, that read Nietzsche and Max Stirner and sang the *Marseillaise* and the *Internationale*.

Had Huneker been a confirmed Wagnerite, he might have wielded influence as a decadent apostate. He was at best a sometime Wagnerite. His "Wagner and Swinburne," published in 1887, reveals a surprisingly inhibited thirty-year-old sensibility: "Shakespeare with his types of humanity and Beethoven with his ever fresh themes, never hysterical, never morbid, are after all the truer and greater artists. . . . Wagner has left the world an imperishable legacy of art but heaven forbid that we should allow the spirit of his music to guide our moralities." By the time he visited Bayreuth, in 1896, however, Huneker was an urbane amoralist. He delighted in comparing the relationship of Amfortas and Parsifal to that of Wagner and the homosexual Ludwig. In a series of short stories and essays, many of which first appeared in the *Musical Courier*, he limned the first prominent portrait by an American of the decadent Wagner, poking savage fun at Wagnerian holiness. Huneker's story "Dusk of the Gods," for instance, recounts the delirium of the music critic Stannum upon hearing the pianist Bech chronologically survey a gamut of famous composers. In this condensed history of music, Wagner occurs as

> a shriller accent, the accent of a sun that has lost its sex and is stricken with soft moon-sickness. A Hybrid . . . this new chromatic blaze, this new tinting of tones—what did it portend? Was it a symbol of the further degradation and effeminization of Music? Gigantic as antediluvian ferns, as evil-smelling and as dangerous,

music in the hands of this magician is dowered with ambiguous attitudes, with anonymous gestures, is color become sound, sensuality in the mask of beauty. This Klingsor tears down, evirates, effeminates and disintegrates. He is the great denier of all things natural, and his revengeful, theatric music is in the guise of a woman. The art nears its end; its spiritual suicide is at hand.

Undoing the work of Theodore Thomas, who molded a manly Wagner, Wagner here appears contrasted with "manly" Handel and Beethoven, neither impotently effete, on the one hand, nor wholly admirable, on the other.[10]

Huneker's stories typically incorporate such reflections into more elaborate fictional narratives, altering and updating Wagnerian plots. In "Tannhäuser's Choice," Henry Tannhäuser is spurned by Miss Elizabeth Landgrave in favor of Henry's friend Wolfram Eschenbach. Other characters include Karl Biterolf, Walter Vogelweise, and Mrs. Venus Holda, all taken from Wagner's opera, as are the selections sung at a musicale. In "Siegfried's Death," two wives appear at the same husband's funeral. "Hunding's Wife" drugs her husband to be alone with a "look-alike lover." A fifth Huneker story, "Brynhild's Immolation," invents the Wagnerian soprano Madame Stock.

Huneker's perception of Wagner as an exemplar of abnormality is so alien to turn-of-the-century American understandings that the only pertinent context is European. Nietzsche—for whom Wagnerian decadence was a source of guilt-laden identification—wrote: "Wagner's art is sick. The problems he presents on the stage—all of them . . . hysterical cases—the convulsive nature of the emotional states he depicts, his overexcited sensibility . . . —all of this taken together represents a profile of sickness that permits no further doubt. Wagner *est une névrose.*"[11] For Huysmans and other decadents, however, Wagner's "sickness" was inspirational: a morbid wellstream of creative insight and narcotic gratification. For Thomas Mann, whose early short stories "Tristan" (1902) and "Blood of the Walsungs" (1905) Huneker's stories superficially resemble, *Tristan und Isolde* and *Die Walküre* occasion an ironic tour de force that both absorbs and critiques Wagnerian sorcery. By this high standard,

Huneker's "feminine" Wagner, far less complex, is often merely titillating or pathetic. Tweaking the acolytes, Huneker the essayist expounds:

> Touching on the acrimonious controversy over *Parsifal*'s blasphemy, I may only say—to every one their belief. No one is forced to see the melodrama, for a mystic melodrama it is, with the original connotations of the phrase. The entire work is such a jumble of creeds that future . . . ethical archeologists will have a terrible task if the work is taken for a relic of some tribal form of worship among the barbarians of the then remote nineteenth century. Here in America, the Land of the Almighty Hysteria, this artificial medley of faded music and grotesque forms is sufficiently eclectic in character to set tripping the feet of them that go forth upon the mountains in search of new, half-baked religions.

Huneker endured *Parsifal* as a mound of pretentious tonnage. Everything about it—even its decadence—seemed insincere.

> You see a lot of women-hating men, deceiving themselves with spears, drugs, old goblets, all manner of juggling formulas, and yet being waited upon by a woman—a poor, miserable witch. You see a silly youth treated as if he had murdered a human being because he shot a swan. You see this same dead bird borne away on a litter of twigs, to noble, impressive music like a feathered Siegfried. Surely Wagner was without a sense of the humorous.

If *Parsifal*, for Huneker, was "the work of a man who had outlived his genius," *Tristan* was a triumph of deranging sorcery, a psychological excavation as fascinatingly modern as a Huysmans novel. "There is something primal, something of the rankness of nature, of life's odor and hum," he rhapsodized in "After Wagner—What?". "It seems almost incomprehensible for a single human brain to have conceived and carried to fruition such a magnificent composition." "And the music—how it searches the nerves." *Tristan* conveyed "the seeds of the morbid, the hysterical, and the merely erotic—hallmarks of most great modern works of art." Comparably heretical, for American readers, were such summary Wagner judgments as:

> Wagner—versatile, mercurial, wonderful Wagner—was a different being every hour of the day. He explained matters to suit his mood of the moment,—a Schopenhauerian one hour, a semi-Christian the next. . . . A German democrat he was—and a courtier, an atheist, and yet a mystic. Wagner was all things to all men, like men of his supple imagination.

> . . . As for the crazy boasts and affirmations of the musical romantics, we who know our Wagner smile at the godlike things claimed for him. He had genius and his music is genuine; but it is music for the theater, for the glow of the footlights; rhetorical music is it, and it ever strives for effect.[12]

Huneker's decadent Wagner may have resonated with the private pleasures of an M. Carey Thomas or a Mabel Dodge Luhan. There was also, as Huneker documents in his autobiography, a surreptitious New York club called "Montsalvat" whose languid adherents, behind doors draped in black velvet, practiced abnegation of the will and suppression of the passions according to Schopenhauer and late Wagner.[13] Publicly, however, Huneker's pronouncements echoed in a void. They meshed not at all with late-nineteenth-century American Wagner rites—rites still practiced during and after the Met's *Parsifal* premiere. Compared to Oliver Huckel's *Parsifal, a Mystical Drama* (1903), Richard Aldrich's *A Guide to Parsifal* (1904), or Richard Heber Newton's *Parsifal: An Ethical and Spiritual Interpretation* (1904), Huneker's taunts—at one point, he conjectured that *Parsifal* was a conscious parody, an "epical" practical joke—sounded, if not a profound twentieth-century voice, a twentieth-century sensibility as blithe, careless, and witty as Krehbiel was earnest, logical, and dour, as worldly as America was innocent.*

---

*A slightly later modernist blast at American Wagnerism was Paul Rosenfeld's in his *Musical Portraits* (New York, 1920):

> For nowhere did the forest of the Nibelungen flourish more lushly, more darkly, than upon the American coasts and mountains and plains. From the towers and walls of

A curious footnote to Huneker's heresies was Upton Sinclair's novel *Prince Hagen*. Today remembered as the socialist author of the muckraking novel *The Jungle* (1906), Sinclair was greatly influenced by Edward MacDowell, whose classes he audited at Columbia University, and whom he considered the first man of genius he had met. MacDowell, Sinclair later reminisced, "hated pretense and formalism, and all things which repress the creative spirit." In the classroom, MacDowell criticized Wagner for long-windedness, but praised his uncanny descriptive powers. Sinclair came away from these lectures consumed by the aspiration to fuse music and literature. In his first novel, *Springtime and Harvest*, musical performances articulate and develop the plot, and certain composers, including Wagner, are discussed at length. This immature effort became the springboard for *Prince Hagen: A Phantasy*, published in 1903. Sinclair once furnished the following synopsis: "Prince Hagen, grandson of the dwarf Alberich . . . brings his golden treasures up to Wall Street and Fifth Avenue and proves the identity between our Christian civilization and his own dark realm. The tale was born of the playing of the score of *Das Rheingold* to so many squirrels and partridges in the forests of the Adirondacks, and in the Fairy Glen on the Quebec lake."

In the course of five substantial chapters embellished with musical examples from *The Ring of the Nibelung*, a real-life underground Nibelheim is discovered. King Alberich seeks help in reforming his problematic grandson, whose father, also named Hagen, is of course the villain of *Götterdämmerung*. The novel's first-person narrator, a poet, proposes to take Prince Hagen to America in the hope of instilling his "savage heart" with the "ideal of a Christian society." King Alberich agrees. But, far from redeemed, the prince is further corrupted by New York businessmen and politicians. Meanwhile, King Alberich dies and Prince Hagen takes possession of his gold arsenal—which he uses to ingratiate himself with Republican

---

New York there fell a great, a grandiloquent language, a stridency and a glory that were Wagner's indeed. His regal commanding blasts, his upsweeping marching violins, his pompous and majestic orchestra, existed in the American scene. . . . American life seemed to be calling for this music in order that its vastness, its madly affluent wealth and multiform power and transcontinental span, its loud, grandiose promise might attain something like eternal being.

bigwigs and to enter Society. He also plots to introduce Christianity
to Nibelheim in order to reconcile the Nibelungs to poverty. He is
killed when the Arabian steeds pulling his carriage are frightened by
an automobile. He is fulsomely eulogized in the press. In sum, the
novel makes a mockery of Christianity and despises its narrator's
uplifting sermons. It suggests the influence of H. G. Wells and of
George Bernard Shaw, whose *Perfect Wagnerite* (1898) similarly
invokes the *Ring* to upbraid rampaging capitalism.[14]

Prince Hagen stands apart from more typical Wagnerian fictions by
American writers, depicting famous sopranos and cultured ladies of
the upper classes. Compared to Willa Cather, Sinclair sows dissi-
dence. Compared to Huneker, he retains a meliorist impulse. He
uses Wagner not merely to reinforce but to heighten the genteel critique of bourgeois materialism.*

No less than the commercialization of *Parsifal*, Huneker and Sinclair
signal the waning of the Gilded Age's constructive, redemptive
"Wagner" and the doom of American innocence. The critic Reginald
De Koven, a lonely abstainer from Wagnerism, reckoned in 1908
that the class of "exclusive" Wagnerites, who admitted the worth
of no other composer, was "now practically done away with." A
younger critic, Lawrence Gilman, challenged De Koven on the rate
of decline, yet conceded that the ranks of the devout were shrink-
ing; he nostalgically recalled when Wagnerites, "impelled by an
apostolic fervor, memorized leitmotives and 'prayerfully studied' the
guidebooks."[15]

For a century and more, Europe—where industrialization was
superimposed on previously feudal societies; where war and revolution discouraged ideals of progress—had generated political and

---

*The less superficial integration of Wagnerian themes and techniques into liter-
ature by such writers as Mann, T. S. Eliot, James Joyce, and Virginia Woolf belongs
to Europe and mainly to a later time.

aesthetic currents more violent than what Americans knew. Now, America was catching up. Melville's *Billy Budd*, unfinished and unpublished at his death in 1891, was one harbinger of the passing of American Siegfrieds. The New Woman, the new poets, the Armory Show of 1913 questioned "eternal" genteel truths. Randolph Bourne, Thorstein Veblen, and H. L. Mencken, hell-raisers all, rejected the "smiling aspects" of American life; Mencken derided "the whole rumble-bumble of the Uplift" (he also called *Parsifal* "an elaborate and outrageous burlesque on Christianity," and characterized its Good Friday music as "lascivious"). Quite suddenly an assortment of European heresies had washed ashore. Ibsen prepared the way for Strindberg, who thrilled and alarmed American audiences in 1912. Constance Garrett's popular translations of Dostoyevsky began appearing the same year. Joyce's *Portrait of the Artist as a Young Man* made a great impression in 1916, as did Diaghilev's Ballets russes. Bergson, Nietzsche, and Freud each enjoyed an American vogue. Naturalism, which denied genteel idealism, was taken up by Frank Norris, Jack London, Stephen Crane, and Theodore Dreiser—and, in painting, by the Ashcan School. Eugene O'Neill, Sherwood Anderson, Alfred Stieglitz, Floyd Dell, all prominently broke with the past. Ruth St. Denis and Isadora Duncan—whose Wagner interpretations were seen at the 1904 Bayreuth Festival at Cosima's invitation—helped inaugurate modern dance.

Aspects of this awakening—admittedly tame in comparison to the more radical subjectivity of more alienated Europeans—might have invigorated the fading cult of Wagner had the Wagner cult been less wholesome. In particular, Wagner's psychological bent—his explorations of incest and mother love, censured or ignored in America—would have complemented the fashion for Freud. And yet, even in Europe, modernism eventually proved antithetical to the Wagnerism that helped spawn it. Debussy likened Wagner to "a beautiful sunset that was mistaken for a dawn"—a famous insight shared by Huneker in 1904 when he wrote "Wagner was the last of the great romantics; he closed a period, did not begin one."[16]

As in Europe, it remained for the Great War to finish off the Wagner movement. More than in Europe, world war signified shattered hope—in an earthly kingdom of love and peace impregnated with New World innocence and optimism. As early as January 1915, a writer for the *New Republic* presciently inquired: "Is it not a possibility that what is taking place marks quite as complete a bankruptcy of ideas, systems, society, as did the French Revolution?"[17] Four years later, millions in America were left wondering why men had died, in Ezra Pound's phrase, "for a botched civilization."

Was Culture civilizing? At the turn of the century, the Germans themselves had seemed its supreme purveyor. With the creation of the wartime Committee on Public Information—the United States Government's first large-scale propaganda machine—Americans were reinstructed to reject the image of the civilizing German. According to a typical CPI advertisement: "In the vicious guttural language of Kultur, the degree A.B. means Bachelor of Atrocities. . . . The Hohenzollern fang strikes at every element of decency and culture and taste." Another CPI advertisement, in the *Saturday Evening Post*, read: "German agents are everywhere, eager to gather scraps of news about our men, our ships, our munitions. It is still possible to get such information through to Germany, where thousands of these fragments—often individually harmless—are patiently pieced together into a whole which spells death to American soldiers and danger to American homes. . . . Do not become a tool of the Hun." As Ludwig Lewisohn observed, American war fever possessed a "peculiarly unmotivated ferocity." Red Cross leaders warned that German Americans had sneaked ground glass into bandages. More than fifteen hundred alleged spies and traitors were arrested. Others were shot or hanged.[18]

And so we should not be amazed that, during the closing months of the war and for some time afterward, Americans lost enthusiasm for German conductors and composers. In Chicago, the Grand Opera abandoned the German repertoire as of fall 1917 and did not return to it for three seasons. Frederick Stock, Theodore Thomas's successor with the Chicago Orchestra, began rehearsing in English rather than German as of 1914. He also asked that the musicians, mainly of German or Bohemian descent, stop reading German newspapers in public. Stock himself, who was born in Jülich, voluntarily retired for a time. The Boston Symphony's Karl Muck—America's most distinguished Wagner conductor when hostilities with Germany commenced—was a Swiss citizen born in Darmstadt. Erect, hawk-nosed, supercilious, Muck was the outward embodiment of a Creel-style "spy." His mail was censored and his house was periodically searched. He was said to have been overheard communicating with German submarines and plotting to blow up the birthplace of Henry Wadsworth Longfellow. In March 1918, he was interned in Fort Oglethorpe, Georgia—where the Cincinnati Symphony's Ernst Kunwald had been living since the previous December.

Josef Stransky, who had succeeded Mahler with the New York Philharmonic, was a Bohemian with much experience in Germany, yet was mainly spared political suspicion. In fact, Wagner figured in three of five Philharmonic request programs performed between 1918 and 1919. At one 1917 concert, the management informed the audience that Wagner had been "as ardent a political revolutionist as he was a musical one. . . . Wagner made speeches and wrote articles in favor of freedom." Eventually, Stransky stopped programming living German composers—in effect, Richard Strauss—for a period of two years. The Philharmonic also anglicized certain Wagner titles: "Prelude and Isolde's Love Death," "*The Mastersingers*." At the opposite extreme from New York's liberality, some smaller orchestras banned German music altogether. A survey of American orchestral programs from 1890 shows Wagner dropping from more than 10 percent of the repertoire to about 6 percent around 1920.[19]

At the Metropolitan Opera, New York again proved more tolerant of wartime German music than the country at large. Business as usual continued through the close of the 1916–17 season, which included thirty-six performances of eight Wagner operas. Count Johann von Bernstorff, the German ambassador, continued to attend. Even America's war declaration, announced midway through *Parsifal* on April 6, proved in no way disruptive. Subsequent performances of *Die Meistersinger* and *Tristan* took place as planned. Ten days before the opening of the following season, however, Gatti-Casazza made it known that there would be no German operas. The directors had decided to risk "nothing that could cause the least offense to the most patriotic Americans." A key proponent of the new policy was Mrs. William Jay, who argued that "given in the

German language and depicting scenes of violence, German opera cannot but draw our minds back to the spirit of greed and barbarism that has led to so much suffering." In a city whose cultural leaders included German Americans of great wealth and influence, Mrs. Jay's opinion was contested. The president of the Metropolitan Opera, Otto Kahn, was German- (and Jewish-)born; he had expected the Met to copy London's Covent Garden, where Thomas Beecham switched to Wagner in English. An editorial in the *Evening Post* contended that:

> For an excited public opinion to try to dictate what opera should be produced and what orchestral numbers played would be a grievous blow to musical art in America. . . . It shows less breadth of tolerance than is to be found in London, where they are giving German opera right along, or in Vienna, where Shakespeare's plays are frequently produced. These great works of art surely rise above international rivalries and warfare. Particularly is this true of Wagner's works. As we have already pointed out, Wagner was one of the most anti-Prussian Germans who ever lived. He hated Prussia and her officialdom, which he frequently denounced, and if he were living could surely be counted upon to be in opposition to-day.

In *Musical America*, a front-page story stressed the continued access to German Romantic music enjoyed by both English and French audiences.[20]

The Met ban lasted two seasons, during which the only German works were Flotow's *Martha* and Mozart's *The Marriage of Figaro*, both given in Italian, and Weber's *Oberon* and Meyerbeer's *Le Prophète*, given in English and French. Gatti-Casazza also discarded Johanna Gadski and five other German singers. The suddenness of the Wagner drought oppressed Henry Krehbiel. To *More Chapters of Opera* (1919), published four years before his death, he appended a plaintive affirmation of genteel codes ruptured by wartime, of "the beautiful and good in art [having] neither geographical nor political boundaries." Krehbiel loathed the German war effort; he called it "the most monstrous crime of a millennium." But he considered the Met's initial resistance to CPI thinking "a record of honor." He agreed with Gatti's dismissal of German artists after 1917, and hoped it might promote the cause of American opera. The prohibition of Wagner and other German composers, however, seemed philistine to him.

> There was little effort to differentiate between the art and its practitioners; between ... the masters who created it with neither knowledge nor premonition that those who came after them would revert to moral savagery, and the practitioners who lived under that savagery and in some cases sympathized with it and upheld it. Yet such distinction ought to be instructive in every intelligent child. To banish Wagner's dramas from the stage of America can as little serve the cause for which the nation pledged its wealth, honor and life, as to bedaub the statues of Goethe and Schiller as was done in some places.[21]

In fact, for Krehbiel—as for the New York Philharmonic and the *Evening Post*—wartime exigency produced a final, defensive, and essentially futile portrait of the genteel Wagner, whose political views, previously less important to Americans, endorsed democracy. Dispatching the violent Francophobia of "A Capitulation" (1870), and Wagner's related attempts to ingratiate himself with Wilhelmite Germany, Krehbiel now wrote:

> [Wagner] was a revolutionary against the monarchical state while living and after his death left no preachments which could bring comfort to those who attempted to destroy the political ideals for which America went into battle. He wrote a silly lampoon on the French Government after the Franco-Prussian War, but its banality avenged itself on his fame. He wrote a march to glorify William I, but his political reputation wrought its rejection at the function for which he had designed it. He also wrote a march to celebrate the century of American Independence, but with it he garnered as little artistic glory as with his foolish French farce.

Notwithstanding his many exegeses of Wagnerian sources, themes, and plots, Krehbiel even soft-pedaled Wagner's extra-musical significance: "The world has learned to smile at Wagner as a philosopher," he wrote in *More Chapters of Opera*. Still, the "underlying purpose" of the *Ring* remained ethical: "to teach that selfish egoism, finding its expression in brute force, must give way to a dispensation of justice and love." *Tannhäuser* taught that salvation lies in the love of pure womanhood. *Parsifal*, preaching compassionate pity, contained nothing "of political or moral obliquity."[22]

Within a few years of the armistice, American orchestral performances of Wagner increased in number, but they never regained prewar levels. At the Met, Wagner gradually resumed—in English,* beginning with *Parsifal*, in Krehbiel's translation, in February 1920. Wagner returned in German in 1921–22, by which time Isadora Duncan had lamented the Wagner ban—"for the work of Wagner flows through every drop of blood in every artist of the world, and his mighty rhythm has become part of every heart-beat of each one of us." In 1923, Siegfried Wagner toured the United States; seeking funding to reopen Bayreuth, he praised the "special friends" from America who understood "the importance of the festivals to the entire world of culture." †[23]

But Wagnerism in America was no more. Gone forever were Albert Niemann, who made Siegmund's melancholy and Tristan's psychosis unbearably real; were the shelves of Wagner books and handbooks, whose painstaking lessons were invariably inspirational; were the special railroad cars for Brighton Beach, where Anton Seidl presided and throngs of acolytes congregated as pilgrims. A related victim was Osward Garrison Villard, editor of the *Nation* and the *New York Evening Post*. His mother had been a leading supporter of the Seidl Permanent Orchestra; since 1916, he had served as president of the New York Philharmonic. A German-born pacifist, Villard had declared in January 1917, speaking in Carnegie Hall: "The pitiful waves of sound that beat across oceans moaning of bloody, unreasoning death pass by this temple of the art. No echo of the strife without can enter, for here is sanctuary for all and perfect peace. . . .

---

*A decision that cost the Met its most magnetic Wagnerian singer: Olive Fremstad insisted on the original German.

†As a young man, Siegfried received instruction about America and learned English so that he might consider moving to the United States.

Musicians who play and musicians who compose are one in devotion to their muse. Before genius of the clefs no prejudice lasts long, even in the tracks of war." The following January, Villard resigned from the Philharmonic board. A letter to the directors explained:

> We are dealing with a hysterical point of view, as is evidenced by the fact that my intensely anti-German book, "Germany Embattled," which led to my being violently denounced in Germany and being notified by my German relatives, with one exception, that they never wished to see me again or to have anything further to do with me, has been banned as pro-German from the Los Angeles Public Library. There is no reasoning with this state of mind, and therefore it is well to take cognizance of it and act in the way least likely to injure so great a cause as that of the Philharmonic.[24]

After 1917, Germans were no longer culture-bearers to America, and "German Americans"—once a proud appellation—preferred to be known as Americans only.

With the end of American innocence, the meliorist American Wagner likewise ended.

The desacralization of Wagner did not dictate Wagner's denial. Rather, it heralded a process of secularization.

Obviously, this did not occur overnight. We have already glimpsed countless manifestations of Wagner more quotidian than spiritual. Four months after mounting the premiere of *Tannhäuser* in 1859, the Stadttheater mounted a *Tannhäuser* burlesque. Wolfram's "Song to the Evening Star" and the "Bridal Chorus" from *Lohengrin* became popular parlor selections. The *Parsifal* Entertainment of 1890 produced a *Parsifal* toque. The American stage premiere of *Parsifal* in 1903 fostered *Parsifal* pastiches and parodies.

Two institutions, in particular, disseminated Wagner to millions of Americans without disseminating high-cultural uplift. These were band concerts and the movies. Patrick Gilmore had programmed the

Tannhäuser Overture and other Wagner selections beginning in the 1870s. With the passing of Gilmore in 1892, the nation's leading bandmaster was John Philip Sousa, whom we have encountered at Manhattan Beach opposite Anton Seidl's Brighton Beach concerts.

Seidl's admirers claimed Sousa's programming was influenced by Seidl's. In fact, Sousa needed no encouragement to play Wagner. He was Sousa's favorite composer, in Sousa's view the "Shakespeare of music." In 1891, Sousa visited Wagner's grave at Bayreuth. Compared to Gilmore, he used a higher proportion of woodwinds and achieved a closer approximation of orchestral textures and balances. His Wagner repertoire was huge. A partial tally of his own band transcriptions (no complete list exists) includes *The Flying Dutchman* Overture, the *Tannhäuser* Overture and Song to the Evening Star, the Prelude to act 3 of *Lohengrin* plus Elsa's Dream and Lohengrin's Narrative, Walther's Prize Song from *Die Meistersinger*, Siegfried's Death, and the Prelude and *Liebestod* from *Tristan und Isolde*.[25]

Like Seidl at Brighton Beach, Sousa would typically perform twice a day, seven days a week. In all other respects, the differences between Seidl and Sousa were vast. With his romantic looks and priestly manner, Seidl was an Artist. Sousa was a populist entertainer who wore tight-fitting uniforms and spotless white gloves. He insisted it was foolish to "try to play above the heads of one's listeners. The audience at big out-door concerts is composed largely of the masses. . . . They don't care for what some folks are pleased to call classical music." On another occasion Sousa said: "I'd just as soon play Kelly as an encore to Siegfried as to play Siegfried as an encore to Kelly."[26]

Like Theodore Thomas, whom Sousa admired, or Toscanini, whose pre–World War I American success occurred while Sousa was still going strong, Sousa embodied military control, discipline, and self-command. His movements were modest and restrained. Wearing "long hair, goggles, an air of mystery," he told the *New York Advertiser* in 1893, did not necessarily connote talent. "Bohemianism has ruined more great minds than any one other thing in the world," he told the *Oakland Enquirer* three years later. No less than Thomas, whose appearance was compared to that of "a substantial banker," or

Toscanini, whom one early American reviewer called "the man who knows his business," Sousa appealed to a mass audience with his manliness and efficiency. A master strategist and organizer, he was also a shrewd promoter who employed a squad of press agents. He posed for photographers riding bicycles and trap shooting. At Manhattan Beach, he was photographed taking boxing lessons. "Here, then, you see bared before the camera the muscular right arm that has wielded the baton to the delight of millions, the sturdy fist that wrote 'El Capitan,'" reported the *New York World*; within a few years of hard training, his teacher testified, "Mr. Sousa could easily develop into a world beater." None of this belittles Sousa's achievement or the sincerity of his democratic and patriotic views; his concerts, as the cultural historian Neil Harris has remarked, engendered a band ritual embodying the "unspoiled benevolence" of American life. But this ritual, employing Wagner, was not remotely Wagnerian.[27]

In principle, the silent film with musical accompaniment more approached the *Gesamtkunstwerk*. In practice, cinema was another popular medium that removed Wagner from the pedestal on which Seidl had placed him. No matter that *Parsifal* was made into an earnest thirty-minute short. More typically, the Ride of the Valkyries was appropriated to accompany galloping Klansmen in D. W. Griffith's *The Birth of a Nation*. Sourcebooks for movie music from 1924 and 1925 suggest the Spinning Song from *The Flying Dutchman* for "Railroad," the *Flying Dutchman* Overture for "Storm," the Bridal Chorus from *Lohengrin* for "Wedding," the Ride of the Valkyries for "Battle Music" and "Gruesome," and the *Parsifal* Prelude for "Religious Music."[28]

After World War I, these secular uses of Wagner were for the first time less challenged than reinforced in the opera house and concert hall—the subject matter of the next chapter.

16

Secularization

During the interwar decades, Wagner revived to varying degrees in the United States. But this revival varied in kind from what had gone before.

One Wagner index only diminished. In 1890, Wagner was the second most performed composer on American orchestral programs, after Beethoven. By 1900, he was number three, after Tchaikovsky. Around 1915, he dropped to fourth place, after Brahms. Around 1950, he was number five, after Mozart. As of 1955, he fell to number six, behind Bach. By then, he accounted for about 2 percent of the repertoire—less than one-fifth the frequency of Wagner concert performances in Seidl's time.[1]

The post–World War I period produced nothing like Walter Damrosch's touring German companies, or the touring *Parsifal* of Henry Savage. But Sol Hurok, still a fledgling immigrant impresario, successfully managed an itinerant Wagner ensemble in 1927–28 and 1928–29. The operas were *The Flying Dutchman*, *Tristan*, the *Ring*, and Mozart's *Don Giovanni*. The cities were Baltimore, Cincinnati, Cleveland, Chicago, Indianapolis, Milwaukee, Philadelphia, Pittsburgh, St. Paul, and Washington. Once, in Milwaukee, Hurok had to mount *Siegfried* without Mime—a remarkable feat of cunning and ruthless abridgement. Johanna Gadski, a member of Hurok's troupe, subsequently toured her own company until she died in an automobile accident in 1932.

In Boston, where Felix Weingartner had triumphed in *Tristan* in 1911–12 and 1912–13 with casts including Burrian, Gadski, Fremstad, Margarete Matzenauer, Nordica, and Jacques Urlus, and where Joseph Urban's designs (as of a huge, billowing sail standing in for Tristan's ship) were singularly adventurous, the Opera Company went bankrupt in 1915; it had lasted four seasons. That left the Chicago Grand Opera, begun in 1910, as the only notable resident company outside New York. Under Cleofonte Campanini—a gifted conductor, formerly artistic director of Oscar Hammerstein's Manhattan Opera—it was more a Franco-Italian than a German house, but by World War I had mounted all the major Wagner operas save *The Flying Dutchman*. Its postwar repertoire—it died in 1932—again de-emphasized German works. The San Francisco Opera, begun in 1923, only became a significant Wagner house with the arrival of Kurt Herbert Adler in 1953. Its interwar repertoire included a 1935–36 *Ring* cycle.

In contrast to these national vicissitudes, New York returned to Wagner with alacrity. By 1922–23, the Met was offering twenty-three performances of *Tannhäuser*, *Lohengrin*, *Die Walküre*, *Tristan*, and *Parsifal*. Meanwhile, a four-week Wagner festival at the Manhattan Opera House, begun in February 1923, featured more than one hundred soloists and choristers from Berlin. The principal singers included Alexander Kipnis, Friedrich Schorr, Meta Seinemeyer, and Urlus; Leo Blech was the principal conductor. Capacity audiences enabled the company to extend its season for three weeks in a second theater. It also made briefer appearances in other American cities.[2]

The following season, the Met restored the complete Wagner canon from *Tannhäuser* to *Parsifal*; a single *Ring* cycle was the company's first since 1917. Wagner casts of the twenties and thirties included Ludwig Hofmann, Maria Jeritza, Kipnis, Marjorie Lawrence, Lotte Lehmann, Freda Lieder, Emanuel List, Matzenauer, Lauritz Melchior, Schorr, and Kerstin Thorborg.

The watershed Wagner event for the interwar period, however, was the American debut of Kirsten Flagstad—as Sieglinde, at the Met on February 2, 1935. She sang Isolde four days later, and the *Walküre* Brünnhilde ten days after that. From the start, Flagstad's prodigious voice exerted a prodigious appeal. She not only revitalized Wagner at the Met; she revitalized the sagging company itself, whose box office receipts had hit bottom. Of Flagstad's 250

Metropolitan Opera performances (excepting concerts and galas), 231 were of Wagner. In fact, in 1936–37, Wagner comprised 37 percent of the Met repertoire—the highest such percentage since Seidl's German seasons ended in 1891. A special World's Fair season, in May 1939, consisted of nine consecutive Wagner operas. Regularly joining Flagstad on these and other occasions was the indefatigable Melchior, who, singing only Wagner, totaled 519 Met performances between 1926 and 1950. And yet this phenomenal level of Wagner activity—unique outside Germany and Austria—signaled no resumption of Wagnerism. Rather, it was a new phenomenon, a different Wagner.

The nature of the new phenomenon has been documented in sound. Beginning in 1931, the Met's Saturday afternoon performances were broadcast, and tapes of these performances date back nearly as far. Flagstad can be heard as Isolde—her signature part (at the Met, she sang it more than twice as often as any other role)—in complete Saturday performances on March 9, 1935, January 2, 1937, March 23, 1940, and February 8, 1941.[3] Her Tristan is always Melchior—in *his* signature part, which he sang 128 times at the Met, as well as opposite Flagstad on tour, and with the companies of Chicago and San Francisco. We enjoy no comparable documentation of Seidl's Wagner, or of the "Golden Age" Wagner of 1891 to 1903. Even so, the interwar performances are so obviously different, in what they attempt and achieve, that comparisons are inescapable.

In the late Gilded Age, Wagner was a religion and the singers were believers. The regal and imperious Lilli Lehmann was a regal and imperious Isolde. Albert Niemann was frightening as the demented Tristan. By this standard, only one singer from the *Tristan* broadcasts passes muster: fifty-one-year-old Alexander Kipnis so inhabits King Marke that every word of his act 2 monologue conveys a spontaneous empathic response to the crisis at hand. Melchior sounds capable of giving this much, but does not. Even so, he remains a committed singing actor, practiced in intercommunicative subtleties of word coloration and *Innigkeit*, and the same can be said of Thorborg, the usual Brangäne, and of Hofmann and List, who sing Marke. Flagstad, by comparison, is a force of nature—and a force unto herself.

Reacting to Marke's sorrow on the afternoon of March 9, 1935, Melchior gives an astounding performance of "O König," transported into the nightworld of oblivion toward which he beckons Isolde. Melchior plays off Hofmann's Marke and Schorr's Kurwenal. He works hand in glove with his conductor, Artur Bodanzky. With his Isolde, the chemistry is nil. Flagstad's answer to the invitation "Wohin nun Tristan scheidet, willst du Isold' ihm folgen?" is no answer at all, but an autonomous intention. Earlier, where Melchior's love-invocation—"Löse von der Welt mich los"—projects a dazed vulnerability, Flagstad's delivery of the same phrase is, if superhuman, impersonal. She possesses a gift divine for phrasing and legato. But Wagner's great duet shrinks; its partners disunited, its essential timelessness, its oceanic forgetfulness, is forgotten. Listening to this skewed exchange, one recalls that Bodanzky was said to have grown bored conducting Wagner at the Met; that Flagstad and Melchior were enemies offstage; that Melchior was prone to play practical jokes on colleagues in performance, and—in *Parsifal*, act 1— would sometimes sneak backstage when he wasn't singing; that Flagstad, after years of singing in the United States, could write of a Zurich recital in the late 1940s: "I found myself suddenly standing there and in the middle of a song realizing that the words themselves meant something to those who were listening." Flagstad also once confided that she lost "a good part of my hearing" for two years after a 1935 laryngitis attack, yet "managed somehow." And why not? She had perfect pitch, and her Isolde was always the same.[*4]

Previous Wagner stars of comparable magnitude had been big, even eccentric personalities. Malvina von Carolsfeld, the first Isolde,

---

[*]Flagstad's Isolde of the 1930s was a recently acquired part. Her famous 1952 *Tristan* recording, under Furtwängler, reveals a more mature artist—as well as a conductor the likes of which she never encountered at the Met.

went mad, and so did Emil Scaria, who created Gurnemanz. Anton van Rooy remained Wotan backstage. The high-tempered Olive Fremstad used to run at full tilt from the furthest backstage wall in order to make a convincing entrance as Kundry. Flagstad—in the words of Charles O'Connell, her record producer at RCA—was "innocent to the point of naiveté," "neither brilliant nor profound, but . . . invariably honest and decent," "vital and vigorous, but hardly vivacious." Wholesome, imperturbable, she exuded "emotional placidity and flaccidity."[5] Flagstad could also be stubborn—and yet Isolde's sarcasm, rage, and erotic languor were not for her. Rather, the pure timbre and indefatigable freshness of her Nordic soprano achieved an elemental impact, an almost preternatural aura transcending missing details of characterization. She delivered the *Liebestod* not as Isolde transfigured, but as a presiding deus ex machina.

The Flagstad/Melchior *Tristan* was notoriously truncated. Bodanzky's cuts may have been the most severe ever inflicted on this four-hour score at the Met. According to David Hamilton's tally, they total 733 measures, or something like 13 percent of the opera. The net effect is surprisingly pervasive: the work seems smaller and less extreme, more focused on exterior narrative, less prone to introversion. In other respects, as well, the performances travestied *Gesamtkunstwerk*. According to Erich Leinsdorf: "Stage directors got literally nothing that would enable them to do any kind of reasonable work for the histrionic part of the operas." Singers came with their own costumes, learned the layout of the stage, and that was it. (Flagstad had no rehearsal for her Met debut.) Joseph Urban's *Tristan* scenery dated from the early twenties; Leinsdorf recalls: "Sets were old and often so tattered that even the best tricks of the chief electrician could not conceal the seaminess of the canvas." The conductors were Bodanzky, who arrived in 1915 from Mannheim, and Leinsdorf himself, who took over (at the age of twenty-seven) when Bodanzky died in 1939. Judging from the *Tristan* broadcasts, both were brisk and efficient leaders. The Bodanzky *Tristan* is notably more plastic, and commands a broader gamut of feeling. But he is no Seidl.[6]

Exigencies imposed by the overtaxed theater must be considered: there were seven weekly performances, plus frequent additional concerts and occasional Wednesday matinees. But the fundamental weakness of the interwar *Tristan* broadcasts is one of understanding, not preparation. *Tristan* is an interior drama. The lovers are not, like Romeo and Juliet, thwarted by external circumstance; they self-destruct in the throes of libidinal excess. The Flagstad/Melchior *Tristan* is, finally, no bigger than the sum of its parts. Whatever one makes of its ravishments—those who heard Flagstad in person testify to the singularity of her voice, its unique combination of size and lustrous beauty—it remains Wagner devoid of Wagnerism, different in kind from the opera whose first New York performances shook Henry Krehbiel's ethical principles and generated an emotional tension "great beyond the bounds of pleasure." One cannot but agree with Hamilton's conjecture that Flagstad "brought into the house many non-Wagnerians, perhaps even non-opera-goers, who came to hear the vocal phenomenon and listened to the work, as it were, in a vacuum."[7] The same could never have been said of Lehmann and Niemann. It may have been true of Jean de Reszke—but, partnered by Seidl or Schalk, de Reszke was the sort of Tristan who would have filled the vacuum and made Wagner matter.

Surveying the Met *Tristan* broadcasts of 1933 to 1943, Hamilton summarizes: "The substance of these performances is not really the music itself, but how excitingly it can be dealt with, now how much electricity can be generated from it."[8] The same generalization fits the performances of Wagner's other central exponent for American audiences of the thirties and forties: Arturo Toscanini.

Not that Toscanini conducted at the Met—or any other American opera house—after 1915. In fact, he conducted no complete Wagner performances after the Salzburg *Meistersinger* of 1936. Rather, Wagner—with Beethoven and Brahms—anchored Toscanini's concert repertoire. Conducting the New York Philharmonic and NBC Symphony between 1926 and 1954, he programmed the *Meistersinger* Prelude fifty-four times—more often than any other composition.* Of his eleven Philharmonic seasons, during four of which he led fewer than thirty New York concerts, nine included performances of the *Meistersinger* Prelude, and seven included performances of the Prelude to *Tristan*. Of his seven NBC Symphony seasons, usually comprising thirteen to twenty concerts, nine included the *Meistersinger* Prelude, eight the *Tristan* Prelude. His longest Wagner extract was the closing scene of *Die Walküre*, act 1, which he led on six occasions with tenor and soprano. Otherwise— unlike Thomas or Seidl, in their concert Wagner performances—he rarely engaged vocal soloists.[9] This abstinence from *Gesamtkunstwerk* did not discourage Lawrence Gilman, of the *New York Herald Tribune*, from writing in 1938:

> Whether Wagner's music is closer to Toscanini's secret heart than any other, it is not possible to say. But certainly he possesses a mastery of its style and a profound identification with its quality that have long seemed his alone. . . .
> Toscanini's conducting of Wagner's music, here and abroad, has always left in the minds of the susceptible the same unshakable conviction: that this was Wagner's music as he himself had dared to dream that it might sound.[10]

That Toscanini was Wagner's greatest interpreter was an article of faith for American audiences and critics of the interwar period. And yet, no less than Flagstad at the Met, Toscanini evinced Wagner without Wagnerism—and not merely because he restricted himself to Siegfried's Rhine Journey, the Ride of the Valkyries, and other "greatest hits." Like the Met's, his performances sacrificed *Innigkeit* for briskness and efficiency—but with twice the power, tension, and virtuosity of a Bodanzky or Leinsdorf. The results were gripping

---

*Picking at random the 1929–30 season—the first for which Toscanini was listed as the Philharmonic's chief conductor—one finds him programming Wagner in twenty-four of fifty-six concerts spanning a total of fifteen weeks. Conducting the orchestra in Europe that spring, he led Wagner on eleven of twenty-three programs.

exercises in maximum overt drama even where overt drama was inappropriate. With its poised, electric tremolos and pointillistic passagework, Toscanini's Forest Murmurs contradicted Wagner's intended sensation of a deep, interior stillness. He made the Prelude to *Lohengrin*, act 3—music celebrating a wedding—excitingly militant. Like Flagstad's thrilling Isolde, Toscanini's thrilling Wagner occupied a contextual vacuum—knowledge of Wagner's writings, plots, and texts was superfluous, even distracting. "Disembodied theater," Virgil Thomson called it.

Another conductor who challenged the diminishing frequency of Wagner in concert was Leopold Stokowski of the Philadelphia Orchestra, whose 1930s symphonic Wagner repertoire was the most comprehensive in America. Unlike Toscanini, Stokowski prepared "symphonic syntheses" of the *Ring* operas, *Tristan*, and *Parsifal* act 3. Though he sometimes employed singers for these performances, he never conducted the operas as such. His lush, technicolored rendering of the act 2 love music from *Tristan*, blending imperceptibly with Tristan's delirium from act 3, would have horrified Krehbiel (who lived just long enough to call Stokowski "a young nincompoop"). Even more than Toscanini's, Stokowski's Wagner extracts acquired a life of their own, oblivious to original meanings.[11] The acceptability of this new norm was doubled by postwar Germanophobia: the orchestras of Boston, New York, and Philadelphia could no longer employ Germanic music directors. The ghosts of Thomas, Seidl, Nikisch, Schalk, Mottl, Weingartner, Mahler, and Muck were laid to rest.

In the days of Thomas and Seidl, Wagner in concert was chiefly a means of introducing and disseminating new music. Stagings of the full operas were either nonexistent or—even in New York—insufficiently frequent to satisfy the curiosity and allegiance of novices and initiates. In the days of Toscanini and Stokowski, Wagner in concert became a means of showcasing music's hottest commodity: what Arthur Farwell in his 1944 Seidl encomium termed the "dazzling virtuoso-conductor." Seidl, to be sure, had been a famous and charismatic figure. But, as thousands of New York reviews testify, he showcased the Music of the Future: it, not him, was the central subject of intense interest. The young Toscanini, too, was such a conductor, espousing Brahms and Wagner in turn-of-the-century Italy. Thirty years later, times had changed. The music appreciation movement of the thirties and forties, which anointed Toscanini its culture-god, placed music at the service of the maestro. Interspersed with overtures, tone poems, and symphonies, the Rhine Journey and Venusberg Bacchanale became opportunities for orchestral display. Reviewing Toscanini's 1926 New York Philharmonic debut (in a program sandwiching Siegfried's Death and Funeral Music between Sibelius's *Swan of Tuonela* and Weber's *Euryanthe* Overture), W. J. Henderson wrote:

> The concert of the Philharmonic Society last night in Carnegie Hall was one of those musical events which might well be turned over to the star descriptive reporter. It was not a concert at all; it was the return of the hero, a Roman triumph staged in New York and in modern dress. The hero was Arturo Toscanini. . . .
>
> For these are days when the plain workaday utterance of music will not suffice for a populace incessantly demanding new ways of saying old truths and ready to sink into apathy unless mental stimulants are liberally administered.[12]

Like Flagstad at the Met, Toscanini at the Philharmonic secularized Wagner. From now on, performers, not composers, would be sacralized.

A last, fatal sacralization of the composer was engineered in Germany, where Hitler worshipped Wagner alongside Beethoven and Bruckner. His swastikas adorned Bayreuth. He befriended Winifred Wagner, who had taken over the festival following the deaths, both in 1930, of her mother-in-law, Cosima, and her husband, Siegfried. Re-experiencing Wagner in exile in the United States, Thomas Mann wrote in 1940:

> [Wagner's] work, created and directed "against civilization," against the entire culture and society dominant since the Renaissance,

emerges from the bourgeois-humanist epoch in the same manner as does Hitlerism. With its Wagalaweia and its alliteration, its mixture of roots-in-the-soil and eyes-toward-the-future, its appeal for a class-less society, its mythical-reactionary revolutionism—with all these, it is the exact spiritual forerunner of the "metapolitical" movement today terrorizing the world.[13]

After World War II, these poisonous associations had to be erased; Wagner had to be rethought.

In his 1915 essay "Shall We Realize Wagner's Ideals?" Carl Van Vechten had complained of laughably old-fashioned Wagner productions in the United States and Europe. The scenery registered "a seemingly absolute ignorance or determined evasion of the fact that there are artists who are now working in the theater." Parts of *Die Walküre*, Van Vechten complained, were already "growing old," weighted down by an anachronistic visual aesthetic. He imagined simplified stage designs, as of mere rocks and clouds, and cited the visionary scenic artist Adolphe Appia as the type of new producer who potentially represented "the salvation of Wagner," "the complete realization of his own ideals."[14]

When Bayreuth reopened in 1951, Appia was twenty-three years dead. But something like his synthesis of stylized forms and creative lighting—a negation of Romantic clutter—was unveiled. Winifred's son, Wieland, the festival's reigning artistic intelligence until his death in 1966, discarded decades of horses, rocks, and winged helmets. He used cyclorama projections to suggest and symbolize mood and meaning. Disowning Wagner's nationalism, he reclaimed instead his credo of innovation.

In the United States, where Wagner was less tainted by Hitler, the war imposed no reformist imperatives. The Met rejected a proposal to boycott Wagner and Strauss. Though Paul Henry Lang, in the *Saturday Review*, reduced Wagner to "Background Music for *Mein Kampf*," Hitler, unlike Kaiser Wilhelm, had no appreciable impact on orchestral programming. Between America's declaration of war on Japan in December 1941 and Germany's surrender in May 1945, John Barbirolli, Howard Barlow, Leonard Bernstein, Fritz Busch, Rudolf Ganz, Vladimir Golschmann, Pierre Monteux, Fritz

Reiner, Artur Rodzinski, George Szell, Arturo Toscanini, and Bruno Walter led Wagner performances with the New York Philharmonic. When Toscanini conducted a 1944 Red Cross benefit concert at Madison Square Garden, an artist for the souvenir booklet reconceived the Valkyries' Ride as a fleet of Allied bombers.[15]

But wartime truncated the American career of the most famous living Wagner singer. In 1941, Kirsten Flagstad returned to Norway to be with her husband, who was later arrested as a Nazi collaborator. Though Flagstad herself was acquitted of political offense, she returned only in 1950 to the Met, where her roles had been taken by Helen Traubel and Astrid Varnay. By that time, the general manager was Rudolf Bing, a British citizen, born in Vienna, who had spent the war years managing the Glyndebourne Opera. Bing disliked Wagner. During his twenty-two-year tenure, *Siegfried* was performed nine times. *Das Rheingold* had thirteen performances, *Götterdämmerung* twenty, *Tannhäuser* twenty-seven. A signature triumph of the Bing era was the least Wagnerian of the canonized Wagner operas: *The Flying Dutchman*, which became a vehicle for George London and Leonie Rysanek. Otherwise, Bing underutilized these galvanizing singing actors in Wagner. Later in his regime, Birgit Nilsson, with her laser soprano, was the Brünnhilde and Isolde. Jon Vickers was an electrifying Siegmund, unforgettably partnered, on seven occasions, by Régine Crespin's Sieglinde. But Bing maintained no Wagner ensemble. He dismissed Hans Hotter, Bayreuth's peerless Wotan, as a comprimario singer. Rather than specialize in Hunding in New York, Hotter abandoned the Met; his brief United States stage career also included appearances in San Francisco and Chicago.

When in 1967 Bing got around to mounting the Met's first new *Ring* cycle since 1947–48, he opted to import the one Gunther Schneider-Siemssen had designed for Herbert von Karajan in Salzburg, with Karajan doubling, as in Salzburg, as conductor and stage director. This was a dark and abstract production à la Wieland, but with nothing like Wieland's originality or incisive detail. In Europe, meanwhile, Wieland's revisionism had proved a Pandora's box; afterward, directors—Karajan being a conspicuous exception—pondered Wagner's meanings by subverting him, refusing to take him on his own terms. This led to another landmark *Ring*: the 1976 Bayreuth centennial production by Patrice Chéreau. Chéreau's method was to assume nothing: to throw out not only Cosima's tradition, but Wieland's as well. The result was a *Ring* at once post-Hitler and postmodern.

Chéreau found himself fascinated by the guile of Mime and Alberich. But he was disgusted by Wotan's more complex opportunism; he gave him grasping gestures and a scowling face, and dressed him as Wagner. Wotan's speeches were tangled in duplicity even where Wagner intended nobility. Chéreau could not believe in Wagner's Siegfried. Here, he overthrew Wotan/Wagner's case for free agentry: the forging of Nothung and killing of Fafner were engineered by Wotan, who literally stalked behind the scenes. The entire drama, so conceived, sought to expose Wagner's own arrogance and rhetorical excess. It poked fun at "heroic" speeches and deeds. It discarded redemption-through-love as a cliché.

Chéreau's un-Romantic playfulness resonated with the stage pictures of Richard Pedruzzi, coolly colored and lit, oscillating between fantasy and realism, whimsy and analysis. Pierre Boulez's conducting was clean, precise, emptied of erotic turmoil. As we have seen, Nietzsche characterized "Wagner as a Danger" in terms of a submissive "swimming and floating" response, versus active "dancing." This condemnation of the Romantic/cathartic Wagner—of the amoral druggist who activates forbidden impulses and paralyzes the mind—documents Nietzsche's own susceptibility to Wagnerian narcosis. Chéreau rejected the Romantic/cathartic Wagner because he is no Romantic: he cannot succumb. It does not occur to him that Art should be moral and ennobling. He discovered a cooler, "dancing" Wagner of which Nietzsche—like Anton Seidl, like Henry Krehbiel, like Wagner himself—was mainly unaware.

If the Met's "answer" to Wieland Wagner in 1967 had been Karajan/Schneider-Siemssen, it answered Chéreau with something both more timid and more risky: a second Schneider-Siemssen *Ring* that would seem new for being old. Otto Schenk, who directed, decried "interpretitis." He aimed "to tell old stories and let the audience find the meanings." For Schenk himself, the meaning of *Die Walküre* was "an immense love story," "the tragedy of a mighty father who must act against his heart." Physically, the Met aimed for a *Ring* as Romantic and naturalistic as Wagner's own stage aesthetic, realized with stage technology Wagner never dreamed of. Advocates of the Met *Ring* had called for a "neutral" staging, a noninterpretive framework that would welcome the individual interpretations of singing actors. But the Schenk/Schneider-Siemssen framework was a lumbering encumbrance, versus a really neutral presentation: in concert. It fulfilled Wieland Wagner's 1966 prophecy that "a naturalistic set today would simply destroy an illusion, not create one." It denied what Carl Dahlhaus has termed Wagner's "aesthetic demand for innovation." Seeking "authenticity," the Met pretended that sin and redemption were concepts whose meanings had not changed in one hundred years, capable of shocking and inspiring as audiences at the first Met *Ring* were shocked and inspired. In 1990–91 Schenk and Schneider-Siemssen even mounted *Parsifal*, at the Met, as pretty pictures and a "good story." Paying innocent allegiance to Wagner's belief that art is moral, they shut, not opened, ears and eyes. Today, thoughtful audiences will find the *Ring* and *Parsifal* darker than the spiritual tracts they once seemed to Gilded Age Americans.[16]

A gradual upsurge in Wagner at the Met during the post-Bing era— since 1972, the company has given twelve *Ring* cycles, versus eight during Bing's twenty-two years—partly reflects the taste of its artistic director, James Levine. Outside New York, regional companies have proliferated: Hartford and Portland, Oregon, have mounted *Tristan*; Tulsa and Baltimore have done *Die Walküre*. This belated dissemination of opera throughout the United States has much to do, I think, with the advent of subtitles for televised opera and of supertitles for live opera. For the first time since the dissipation of the German-American presence, Wotan's speeches can actually be understood. Suddenly, America's failure to establish a tradition of opera in the vernacular—and, concomitantly, its exaggerated preoccupation with operatic glamour and vocal display—matters less than before. Not since the days of Seidl and Mahler, Niemann and Fremstad, has German opera been so widely appreciated by Americans as a form of theater.

To date, the United States has not welcomed the deconstructionist stagings that fascinate Europe. But there have been notable initiatives. Under Kurt Herbert Adler, the San Francisco Opera stressed Wagner for twenty-eight years; as at Bing's Met, the performances were more memorable for outstanding individual singers than for integrated impact, or for subtleties of production. But Adler's successor, Terence McEwen, conceived a visually distinguished "Romantic" *Ring* designed by John Conklin. In Chicago, the Lyric Opera is moving toward an unprecedented frequency of Wagner productions, including its first *Ring* cycle (the company has never given the four *Ring* operas in a single season), with Conklin as designer. Its boldest Wagner production to date has been Peter Sellars's 1988 *Tannhäuser*, whose hero was a televangelist. In Houston, the Grand Opera presented a hallucinatory 1992 *Parsifal*, staged by Robert Wilson. David Hockney designed the Los Angeles Opera's painterly 1987 *Tristan und Isolde*.

But the most concentrated Wagner venue in the United States in recent years has been Seattle, where Glynn Ross began presenting summer *Ring* cycles in 1975. Like Leopold and Walter Damrosch bringing Wagner to New York ninety years before, this effort represented a triumph of willpower and enterprise—and it took hold. Ross departed in 1983, to be succeeded, as general manager, by another Wagnerite, Speight Jenkins. Jenkins opted for a classier, costlier *Ring*, one he could not afford to mount every summer, but more carefully cast, more strongly conducted, and staged with panache and a point of view. The resulting production, directed by François Rochaix and designed by Robert Israel, has been given seven times, with two cycles in 1986 and 1987, and three in 1991.

Rather like Chéreau, Rochaix makes Wotan/Wagner the central actor in a play he himself directs. As in Chéreau, Wotan's mania for control is stressed. So is Siegfried's dependency: as in Chéreau, the Forest Bird is an inanimate prop, a toy on a stick. Like Wagner, like

Wotan, like Chéreau, Rochaix eventually finds himself ensnared by contradictions of his own devising. But his *Ring* is not really deconstructive. His use of a side-stage, for instance, is not a distantiation device à la Brecht. When Wotan, vigilant in his side-stage chair, watches the whole of *Die Walküre*, act 1, we empathize with an embattled father observing his harried and beloved offspring. Rochaix's response is not esoteric but fresh, not complex but sincere.

And the same can be said for the Seattle Wagner enterprise as a whole. Jenkins has aimed for a balanced Wagner ensemble. He has not courted celebrity performers, pedigreed by Deutsche Grammophon, Salzburg, and Columbia Artists Management. Rather, he has stressed world-class *Ring* lectures, four-hour *Ring* symposia, and a serious bookstore. His English supertitles, an innovation so far shunned by the Met, transform the ambience of the house.

Wagner eyed the New World and perceived virgin terrain unshackled by Old World history and tradition. Anton Seidl, Lilli Lehmann, and Albert Niemann helped to actualize Wagner's vision in New York. A century later, it is the young Northwest, not old New York, that resembles a Wagnerian New World. If Jenkins's Seattle Opera is not remotely Seidl's Metropolitan Opera reborn, something special has been rekindled: a company whose mission transcends self-promulgation.[17]

I have so far slighted one aspect of Wagner's recent fate at the Met. In his time, Wagner saw opera reduced to an article of extravagant consumption. He railed against the complacency of bourgeois culture, the commercialization of art, the squandering of vast institutional resources, the fondness for easy effect and resistance to innovation. These tables have turned. If Seattle recalls, however distantly, something like the idealism of the Gilded Age, at the Met Wagner has become big business. The commercialization of *Parsifal*, decried by Krehbiel in 1903, foreshadowed the machinations of today's media mart. The Met spent millions creating its current *Ring*.

But, with DG, it has packaged the production on fifteen CDs, and also videotaped it for television, and for VHS and laser disc sales. All of this correlates with marketing strategies for the house as a whole, as well as with the international career strategies of James Levine and other star performers, as plotted by Columbia Artists' Ronald Wilford and other music businessmen. Wagner's new commercial possibilities have also created new promotional possibilities. Not since the days of Heinrich Conried has the Met been so prone to hyperbolic self-acclaim. Wagner attains a scale of operation that holds innovation hostage: theoretically, the lowest common denominator of taste achieves a maximum return.

The commercialization of high culture—the marketing of mid-culture—proceeds apace. The organic interplay of the life of art with the life of the mind, a signature of Wagnerism, has splintered; this sword of civilization is not now reforged. The Gilded Age produced shelves of Wagner books, pamphlets, and lectures. Today's TV discourse of terse sound bites could not be less Wagnerian. A publication called *Pulse!* tells its readers "everything you ever needed to know about classical music." What do you need to know about Wagner? According to *Pulse!*, Jon Vickers "summed up Wagner, the man, when he said, 'He was bad news . . . he really was.'"[18]

These are some of the challenges confronting Wagner today. They lay heavy odds, but so does Wagner's potency as a resonator. The examples of Chéreau and Rochaix suggest strategies of renewal. A century ago, the sacralization of Wagner was necessary and timely. It resulted in an unprecedented standard of performance. It proved inspirational to Gilded Age Americans in search of spiritual uplift. Today, sacralization is a dead end. We should not attempt to ennoble Wagner, or his deity Wotan, or his superman Siegfried, or the celebrity conductors and singers who interpret his works. Intellectually, a merely meliorist *Ring* or *Parsifal* is today impossibly glib. Productively construed, the Wagner operas are not religious relics or museum pieces or vehicles for Great Performers. Rather, their restless mutability tells. They manage to sustain art as a hands-on experience, as a workable clay.

Wagner lives because Wagnerism is dead.

The Gilded Age Reobserved

T he very least this book accomplishes is to demonstrate how little Americans have investigated or appreciated their musical high culture of a century ago. My study of Wagnerism is a beginning. Before closing, I start three topics—Wagnerism outside New York, Wagnerism and racism, Wagnerism and modern dance—that others may choose to finish.

I have concentrated on New York City. Other writers will, I hope, inquire more than I have how Wagnerism fared elsewhere in the United States. To date, our understanding of late-nineteenth-century institutions of culture is spotty at best. Such scholars as Paul DiMaggio, Helen Horowitz, and Lawrence Levine have emphasized the role of "native-born elites"—of WASP wealth—in the creation of the Chicago and Boston Symphonies, of the Art Institute of Chicago and the Boston Museum of Fine Arts. Their picture is one of philanthropists shackled by conservative taste and psychological need, of influential citizens whose notions of cultural uplift revealed anxious disapproval of restless immigrant masses. Chicago's Anglo-Saxon cultural benefactors, writes Horowitz, attempted "to use art to alter what disturbed them about American life." Elevating the civitas, they would elevate or ignore the unwashed. In Boston, writes DiMaggio, the orchestra and art museum were "creations of Brahmins alone," "cultural Capitalists" for whom high culture, which they defined and segregated, represented "refuge from slings and arrows of the troubled world around them." In a similar vein, Charles Hamm, surveying America's late-nineteenth-century musical high culture, writes of a "mystifying ritual of dress, behavior and repertory" prized by an elite determined to maintain class privilege.[1] This perspective has merit yet supplies a flawed general model. It certainly does not fit the early Metropolitan Opera or New York Philharmonic. Vast, cosmopolitan, diverse, dynamic, New York offered scant opportunity for "refuge," even for its patrician culture-bearers.

Boston was a fortress of respectability and tradition, a place of settled habits whose idealism was unsullied by the quotidian. It was the city of John Sullivan Dwight, whose ghost stirred when Philip Hale, of the *Boston Post*, wrote of *Parsifal* in 1891: "Long drawn out monotony is the result of the frantic efforts to rivet the attention and inflame the imagination. The limits of the hearer's capacities are ignored. Every episode is treated at too great a length." From 1889 to 1893—years during which New York feted Anton Seidl—Boston was unready for Arthur Nikisch; Hale condemned his interpretive meddling and "overstress." In Chicago, the orchestra had, in Theodore Thomas, a conductor immune to excess. It also had an orchestra board that kept ticket prices high, did not advertise in the German-language press, and did not offer complimentary tickets to German critics. When the *Freie Presse* complained, Charles Norman Fay, who among the orchestra's trustees had crucially supported its formation, replied that "Germans who have contributed to the support of the Orchestra, either in the purchase of tickets or by direct donation, [have been] few in number, and their donations have been . . . small in amount."[2]

Thomas himself, of course, was German-born, and conducted rehearsals in German. And yet he was not the type to cultivate special ties to Chicago's large German community. His second wife, as of 1890, was Rose Fay—Charles's sister, the prominent daughter of an Episcopal clergyman and granddaughter of the presiding bishop of the Episcopalian house of Bishops.* Like Margaret Blaine

---

*A third sibling, Amy Fay, was a well-known American pianist and teacher.

Damrosch, Rose Fay Thomas conferred pedigree. Like Walter Damrosch, Thomas was rapidly mobilized upward. In his memoirs, he turned his back on Carl Bergmann, whose milieu had been more German than American.

For Seidl, in New York, this scenario of professional advancement was both unthinkable and unnecessary. He spoke German not only with his orchestra but with his wife and his close friends. He did not pursue money. And yet the philanthropists, Anglo and German, ultimately came to him.

New York, a "foreign" city, teemed with Jews and Italians, with Hungarian and Russian cafes, with artists and musicians, atheists and anarchists. "There are lots of interesting young painting and writing fellows, and the place is lordly free, with foreign touches of all kinds," wrote William Dean Howells from New York to a Boston friend. "Boston seems of another planet." "In New York, where there is no civic pride, . . . the mixture of population prevents a consolidation of any one artistic direction," remarked the *Musical Courier*. The great elitist orchestras of Boston and Chicago ruled the roost; the Boston Symphony's Henry Higginson suppressed potential rivals. In New York, Thomas and Leopold Damrosch, Seidl and Walter Damrosch, the Metropolitan and Manhattan Operas, the New York Philharmonic and New York Symphony jockeyed for position. At the Met, new wealth, locked out of the Academy of Music, elbowed a place to parade its diamonds—only to find the opera company overtaken by Wagnerite Germans. And the Germans—whose cultural contributions, incredibly, still await the lucky historian who will scrutinize the singing societies, the theaters, and the German-language press—were a mixed lot: affluent or proletarian, traditional or progressive, Catholic, Protestant, or Jewish, sometimes displacing, sometimes intermingling with a genteel elite itself more fragmented and unstable than in other cities.* Concerts and opera in New York cannot be pigeonholed as social rites; rather, they served multiple

*William Steinway, a cultural power broker in the German community, was a friend to Theodore Thomas and the American Opera Company, but—as his diary (a copy of which may be examined at the New York Historical Society) makes clear—

social, aesthetic, and emotional purposes. To varying degrees, performances were commercially viable. Barbarian benefactors were, to varying degrees, dispensable.*[3]

Paralleling the work of DiMaggio, Lawrence Levine has portrayed the sacralization of American culture at the end of the nineteenth century. In a compassionate polemic, he decries its bifurcation into "high" and "low." The raucous vitality of heterogeneous audiences for theater, concerts, and opera, he argues, was undermined around the turn of the century, when Shakespeare and Verdi were transformed into difficult "culture," distinct from popular entertainment. Propped on a pedestal, frozen in time, *Hamlet* and Beethoven's Ninth were revered as sacred artifacts only initiates could worship. Like DiMaggio and Helen Horowitz, he argues that the important agents of this transformation included upper-class snobs who spurned the rabble.

---

was not part of Seidl's circle. A member of the Liederkranz Society, he found the Arion Society's balls "disgustingly indecent." Politically, he was affiliated with the Democrats. Other prominent German Americans were Republicans. As Stanley Nadel has summarized, New York's Kleindeutschland was "a fully heterogeneous and internally differentiated ethnic community, home to workers and artisans, intellectuals and entrepreneurs, devout Catholics, Protestants, and Jews, and freethinking radicals and socialists" (Nadel, "Kleindeutschland: New York City's Germans, 1845–1880" [Ph.D. diss., Columbia University, 1981]).

*Paul DiMaggio, in "Classification in Art," (*American Sociological Review*, 1987, pp. 440–55), briefly but trenchantly explores differences in high culture between turn-of-the-century Boston and New York:

> Where elites were fragmented, artistic genres remained more highly differentiated and weakly bounded for a longer time. New York elites, for example, were less successful than Boston's in reproducing their status intergenerationally and in controlling positions of influence. . . . Although New York's population was larger, wealthier, and included more artists than Boston's, the greater cohesion of Boston's upper class facilitated cultural entrepreneurship, while the size and fragmentation of New York's elite impeded it. . . .
>
> Moreover, the segmentation of musical labor markets between "classical" and "popular" sectors, which [the Boston Symphony's Henry] Higginson effected when he offered extended contracts but forbid players to work in other ensembles, was delayed in New York, where competing patrons could neither offer sufficient security nor wield enough power to deter players from succumbing to the lure of the summer garden and the theater pit.

DiMaggio intends to elaborate these contrasts in a forthcoming book.

As a point of reference, Levine's model is heuristic and humane. His ideal is not uplifting Culture—as in the Wagner cult—but a more democratic, less moralistic communalism. He illuminates shortcomings of the genteel agenda and supplies a useful narrative framework. Nothing could more buttress his lowbrow-to-highbrow scenario than the trajectory that, in the course of three decades, propelled Wagner uptown from the Stadttheater, where sausages were consumed and *Tannhäuser* was both staged and parodied, to the Met with its Diamond Horseshoe. Levine is surely correct when he generalizes: "Opera was performed in isolation from other forms of entertainment to an audience that was far more homogeneous than those which had gathered earlier." But he overdraws the audience transformation when he continues: "More and more, opera in America meant foreign-language opera performed in opera houses like the Academy of Music and the Metropolitan Opera House, which were deeply influenced if not controlled by wealthy patrons whose impresarios and conductors strove to keep the opera they presented free from the influence of other genres and other groups."[4] In fact, though they may have paid the bills, Mrs. Belmont and other fashionables could not call the tune. The Germans who had patronized Wagner on the Bowery followed him uptown to the Met. They ate no sausages there, yet remained a vociferous presence, shushing the boxholders and cheering their heroines and heroes. When *Die Meistersinger* was given, their singing societies participated on stage. After the boxholders rebelled and terminated German opera in 1891, the house was flooded by Italians. Renewed Germanic pressure forced the Met to take Wagner and Seidl back. After 1900, the company's president, board chairman, and dominant shareholder was the shrewd and sophisticated Otto Kahn, an immigrant German investment banker who acted as Gatti's de facto artistic adviser yet was denied a box because his parents were Jewish. By World War I, Mrs. Jay and her Society cohorts succeeded in suppressing Wagner—but not without igniting a hue and cry. The Wagnerite army that turned out for Leo Blech's touring Berlin troupe in 1923 may have forced the Met's hand; in any event, Wagner in German was thoroughly restored the following season. Twenty blocks uptown, at Carnegie Hall, the New York Philharmonic was also more a battleground than a WASP preserve. It had begun as a musicians' cooperative. As at the Met, immigrant Germans and native Anglo-Saxons sometimes sparred, sometimes merged in determining its course. Only in 1909, when Mrs. Sheldon and the guarantors took charge, did commercial considerations empower the kind of elitist wealth that had initiated the Boston and Chicago Symphonies.

The Wagner cult was nothing if not an example of late-nineteenth-century sacralization: Wagner was a holy cause, and his operas were considered exercises in uplift. Wagner did inculcate a reverent audience that haughtily spurned Bellini and Donizetti and other "lightweight" fare. But it does not follow that sacralization was mainly stultifying, as Levine assumes. The reverent Wagner audience was impassioned, not fashion-enslaved. Seidl's "highbrow" performances represented an astonishing improvement over the dedicated efforts of Bergmann and Neuendorff. The Wagner cause—the Music of the Future—was actually progressive. Wagnerites did not deify dead European masters, as John Sullivan Dwight had done, but espoused brave contemporary music. To a notable degree, they even espoused American music and opera in English—causes taken up by Clara Louise Kellogg and Henry Savage, by Thomas and Seidl, by Henry Krehbiel. Levine's indignation better applies to the lazy and prestige-hypnotized audiences of today. It was after World War I that sacralization metastasized into an insidiously popular movement—a midculture based on mass snob appeal—which rejected contemporary culture, enshrined celebrity performers, and canonized aged European masterworks.[5]

All of which invites reconsideration of the question: Could Boston and Chicago have been so drastically different from New York? Do we risk confusing the instigators of Gilded Age culture—the Higginsons and Fays—with its actual audiences? The Wagner cult was hardly restricted to its base in New York. Granted, Wagner's operas were hard to tour. And Walter Damrosch's company, which toured widely, found sparse audiences for Wagner in the South, excepting New Orleans. But there must have been many American cities in which Wagner intoxicated genteel intellectuals, and Gilded Age housewives, and masses of immigrants.

Wagnerism was not decadently elitist, but formidable and complex. It gripped the New World at least as much as the Old. It could not have relied on Gilded Age WASPs who sought shelter from immigrant tumult and class unrest.

As everyone knows, there is a dark side to Wagner and Wagnerism. If I have not paid much attention to it in this account, it is because Americans did not pay much attention to it during the period when Wagnerism was at its height.

The topic is a vexing one. Hitler, who patronized Bayreuth, altered the meaning of Wagner forever. Wagner himself was no Hitler. And Wagnerism, as I have commented, was not inherently protofascist.* But Wagner was a virulent racist and anti-Semite, and some of his influential followers, notably Houston Stewart Chamberlain, were worse. Wagner's most noxious theories and opinions, moreover, are not confined to his writings; they infiltrate the operas. The desirable preservation of pure racial stock figures among the confusion of themes entangling *Parsifal*. To my way of thinking, Mime, in the *Ring*, is an especially "Jewish" villain—whose models, however, included Wagner himself: small, hyperactive, scheming.†

Wagner's racism and anti-Semitism were relatively little discussed during the Gilded Age. His "Judaism in Music," now notorious, first came to the attention of English-speaking readers in 1855, when it was mentioned in an article in the *New York Musical Gazette*. In 1869,

---

*See page 279.

†The Jewish-born Gustav Mahler, in an unforgettable commentary, once remarked: "No doubt with Mime, Wagner intended to ridicule the Jews with all their characteristic traits—petty intelligence and greed—the jargon is *textually and musically* so cleverly suggested; but for God's sake it must not be exaggerated and overdone. . . . I know of only one Mime and that is myself. . . . You wouldn't believe what there is in that part, nor what I could make of it." (Henry Louis de La Grange, *Mahler* [New York, 1973], vol. 1, p. 482.)

Dwight's Journal, as we have seen, called Wagner's essay "ignoble," "small-minded," and "a disgrace." Edward Burlingame omitted it from his 1875 edition of Wagner's writings as among those efforts "of too temporary and merely national interest to survive." At least one Christian Wagnerite, Albert Ross Parsons, parroted Wagner's harsh view of Old Testament Judaism. The *Nation* vehemently rejected the anti-Semitic allusions in Wagner's *North American Review* article of 1879, which it found "mild in comparison with the tone of his scandalous pamphlet 'Das Judenthum in der Musik'" (and yet called Wagner a grand genius). To my knowledge, the fullest American treatment of Wagner's anti-Semitism during the Wagnerism years appeared in Henry Finck's Wagner biography of 1893. Finck calls "Judaism in Music" "exaggerated," "notorious," and "deplorable." Essentially, however, he more exonerates than blames its author. He cites extenuating circumstances: early impressions in Leipzig's Jewish ghetto, the undeserved success of Meyerbeer and Mendelssohn. Can we blame Wagner, Finck asks, "for having taken up the cudgel on behalf of German classical art and his own music-drama?" What is more:

> Among Wagner's other personal friends there were many Jews—men and women who were intelligent enough to see that his tirades were directed against certain disagreeable general traits of their nation, and therefore not applicable to individuals who were free from those traits. And this is a point on which too much emphasis cannot be laid. Again and again Wagner dwells on the fact that nothing could have been farther from his intentions than a desire to hurt anyone's feelings. His great enthusiasm for his idea . . . caused him to "forget all regard for personal considerations"—a characteristic of men of genius, by the way, which ordinary individuals, who are never guided by other than personal motives, find it very difficult to comprehend.

It bears stressing, once again, that the Gilded Age Wagner—democrat, entrepreneur, benign uplifter of the spirit—was the antithesis of Hitler's Wagner. The German neighborhoods of New York in which Wagnerism flourished were full of Jews. Many Wagnerites of the late Gilded Age were Jewish.* James Gibbons Huneker, a self-described lover of Jews, firmly believed that Wagner himself was of Jewish extraction. That the same was true of Seidl was rumored widely and persistently (and perhaps correctly, for all we know). Huneker once wrote: "In Europe there is room for race prejudice, but not in America. . . . We need the Jewish blood as spiritual leaven; the race is art-loving."[6]

The more significant, more elusive question is whether, below the surface of public discourse, the darker Wagner appealed to darker aspects of the genteel curriculum. The period was one of glaring inequality and economic hardship. An immigrant wave, continuously strong, stirred fear and resentment. In polyglot America, notions of racial type—of ethnic culture correlating with personality and character traits—were commonplace. White Protestant custodians of culture, alienated by "barbarian" nouveau riches, by Irish politicians and Jewish financiers, by the seeming chaos of urban, industrial America, championed "Anglo-Saxon" stock as an inherently moral, essentially American inheritance. To them, Uncle Sam was a universalized Yankee, traceable to a Puritan bloodline.

This type of thinking obviously resonated with Wagnerian thought. Wagner himself, in his *North American Review* article, had argued that "the strongest Teutonic races" had implanted Germanic civilization in the United States, where the German mind could develop unfettered by hostile history and tradition. American Wagnerites championed German culture. In a period of heavy immigration from Italy, they specifically condemned Italian opera as unrefined "hurdy gurdy" music—a Mediterranean mockery whose melodies belonged in the street. German singers, wrote Finck in a typical 1890 commentary, "are, as a rule, superior to Italians, not only in the

---

*Though it is impossible to know how many of New York's cultured German Americans were Jewish, Jews occupied a prominent place in the German community. German-language theaters, for instance, depended on Jewish theatergoers. Certain German Jews were widely recognized as leaders of the German community. (See Nadel, "Kleindeutschland," pp. 202–13.) Marc Blumenberg of the *Musical Courier* was one prominent Jewish Wagnerite. Lilli Lehmann, according to Henry Finck and others, was of Jewish extraction.

more sonorous and richer timbre of their voices, but in their use of them."[7] And, as we have observed, Heinrich Conried and other Jews were accused of insensitivity when the Met staged *Parsifal* in 1903.

The racial philosophy of American Wagnerites may be observed in microcosm in the person of Henry Krehbiel. Krehbiel was not only a pronounced Germanophile; he was a student of race. In an age during which Americans pondered where to find their national voice, Krehbiel was one of many who believed that "like tragedy in its highest conception, music is of all times and all peoples; but the more the world comes to realize how deep and intimate are the springs from which the emotional element of music flows, the more fully will it recognize that originality and power in the composer rest upon the use of dialects and idioms which are national or racial in origin and structure." Krehbiel's own ethnomusicological investigations were industrious. Applying "scientific observation" to the relationship of folksong to national schools of composition, he researched and wrote about the folk music of Magyars, Slavs, Scandinavians, Russians, Orientals, and American Indians. Of special interest are his findings regarding "Afro-American folksongs," which influenced Dvořák and eventually generated a 155-page book—not an armchair rumination, but a closely argued report packed with scrutiny of modes, rhythms, and the like. "That which is most characteristic, most beautiful and most vital in our folk-song," he believed, "has come from the negro slaves of the South, partly because they lived a life that prompted utterance in song and partly because as a race the negroes are musical by nature." Krehbiel hoped America's composers would appropriate plantation songs and other such tunes, and rebuked as "ungenerous and illiberal" those culture-bearers—presumably of Anglo-Saxon pedigree—who blanched at equating "negro" and "American."* He deplored ragtime as a gross popularization that nevertheless proved "that a marvelous potency lies in the

---

*In a similar vein, W. J. Henderson wrote in the *New York Times* (Dec. 17, 1893):

In spite of all assertions to the contrary, the plantation songs of the American negro possess a striking individuality. No matter whence their germs came, they have in their growth been subjected to local influences which have made of them a new species. That species is the direct result of causes climatic and political, but never anything else than American. Our South is ours. Its twin does not exist. Our system

characteristic rhythmical element of the slave songs." He associated
jazz with "Negro brothels of the south" and affirmed that it encouraged instrumental techniques—"unnatural contortion of the lips and
forcing of the breath"—unsuited to the higher purposes he wished
African American music to serve.[8]

It is perfectly conceivable, even likely, that Krehbiel influenced
Dvořák, who—as we have seen, with respect to his relationship to
Seidl in New York—decided that Americans should adapt "negro
melodies" toward creating an "original school of composition."
There is no doubt that Krehbiel acted as Dvořák's advocate in this
endeavor. Around the time of Seidl's premiere performance of the
New World Symphony, Krehbiel and Dvořák corresponded almost
daily, and also visited one another often.[9] The day of the performance, the *Tribune* carried a long article by Krehbiel describing and
extolling the new work, and citing such details as its pentatonic flavor and the "Scot's snap" of its recurrent principal theme—both
being pervasive elements in "African music."

Jewish music was another area of special fascination for Krehbiel.
As always, he devoured the pertinent literature. His "field research"
included visits to synagogues, where he transcribed shofar blasts and
cantorial chant. According to what he inferred from the Old Testament, the ancient Hebrews had attained an unprecedented musical
culture—exemplified, for instance, by David's psalms, which were
"doubtless set to music." Eighteen centuries of silence followed.
Then, abruptly, Jews again achieved eminence in music, beginning
with Meyerbeer, Mendelssohn, and Moscheles, and continuing with
a "brilliant phalanx" including Ernst, Goldmark, Halévy, Hiller,

---

of slavery, with all its domestic and racial conditions, was ours, and its twin never
existed. Out of the heart of this slavery, environed by this sweet and languorous
South, from the canebrake and the cotton field, arose the spontaneous musical utterance of a people. . . . If those songs are not national, then there is no such thing as
national music.

By comparison, Philip Hale of Brahmin Boston conjectured that the negro was
not "inherently musical" and that his songs were in fact imitations of sentimental
ballads sung by white women on the plantation. Hale parodied Dvořák for prescrib-
ing a future American music based on "the use of Congo, North American Indian,
Creole, Greaser, and Cowboy ditties, shinneys, yawps, and whoopings." (Boston
Symphony program note, Dec. 23, 1910.)

Joachim, Offenbach, Rubinstein, and Wieniawski. "How could Jewish musical culture recur so suddenly?" Krehbiel inquired. The only apparent explanation "lies in that racial trait that has made them the miracle of history"—that "their physical type and mental attitudes," surviving "such mutations as no other race has been subjected to," seem as distinct as in the days of Moses. "They have maintained their individuality as a race inviolate." This "singular devotion to its own entity of a wonderfully gifted people" must then account for the survival of its "phenomenal" musical gift.

At the same time, Krehbiel accurately predicted that, as composers, all the Jewish musicians he had listed "will be judged evanescent" with the exception of Mendelssohn, of whose family he wrote: "I know of no more amicable chapter in the history of intellectual culture than that which recalls the life of the Mendelssohn family from the coming of the philosopher, who was its vigorous root, to the passing of the musician, who was its beautiful flower." And yet Krehbiel distanced himself from the "disproportionate praise" once bestowed on Mendelssohn in Germany, and "still lavished on him in England." Of Meyerbeer, Rubinstein, and Goldmark he remarked that they "have been ranked with the best of their contemporaries except Richard Wagner." He found evidence of Jewish melodies, which themselves reflect "their Oriental origin," in Goldmark's *Die Königin von Saba*—and recommended that other Jewish composers explore such synagogue tunes as "Kol nidre," "Ovenu Malkenu Kosvenu," "Hayom Harasolom," and "An Hamelech." "What Sulzer in Vienna, Naumburg in Paris, Lowenstamm in Munich, and other cantors have accomplished by utilizing traditional melodies in their settings of Hebrew services," he continued, "ought to stimulate composers who are not cantors to turn to this all-but buried treasure for material to be otherwise applied."[10]

Krehbiel viewed the United States as a "hotch-potch of peoples." But he also referred to America's Teutonic "ancestors," and to its special receptivity to Teutonic myth. I have earlier cited his opinion that the heroes of the *Ring*, "in their rude forcefulness and freedom from restrictive conventions," might be called "representative of the American people," that Siegfried is American "in being an unspoiled nature." Krehbiel's reasoning included the following:

This is not altogether a fanciful idea, nor is the share which the American people (in common with the other races of Teutonic origin) have in the poetical heritage that Wagner has striven to preserve in his dramas altogether fictitious. We would not assert that the tales of Northern mythology have any peculiar force for us in themselves, but only that their presentation in an idealized form which lifts into prominence the ethical and other elements that are characteristic of the stock from which we are sprung is naturally near to our sympathies. We have not preserved Siegfried in the character of a popular hero, as the peoples who occupy our ancestral homes have done, but we have put his manliness and strength, and even his frank lawlessness into many of the heroes of our fairy tales, while in Sir Walter Scott's Gyneth, who was put into a magic sleep by Merlin, in Tennyson's Enchanted Princess and in the story of the Sleeping Beauty, which we early made a part of our literature, we have retained memories of Bruennhilde's sleep and awakening.[11]

Read today, these remarks are chilled by other retained memories: of Germany's Third Reich. And there is no denying that Krehbiel's views on Jewish music, on Meyerbeer and even on Mendelssohn, parallel Wagner's emphasis on soil and folk, on the modern Jew's estrangement from the sources of creativity. But these parallels hold up to a point and no further. It is enough to know that most of Krehbiel's opinions on Jews and music cited above come from an article he wrote on commission for the journal *The American Hebrew*. He was not a reckless polemicist of intolerance but a disinterested scholar appreciative of a gamut of races and their alleged attributes. His views on the uses of folk music are much less close to the contentious Wagner than to the amiable Dvořák—who believed that every artist has a nation to which he must be true, that music reflects national characteristics and an almost intangible message of locale, that African Americans were innately musical. Krehbiel's advice to Jewish composers—that they attend to the cantorial song of their own people—is pure Dvořák. His condemnation of ragtime and jazz was shortsighted. So was his antipathy to modernism and to the denial of cultural nationalism he discerned in Mahler's polyglot symphonies. But I detect nothing mean-spirited or malicious in his writings on negroes, Jews, or Teutons. He does not proclaim a hierarchy of races. He does not decry commingled bloods.

Nor does the turn-of-the century Wagner literature buy into a laissez-faire and racist Social Darwinism, exulting in hereditary inequality.* More characteristic and predictable are Social Gospel Wagnerites like the churchman Washington Gladden, who attempted to reconcile the theory of evolution with a philosophy of humane intervention on behalf of the weak. Even if the Anglo-Saxonism of certain Wagnerites—of the architect Ralph Adams Cram or the critic Joseph Sohn—seems somewhat more disturbing than Krehbiel's writings on race, "scientific racism" of the sort Wagner imbibed from Count Joseph-Arthur de Gobineau did not reach high tide in the United States until the 1920s—by which time Wagnerism was finished. As John Higham has summarized in his history of American nativism, the "vague and somewhat benign racial concepts of romantic nationalism"—of the Anglo-Saxonists—gave way to racism "as an ideology," stressing heredity and physiology, warning of Darwinian combat leading to the destruction of one species by another. The pivotal figure in this trajectory was Madison Grant, who hated Mediterraneans and Jews and claimed that the blond "Nordic" exemplified the "white man par excellence." In contrast to earlier Anglo-Saxonists, who had undertaken a patronizing mission to help newcomers assimilate, and who respected an American tradition of humanistic democracy, Grant preached racial purity. His *The Passing of the Great White Race*, published in 1916, achieved a vogue in the twenties. Grant was no Wagnerite but was influenced by one: Houston Stewart Chamberlain, whose *Foundations of the Nineteenth Century* was first printed in English in 1920. And yet Chamberlain's book, a sensation in Europe, was barely noticed in American intellectual circles. The most prominent anti-Semite among American musicians and writers on music was Daniel Gregory Mason, whose

---

*Darwinian thought, however, typically endorsed Wagnerian music-drama as an evolutionary necessity. Here, for instance, is Mariana Van Rensselaer in the March 1883 *Harper's*: "[Wagner's] art is the rational, direct, unforced expression of the aesthetic feeling of his time and race—not a willful eccentricity, an eccentric development, attractive by its novelty and destined speedily to decline and leave no trace behind."

phobia peaked after 1920, and who was a Brahmsian, not a Wagnerite.[12]

In sum: Wagner's racism resonated with genteel notions of cultural nationalism. More research may extrapolate and refine this relationship; certain writers, I am sure, will find the Wagner equals racism bandwagon irresistible. But, in fact, Wagnerism in America was not remotely a racist political cult. It originated with freedom-loving refugees of the revolutions of 1848 and 1849. It sustained a complex amalgamation of Yankee and German, native and immigrant. Robert Ingersoll, a confirmed Wagnerite, spoke up for Jews and negroes. W. J. Henderson was as devoted to Italian *bel canto* as to *Tristan* and the *Ring*. Even Krehbiel, after his fashion, proclaimed the greatness of late Verdi.

When Siegfried Wagner visited the United States in 1923 to raise money for Bayreuth, he traveled to Dearborn, Michigan, and met Henry Ford. Ford was a voluble anti-Semite. Siegfried must have reasoned that he might also be a wealthy Wagnerite. He left Dearborn empty-handed.

In the course of this account, I have correlated Wagnerism with the American Renaissance and with the New Woman, with a raised artistic consciousness and a hunger for intense experience. The essential context for America's Wagner cult is fin-de-siècle ferment.

Obviously, the late-nineteenth-century assault on genteel culture was less direct, less dramatic in the United States than in Paris or Vienna. There was a time when chroniclers of cultural change denied that any such American upheaval occurred before 1900. But in the four decades since Henry Steele Commager called the 1890s the "watershed of American history," this denial has been effectively reversed. The tensions of economic stress and social change accompanied a restlessly dynamic artistic climate, more passionate than what had gone before.

Two musicians, I have suggested, symbolize this transformation, of which the Wagner cult was an integral part. Theodore Thomas was "brown" and Victorian. Anton Seidl was sensuous and cosmopolitan. Thomas embodied a defensive postulation of Culture, discarding wimps and sissies. Moral, manly, strenuous, he hardened his body with icy baths and daily gymnastics. A tireless optimist, he would infuse the demos with Beethoven and Wagner. He took charge of music at the Philadelphia Exposition of 1876—where William Dean Howells chiefly admired the "vast and almost silent grandeur" of the Corliss engine. "Yes, it is still in these things of iron and steel that the national genius most freely speaks by."

Seidl, who ignored his health and never exercised, embodied Art without special pleading. Granted, he was no protomodernist for whom Culture served no necessary social purpose. But Seidl was romantically melancholy; he wept when he conducted the *Pathétique* Symphony. He seemed possessed by some secret grief. That ladies would have swooned for Thomas was as unthinkable as the image of Seidl presiding over monster concerts at patriotic expositions. Diluted earlier in the Gilded Age, America's musical high culture achieved unprecedented—and subsequently unsurpassed—focus and concentration during the fin de siècle.

Compared to Europe, with its decadents and symbolists, America fostered a more genteel Wagnerism, "without bad after-effects." And yet, stretching genteel norms to the breaking point, Wagnerism freed the way to a modernism that rejected it. Like Albert Pinkham Ryder, who attended Wagner at the Met, and whose Romantic anxiety contradicted the postcard Romanticism of the Hudson River school, it infiltrated with a searing intensity.

Wagnerism's residual reach, into the early twentieth century, was subtle and complex. One area that deserves study is its relationship to modern dance. Most American Wagnerites were women. Some, like M. Carey Thomas, were New Women. Wagner addressed buried emotional needs and private emotional lives. Brünnhilde and Isolde, Lilli Lehmann and Lillian Nordica, were influences en route to liberation. After 1900, Ruth St. Denis and Isadora Duncan consummated this opportunity. Self-expressive, self-created solo dancers, they were individualists no corps de ballet could have satisfied. In effect, they capitalized on the New Woman's agenda of dress reform, open air, aesthetic exercise, and artistic pursuit. They "represented

America's emergence from its Victorian cocoon into a confused realm of beauty and moral uncertainty," writes Elizabeth Kendall in her indispensable *Where She Danced*. They entered the theater "at a time when a giddy aura of license reigned, especially for women's acts. . . . All the women headliners were idiosyncratic performers. The legendary ones at the turn of the century—Lillian Russell, Nora Bayes, Elsie Janis, Gertrude Hoffman, Eva Tanguay . . . all displayed the desperate raw energy of their era—the kind of energy that devastated their personal lives but expanded and transformed the stages they played on." Exuding an astonishing physicality, St. Denis, Duncan, and their disciples thrilled a female public—a ladies' matinee audience, at Carnegie Hall and the Metropolitan Opera House— "already sensitized to a whole range of exotic phenomena." They eventually inspired dramatically public "after-effects" Wagnerism did not: exhibitionistic social dancing, ragtime and tangos in dance halls helplessly denounced as gates of Hell.[13]

Duncan herself suggests linkage to Wagnerism; her Wagner repertoire included excerpts from *Tannhäuser, Die Walküre, Siegfried, Götterdämmerung, Tristan, Die Meistersinger*, and *Parsifal*. Like her mother and siblings, like the father of Ruth St. Denis, she fervently followed Robert Ingersoll—himself a Wagnerite committed to innovative art and fullness of expression. Another influence on the new dance was the actor-director Steele MacKaye, who was America's central prophet of the Delsarte movement that fired both St. Denis and Duncan, and whose son, Percy MacKaye, conceived epic "pageant-rituals" that, as he himself said, were Wagnerian in theme and scale.* Sarah Bernhardt, who helped create a climate of serious theatrical extravagance, chose strong "bad women" for her heroines: Adriana Lecouvreur, La Tosca, Fedora, La Dame aux Camélias—all of whom became sopranos. Beginning in the late 1880s, Americans flocked to Bernhardt's touring performances "as though to an opera—for the awesome alien rituals."[14] David Belasco wrote and mounted a play called *Madame Butterfly*—which in turn became a solo dance for Ruth St. Denis, a Belasco protégé.

---

*Arthur Farwell, in some respects a follower of the MacKayes, also created musical pageants influenced by Bayreuth.

In opera, Geraldine Farrar was the Bernhardt equivalent who bewitched New York—and its ardent young "Gerry flappers"—as Tosca, Butterfly, Mimi, Marguerite, and Manon between 1906 and 1922. Farrar herself had a Wagner-equivalent: Olive Fremstad. It is Fremstad who, finally, connects Wagnerism with the stage world of the pioneer solo dancers. An actress of limitless resource and intensity, she was not histrionic (as Farrar could sometimes be), but true. Her Carmen, in Henderson's words, was "plucked from the heaps of eccentricity, bizarrerie and sensationalism, garbed in the robes of genuine dramatic art." Compared to her teacher Lehmann (who also taught Farrar), Fremstad was sensuous and exotic, not noble or monumental. For Isolde, she wore a Secessionist-style robe of deep green; Lehmann's Isolde had been clad in white. And Lehmann is unimaginable as Salome, whom Fremstad (as we have seen) introduced to America. To prepare, she visited a New York morgue to find out how it felt to carry a human head. While she did not perform the Dance of the Seven Veils—the Met's prima ballerina, Bianca Froehlich, stepped in—her Salome, according to Krehbiel, was "a miracle, a sleek tigress with seduction speaking in every pose, gesture, look and utterance, she grew steadily into the monster which sank under the shield of the soldiers." There can be no doubt that the shock of Strauss's opera, and its instant banning, were partly due to Fremstad's interpretation.

Fremstad was an illegitimate child, born in Stockholm in 1871. Adopted by Americans, she lived in Minneapolis and New York before moving on to Lehmann and Berlin. She succeeded at Covent Garden before coming to the Met, where she was the leading Wagner soprano from 1903 to 1914. High-tempered, moody, restless away from the stage, she twice married abortively. She identified with Ibsen's women; she learned to drive a car. In the summers, in Scandinavia, she chopped wood, cleared underbrush, and preferred to swim "when the wind is high and angry and I can struggle with the waves and beat them down or let them hurtle against me until my flesh glows red with their pounding."[15] Her acquaintances included Willa Cather, whose memorable *The Song of the Lark* (1915) is to some degree her fictional portrait. Huneker, smitten by Fremstad's auburn hair and deep-set blue eyes at Bayreuth in 1896, celebrated her in his short story, "The Last of the Valkyries"; in his novel *Painted Veils* (1921), the lesbian soprano Easter Brandes is largely a composite of Fremstad and Mary Garden.* Fremstad's loyalest companion was Mary Cushing, her secretary and adoring yet credible biographer. Cushing's *The Rainbow Bridge* (1954) documents Fremstad's impact on the daughter of a Vermont clergyman who ventured to New York for half-hearted studies at the Art Students League. Cushing became an operagoer—and discovered, "to my own surprise and the grudging admiration of my fellow art-students," that she adored Wagner to the exclusion of everything else.

> In the natural course of events . . . I decided to attend a matinee cycle of the entire *Ring of the Nibelungen*. At the second performance, *Die Walküre* . . . there was an innovation in casting. Johanna Gadski, the usual Brünnhilde, whose staid and cautious deportment and unbecoming tight metal corset had much upset my notions of a romantic Wish-Maiden, was not singing. . . . Olive Fremstad, already one of my special favorites, was cast as Brünnhilde. It was her debut in the role. . . . There was more than the usual applause when the stage picture was revealed, for such a Brünnhilde as no Metropolitan audience had ever seen before stood poised on the rocks above her parent Wotan, laughing and exultant. The toss of her head was wild and free, and girlish mischief shone in her eyes.
>
> In her youth Fremstad also had been tortured by the steel bodices of Bayreuth and apparently was now determined to flout tradition and the possible disapproval of Cosima Wagner. . . . This new Brünnhilde required something a little more suitable for an athletic young goddess whose common means of transportation was a winged horse, and whose arms must be free for spear and shield, and for slinging across her saddlebrow the slain heroes from the battlefield. In connivance with Professor [Alfred] Roller, Chief Designer of the Court Opera in Vienna . . . she had evolved an outfit for the warrior maiden which even the leading seamstresses of Walhalla itself could not have improved upon. At one glance the

---

*Gertrude Atherton's obscure *The Tower of Ivory* (1910) is another American novel portraying a fictional Wagnerian soprano, the goddess-like Margarethe Styr. She rejects her beloved rather than sacrifice her art. Then, during a performance of *Götterdämmerung*, she commits suicide by jumping upon Siegfried's flaming bier.

whole familiar scene was lifted into the realm of the highest poetic imagination.

Fremstad was not then slim and slight, although she contrived to give that impression whenever she wished; neither was she large and heroic as most people thought. She was of ordinary size except for a thickness of diaphragm which she once explained by saying— with as near an approach to the vulgar as she ever permitted herself—"that is my *bellows*, I'd have you know, not my *belly*!" She had, however, admirably molded hips, thighs, and ankles, as the new costume plainly revealed. She had reduced the old armored corset to a mere bandeau slung to her shoulders with leather straps; more of these straps made her girdle, in which her gray-white kirtle was caught up out of her equestrian way. From her waist, to give variety and brilliance to her movements, swung a series of copper disks and triangles which caught the glint of the footlights. Her cloak, clasped with polished steel, was gray, the color of the clouds where she was most at home. Her sandals were heelless (a striking innovation) and her handsome legs were crosshatched with leather thongs. On her dark red hair, short and wind-tossed, was a white-winged helmet, a wreath of the traditional leaves softening its line across her brow.[16]

In Fremstad's Sieglinde, Cushing perceived a housewife transfigured by previously repressed stirrings:

She gave to the frightened wife of Hunding, the rapturous bride of Siegmund, a tender, womanly quality which touched the heart. I always loved to watch her set the table in act 1, the loaf of bread tucked under her arm like any Hausfrau; and I could never see without a smile, the wifely way in which she took from Hunding his spear and shield and hung them in the primitive equivalent of the hall closet. When she and the two men sat down to their meal I waited impatiently for that dream-like moment when the orchestra confides, on the Walhalla motif, the secret parentage of the enamored brother and sister. Fremstad's Sieglinde here leaned gently back and closed her eyes, as if her whole being concentrated upon some mysterious stirring deep within her heart. Then, as the motif rolled majestically on to its end she lifted her head, alert, eyes shining, as if a god had touched her lightly in passing. No other Sieglinde I have ever seen . . . has conveyed to an audience such vibrant and poetic imagery. Later, in her dialogue with Siegmund, there came another such breathless moment as she listened inwardly to echoes of a voice half recalled from a happier past.

Even as Elsa—-Wagner's palest, most reticent heroine—Fremstad conveyed an affirmative personality:

> She battled tirelessly against the popular conception of the part which was so foreign to her own nature, and through an alchemy of mind and imagination actually succeed in transmuting the weakness into a kind of strength. She created thereby an entirely new Elsa poetically symbolic and enormously fascinating, especially to the women in her audience. Conscience-stricken housewives saw their own misdeeds reflected in the tragic implications of Elsa's curiosity, and doubtless made secret vows never again to look through their husbands' pockets or ask whiningly why their men had stayed so late at the office. Fremstad's Elsa ... became imbued with a kind of fiery tenderness and dignity which ennobled and made poignant the suffering she seemed to have brought upon herself.

Fremstad's pièce de résistance was Wagner's most extreme, most exotic female creation: the schizoid Kundry. As the wild woman of act 1, she stained her skin a dirty, sulfurous brown. Her short, tattered dress "permitted her legs a fascinating freedom as she darted about the stage on errands of mercy, or thrashed in shuddering fatigue upon the ground." As I have mentioned, for her urgent entrance she started her run from the furthest backstage wall so that she would come into view at full speed.* It took most of the remainder of act 1 for Cushing and her helpers to remove the body stain and apply Fremstad's act 2 make-up, as weirdly alluring as Nordica's act 2 Kundry was chic and Parisian:† "A white line down the nose, brows of dark purple, carmine in the corners of the eyes, the nostrils,

---

*Fremstad employed the same technique as Isolde (acts 2 and 3), Sieglinde (act 2), and the *Walküre* Brünnhilde (act 2).

†While Lillian Nordica was no Fremstad, her identification with Brünnhilde and Isolde may not be irrelevant to her prominent advocacy of women's suffrage after 1900. She even appeared as Columbia at a women's suffrage pageant at the Metropolitan Opera House in 1912.

and on the ear lobes; vivid rouge spread to the temples; the rest of the face and neck a milky lavender; the lashes—extended a full half inch—terminating in little blobs of black wax; the mouth a slice of tangerine." For act 3, Fremstad whitened her face and darkened her eye sockets.[17]

The last word on Fremstad's Kundry was spoken by Willa Cather in her article "Three American Singers" for the December 1913 *McClure's* magazine:

> [Kundry] is a summary of the history of womankind. [Wagner] sees in her an instrument of temptation, of salvation, and of service; but always an instrument, a thing driven and employed. Like Euripedes, he saw her as a disturber of equilibrium, whether on the side of good or evil, an emotional force that continually deflects reason, weary of her activities, yet kept within her orbit by her own nature and the nature of men. She can not possibly be at peace with herself. Mme. Fremstad preserves the integrity of the character through all its changes. In the last act, when Kundry washes Parsifal's feet and dries them with her hair, she is the same driven creature, dragging her long past behind her, an instrument made for purposes eternally contradictory. She had served the grail fiercely and Klingsor fiercely, but underneath there was weariness of seducing and comforting—the desire not to be. Mme. Fremstad's Kundry is no exalted penitent, who has vision and ecstasies. Renunciation is not fraught with deep joys for her; it is merely—necessary, and better than some things she has known; above all, better than struggle. Who can say what memories of Klingsor's garden are left on the renunciatory hands that wash Parsifal's feet?

For her "raw energy" and "aura of license," freedom of movement and individuality of gesture, Fremstad was a presence to parallel St. Denis and Duncan. To ponder the faces of Wagner in America for half a century, it is enough to ponder the succession from the grandeur of Lehmann, to the liberating after-effects of Fremstad, to the vocal phenomenon Flagstad.

This book began with a funeral cortege on a drizzly March day in 1898. The mass of tearful women, some of whom clasped hands to force their way into the Metropolitan Opera House, may have appeared melodramatic. In fact, their grief was real. The huge German band that joined the procession at 40th Street may have seemed a quaint intrusion. In fact, it signified a Gilded Age confluence of native wealth and foreign blood. The Fifth Avenue mansions along the route may have seemed a foolish pastiche of Gothic and Renaissance, French and Italian styles. In its time, Vanderbilt Row, with interior decors by La Farge and St. Gaudens, exuded energy and resourcefulness.

Though the funeral of Anton Seidl was tragically sad, its backdrop was a world of optimism and achievement, of moral consensus and organic community. The innocence sustaining this world would shortly dissipate—which, everything considered, was both right and inevitable. But we should not look back at it and scoff.

APPENDIX

THE WAGNER OPERAS: SYNOPSES AND PREMIERES

Richard Wagner was born in 1813. His two earliest operas, now little remembered, are *Die Feen* (1834) and *Das Liebesverbot* (1835). *Rienzi* (1840), famous in Wagner's lifetime, has since faded from the repertoire. The first performance was in Dresden on October 20, 1842, the American premiere at New York's Academy of Music on March 4, 1878. The first Metropolitan Opera performance, conducted by Anton Seidl, took place on February 5, 1886. The cast included Eloi Sylva, Lilli Lehmann, Adolf Robinson, Marianne Brandt, and Emil Fischer.

All ten subsequent Wagner operas hold the stage today. The earliest is *The Flying Dutchman* (*Der fliegende Holländer*). A seaman, condemned for blasphemy, must sail the ocean until redeemed by a woman's true love. He is permitted to dock every seven years. In port, he encounters Senta, who vows to save him. But overhearing her suitor, Erik, he misconstrues her intentions. He sets to sea; she leaps from a cliff. Her fidelity redeems him.

First performance: Dresden, Jan. 2, 1843
First American performance (in Italian):
Philadelphia Academy of Music, Nov. 8, 1876.
First Metropolitan Opera performance:
Nov. 27, 1889, conducted by Anton Seidl

DUTCHMAN: Theodor Reichmann
SENTA: Sophie Wiesner
ERIK: Paul Kalisch
DALAND: Emil Fischer

In *Tannhäuser*, the title role is that of a thirteenth-century Minnesinger. Sequestered in the Venusberg, he sings a hymn to sensual pleasure. Yet he longs to return to the world. Trusting in the Virgin Mary, he eventually finds himself transplanted to the Wartburg, where he participates in a song tournament. The prize is the hand of Elisabeth, the Landgrave's niece. Tannhäuser's friend Wolfram sings of selfless love; in an impatient outburst, Tannhäuser praises Venus. The knights turn against him, but Elisabeth vows to pray for him. Tannhäuser joins a pilgrimage to seek absolution from the Pope in Rome. He returns haggard and distraught— the Pope has proclaimed Tannhäuser's soul as barren as the staff the Pope holds in his hand. Tannhäuser considers returning to the Venusberg, but his repentance holds. A funeral procession conveys the bier of Elisabeth. Guilt-stricken, Tannhäuser sinks to his death. As morning dawns, pilgrims arrive bearing the Pope's staff. It has miraculously sprouted leaves.

First performance: Dresden, October 19, 1845
First American performance: Stadttheater, New York,
April 4, 1859, conducted by Carl Bergmann
First Metropolitan Opera performance:
Nov. 17, 1884, conducted by Leopold Damrosch

TANNHÄUSER: Anton Schott
ELISABETH: Auguste Seidl-Kraus
WOLFRAM: Adolf Robinson
VENUS: Anna Slach

In *Lohengrin*, set in tenth-century Antwerp, Count Frederick of Telramund accuses his ward, Elsa, of having murdered her brother, Gottfried, in order to bid for the throne. Elsa prays for a defender. Drawn by a swan-boat, Lohengrin appears. He offers to marry Elsa on condition she never ask his name or origin. He defeats Telramund in a duel. Telramund and his wife, Ortrud, accuse Lohengrin of sorcery, shaking Elsa's trust. Lohengrin and Elsa marry, but Elsa insists on knowing his real identity. Telramund bursts into the bridal chamber and is slain by Lohengrin. Lohengrin now sadly agrees to reveal that he is a knight of the Grail, son of Parsifal. His swan-boat appears. Ortrud announces that the swan is actually Gottfried, transformed by her. Lohengrin restores Gottfried to human form. A dove of the Grail draws his boat away. Elsa collapses.

First performance: Weimar, August 28, 1850
First American performance: Stadttheater, New York,
April 3, 1871, conducted by Adolf Neuendorff
First Metropolitan Opera performance: October 26, 1883
(in Italian), conducted by Auguste Vianesi

LOHENGRIN: Italo Campanini
ELSA: Christine Nilsson
ORTRUD: Emmy Fursch-Madi
TELRAMUND: Giuseppe Kaschmann

Following a hiatus, during which his artistic views ripened, Wagner embarked on *The Ring of the Nibelung* (*Der Ring des Nibelungen*). This cycle of four operas consists of *Das Rheingold, Die Walküre, Siegfried*, and *Götterdämmerung*.

Das Rheingold, "Prelude" to the *Ring* in one huge act, begins at the bottom of the Rhine. Three Rhinemaidens guard the Rhinegold. He who renounces love and fashions the gold into a Ring becomes master of the world. The dwarf Alberich renounces love and seizes the gold. On a mountaintop, the giants Fasolt and Fafner finish building Wotan's new palace, Valhalla. As compensation, Wotan had promised them Freia, sister of his wife Fricka. Wotan now protests that he was jesting. The giants insist, but are distracted by Loge, who describes Alberich's Ring. The giants agree to accept this substitute payment. Wotan and Loge descend to Nibelheim, Alberich's underground realm. They trick Alberich and acquire the Ring. Wotan now refuses to relinquish it to the giants. The earth-goddess Erda warns him of terrible consequences. He relents and adds the Ring to the giants' hoard. The giants quarrel; Fafner kills Fasolt. The gods cross a rainbow bridge to Valhalla.

First performance: Munich, Sept. 22, 1869
First American performance: Metropolitan Opera,
Jan. 4, 1889, conducted by Anton Seidl

WOTAN: Emil Fischer
FRICKA: Fanny Moran-Olden
ALBERICH: Joseph Beck
LOGE: Max Alvary

Appendix

ERDA: Hedwig Reil
FASOLT: Ludwig Mödlinger
FAFNER: Eugene Weiss

By the time of *Die Walküre* (*The Valkyrie*), Wotan has fathered nine warrior-maidens, or Valkyries. He has also fathered two human children, the twins Siegmund and Sieglinde. Siegmund, he hopes, will some day kill Fafner and take the Ring. The twins are separated at birth. Sieglinde marries Hunding. In the first act of *Die Walküre*, Siegmund is driven by a storm to seek shelter in an unfamiliar house. It is Hunding's. Siegmund and Sieglinde acknowledge their love and their sibling bond. Siegmund withdraws a sword, Nothung, from a tree trunk; a one-eyed Wanderer (Wotan) had prophesied that only a hero could so remove it. The twins escape into the night. Fricka, on high, protests this incest. She forces Wotan to desist from aiding Siegmund in his looming contest with Hunding. Broken, Wotan confides in his favorite daughter, the Valkyrie Brünnhilde. She compassionately resolves to disobey him and protect Siegmund. Wotan intervenes to insure Siegmund's death. Brünnhilde flees with Sieglinde and with Siegmund's shattered sword. Wotan, enraged, punishes Brünnhilde by ending her divinity and setting her asleep within a ring of magic fire. The first man to penetrate these flames will become her husband.

First performance: Munich, June 26, 1870
First American performance: Academy of Music, New York,
April 2, 1877, conducted by Adolf Neuendorff
First Metropolitan Opera performance: Jan. 30, 1885,
conducted by Leopold Damrosch

BRÜNNHILDE: Amalie Materna
SIEGMUND: Anton Schott
SIEGLINDE: Auguste Seidl-Kraus
WOTAN: Josef Staudigl
FRICKA: Marianne Brandt

In *Siegfried*, the hero is Siegmund and Sieglinde's orphan son. He is raised in the wild by the dwarf Mime, Alberich's brother. Like Wotan and Alberich, Mime covets the Ring. Like Wotan, he hopes Siegfried will slay Fafner and take it. Fafner, meanwhile, has turned himself into a dragon, the better to guard his treasure. Siegfried forges the splintered Nothung and uses it to kill Fafner. Upon sucking the dragon's blood, he understands the song of a Forest Bird, who warns that Mime is plotting against him. Siegfried slays Mime. The Forest Bird now leads him to the mountaintop where Brünnhilde lies sleeping. Wotan, his ego aroused, appears as the Wanderer and attempts to bar Siegfried's way. Wielding Nothung, Siegfried shatters Wotan's spear, the symbol of his authority. He passes through the magic fire and awakens Brünnhilde with a kiss. Goddess no longer, she experiences a new vulnerability before submitting to his entreaties.

First performance: Bayreuth, Aug. 16, 1876
First American performance: Metropolitan Opera,
Nov. 9, 1887, conducted by Anton Seidl

SIEGFRIED: Max Alvary
BRÜNNHILDE: Lilli Lehmann
WANDERER: Emil Fischer
ERDA: Marianne Brandt
MIME: José Ferenczy
ALBERICH: Rudolph von Milde
FAFNER: Johannes Elmblad
FOREST BIRD: Auguste Seidl-Kraus

Götterdämmerung (*Twilight of the Gods*) opens with the three Norns spinning fate; the thread breaks, foretelling doom. Dawn breaks; Siegfried and Brünnhilde emerge from a cave. Siegfried sets off to seek adventure. At the Hall of the Gibichungs, the Gibichung king, Gunther, is advised by his half-brother, Hagen, to marry Brünnhilde. Hagen, who is Alberich's son, is in fact scheming to steal the Ring. Siegfried arrives. Hagen serves him a potion that causes him to forget Brünnhilde and fall in love with Gutrune, Gunther's sister. Siegfried is told that, to obtain Gutrune, he first must secure Brünnhilde as Gunther's bride. Disguised as Gunther,

Siegfried returns to Brünnhilde, tears the Ring from her finger, and seizes her. Later, when Brünnhilde identifies Siegfried as her kidnapper, she plots with Hagen to kill him. Siegfried is slain by Hagen during a hunt. Hagen also kills Gunther. When he attempts to take the Ring, Siegfried's dead hand rises threateningly. Brünnhilde, who now comprehends Hagen's treachery, orders a funeral pyre built and sets it aflame. In the course of her immolation, the Gibichung Hall crumbles, as does Valhalla. The Rhine overflows, returning the Ring to the Rhinemaidens.

First performance: Bayreuth, Aug. 17, 1876
First American performance: Metropolitan Opera,
Jan. 25, 1888, conducted by Anton Seidl
BRÜNNHILDE: Lilli Lehmann
SIEGFRIED: Albert Niemann
GUNTHER: Adolf Robinson
GUTRUNE: Auguste Seidl-Kraus
HAGEN: Emil Fischer
ALBERICH: Rudolph von Milde

During a break in the composition of *Siegfried*, Wagner composed *Tristan und Isolde* and *Die Meistersinger*. Tristan is a Cornish knight. He has fetched the Irish princess, Isolde, who is to marry his uncle, King Marke of Cornwall. On Tristan's ship, Isolde recalls to Brangäne, her attendant, how she once restored Tristan to health after he had killed her beloved, Morold. She orders Brangäne to prepare a death potion, which she then offers Tristan as a cup of atonement. They drink not the death potion, as Isolde thinks, but a love potion, which Brangäne has disobediently substituted. In Cornwall, they are discovered by Marke and his courtier, Melot, in passionate embrace. Melot draws his sword and wounds Tristan, who offers no resistance. In his castle in Brittany, Tristan awakens from a long stupor. He hallucinates Isolde's arrival. This moment passes, but a second sighting is true. While Isolde rushes toward him, Tristan tears off his bandages and dies. She unites with him in blissful death.

First performance: Munich, June 10, 1865
First American performance: Metropolitan Opera,
Dec. 1, 1886, conducted by Anton Seidl

TRISTAN: Albert Niemann
ISOLDE: Lilli Lehmann
KURWENAL: Adolf Robinson
BRANGÄNE: Marianne Brandt
MARKE: Emil Fischer

Die Meistersinger von Nürnberg (*The Mastersingers of Nuremberg*) is set in the sixteenth century. Walther von Stolzing, a knight, is smitten by Eva, daughter of the goldsmith Pogner. He learns from her of a song contest whose winner she is to marry. But only members of the mastersingers' guild may compete. When Walther applies for membership, his improvised trial song is rejected by the guild with the pedantic Beckmesser, a town clerk, in the lead. Of the mastersingers, only the cobbler Hans Sachs senses the artist in Walther. That night, Beckmesser, who seeks Eva's hand, attempts to serenade her, but Sachs interrupts with his cobbling. A riot ensues. The next day, Walther composes a song coached by Sachs, who transcribes it. Beckmesser happens upon the manuscript and takes it with Sachs's permission. At the tournament, he disgraces himself attempting to sing Walther's song. Walther sings it properly and is named victor, mastersinger, and husband-to-be. When he spurns membership in the mastersingers' guild, Sachs counsels him to honor tradition, and Walther changes his mind. Sachs's closing speech praises sacred German art.

First performance: Munich, June 21, 1868
First American performance: Metropolitan Opera,
Jan. 4, 1886, conducted by Anton Seidl

SACHS: Emil Fischer
EVA: Auguste Seidl-Kraus
WALTHER: Albert Stritt
MAGDALENE: Marianne Brandt
DAVID: Felix Krämer
BECKMESSER: Otto Kemlitz
POGNER: Josef Staudigl

Parsifal is a "stage-consecrating festival drama" set in and around the Castle of Monsalvat in the Spanish Pyrenees in the Middle Ages. Gurnemanz, a Knight of the Grail, describes how Amfortas, who rules the Knights, suffers from a wound inflicted by the magician Klingsor, himself once a Knight and now possessor of the Sacred Spear whom only a "pure fool" can regain. Parsifal now appears, seeking a swan he has shot. Gurnemanz conducts him to a hall where he witnesses the unveiling of the Grail by Amfortas. Parsifal evidently fails to understand this ritual, and is driven away by Gurnemanz. Klingsor, in his castle, summons Kundry, a sorceress in his power. She seduces Parsifal, whom Klingsor recognizes as a threat. Parsifal suddenly intuits that he is in the presence of Amfortas's adversary. Klingsor hurls the Sacred Spear at Parsifal; Parsifal seizes it and makes the sign of the cross. Klingsor's castle falls in ruins. Many years later, returning to Monsalvat, Parsifal is identified by Gurnemanz and the repentant Kundry as the long-awaited holy fool. With the Sacred Spear, he heals Amfortas's wound and takes his place as leader. A white dove ascends as Kundry falls lifeless.

First performance: Bayreuth, July 26, 1882
First American stage performance: Metropolitan Opera,
Dec. 24, 1903, conducted by Alfred Hertz

KUNDRY: Milka Ternina
PARSIFAL: Alois Burgstaller
GURNEMANZ: Robert Blass
AMFORTAS: Anton van Rooy
KLINGSOR: Otto Goritz

NOTES

INTRODUCTION: WAGNERISM AND AMERICA

1. Romain Rolland, *Musicians of Today*, translated by Mary Blaiklock (London, 1915), p. 67.

2. Spanuth and Nordica quoted in Henry Finck, ed., *Anton Seidl: A Memorial by His Friends* (New York, 1899; rpt. 1983), pp. 149, 250.

3. "Leading historian" is Gilbert Chase, *America's Music* (New York, 2nd ed., 1966), p. 164. "Prominent commentator" is Irving Lowens, *Music and Musicians in Early America* (New York, 1964), pp. 269–70. Jeffrey Gantz, "The Mahler Years," *Stagebill* (New York Philharmonic program book), April 23, 1992, p. 36. Levine quote from "The Maestro," a television documentary produced by Peter Rosen.

4. Lilli Lehmann, *My Path Through Life* (New York, 1914), p. 378.

5. George Santayana, "The Genteel Tradition in American Philosophy," in *Winds of Doctrine: Studies in Contemporary Opinion* (New York, 1913).

6. Santayana quoted in Macdonald Smith Moore, *Yankee Blues: Musical Culture and American Identity* (Bloomington, Ind., 1985), p. 16.

7. Theodore Dreiser, *The Color of a Great City* (New York, 1923), pp. 284–85. Riis quoted in Page Smith, *The Rise of Industrial America* (New York, 1984), p. 366.

8. Adams quoted in Smith, *Rise*, pp. 586, 912. William Dean Howells, *A Boy's Town* (New York, 1890), p. 171.

9. John Higham, *Writing American History* (Bloomington, Ind., 1970).

10. Alexis de Tocqueville, *Democracy in America*, translated by Henry Reeve (New York, 1945), vol. 2, ch. 9, p. 41.

PRELUDE: A GILDED AGE FUNERAL

1. My account of Seidl's funeral incorporates information from the detailed descriptions in various New York newspapers and from Henry Finck, ed., *Anton Seidl: A Memorial by His Friends* (New York, 1899; rpt. 1983), pp. 85–100.

2. Finck, *Seidl*, p. vii.

3. Ibid., pp. 114–16. A somewhat different version of Huneker's eulogy appeared in the *Musical Courier*, April 6, 1898.

4. Finck, *Seidl*, p. 250.

5. *Brooklyn Daily Eagle*, undated clipping (late March 1898), Seidl Society archive, Brooklyn Historical Society.

6. *Musical Courier*, June 22, 1922.

CHAPTER ONE: THE ASCENDANCY

1. Martin Gregor-Dellin and Dietrich Mack, eds., *Cosima Wagner's Diaries*, translated by Geoffrey Skelton (New York, 1980), vol. 2, pp. 431–34.

2. Ibid., p. 435.

3. Ibid., pp. 436–37.

4. On Dr. Jenkins: Newell S. Jenkins, *Reminiscences* (Princeton, 1924), pp. 191–204. For Wagner's letter, see Stewart Spencer and Barry Millington, eds. and trans., *Selected Letters of Richard Wagner* (New York, 1987), pp. 899–900.

5. Spencer and Millington, *Letters*, pp. 179, 243.

6. A valuable account of Wagner's writings about the United States, from which my narrative draws for 1854–58, is Rudolf Sabor, *The Real Wagner* (London, 1987), pp. 226–38. For letter to Klindworth, see Spencer and Millington, *Letters*, p. 450.

7. On Wagner and Chicago, see Henry Finck, *Wagner and His Work* (New York, 1893; rpt. 1968), vol. 2, p. 506. "I am dragging myself" and "set sail," in Spencer and Millington, *Letters*, pp. 802, 866. Ludwig quoted in Sabor, *Real Wagner*, p. 234.

8. Jenkins, *Reminiscences*, pp. 191–204. G. W. Cooke, *John Sullivan Dwight: Brook-Farmer, Editor, and Critic of Music* (Boston, 1898; rpt. 1969), p. 230.

9. For background on music and the genteel tradition, see Joseph Mussulman, *Music in the Cultured Generation: A Social History of Music in America, 1870 to 1900* (Evanston, Ill., 1971).

10. Ibid., p. 165.

11. *Dwight's Journal of Music*, Nov. 27, 1858.

12. For a detailed treatment of Dwight's writings on Wagner, see Harold E. Briggs, *Richard Wagner and American Music-Literary Activity from*

1850 to 1920 (Ph.D. diss., Indiana University, 1989; published by UMI Dissertation Services, Ann Arbor, 1992), pp. 147–235.

13. *Dwight's Journal of Music*, May 22, 1869.

14. Josiah Hollard, "Wagner at Bayreuth," *Century* Magazine, November 1876, pp. 124–25.

15. Samuel Osgood, "Social Art," *Harper's* magazine, October 1873, p. 774.

16. Richard Wagner, "The Work and Mission of My Life," *North American Review*, August and September 1879.

CHAPTER TWO: THE FIRST MISSIONARIES

1. Louis Moreau Gottschalk, *Notes of a Pianist* (Philadelphia, 1881; rpt. 1979), pp. 63, 127.

2. The best source on German American population is Ira Rosenwaike, *Population History of New York City* (Syracuse, N.Y., 1972).

3. *New York Staats-Zeitung*, July 19, 1860. Cited in Stanley Nadel, "Kleindeutschland: New York City's Germans, 1845–1880" (Ph.D. diss., Columbia University, 1981), p. 239. Nadel comments that, though the *Staats-Zeitung* may overstate reality, the singing societies nevertheless played a singular role in "maintaining community cohesion in spite of growing class divisions" in the 1860s and 1870s.

4. Nadel, "Kleindeutschland." Also see James S. Lapham, *The German-Americans of New York City, 1860–1890* (Ann Arbor [UMI Dissertation Services], 1977); La Vern J. Rippley, *The German-Americans* (Boston, 1976); Joseph Wandel, *The German Dimension of American History* (Chicago, 1979).

5. George W. Curtis, "Choral Music in New York," *Harper's* magazine, July 1881, p. 305.

6. The central account of the New York Philharmonic's early history is Howard Shanet, *Philharmonic: A History of New York's Orchestra* (Garden City, N.Y., 1975). For prospectus, see p. 85.

7. Ibid., pp. 34–39.

8. Gottschalk, *Pianist*, p. 239. For background on "ballyhoo" and "Germanic" traditions, see Joseph Horowitz, *Understanding Toscanini: How He Became an American Culture-God and Helped Create a New Audience for Old Music* (New York, 1987), pp. 17–35.

9. George Upton, ed., *Theodore Thomas: A Musical Autobiography* (New York, 1905; rpt. 1964), p. 36.

10. Ibid., p. 126.

11. H. Earle Johnson, "The Germania Musical Society," *Musical Quarterly*, 1953, pp. 75–93.

12. *Dwight's Journal of Music*, Dec. 10, 1853; Johnson, "Germania," pp. 88–89.

13. Upton, *Thomas*, p. 36; *New York Musical Review*, April 26, 1855.

14. *New York Musical Review*, March 22, April 5, April 19, May 3, May 17, May 31, 1856.

15. *New York Evening Post* quoted in *Dwight's Journal of Music*, April 23, 1859. Allan Nevins and Milton Halsey Thomas, eds., *The Diary of George Templeton Strong* (New York, 1952), vol. 2, pp. 445–46.

16. Funeral report in *Dwight's Journal of Music*, Aug. 19, 1876. Doremus quote in *Dwight's Journal of Music*, Dec. 9, 1876. For background, see Shanet, *Philharmonic*, pp. 154–55.

17. Frédéric L. Ritter, *Music in America* (New York, 1883), p. 370. W. J. Henderson, "Who Discovered Wagner," *Munsey's* magazine, 1905, p. 673.

18. Johnson, *Germania*, pp. 83–84. Upton, *Thomas*, p. 42.

19. *New York Musical Review*, Feb. 17, 1866.

20. Ritter, *Music in America*, p. 461. Cincinnati review quoted in H. Earle Johnson, *First Performances in America to 1900* (Detroit, 1979), p. 376; Gustav Kobbé, "Wagner in New York," *Review of Reviews*, 1899, p. 688; Josiah Holland, "Wagner at Bayreuth," *Century* magazine, November 1876, p. 125.

21. *New York Sun*, Nov. 17, 1875.

22. Upton, *Thomas*, p. 35.

23. Ritter, *Music in America*, p. 465. "Wagner in the Bowery," *Century* magazine, June 1871, pp. 214–16.

24. Henry Krehbiel, *Chapters of Opera* (New York, 1909; rpt. 1980), pp. 134, 132. Kobbé, "Wagner in New York."

25. Henderson, "Who Discovered Wagner?" p. 673. "Music," *Century* magazine, June 1874, p. 246. William F. Apthorp, "*Lohengrin* by the Strakosch Troupe," *Atlantic* magazine, March 1875, p. 378.

26. Clara Louis Kellogg, *An American Prima Donna* (New York, 1913), pp. 263–65.

CHAPTER THREE: THE MASTER BUILDER

1. Essential sources for Theodore Thomas include George Upton, ed., *Theodore Thomas: A Musical Autobiography* (Chicago, 1905; rpt. 1964); Rose

Fay Thomas, *Memoirs of Theodore Thomas* (New York, 1911; rpt. 1971); Charles E. Russell, *The American Orchestra and Theodore Thomas* (Garden City, N.Y., 1927); Ezra Schabas, *Theodore Thomas: America's Conductor and Builder of Orchestras, 1835–1905* (Urbana, Ill., 1989).

2. Schabas, *Thomas*, p. 52.

3. Lilli Lehmann, *My Path Through Life* (New York, 1914), p. 346.

4. Richard Aldrich, "Theodore Thomas," in Aldrich, *Musical Discourse* (New York, 1928).

5. Upton, *Thomas*, pp. 216, 221; *Chicago Evening Post*, Dec. 21, 1895.

6. Van Wyck Brooks, *America's Coming of Age* (New York, 1915), p. 79.

7. On "little extravagances," Upton, *Thomas*, p. 54. On *Träumerei*, Russell, *American Orchestra*, pp. 2–3.

8. Gilmore's Wagner repertoire according to Frank J. Cipolla (State University of New York at Buffalo). Thomas on "modern school" quoted in Schabas, *Thomas*, p. 29. Thomas on "pillars" quoted in Upton, *Thomas*, p. 333.

9. *New York World* quotation in Earle Johnson, *First Performances in America to 1900: Works with Orchestra* (Detroit, 1979), p. 377; *New York Tribune*, May 15, 1862; *New York Times*, Feb. 12, 1866; *New York Musical Review*, Feb. 17, 1866.

10. Schabas, *Thomas*, p. 38.

11. Ibid., p. 59.

12. Harold E. Briggs, *Richard Wagner and American Music-Literary Activity from 1850 to 1920* (Ph.D. diss., Indiana University, 1989; published by UMI Dissertation Services, Ann Arbor, 1992), p. 16.

13. For various perspectives on Thomas's commission, see Upton, *Thomas*; Schabas, *Thomas*; and Abram Loft, "Richard Wagner, Theodore Thomas, and the American Centennial," *Musical Quarterly*, April 1951, p. 184. For Hassard article, see Loft, ibid., p. 190.

14. *New York Times* and Wagner quoted in Loft, "Wagner, Thomas, and the Centennial," p. 192.

15. Schabas, *Thomas*, p. 74.

16. Howells quoted in Alan Trachtenberg, *The Incorporation of America: Culture and Society in the Gilded Age* (New York, 1982), p. 47.

17. For Thomas's New York Philharmonic programs, see Henry Krehbiel, James Gibbons Huneker, and John Erskine, *Early Histories of the New York Philharmonic* (New York, 1974). For breakdown by composer, see Howard Shanet, *Philharmonic: A History of New York's Orchestra* (Garden City, N.Y., 1975), p. 439.

18. Thomas quoted in Schabas, *Thomas*, p. 117, and Upton, *Thomas*, p. 91. George W. Curtis, "Editor's Chair," *Harper's* magazine, July 1882, pp. 306–8.

19. Cincinnati and Chicago quotations in Schabas, *Thomas*, pp. 134, 136.

20. Upton, *Thomas*, p. 94.

21. Hone quoted in Henry Krehbiel, *Chapters of Opera* (New York, 1909, rpt. 1980), p. 21.

22. A central authority on the popularity of English-language opera is Katherine Preston (College of William and Mary), whose work is not published at this writing. Also see Charles Hamm, *Yesterdays: Popular Song in America* (New York, 1979), ch. 4.

23. Henry Krehbiel, *Review of the New York Musical Season, 1885–86* (New York, 1886), p. 116. Krehbiel, *Chapters of Opera*, p. 44.

24. Upton, *Thomas*, pp. 186–87.

25. Articles in *Century* and *Harper's* quoted in Joseph Mussulman, *Music in the Cultured Generation: A Social History of Music in America, 1870 to 1900* (Evanston, Ill., 1971), p. 139.

26. Boston reviews from Jeannette Thurber scrapbooks, Performing Arts branch of New York Public Library (*ZAN*M28, reel 41).

27. For differing views of the American Opera Company, see Krehbiel, *Chapters of Opera*; Schabas, *Thomas*, ch. 8; and Emanuel Rubin, "The Dream that Failed: The Collaboration of Theodore Thomas and Jeannette M. Thurber" (unpublished paper).

28. Upton, *Thomas*, p. 280.

29. Thomas quotations in ibid., pp. 104, 333–51; and Schabas, *Thomas*, p. 163.

30. Thomas and Rose Fay quoted in Lawrence Levine, *Highbrow/Lowbrow: The Emergence of Cultural Hierarchy in America* (Cambridge, Mass., 1988), pp. 115–19.

31. Upton, *Thomas*, pp. 99, 105.

32. Sauer quoted in ibid., p. 240. Thomas on *Tristan* quoted in Philip Hart, *Orpheus in the New World: The Symphony Orchestra as an American Cultural Institution* (New York, 1973), p. 25.

33. *New York Times* and *Musical Courier* quoted in Joseph Horowitz, *Understanding Toscanini: How He Became an American Culture-God and Helped Create a New Audience for Old Music* (New York, 1987), p. 41.

34. Lewis Mumford, *The Brown Decades: A Study of the Arts in America, 1865–1895* (New York, 1931; rpt. 1971), pp. 3–4.

CHAPTER FOUR: GERMANIZED OPERA

1. On solidifying the patriciate, Bruce A. McConachie, "New York Opera-Going, 1825–50: Creating an Elite Social Ritual," *American Music*, Summer 1988; Allan Nevins and Milton Halsey, eds., *The Diary of George Templeton Strong* (New York, 1952), vol. 2, p. 59; Mark Twain, *The Innocents Abroad* (New York, 1869; rpt. 1966), ch. 23, p. 167.

2. Whitman and New Orleans cited in Lawrence Levine, *Highbrow/Lowbrow: The Emergence of Cultural Hierarchy in America* (Cambridge, Mass., 1988), p. 25. Thomas quoted in George Upton, ed., *Theodore Thomas: A Musical Autobiography* (Chicago, 1905; rpt. 1964), p. 25.

3. Henry Krehbiel, *Chapters of Opera* (New York, 1909; rpt. 1980), pp. 71–72; James Gibbons Huneker, *Steeplejack* (New York, 1923), vol. 2, p. 32.

4. Martin Mayer, *The Met: One Hundred Years of Grand Opera* (New York, 1983), p. 12.

5. Ibid., p. 33. Krehbiel, *Chapters of Opera*, pp. 93, 100.

6. Krehbiel, *Chapters of Opera*, p. 138.

7. Frédéric L. Ritter, *Music in America* (New York, 1893), p. 453. A central, if insufficiently critical, source for Damrosch is George Martin, *The Damrosch Dynasty* (Boston, 1983).

8. For complete information on Metropolitan Opera repertoire and casts, see Gerald Fitzgerald, ed., *Annals of the Metropolitan Opera* (Boston, 1989).

9. George W. Curtis, "The Coming Opera Season," *Harper's* magazine, November 1884.

10. Krehbiel, *Chapters of Opera*, p. 129. On Materna: unidentified clipping, "New York Scrapbooks," Performing Arts branch of New York Public Library (*ZAN*M28, reel 24).

11. Krehbiel, *Chapters of Opera*, p. 121. For daily press, see "New York Scrapbooks."

12. Krehbiel, *Chapters of Opera*, p. 124.

13. Schott quoted in *New York Times*, Feb. 20, 1885. For an account of the reorganization under Stanton, see Paul D. Eisler, *The Metropolitan Opera: The First Twenty-five Years, 1883–1908* (Croton-on-Hudson, N.Y., 1984), pp. 112–27.

14. *New York Tribune*, Feb. 27, 1887.

15. Ernest Newman, *The Life of Richard Wagner* (New York, 1946; 1976), vol. 4, p. 359.

16. All Seidl quotations from *New York Tribune*, Feb. 27, 1887.

17. Martin Gregor-Dellin and Dietrich Mack, eds., *Cosima Wagner's Diaries*, translated by Geoffrey Skelton (New York, 1980), vol. 1, pp. 949, 993; vol. 2, pp. 26, 27, 29, 30, 39, 55, 62, 74, 75, 89, 111.

18. *Bayreuther Blätter*, 1898, *Stück* 6, p. 137; poem in Henry Finck, ed., *Anton Seidl: A Memorial by his Friends* (New York, 1899; rpt. 1983), p. 198.

19. Fridberg quote from Francis Neilson, *My Life in Two Worlds* (Appleton, Wis., 1953), vol. 1, p. 195.

20. Finck, *Seidl*, p. 187.

21. Angelo Neumann, *Personal Recollections of Wagner* (New York, 1908; rpt. 1976), pp. 70, 74, 77, 85, 88.

22. Gregor-Dellin and Mack, *Cosima*, vol. 2, p. 662. Wagner's letter quoted in Finck, *Seidl*, pp. 14–15.

23. Finck, *Seidl*, p. 105.

24. Mrs. Seidl's memoir appears in ibid., pp. 17–29.

CHAPTER FIVE: THE COMING OF THE DISCIPLE

1. Henry Finck, ed., *Anton Seidl: A Memorial by His Friends* (New York, 1899; rpt. 1983), pp. 115, 106.

2. Ibid., p. 117.

3. Ibid., pp. 243, 259.

4. Finck in *New York Evening Post*, Feb. 26, 1886. Apthorp quoted in Finck, *Seidl*, p. 68.

5. *Musical Courier*, March 30, 1898. Krehbiel quoted in Finck, *Seidl*, p. 135.

6. Seidl's essay is reprinted in Finck, *Seidl*, pp. 215–40. It originally appeared in the two-volume *The Music of the Modern World*, a collection of articles and music for which Seidl is listed as "editor-in-chief." The title was honorific, however.

7. William Ashton Ellis, ed. and trans., *Richard Wagner's Prose Works* (London, 1891; rpt. 1972), vol. 3, pp. 210–12.

8. Huneker and Herbert in Finck, *Seidl*, pp. 117, 168.

9. *New York Staats-Zeitung*, March 29, 1898. Krehbiel in Finck, *Seidl*, p. 133.

10. On rush for tickets, see Paul D. Eisler, *The Metropolitan Opera: The First Twenty-five Years, 1883–1908* (Croton-on-Hudson, N.Y., 1984), p. 125. On paid attendance, see Irving Kolodin, *The Story of the Metropolitan Opera, 1883–1950: A Candid History* (New York, 1953), p. 93.

11. Henry Krehbiel, *Review of the New York Musical Season, 1885–86*

(New York, 1886), p. 42. Finck, *Seidl*, p. 165. On errors, see Martin Mayer, *The Met: One Hundred Years of Grand Opera* (New York, 1983), p. 59.

12. Unidentified clippings (*New York Evening Post?*), New York Scrapbooks, Performing Arts branch of New York Public Library (*ZAN*M28, reel 24).

13. *New York Evening Post*, Jan. 5, 1886.

14. Krehbiel, *Musical Season*, pp. 95–101.

15. See Barry Millington, "Nuremberg Trial: Is There Anti-Semitism in *Die Meistersinger?*" *Cambridge Opera Journal*, vol. 3, no. 3 (1992), pp. 247–60.

16. *Musical Courier*, Feb. 9, 1887.

17. Ibid., Dec. 16, 1885.

18. Ibid., Jan. 20, 1886.

19. Krehbiel, *Musical Season*, pp. 132–33.

20. Ibid., pp. 150–51. Seidl quoted by Krehbiel in *New York Tribune*, Feb. 27, 1887. Finck in *New York Evening Post*, Feb. 26, 1886.

21. Richard Guy Wilson in *The American Renaissance, 1876–1917*, a catalogue published by the Brooklyn Museum, 1979, p. 63.

22. Henry James, *The American* (Cambridge, Mass., 1907), pp. 29, 45.

CHAPTER SIX: *TRISTAN UND ISOLDE*

1. Stewart Spencer and Barry Millington, eds. and trans., *Selected Letters of Richard Wagner* (New York, 1987), p. 452.

2. Schnorr von Carolsfeld quoted in Ernest Newman, *The Life of Richard Wagner* (New York, 1941; rpt. 1976), vol. 3, p. 380. Bülow quoted in Elliott Zuckerman, *The First Hundred Years of Wagner's "Tristan"* (New York, 1964), p. 60.

3. *Musical Courier*, Dec. 8, 1886; Henry Krehbiel, *Chapters of Opera* (New York, 1909; rpt. 1980), p. 167.

4. Newman, *Life of Wagner*, vol. 3, p. 380.

5. Henry Finck, *Wagner and His Works* (1893; rpt. 1968), vol. 2, pp. 163–70.

6. For Krehbiel on *Tristan*, see his *Studies in Wagnerian Drama* (New York, 1904), pp. 68–69; *Review of the New York Musical Season, 1886–87* (New York, 1887), pp. 38–56; "How to Listen to Wagner's Music," *Harper's* magazine, March 1890, pp. 530–36; *The Portable Nietzsche*, ed. and trans. Walter Kaufmann (New York, 1954), pp. 666–67.

7. Finck, *Wagner*, vol. 2, p. 168.

8. Krehbiel, *Musical Season*, p. 53.

9. William J. Henderson, *Richard Wagner: His Life and His Dramas* (New York, 1901), pp. 300–16.

10. Krehbiel, *Musical Season*, pp. 52, 49. William Ashton Ellis, ed. and trans., *Richard Wagner's Prose Works* (London, 1899), vol. 8, pp. 386–87.

11. See T. J. Jackson Lears, "From Salvation to Self-Realization," in Richard W. Fox and T. J. Jackson Lears, eds., *The Culture of Consumption* (New York, 1983), p. 16.

12. Lilli Lehmann, *My Path Through Life* (New York, 1914), p. 366.

13. William J. Henderson, *The Art of Singing* (New York, 1938), p. 360.

14. Krehbiel, *Chapters of Opera*, p. 150.

15. Henry Pleasants, *The Great Singers* (New York, 1966), p. 234.

16. Lehmann, *My Path*, pp. 366–67.

17. Henderson, *Art of Singing*, p. 366.

18. Lehmann, *My Path*, pp. 343, 363, 337.

19. Wagner quoted in Newman, *Life of Wagner*, vol. 4, p. 19.

20. Krehbiel, *Chapters of Opera*, pp. 171, 167.

21. *Musical Courier*, Dec. 8, 1886. Lehmann quoted in Newman, *Life of Wagner*, vol. 4, p. 489.

22. Saint-Saëns quoted in Newman, *Life of Wagner*, vol. 4, p. 490. Grieg quoted in Robert Hartford, ed., *Bayreuth: The Early Years* (New York, 1980), p. 68. Neumann quoted in ibid., p. 71. Lehmann quoted in Newman, *Life of Wagner*, vol. 4, p. 489; and in Hartford, *Bayreuth*, p. 213.

23. Krehbiel, *Chapters of Opera*, pp. 170–72.

24. Henderson quoted in William H. Seltsam, ed., *Metropolitan Opera Annals* (New York, 1947), p. 22.

25. Krehbiel, *Chapters of Opera*, pp. 172–73.

26. Undated clipping, Anton Seidl archive, Columbia University (Butler Library: Rare Books), box 4. Krehbiel, *Chapters of Opera*, p. 168.

27. Krehbiel, *Chapters of Opera*, p. 168.

CHAPTER SEVEN: *DER GROSSE SCHWEIGER*

1. Henry Finck, ed., *Anton Seidl: A Memorial by His Friends* (New York, 1899; rpt. 1983), p. 40.

2. Henry Krehbiel, *Chapters of Opera* (New York, 1909; rpt. 1980), p. 152. *New York Times*, Feb. 7, 1886. Henry Finck, "German Opera in New York," *The Cosmopolitan*, March 1888, p. 63. Finck, *Seidl*, p. 33. Krehbiel, *Chapters*, p. 193.

3. Henry Krehbiel, *Review of the New York Musical Season, 1886–87* (New York, 1887), p. 121. *New York Tribune*, March 2, 1887.

4. Seidl quoted in unidentified clipping, *Brooklyn Daily Eagle*, August 1896, Seidl Society archive, Brooklyn Historical Soceity. Huneker in *Musical Courier*, April 6, 1898. Steinberg in Finck, *Seidl*, p. 107.

5. *New York Tribune*, Feb. 27, 1887.

6. Finck, *Seidl*, pp. 145, 44.

7. Huneker in ibid., p. 116.

8. Anton Seidl, "Wagner's Influence on Present-Day Composers," *North American Review*, January 1894, pp. 86–93.

9. Finck, *Seidl*, p. 127.

10. Huneker in ibid., p. 115.

11. Ibid., p. 54.

12. Francis Neilson, *My Life in Two Worlds* (Appleton, Wis., 1953), vol. 1, pp. 143–57, 195.

13. Ibid., p. 55

14. Ibid., pp. 52–54.

15. *New York Herald*, Feb. 5, 1894.

16. *New York Morning Journal*, Oct. 18, 1891. *New York Sun* quoted in Finck, *Seidl*, p. 32.

17. For New York in the 1890s, see James Gibbons Huneker, *New Cosmopolis* (New York, 1915), pp. 67, 72, 75–81; Huneker, *Steeplejack* (New York, 1923), vol. 2, pp. 10, 13, 73, 78–79, 202, 219; Neilson, *My Life in Two Worlds*, pp. 93–97, 143–53. A vivid, affectionate, and nostalgic evocation of New York in the 1880s is Jack Finney, *Time and Again* (New York, 1970).

18. Frank Smith, *Robert Ingersoll: A Life* (Buffalo, 1990), esp. pp. 381–82. Lotus Club speech in *The Works of Robert G. Ingersoll* (New York, 1912), vol. 12, pp. 171–78.

CHAPTER EIGHT: *DER RING DES NIBELUNGEN*

1. Robert Hartford, ed., *Bayreuth: The Early Years* (New York, 1980), pp. 92, 170.

2. *New York Sun*, Aug. 13, Aug. 18, Aug. 23, Aug. 26, Sept. 3, 1876.

3. *New York Tribune*, Aug. 18, Aug. 28, 1876. Henry Finck, *My Adventures in the Golden Age of Music* (New York, 1926), p. 123.

4. *Dwight's Journal of Music*, Sept. 2, 1876.

5. Hartford, *Bayreuth*, pp. 72–85.

6. Elise Kirk, "RingMaster," *Opera News*, March 27, 1993.

7. Henry Finck, ed., *Anton Seidl: A Memorial by His Friends* (New York, 1899; rpt. 1983), pp. 209–10. Martin Gregor-Dellin and Dietrich Mack, eds., *Cosima Wagner's Diaries*, translated by Geoffrey Skelton (New York, 1980), vol. 2, p. 585. Henry Krehbiel, *Chapters of Opera* (New York, 1909; rpt. 1980), p. 182.

8. *Musical Courier*, Aug. 5, Aug. 12, 1896.

9. Adams and Homer quoted in John Diziges, *Opera in America: A Cultural History* (New Haven, 1993), p. 243.

10. Carl Dahlhaus and John Deathridge, *The New Grove Wagner* (New York, 1984), p. 84.

11. George Bernard Shaw, *The Perfect Wagnerite* (London, 1899; rpt. 1967). *New York Tribune*, Aug. 18, 1876.

12. William J. Henderson, *Richard Wagner: His Life and His Dramas* (New York, 1901), pp. 421–22. Henry Krehbiel, *Studies of the Wagnerian Drama* (New York, 1904), p. 158. Freda Winworth, *The Epic of Sounds* (New York, 1898), p. 158. Henry Finck, *Wagner and His Works* (New York, 1893; rpt. 1968), vol. 2, pp. 365–66.

13. Krehbiel quoted in William H. Seltsam, ed., *Annals of the Metropolitan Opera* (New York, 1947), p. 29. Finck, *Wagner and His Works*, vol. 2, p. 365.

14. Finck, *Wagner and His Works*, vol. 2, p. 349.

15. *New York Tribune*, Feb. 22, 1888.

16. Turner quoted in Alan Trachtenberg, *The Incorporation of America: Culture and Society in the Gilded Age* (New York, 1982), p. 14. William J. Henderson, *Preludes and Studies* (New York, 1892), p. 28.

17. Mark Twain, *The Innocents Abroad* (New York, 1869; rpt. 1966), chs. 22–23. Twain on Bayreuth: "At the Shrine of Saint Wagner," *"What Is Man?" and Other Essays* (New York, 1917).

18. Justin Kaplan, *Mr. Clemens and Mark Twain* (New York, 1966), p. 30.

19. John S. Dwight, "The Intellectual Influence of Music," *Atlantic* magazine, November 1870, p. 615.

20. Finck, *Wagner and His Works*, vol. 2, pp. 456–67.

21. William F. Apthorp, "Finck's Wagner and His Works," *Atlantic* magazine, October 1893, p. 559. Henderson, *Wagner*, p. 154.

22. Winworth, *Epic of Sounds*, pp. 38–39.

23. Lilli Lehmann, *My Path Through Life* (New York, 1914), p. 385.

24. Henderson quoted in Seltsam, *Annals of the Met*, p. 45. Fischer and Seidl quoted in Krehbiel, *Chapters of Opera*, p. 207.

25. Paul D. Eisler, *The Metropolitan Opera: The First Twenty-five Years, 1883–1908* (Croton-on-Hudson, N.Y., 1984), p. 163.

26. Martin Mayer, *The Met: One Hundred Years of Grand Opera* (New York, 1983), p. 63.

27. *New York Staats-Zeitung*, March 22, 1891. Krehbiel, *Chapters of Opera*, pp. 202, 207.

CHAPTER NINE: PARTIAL ECLIPSE

1. Henry Finck, *My Adventures in the Golden Age of Music* (New York, 1926), p. 177.

2. Howard Shanet, *Philharmonic: A History of New York's Orchestra* (Garden City, N.Y., 1975), pp. 165–86.

3. An excellent clippings file for Seidl's tours may be found in the Anton Seidl archive, Columbia University (Butler Library: Rare Books).

4. Richard Wagner, *On Conducting*, translated by Edward Dannreuther (London, 1887; rpt. 1989).

5. *New York Tribune*, Feb. 27, 1887.

6. Henry Krehbiel, *Review of the New York Musical Season, 1886–1887* (New York, 1887), pp. 203–04.

7. *Don Giovanni* review from unidentified clipping, "Anton Seidl" clipping file, Performing Arts branch of New York Public Library. Schubert review in *Brooklyn Daily Eagle*, March 6, 1892.

8. Henry Finck, ed., *Anton Seidl: A Memorial by His Friends* (New York, 1899; rpt. 1983), pp. 135, 175. *Musical Courier*, March 30, 1898.

9. *New York Herald*, May 21, Dec. 17, 1893. "Tremendous energy and vivacity," *Brooklyn Daily Eagle*, Jan. 12, 1894. Henry Krehbiel, "Antonin Dvořák," *Century* magazine, September 1892, pp. 657–80.

10. Paine in *Boston Herald*, May 28, 1893 (cited in Adrienne Fried Block, "Dvořák's Long American Reach," in John Tibbetts, ed., *Dvořák in America* [Portland, Ore., 1993]). Apthorp quoted in Joseph Mussulman, *Music in the Cultured Generation: A Social History of Music in America, 1870–1900* (Evanston, Ill., 1971), pp. 114–15.

11. Joseph Horowitz, "Dvořák in New York: A Concentrated Moment," in Michael Beckerman, ed., *Dvořák and His World* (Princeton, 1993).

12. Waller and Huss in Finck, *Seidl*, pp. 118–21. Policy frustrated, according to August Spanuth in ibid., p. 157. (The work in question was Harry Roe Shelley's Second Symphony, which the Philharmonic allegedly refused to program.)

13. See Harold Briggs, *Richard Wagner and American Music-Literary Activity from 1850 to 1920* (Ph.D. diss., Indiana University, 1989; published by UMI Dissertation Information Service, Ann Arbor, 1992), pp. 42–47; and Briggs, "Indians!" *Opera News*, June 1976.

14. Francis Neilson, *My Life in Two Worlds* (Appleton, Wis., 1953), vol. 1, pp. 143–45. Neilson, *Manabozo*, with author's preface (London, 1899). *Boston Transcript*, Oct. 6, 1906.

15. Anton Seidl, "The Development of Music in America," reprinted in Finck, *Seidl*, pp. 206–09.

16. Finck, *Seidl*, pp. 209, 224.

17. William G. Curtis, "The Humors of Opera," *Harper's* magazine, April 1891, p. 797.

18. Finck, *Seidl*, p. 37. Henry Krehbiel, *Chapters of Opera* (New York, 1909; rpt. 1980), p. 219.

19. Krehbiel, *Chapters of Opera*, p. 246. Antonin Dvořák, "Music in America," *Harper's* magazine, February 1895, pp. 429–34. Finck, *Seidl*, p. 41. Seidl letter to Laura Langford, April 2, 1894, Seidl Society archive, Brooklyn Historical Society.

20. Finck, *Seidl*, p. 246. Krehbiel quoted in William H. Seltsam, ed., *Annals of the Metropolitan Opera* (New York, 1947), p. 78.

21. Krehbiel quoted in Seltsam, *Annals*, p. 78.

22. William J. Henderson, *The Art of Singing* (New York, 1938), p. 336.

23. Krehbiel quoted in Seltsam, *Annals*, p. 87. Henderson in *New York Times*, Dec. 31, 1896.

24. Finck, *Seidl*, p. 36.

25. Walter Damrosch, *My Musical Life* (New York, 1923), p. 111. Krehbiel, *Chapters of Opera*, p. 256.

26. Krehbiel, *Chapters of Opera*, p. 268.

CHAPTER TEN: THE *PARSIFAL* ENTERTAINMENT

1. Clippings on the *Parsifal* Entertainment may be found in the Anton Seidl archive, Columbia University (Butler Library: Rare Books) and the Seidl Society archive, Brooklyn Historical Society.

2. Neumann quoted in Robert Hartford, ed., *Bayreuth: The Early Years* (New York, 1980), p. 120. H. R. Haweis, *My Musical Life* (London, 1886), p. 486.

3. Mariana Van Rensselaer, *"Parsifal,"* *Harper's* magazine, March 1883, pp. 540–57. Charles Dudley Warner, *A Roundabout Journey* (Hartford, Ct., 1904), p. 313.

4. *New York Evening Post*, March 5, 1886.

5. *New York Tribune*, April 1, 1890. Lehmann in *New York Post*, Jan. 29, 1904; and Lilli Lehmann, *My Path Through Life* (New York, 1914), pp. 279–81.

6. Henry Finck, ed., *Anton Seidl: A Memorial by His Friends* (New York, 1899; rpt. 1983), p. 133.

7. Nietzsche and Hanslick quoted in Lucy Beckett, ed., *Parsifal*, Cambridge Opera Handbooks (New York, 1981), pp. 105–07.

8. Henry Finck, *Wagner and His Work* (New York, 1893; rpt. 1968), vol. 2, p. 413. William J. Henderson, *Richard Wagner: His Life and His Dramas* (New York, 1901), p. 474.

9. Henry Krehbiel, *Studies in Wagnerian Drama* (New York, 1904), pp. 162–63.

10. *New York World*, March 16, 1890.

11. Washington Gladden, *Witnesses of Light* (Boston, 1903), p. 222. Haweis, *My Musical Life*, pp. 477, 484.

12. Abbott quoted in Page Smith, *The Rise of Industrial America* (New York, 1984), p. 561. Ibid., p. 210.

13. On Wagner and Schopenhauer, see Bryan Magee, *The Philosophy of Schopenhauer*, pp. 326–78.

14. For background on Laura Langford and the Seidl Society, the Seidl Society archive, Brooklyn Historical Society, contains letters, programs, clippings, and pictures. On Laura Langford, see *Brooklyn Daily Eagle*, Sept. 1, 1890.

15. Finck, *Seidl*, p. 42. Seidl Society constitution in Seidl Society archive.

16. *New York World*, April 1, 1890.

17. Ira Rosenwaike, *Population History of New York City* (Syracuse, N.Y., 1972), p. 70.

18. *Brooklyn Daily Eagle*, March 6, 1891.

19. Ibid., Aug. 5, 1894.

20. Ibid., April 29, 1894.

21. Ibid., Nov. 24, 1895.

22. Ibid., clippings, Seidl Society archive. *Musical Courier*, April 27, 1896.

23. Correspondence between Seidl and Langford in Seidl Society archive.

24. *Brooklyn Daily Eagle*, May 2, 1896. *Musical Courier*, May 6, 1896.

CHAPTER ELEVEN: WAGNER NIGHTS

1. *Brooklyn Daily Eagle*, Sept. 4, 1894. For more on Brighton Beach concerts, see Seidl Society archive, Brooklyn Historical Society.

2. *Brooklyn Daily Eagle*, June 6, 1889.

3. *Spirit of the Times*, July 26, 1890. I am grateful to Paul Charosh for bringing this article to my attention.

4. Seidl quoted in *Brooklyn Daily Eagle*, June 3, 1891. "To pray" from letter to the editor, *New York Mirror*, undated clipping (August 1890), Seidl Society archive.

5. *Brooklyn Daily Eagle*, June 24, 1894. Undated clipping, *Musical Courier*, Seidl Society archive.

6. *Brooklyn Daily Eagle*, undated clipping (late August 1895), Seidl Society archive.

7. *Brooklyn Daily Eagle*, July 28, 1895.

8. Unidentified clipping, dated July 28, 1889, in clippings file "Anton Seidl," Performing Arts branch of New York Public Library.

9. *Brooklyn Daily Eagle*, June 15, 1889.

10. Ibid., June 20, 1894.

11. Ibid., Aug. 5, 1894. "Coney Island," *Scribner's* magazine, July 1896. *Brooklyn Daily Eagle*, June 21, 1894. *Musical Courier*, April 27, 1896.

12. David Nye, *Electrifying America* (Cambridge, Mass., 1990), p. 50. I am grateful to Kathleen Hulser for bringing this reference to my attention.

CHAPTER TWELVE: PROTOFEMINISM

1. *Brooklyn Daily Eagle*, June 20, 1894.

2. Unidentified clipping, Jan. 13, 1890, in "New York Scrapbooks," Performing Arts branch of New York Public Library (*ZAN*M28, reel 24).

3. Henry Krehbiel, *Review of the New York Musical Season, 1886–1887* (New York, 1887), p. 47.

4. "Jealous husbands" in clipping (*Brooklyn Daily Eagle*?), July 27,

1889, Seidl Society archive, Brooklyn Historical Society. *Musical Courier*, June 22, 1922.

5. T. J. Jackson Lears, *No Place of Grace: Antimodernism and the Transformation of American Culture, 1880–1920* (New York, 1981), p. 32.

6. For background, see, e.g., Page Smith, *The Rise of Industrial America* (New York, 1984), pp. 661–95.

7. Lears, *No Place of Grace*, p. 172.

8. Clare Benedict, *The Divine Spark* (Philadelphia, 1913), pp. 7–10. Ella Wheeler Wilcox, "The Prelude to 'Tristan und Isolde,'" *Munsey's* magazine, December 1894, p. 288. Charlotte Teller, *The Cage* (New York, 1907), pp. 98–99. Mabel Dodge Luhan, *Intimate Memories* (New York, 1933), vol. 1, pp. 267–72.

9. Willa Cather, "A Wagner Matinee," *The Troll Garden* (New York, 1905). Originally published in *Everybody's* Magazine.

10. Angelo Neumann, *Personal Recollections of Wagner* (New York, 1908; rpt. 1976), pp. 9–13.

11. "Man and Woman," in Stewart Spencer and Barry Millington, eds. and trans., *Selected Letters of Richard Wagner* (New York, 1988), p. 303. Richard Wagner, *Die Walküre*, act 1, scene 2.

12. "Nietzsche Contra Wagner," in Walter Kaufmann, ed. and trans., *The Portable Nietzsche* (New York, 1954), p. 663. "The Sorrows and Grandeur of Richard Wagner," in Thomas Mann, *Pro and Contra Wagner* (Chicago, 1985), p. 96.

13. Wagner quoted in Mann, *Pro and Contra Wagner*, p. 115.

14. Bryan Magee, *Aspects of Wagner* (New York, 1969), p. 71.

15. Carroll Smith-Rosenberg, *Disorderly Conduct: Visions of Gender in Victorian America* (New York, 1985), p. 76.

16. Helen Horowitz, "'Nous Autres': Reading, Passion, and the Creation of M. Carey Thomas," *Journal of American History*, June 1992.

17. M. Carey Thomas Papers, Bryn Mawr College. Letters dated March 3 and Aug. 23, 1891; Dec. 17, 1893.

18. Richard Wagner, *Siegfried*, act 3, scene 3.

19. Michael T. Steinberg, Cornell University, was helpful in suggesting this formulation.

20. Ann Douglas, *The Feminization of American Culture* (New York, 1977), p. 8.

21. Ibid., pp. 10, 243.

22. According to the Americanist/musicologist Charles Hamm, in correspondence with the author.

23. Douglas, *Feminization*, pp. 9, 255.

24. Kathleen McCarthy, *Women's Culture: American Philanthropy and Art, 1830–1930* (Chicago, 1991), esp. pp. 113–15.

25. Thomas quoted in *St. Paul Post-Dispatch*, Dec. 2, 1898. Ann Firor Scott, *Natural Allies: Women's Associations in American History* (Urbana, Ill., 1991), p. 27.

26. Scott, *Natural Allies*, pp. 2, 4.

27. Laura Holloway, *Adelaide Neilsen: A Souvenir* (New York, 1885), pp. 5, 6, Introduction.

28. Laura Holloway, *Ladies of the White House* (New York, 1884), Introduction, p. 566.

29. Correspondence between Laura Langford and Anton Seidl, Seidl Society archive.

30. "Applauded wildly," *Brooklyn Daily Eagle*, Sept. 8, 1895. "Queen of the musical world," letter from Seidl to Langford, May 15, 1893, Seidl Society archive.

31. Alma Mahler, *Gustav Mahler: Memories and Letters* (London, 1946), p. 160.

CHAPTER THIRTEEN: *TRAUERMUSIK*

1. *Chicago Times*, Feb. 6, 1876.

2. *Musical America*, Jan. 30, 1909. Quaintance Eaton, *The Boston Opera Company* (Boston, 1965), p. 41.

3. For an overview, see Ronald C. Davis, *Opera in Chicago* (New York, 1966).

4. Ibid., pp. 38–39, 64, 57.

5. Louis Sullivan, *The Autobiography of an Idea* (New York, 1922), p. 208.

6. Davis, *Opera in Chicago*, p. 43.

7. John Dizikes, *Opera in America: A Cultural History* (New Haven, 1993), p. 256.

8. E. C. Moore, *Forty Years of Opera in Chicago* (New York, 1930; rpt. 1977), p. 36.

9. Henry Finck, ed., *Anton Seidl: A Memorial by His Friends* (New York, 1899; rpt. 1983), pp. 64–68.

10. *Bayreuther Blätter*, 1898, *Stück* 6, pp. 137–42. That Seidl did not visit Wahnfried or Wagner's grave is documented in Francis Neilson, *My Life in Two Worlds* (Appleton, Wis.), vol. 1, p. 161. Arthur Farwell, "America's Gain from a Bayreuth Romance: The Mystery of Anton Seidl," *Musical Quarterly* (October 1944). Curtis quoted in *New York Evening Mail*, Jan. 13, 1906.

11. Finck, *Seidl*, p. 75.

12. Ibid., p. 76.

13. Ibid., p. 77.

14. Ibid., p. 80.

15. Ibid., pp. 80–83, and newspaper accounts.

16. *New York Staats-Zeitung*, Feb. 29, 1898. *Musical Courier*, March 30, 1898.

17. Farwell, "America's Gain."

18. *Musical America*, Feb. 6, 1909.

19. Ibid., Feb. 16, 1887.

20. Farwell, "America's Gain."

CHAPTER FOURTEEN: *PARSIFAL* REVISITED

1. An excellent clippings file on the Met's first *Parsifal* may be found in the Metropolitan Opera archives. *New York Telegraph*, Aug. 29, 1903.

2. *New York Journal*, Feb. 28, 1903. *New York Telegraph*, Sept. 1, 1903.

3. *Musical Courier*, Sept. 30, 1903.

4. Martin Mayer, *The Met: One Hundred Years of Grand Opera* (New York, 1983), p. 90.

5. *Musical Courier*, Oct. 7, Oct. 14, Nov. 11, 1903. *New York Daily News*, Nov. 18, 1893.

6. *New York Telegraph*, Nov. 23, 1903. *Musical Courier*, Nov. 25, 1903.

7. *New York Times*, Nov. 26, 1903.

8. Damrosch in *Musical Courier*, Dec. 30, 1903. Aldrich in *New York Times*, Dec. 26, 1903.

9. Aldrich quoted in *Musical Courier*, Dec. 30, 1903. Henry Krehbiel, *Chapters of Opera* (New York, 1909; rpt. 1980), p. 334.

10. The 1904 film has been revived by the conductor Gillian Anderson. For Lee Avenue production, see *Brooklyn Daily Eagle*, March 13 and 15, 1904. (I am indebted to Evan Baker for bringing these articles to my attention.)

11. William James Henderson, *The Art of Singing* (New York, 1938), p. 363.

12. Henderson quoted in William H. Seltsam, *Metropolitan Opera Annals* (New York, 1947), p. 118.

13. Krehbiel, *Chapters of Opera*, p. 329. Carl Van Vechten, *Music and Bad Manners* (1916), p. 164.

14. Dohn Dizikes, *Opera in America: A Cultural History* (New Haven, 1993), pp. 321–36.

15. Alma Mahler, *Gustav Mahler: Memories and Letters* (London, 1946), p. 107.

16. *New York Times*, Dec. 2, 1908.

17. *New York Sun*, Dec. 11, 1908. *New York Tribune*, April 14, 1913.

18. *New York Tribune*, Jan. 2, 1908.

19. *Musical America*, Oct. 30, 1909.

20. *New York Sun*, Dec. 27, 1908.

21. For "public relations juggernaut," see Joseph Horowitz, *Understanding Toscanini: How He Became an American Culture-God and Helped Create a New Audience for Old Music* (New York, 1987), pp. 60–65.

22. Krehbiel, *Chapters of Opera*, p. 47. Henry Krehbiel, *More Chapters of Opera* (New York, 1919), pp. 5–7.

23. Henry Finck, ed., *Anton Seidl: A Memorial by His Friends* (New York, 1899; rpt. 1983), p. 125. Mahler in a letter to Bruno Walter (December 1909), quoted in Kurt Blaukopf, ed., *Mahler: A Documentary Study* (New York, 1976), p. 262.

CHAPTER FIFTEEN: ENTER MODERNISM

1. The principal source for my overview is David Large and William Weber, eds., *Wagnerism in European Culture and Politics* (Ithaca, N.Y., 1989).

2. Gerald Turbow, "Art and Politics: Wagnerism in France," ibid., p. 165.

3. For Krehbiel on the Met's first *Salome*, including audience's "strange horror or disgust," see Henry Krehbiel, *Chapters of Opera* (New York, 1909; rpt. 1980), pp. 343–57.

4. Ibid., p. 396.

5. Aldrich in *New York Times*, April 8, 1923. Henry Finck, "Why Make Music Hideous?" *Etude*, January 1925, p. 11. Also see Barbara Mueser, *The Criticism of New Music in New York: 1919–1929* (Ph.D. diss., CUNY, 1975; published by UMI Dissertation Services, Ann Arbor, 1990).

6. Henderson quoted in Paul Shurtz, *William James Henderson: His Views on the New York Musical World, 1887–1937* (Ph.D. diss., University of Colorado, 1980; published by UMI Dissertation Services, Ann Arbor, 1990), pp. 45, 48, 52, 58.

7. Ibid., pp. 212, 215–17.

8. *New York Sun*, Jan. 15, 1926.

9. For more on Krehbiel and Henderson, see Joseph Horowitz, *Understanding Toscanini: How He Became an American Culture-God and Helped Create a New Audience for Old Music* (New York, 1987), pp. 246–49.

10. James Gibbons Huneker, "Wagner and Swinburne," *American Art Journal*, Oct. 1, 1887. Cited in Arnold T. Schwab, *James Gibbons Huneker: Critic of the Seven Arts* (Stanford, Calif., 1963), p. 41. "Twilight of the Gods" in James Gibbons Huneker, *Melomaniacs* (New York, 1902), pp. 291–92.

11. Translation, from *The Case of Wagner*, by Thomas Grey in "Sickness or Redemption? Wagnerism and the Consequences" (unpublished paper, 1990).

12. James Gibbons Huneker, "Parsifal: A Mystic Melodrama" and "After Wagner—What?" in Huneker, *Overtones* (New York, 1904; rpt. 1970). See esp. pp. 66, 71, 308.

13. James Gibbons Huneker, *Steeplejack* (New York, 1923), vol. 2, pp. 99–108.

14. For background: Harold Briggs, *Richard Wagner and American Music-Literary Activity from 1850 to 1920* (Ph.D. diss., Indiana University, 1989; published by UMI Dissertation Services, Ann Arbor, 1992), pp. 94–120.

15. DeKoven and Gilman cited ibid., pp. 294–97.

16. Huneker, *Overtones*, p. 310.

17. Frank H. Simonds, "1914: The End of an Era," *New Republic*, Jan. 2, 1915. Cited in Henry F. May, *The End of American Innocence: The First Years of Our Own Time, 1912–1917* (New York, 1959), p. 361.

18. CPI and Lewisohn cited in Horowitz, *Understanding Toscanini*, pp. 78–79.

19. Barbara Tischler, *An American Music: The Search for an American Musical Identity* (New York, 1986), p. 75. Kate Mueller, *Twenty-seven Major American Orchestras* (Bloomington, Ind., 1971), p. xxxiii.

20. On directors' policy, Henry Krehbiel, *More Chapters of Opera* (New York, 1919), p. 393. Mrs. Jay, *Evening Post*, and *Musical America* cited in Tischler, *An American Music*, p. 87.

21. Krehbiel, *More Chapters of Opera*, pp. 413–17.

22. Ibid., pp. 414–15.

23. Duncan and Siegfried Wagner quoted in Large and Weber, *Wagnerism*, pp. 275, 128.

24. Villard letter and speech (Jan. 17, 1917, at Carnegie Hall), New York Philharmonic archives.

25. Paul E. Bierley, *John Philip Sousa: A Descriptive Catalog of His Works* (Urbana, Ill., 1973).

26. Sousa quoted in *New York World*, Aug. 6, 1893; and in John Philip Sousa, *Marching Along: Recollections of Men, Women, and Music* (Boston, 1928), p. 341.

27. *New York Advertiser*, Aug. 17, 1893. *Oakland Enquirer*, March 18, 1899. *New York World*, Aug. 18, 1899. Neil Harris, *Cultural Excursions: Marketing Appetites and Cultural Tastes in Modern America* (Chicago, 1990), p. 222. (Harris's chapter on Sousa is also the source of the newspaper citations above.)

28. Erno Rapee, *Motion Picture Moods for Pianists and Organists* (New York, 1924). *Erno Rapee's Encyclopedia of Music for Pictures* (New York, 1925).

CHAPTER SIXTEEN: SECULARIZATION

1. John Mueller, *The American Symphony Orchestra* (Bloomington, Ind., 1951), pp. 193–95. Kate Mueller, *Twenty-seven Major American Orchestras* (Bloomington, Ind., 1973), p. xxxiii.

2. The tour was closely followed in *Musical America*, February–March 1923.

3. A recording of the Feb. 8, 1941, performance is available from the Metropolitan Opera Fund. Tapes of all four performances may be heard at the Rodgers and Hammerstein archive, Performing Arts branch of New York Public Library.

4. For a detailed examination (and similar conclusions), see David Hamilton, "Tristan in the Thirties," *Musical Newsletter*, Fall 1976 and Spring 1977. See also David Breckbill in Barry Millington, ed., *The Wagner Compendium* (New York, 1992), p. 366. Flagstad quoted in David Hamilton, "The Great Opera Controversy," *Keynote*, April 6, 1982.

5. Charles O'Connell, *The Other Side of the Record* (New York, 1947), pp. 143–58.

6. Erich Leinsdorf, *Cadenza: A Musical Career* (Boston, 1976), p. 64.

7. Hamilton, "Tristan in the Thirties," pt. 2, p. 19.

8. Ibid., p. 17.

9. Joseph Horowitz, *Understanding Toscanini: How He Became an American Culture-God and Helped Create a New Audience for Old Music* (New York, 1987), pp. 132, 182.

10. Lawrence Gilman, *Toscanini and Great Music* (New York, 1938), pp. 178–80.

11. J. Mueller, *American Symphony Orchestra*, p. 194. Krehbiel quoted in Norman Lebrecht, *The Maestro Myth* (New York, 1991), p. 141.

12. *New York Sun*, Jan. 15, 1926.

13. Thomas Mann, *Pro and Contra Richard Wagner* (Chicago, 1985), p. 202.

14. Carl Van Vechten, *Music and Bad Manners* (New York, 1916), p. 147.

15. Lang in *Saturday Review*, Jan. 20, 1945. Horowitz, *Understanding Toscanini*, p. 180.

16. For more on Met and Chéreau stagings, see Joseph Horowitz, "Of Swimming and Dancing: Staging Wagner's *Ring*," *Opus*, April 1987. Dahlhaus quote from Carl Dahlhaus and John Deathridge, *The New Grove Wagner* (New York, 1984), p. 104.

17. For more on the Seattle *Ring*, see Horowitz, "Of Swimming and Dancing."

18. *Pulse!* Sept. 1991, p. 102.

POSTLUDE: THE GILDED AGE REOBSERVED

1. Lawrence Levine, *Highbrow/Lowbrow: The Emergence of Cultural Hierarchy in America* (Cambridge, Mass., 1988). Helen Horowitz, *Culture and the City: Cultural Philanthropy in Chicago from the 1880s to 1917* (Chicago, 1976). Paul DiMaggio, "Cultural Entrepreneurship in Nineteenth Century Boston," pts. 1 and 2, in *Media, Culture, and Society*, 1982, vol. 4. Charles Hamm, "United States of America," in Jim Samson, ed., *Music and Society: The Late Romantic Era* (Englewood Cliffs, N.J., 1991).

2. Hale in *Boston Post*, April 16, 1891; and *Musical Courier*, Sept. 9, 1897. Fay quoted in Helen Horowitz, *Culture and the City*, p. 111.

3. William Dean Howells, *Selected Letters* (Boston, 1983), vol. 3, p. 223. *Musical Courier*, Dec. 23, 1903. Stanley Nadel, "Kleindeutschland: New York City's Germans, 1845–1880" (Ph.D. diss., Columbia University, 1981).

4. Levine, *Highbrow/Lowbrow*, pp. 101–2.

5. On new audience and music appreciation, see Joseph Horowitz, *Understanding Toscanini: How He Became an American Culture-God and Helped Create a New Audience for Old Music* (New York, 1987).

6. *The Nation*, July 31, 1879. Henry Finck, *Wagner and His Work* (New York, 1893; rpt. 1968), vol. 1, p. 334. James Gibbons Huneker, *Overtones* (New York, 1904; rpt. 1970), p. 64. Huneker, *New Cosmopolis* (New York, 1915), p. 70.

7. Finck in *New York Evening Post*, April 1, 1890.

8. Henry Krehbiel in *Century* magazine, September 1892, pp. 657–60. Henry Krehbiel, *Afro-American Folksongs: A Study in Racial and National Music* (New York, 1911), p. v.

9. Michael Beckerman, "Dvořák's 'New World' Largo and the Song of Hiawatha," *19th-Century Music*, Summer 1992, p. 38.

10. Henry Krehbiel, "The Jew in Music," *The American Hebrew*, May 22, 1891. Also, Krehbiel in *New York Tribune*, Aug. 20, 1899.

11. *New York Tribune*, Feb. 2, 1888.

12. On Gladden and Abbott, see Thomas F. Gossett, *Race: The History of an Idea in America* (New York, 1963), pp. 176, 194. John Higham, *Strangers in the Land* (New Brunswick, N.J., 1955), pp. 131–33. Geoffrey G. Field, *Evangelist of Race: The Germanic Vision of Houston Stewart Chamberlain* (New York, 1981), p. 459.

13. Elizabeth Kendall, *Where She Danced: The Birth of American Art-Dance* (Berkeley, 1979), pp. 80, 38, 77, 95.

14. Ibid., p. 44.

15. Henderson in *New York Sun*, Nov. 26, 1904. Krehbiel quoted in W. R. Moran, "Olive Fremstad: A Short Biography," an addendum to Mary Cushing, *The Rainbow Bridge* (New York, 1954; rpt. 1977), p. v. Fremstad quoted in *Boston Advertiser*, Sept. 18, 1915.

16. Cushing, *Rainbow Bridge*, pp. 12–14.

17. Ibid., pp. 216, 127, 134.

INDEX

Designer:	Sandy Drooker
Compositor:	TBH/Typecast, Inc.
Text:	10.5/14 Caslon 540
Display:	Caslon 540
Printer and Binder:	Edwards Brothers, Inc.